# The Near West

# The Near West

A History of Grey Lynn, Arch Hill and Westmere

# Tania Mace

MASSEY UNIVERSITY PRESS

**PREVIOUS PAGES:** Map showing extent of residential subdivision in 1924. Parts of Westmere have been subdivided and the remaining land will soon follow.
AUCKLAND LIBRARIES HERITAGE COLLECTIONS, MAP 77

# Contents

Preface / 6

Introduction / 11

01. Geological and Māori history / 21
02. Farming / 35
03. Residential development / 57
04. Infrastructure and local government / 91
05. Industry and business / 131
06. Education / 197
07. Sport and recreation / 231
08. Faith / 277
09. The visual arts / 313
10. The performing and literary arts / 343

Afterword / 370
Notes / 372
Acknowledgements / 408
About the author / 409
Index / 410

# Preface

Sitting on the sun-warmed front steps in the early evening, accompanied by flatmates, glass of wine in hand, looking out across Grey Lynn Park, with the neighbourhood kids playing in the street out front — this is my enduring memory of Grey Lynn in the 1990s. To some extent my flatmates and I lived our lives on those sun-bathed steps. It was the place we drank coffee in the morning and ate breakfast or lunch, and in our non-smoking flat it served as the smoking lounge.

On still days we would hear the opera singer across the park running through her scales, or the neighbours' kid practising the drums. Just before Christmas the Salvation Army band would perform in our street as part of its tour around the neighbourhood, and when the wind was blowing in the right direction the concerts at Western Springs were clearly audible, as were the screaming engines of the cars at the Speedway.

The day of the Grey Lynn Park Festival was always loud and busy at our house: the windows vibrated with the sound system, and friends arrived to park in the driveway, use the loo or stop for a cup of tea. There was always something going on in the park: games of kilikiti and rugby league, and in the lead-up to the annual Hero Parade (later known as the Pride Parade) the marching boys practised their routines.

It was a flat with the usual collection of people. Some stayed for just a few months while others remained for years. Some flatmates worked regular 40-hour weeks, others were students with part-time jobs. Everyone had a creative hobby of some sort. Along with the usual assortment of students and graduates at the beginning of their careers there was a computer programmer and part-time shaman, an art teacher and part-time fire eater and an American Fulbright scholar.

The neighbourhood was a mix. Some nuns lived over the road. Lovely Sister Antoinette was always happy to talk about gardening with me; I was one of the few people my age who attempted to grow vegetables — at first largely unsuccessfully. I had more luck with the grapefruit tree that was already well established when I moved in. It thrived on neglect. In season I would answer the door to one of the neighbourhood kids, who'd ask, 'Excuse me, miss, can we have some fruits?' We were always happy to share.

For a while a couple of drag queens lived next door and practised their routines in the driveway. Every time I hear Natalie Imbruglia's 'Torn' I am reminded of them. And on the weekend someone in the neighbourhood would always be having a party.

Life changed for me in the early 2000s. My flatmates were replaced by a husband and children and I experienced my suburb in different ways — now life was dominated by my children's needs, kindergarten and school. Parenting opened up a different world. I knew lots of children and their parents and some became good friends.

Meanwhile, Grey Lynn, too, was changing. Suddenly everyone was talking about house prices and there was a continuous exodus of the Pasifika families who had lived there for generations, and a subsequent influx of people well-established in their professional careers, many of whom had either started, or were about to start, families.

Houses were renovated, there were more late-model cars in the streets, the playground at Grey Lynn Park was increasingly busy. Even the dogs were different: the free-range mongrels of the 1990s giving way to pedigree and designer crossbreeds — cavoodles and wheaten terriers kitted out in fancy collars.

So much has changed in the years I've lived here, but so much is also the same. Grey Lynn has always had a quirky vibe — the people are friendly and it's a great place to live. The history of this area has always interested me and so it's been an absolute pleasure to write this book. I hope you enjoy reading it.

Tania Mace
Grey Lynn
2024

# A note on place names

Newton, Newtown, Newton West, Surrey Hills, Richmond, Grey Lynn, Coxs Creek, Arch Hill . . . where?

Parts of the suburbs we now know as Arch Hill, Grey Lynn and Westmere have gone by a variety of names over the past 170 years. In the days when settlers were few and far between, places were often described in relation to the nearest well-settled area. So in the late 1850s and early 1860s when land was subdivided on the southern side of Great North Road, including the streets we now know as Commercial Road and Cooper, Bond, King, Brisbane, Waima, Kirk and Burns streets, subdivision plans were named Newtown West (west of Bond Street) and South Newtown (east of Bond Street), though the area was most commonly known as Newtown/Newton West — the area being west of Newton/Newtown Road. Newtown lost its second 'w', becoming Newton, when the area became part of the electorate of Newton in 1861.

This area later became known as Arch Hill when local government came to the area with the election of the Arch Hill Highway Board in 1871 — named after Joseph Young's farm 'Arch Hill' on the eastern side of Tuarangi Road, and at the centre of the extensive Arch Hill Highway Board area which included Newton West (Arch Hill), and also originally stretched west of Young's farm all the way to Point Chevalier.

On the northern side of Great North Road was the extensive Surrey Hills farm with Richmond beyond. These areas became part of the Newton Highway District in 1868. So there was now the suburb of Newton, south of Karangahape Road, Arch Hill (also known as Newton West), and now the Newton Highway District (later known as the Newton Road District, Newton Borough and Grey Lynn Borough), which included the areas we now know as Grey Lynn and Westmere. These names, when found in nineteenth-century sources, can be the cause of considerable confusion to those unfamiliar with the local history of the area.

Many streets have also been renamed, and in the case of two of our main thoroughfares there have been two significant changes. Great North Road originally ran down the line of Tuarangi Road — steep and difficult to keep in reasonable order. In the early twentieth century Deviation Road was formed, taking the easier line through the valley between Tuarangi Road and Surrey Crescent. This became the new line of Great North Road.

Many an unwary researcher has been tripped up by the three names originally given to sections of Richmond Road. In the nineteenth and early twentieth century Richmond Road was known as Richmond Avenue at the Surrey Crescent end, Richmond Road at the Ponsonby Road end, and Richmond Hill for the section between the two.

Other streets were renamed after the amalgamation of the Arch Hill Road Board and Grey Lynn Borough with Auckland City Council in 1913 and 1914 respectively. To avoid confusion, Auckland City Council renamed certain roads where there was duplication of names, including King Street in the former Grey Lynn Borough, which was renamed Kingsley Street to avoid confusion with King Street in Arch Hill.

More recent changes have seen the expansion of the area known as Westmere. The name comes from the 1920s subdivisions on either side of Garnet Road and west of Edgars Creek. In recent times the name Westmere has been given to the adjoining stretch of land between Edgars and Coxs creeks north of Richmond Road, an area formerly known as Coxs Bay, Grey Lynn and, back in 1860s, Richmond Village.

This book tries to be clear when describing locations, particularly where names have changed over time.

# Introduction

**PREVIOUS PAGES:** A view of Arch Hill in 1989. Brisbane Street runs diagonally up the hill. Number 10 Home Street can be seen on the left of Brisbane Street, halfway up the hill. Number 12 is obscured by the Norfolk Island pine. AUCKLAND LIBRARIES HERITAGE COLLECTIONS, 273-HAR050-09

This book is about three adjoining Auckland suburbs — Grey Lynn, Arch Hill and Westmere — and the people who have lived here.

As in all suburbs, their buildings and places have stories to tell, as two neighbouring houses, 10 and 12 Home Street in Arch Hill, exemplify. One, a modest cottage, is perched on a steep section at the corner of Home Street and Brisbane Street, its façade partly obscured by a picket fence above a retaining wall that appeared long after the house was built, in order to provide a level road and footpath. Its larger neighbour, while still modest, features a hip roof and narrow verandah. Both houses were built just inside the southwest boundary of the 3000-acre block of land that was gifted in 1840 by Ngāti Whātua for the new capital of the young colony, New Zealand. The acreage was initially cut up into town sections with suburban farms beyond.

The land where the houses stand was purchased from the Crown in 1844 by Thomas Poynton, an ex-convict who had arrived in New Zealand from Australia with his wife, Mary, in 1828 and set up a store and sawmill in the Hokianga.[1] His property at Arch Hill was one of a number of suburban farms Poynton bought in the 1840s as he took advantage of a government scheme that allowed pre-Treaty land claimants in remote areas to swap their low-value properties for higher-value land in the growing town. This encouraged settlers to relocate to Auckland, where settlers were needed, while also removing them from areas where there was no colonial government presence to protect them or stop them getting into quarrels with local Māori.[2]

Poynton didn't ever settle the land, selling it in 1845 to butcher William Thorne Buckland. In 1853 it was bought by David Burn, who in 1859 subdivided it into residential sections, no doubt hoping to make a good profit. Close to the city, and relatively small, the sections were ideal for city workers. However, Burn was one of many vendors of newly subdivided land near

**Introduction | 13**

the city, and with supply outstripping demand, it would be decades before his land was all sold.[3] The purchaser of the two adjoining sections fronting Home Street on the southwestern corner of Brisbane Street was Nathaniel Gow, a bootmaker who had recently arrived from Barrhead in Scotland with his wife Margaret and their eight children, and who, like many other plucky immigrants before and since, had made the decision to sail to the opposite side of the world, away from all they had ever known in the hope of building a better future for their family. They arrived in Auckland on the *Ganges* in 1863 and, not long after, Gow agreed to sell one section to William Baildon, an immigrant from Huddersfield. Evidently love was in the air; in 1867 William Baildon married Nathaniel and Margaret's third daughter, Isabella, at the Gow residence.[4]

Like many new Aucklanders, the young couple moved to Thames after gold was discovered there. They returned a few years later and Baildon, a builder, erected a house not far from his in-laws at the western end of Dean Street (then known as Stanley Street), where he and Isabella raised a family.[5]

William Baildon and Nathaniel Gow were both active in local body politics, serving on the Arch Hill Highway Board as it struggled to build and maintain roads and keep the area in a sanitary condition.[6] This was no easy task in the days before piped water and sewerage; local nuisances included stinking piles of manure and bloated horse carcasses abandoned on roadsides, resulting in letters from the highway board demanding residents clean up their mess. Keeping order and making improvements was difficult when there was limited rating revenue and where the hilly terrain meant that roads could often only be formed by digging away banks and filling in ditches by hand.

On Sundays the Baildons and Gows attended St James Presbyterian Church, a little over 2 kilometres away, on Wellington Street in Freemans Bay.[7] From 1877 the children of both families attended nearby Newton West School, a one-room public school on Great North Road that also served a variety of community purposes, from meetings and church services to social events.[8]

But there was another side to this suburb. William Crowe's brothel in nearby Waima Street (then known as Oxford Street) disturbed the peace of the quiet neighbourhood in the 1870s and early 1880s, with one neighbour complaining that 'midnight brawls and curious noises made night hideous, and banished sleep from the locality'.[9] At the time the nearest police presence was the sole-charge Newton Station in West Street (now West Terrace) off Karangahape Road. The fledgling police force generally left brothelkeepers and prostitutes to their own devices unless there was public misconduct or complaints from neighbours. Crowe's establishment clearly attracted police attention, as did the larrikins who disrupted the peace of the neighbourhood by swearing, beating kerosene tins and vandalising property.[10] By 1887 there was sufficient trouble in the district to warrant a police station, which was located in a rented house

A subdivision plan showing the Gow and Baildon properties in Home Street, c. 1859. Rather confusingly, this subdivision was initially named South Newtown — located east of a subdivision called Newtown West and west of a subdivision called West Newtown. This area would soon become known as Newton West (having lost its second 'w' after the electorate of Newton was proclaimed in 1861) and later Arch Hill. Many of the streets would be renamed in the twentieth century.
AUCKLAND LIBRARIES HERITAGE COLLECTIONS, MAP 4495-8

# SOUTH NEWTOWN

## GREAT NORTH ROAD

1 2 3 4 5  6 7 8 9 10 11  12 13 14 15 16 17

34 33 32 31 30  29 28 27 26 25 24  27 22 21 20 19 18

### STANLEY STREET

35 36 37 38 39  40 41 42 43 44 45  46 47 48 49 50 51

68 67 66 65 64  63 62 61 60 59 58  57 56 55 54 53 52

### HOME STREET

69 70 71 72 73  74 75 76 77 78 79  80 81 82 83 84

102 101 100 99 98  97 96 95 94 93 92  91 90 89 88 87 86

### KEPPELL STREET

103 104 105 106 107  108 109 110 111 112 113  114 115 116 117 118 119

  131 130 129 128 127 126  125 124 123 122 121 120

### NIGER STREET

on the north side of Great North Road between Turakina and Ariki streets (then known as Tennyson and Princep streets).[11]

Alcohol was the cause of many social ills, and the temperance movement grew strong in Arch Hill. In 1886 William Baildon stood as one of five temperance candidates for the Arch Hill Licensing District elections, pledging if elected to close the only hotel in the district.[12] Although unsuccessful, he continued to support the temperance cause, and in the early twentieth century Grey Lynn electorate (including Arch Hill, Grey Lynn and Westmere) became the first North Island electorate to ban the sale of alcohol when the residents voted the district 'dry'. It would remain so for much of the twentieth century; in 1996 it was one of the last areas to vote 'wet', ending one of the longest dry spells in New Zealand.[13]

By the late 1880s the Baildon family was living on the south side of Great North Road between King and Bond streets, the ridge-top position giving magnificent views to the north across the vast Surrey Hills Estate and on to Coxs Creek, with the Waitematā Harbour and North Shore beyond.[14]

Only a few houses dotted this landscape. Prominent features included the Warnock Brothers' soap and candle works on the south side of Richmond Road, at the edge of Coxs Creek, and Hellaby's slaughterhouse and meatworks on the coastal land beyond. To the northwest the distant chimney of the municipal abattoirs towered above Western Springs, where West View Road runs today.[15] These were just some of the noxious industries that were no longer tolerated in the increasingly populous city and so were relocated to the open fields beyond.

But the view north from the Baildon's ridge-top home would change. The belching chimneys were gradually overwritten by residential development that staggered, in fits and starts, across the landscape, and the evolution of less offensive industrial concerns that provided local jobs for residents.

William and Isabella Baildon's eldest son, George, married Maggie Kerr in 1893 and the couple moved to a house (likely built by George with the help of his father) on the property adjoining the Gows' in Home Street.[16] Two years later George followed his father into local politics. He was elected to the Arch Hill Road Board and later the Grey Lynn Borough Council and Auckland City Council, and served as mayor of both Grey Lynn Borough and Auckland City councils. In the early twentieth century George and Maggie moved to Great North Road, at the western corner of Northland Street (then known as Northcote Street), where they would remain for the rest of their lives.[17]

16 | **The Near West**

Numbers 10 (left) and 12 Home Street. PATRICK REYNOLDS

Subsequent residents of the former Baildon property at 12 Home Street included a tramways company employee who helped transport workers from the suburbs to city workplaces, something that had been part of the pattern of life in Grey Lynn and Arch Hill since 1903 when the first electric trams made their way along Great North Road, stirring up a cloud of dust in their wake.[18]

In the 1940s Daisy and William Ellis made their home in the former Gow residence at 10 Home Street. During the Second World War William joined the Royal Air Force and flew missions over Germany. When the news came that he had been shot down Daisy was no doubt bereft. The Gows and Baildons knew the feeling — George Baildon had lost a brother and a son in the previous war.[19]

From the mid-1950s to the mid-1960s, the Baildons' former home at 12 Home Street was the residence of the artist Theo Schoon, an immigrant of Dutch heritage who had grown up in Indonesia. At this time Arch Hill was home to several departments of the Elam School of Art, which had been relocated to the former Newton West School after fire destroyed part of the art school's Symonds Street premises.[20] The neighbourhood was becoming more culturally diverse than it had been in William Baildon's time, and now included people from rural Māori communities and the Pacific Islands.

The government encouraged Pacific Islanders to come to New Zealand to ease the labour shortage, and many Pasifika peoples now made their homes in the increasingly rundown housing of the inner-west suburbs, including Arch Hill and Grey Lynn, where buying or renting were cheap and the commute into the city was relatively easy. In 1961 Niuean timber worker Langi Sipley bought the former Gow residence in Home Street; it would remain connected to the Sipley (Sipeli) family for almost 60 years.[21]

Introduction | 17

The challenges of adapting to life in New Zealand were eased by the Pacific Island churches and their communities. Grey Lynn and Arch Hill were close to the Pacific Island Presbyterian Church in Newton, where people gathered to worship in their own languages. Other congregations gathered closer to home, raising funds for church buildings including the Sione Uesile (John Wesley) Samoan Methodist Church and community centre in King Street.

Local schools adapted to teaching children who were recent arrivals from the various island nations of the Pacific. Many spoke little or no English, so new methods evolved to help them learn.

Facing discrimination, young members of these communities banded together to support Polynesian people and fight racial prejudice, and formed the Polynesian Panthers, who first met in a house in Keppell Street, just a stone's throw from the former Gow and Baildon residences in Home Street.[22]

Auckland was growing, and better connections between west Auckland and the city were needed. Soon a thick ribbon of black asphalt worked its way along the Arch Hill gully, blanketing part of the Newton Central School playground, and by the late 1970s the hum of cars speeding along the new motorway was added to the sounds of the suburb. The industrial landscape also changed as light industry marched west from the Newton Road end of Arch Hill — many houses at this end of the district were demolished to make way for commercial buildings.

In 1977 Neil French, a car-yard manager, bought 12 Home Street and lived there for several years, and in 1987 the property was purchased by the Presbyterian Church and later became the home of Presbyterian minister Mua Strickson-Pua, who had grown up in Grey Lynn as the son of Samoan immigrants, and his wife Linda.[23]

Through the closing decades of the twentieth century and into the twenty-first, house prices in this part of the city rose dramatically. Many rundown rental properties were sold to owner-occupiers who renovated them, further increasing their value and the desirability of the area.

Well over a century has passed since the little houses at 10 and 12 Home Street were first built. Their survival has been remarkable, and they are a tangible reminder of the history of this part of the city and of the people who have lived here.

The growth of the local Pasifika population led to a wider variety of vegetables, including those imported from the Pacific Islands, being stocked by shops. Here several tubers of the enormous Tarua taro (*Xanthosoma sagittifolium*) are displayed at the front of a dairy on Great North Road, Grey Lynn, in **1989.** AUCKLAND LIBRARIES HERITAGE COLLECTIONS, 273-HAR009-14

Introduction | 19

# Geological and Māori history

**PREVIOUS PAGES:** An aerial view from 1946 showing Westmere in the foreground and Te Tokaroa Meola Reef stretching out across the Waitematā Harbour, and almost touching the North Shore. ALEXANDER TURNBULL LIBRARY, WA-02359-G

Grey Lynn, Arch Hill and Westmere lie within sight of several of the more than 50 cones that make up Auckland's volcanic field, formed through a series of eruptions over the past 250,000 years. During this time the earth witnessed two ice ages. As the last of these ended, the earth warmed and ice sheets melted, causing sea levels to rise and inundate the forests that grew on what are now the beds of the Manukau and Waitematā harbours, and defining the coastal edges of the area we know today as Auckland.[1]

One of the Māori origin stories of the Auckland volcanic field centres on the relationship between two patupaiarehe (mythical fairy people known for their mischievousness) and their respective tribes. Hinemairangi, daughter of the chief of the Hūnua tribe of patupaiarehe, fell in love with Tamaireia, son of the chief of the Waitākere tribe. The couple eloped and went to live with Tamaireia's people at Hikurangi (Te Rau-o-te-Huia Mount Donald McLean), the highest point in the Waitākere Ranges.

Hinemairangi's father opposed the union and gathered a war party intent on returning his daughter to her people. As they headed across the isthmus they were seen by the Waitākere tribe, who gathered their tohunga (priests) in a line across Hikurangi, delivering powerful incantations that not only incapacitated the Hūnua war party but also caused the isthmus to erupt, forming the volcanoes and craters of Auckland.[2]

Another story tells of the deity Mataaho stepping across from the North Shore to Māngere, where his footsteps left the indentations Ngā Tapuwae (the footsteps), the two lagoons in the vicinity of Barrys Point Road, and Te Pūkaki Tapu Lagoon in Māngere. Volcanoes sprang up in between.[3]

Skirting the west of Grey Lynn and Westmere are the lava flows from Te Kōpuke Mount St John and Te Tātua Riukiuta/Te Tātua o Mataaho Three Kings. Te Kōpuke (the prominent mound) is one of Auckland's oldest volcanoes and its 11-kilometre lava flow, Auckland's longest, formed a thick ribbon of stone running west along a valley, through the site where Maungawhau Mount

**Geological and Māori history** | 23

v.Hochstetter's & Petermann's Geol.-topogr. Atlas of New-Zealand.

3.

Long. E. 172° 30' of Paris

HAURAKI GULF

TAPUI.

THE ISTMUS OF AUCKLAND
with its extinct Volcanoes,
by
Dr. Ferdinand von Hochstetter
1859.

The Drawing & geographical Foundation compiled
principally from the Surveys of Stokes & Drury
by A. Petermann.

Scale 1:120.000.

½ German geogr. Mile (15. 1°)
1 Engl. Mile (69.16. 7°)
Heights in Engl. Feet.
Soundings in fathoms.
Lava streams.

Tufferater

Skoal
Bay

Mud Flat

Onepoto Pt

Black Cork Buoy

Tanapona Head

Rough Pt
White
Beach

North Head 216 (Takarunga)
Cook Pt

Motukorea Channel

Rangitoto Channel

Motukorea (Brown I.)

36°50'

Boat Rock

Sentinel Rock

Waitemata or Auckland Harbour

Bean Rocks
Bastion Reefs
Bastion Rock

AUCKLAND

Hobson B.

Orakei Bay (Tufferater)

Tamaki Head

Tenaupata Pt

Newmarket

Mount or Rangitoto

St. John's College

Taylor Hill
Farm

Maunga Wau

Mt Hobson

Mt St. John 400

Epsom

Purchas Hill
Maunga Rei
Mt Wellington

Pigeon Hill

HOWICK

Mt Albert

Three Kings

Maunga Kiekie

Mt Kennedy

Pannure

Wai Magoia
(Pannure Basin)

ONEHUNGA

Mt Smart

Otahuhu

Green Hill
Bessy Bell

Otara Hill
Mary Grace

Pt Richard
Robertson Hill

MANUKAU HARBOUR

Te Tau Bank

Puketutu (Weekes I.)

Mangere
Mt Eden

Tufferater

Tufferater with Swampy bottom

The five Tufferaters of Kohimara

Great South Road

Pukeiti

Waitomokin

Matukarua

Owhata Pt

Karore Bank

Mamurewa 300

Mt Taketake
300

Tamalao Pt

Kolua I.

Long. E. 174° 50' of Greenwich

Stratified Volcanic Tuff and
Breccias, with numerous Craters

Scoria & Cones marking Craters
or Centres of Eruption.

Basaltic Lava streams.

Tertiary Clay, Marl and Sandstone.

Quatern. Lignitformation with
plastic clay and Sandstone.

Lignite.

Swamps.

A. Welker del.

Lith. og. by C. Hellfarth, Gotha.

GOTHA. JUSTUS PERTHES
1865.

Eden would later erupt, then turning to the north around where Morningside is today and flowing on to form Te Tokaroa Meola Reef.[4]

Māori explain the formation of the reef, visible only at low tide, through the story of conflict between two tribes of patupaiarehe. The weaker tribe built a stone causeway across the Waitematā Harbour that would enable them to escape at low tide but would become submerged as the tide rose, foiling any attempt by their enemies to pursue them. However, as they worked to build their escape route the sun rose, destroying the patupaiarehe, who were unable to endure its rays, and leaving the causeway partly finished.[5]

An early name of the reef was Te Whakapekapeka o Ruarangi (the pathway or diversion of Ruarangi) recalling an escape over the reef by Ruarangi, of Tainui. Ruarangi had quarrelled with his brother Ohomatakamokamo over cultivations near Rarotonga (Mount Smart), and in the ensuring battle Ruarangi and his people were besieged at Ōwairaka (Mount Albert). They escaped through a lava tunnel and headed north, crossing the Waitematā Harbour over Meola Reef.[6] The reef later became known as Te Tokaroa (the long rock).[7]

A large lava flow from Te Tātua Riukiuta/Te Tātua o Mataaho followed, many thousands of years after Meola Reef was formed. This volcano initially erupted 28,500 years ago. During a second round of eruptions, when a series of cones were formed, lava poured out from a breach in the tuff ring created by the first eruption.

The lava flowed down a stream bed to Western Springs, burying the stream. It continued to flow as a subterranean waterway, percolating through cooling cracks in the lava before emerging to form Te Wai Ōrea (Western Springs lake), named for its plentiful eels.[8]

These eruptions and others in the Auckland volcanic field provided volcanic rock and fertile soils rich in minerals. Combined with a climate that was warm in summer and cool in winter, with adequate rainfall, these provided ideal conditions for flora and fauna to flourish, and the coastal margins and waterways supported an abundance of aquatic life. This flora and fauna had developed its own unique character in the time since the Aotearoa New Zealand landmass broke away from the edge of the Gondwana supercontinent around 80 million years ago.[9]

An 1859 map of the Auckland volcanic field by Dr Ferdinand von Hochstetter. AUCKLAND LIBRARIES HERITAGE COLLECTIONS, MAP 5694B

✕

Humans first set eyes on this unique environment around 800 years ago when Polynesian explorers, the ancestors of today's Māori, began arriving in a series of migrations. The riches of this new land must have been a welcome sight after their arduous sea voyage.[10] Known as Tāmaki

Herenga Waka (where waka are tied), the narrow Auckland isthmus became the most heavily populated part of Aotearoa.[11]

Polynesian navigators brought with them new plants and animals, including the kūmara (sweet potato), and the kiore or Polynesian rat. The kūmara was one of the few Polynesian plants that grew well here, able to survive in the cooler climate. The kiore adapted readily to its new environment and rapidly wreaked havoc on Aotearoa's ground-nesting birds, reptiles and frogs. But the impact of the kiore on native species was dwarfed by that of humans, who hunted several species of large birds, including moa, to extinction.[12] Bones from these avian giants would be found in volcanic caves at Western Springs in the twentieth century, long after their demise.[13]

With its eight portages connecting the east and west coasts, the isthmus was a frequent transit point for travellers, who made use of local food sources and fresh water.[14] The presence of middens across the coastal edges of Westmere and Coxs Bay attests to the enjoyment of plentiful seafood over the centuries. Local place names refer to food sources, including Waitītiko Meola Creek (water of the periwinkles) and Te Wai Ōrea (water of the eels). Eels were an important food source, and both long-finned and short-finned native eels still exist in Te Wai Ōrea.[15] The pattern of life revolved around seasonal journeys to carry out gardening, fishing, hunting and harvesting.[16]

Opoutukeha Coxs Creek originally ran from a spring in upper Pollen Street, wending its way through what is now Grey Lynn Park to Coxs Bay. The part of the creek south of Richmond Road now runs through underground pipes and emerges on the north side of Richmond Road to meander through the Coxs Bay Reserve before spilling into Coxs Bay under West End Road. It was named after Poutukeha (also spelled Poutukeka), an ancestor from the *Tainui* waka. Opoutukeha formed the boundary between the early tribes Ngāti Riu and Ngāti Huarere.[17]

Seasonal kūmara plantations flourished on the sun-warmed north-facing slopes of Grey Lynn above Opoutukeha, and flax grew in abundance in the wetlands around Coxs Bay, much of which was later reclaimed to become Coxs Bay Reserve.[18] Tukituki Muka (to prepare flax) is the name given to the area where flax harvested from the wetlands was processed and dried, to be turned into rope and clothes. The location of Tukituki Muka is described in different sources as the north-facing slope at the end of Jervois Road in Herne Bay, or the area just east of the cul-de-sac of Webber Street.[19]

Other locations in the district are associated with intertribal conflict. In the late seventeenth or early eighteenth century, the great Tainui warrior Kāwharu was enlisted to lead Ngāti Whātua on a series of raids that became known as Te Raupatu Tīhore (the stripping conquest).[20] One of the battles in this campaign appears to have occurred at Ngā Kauaewhati (the broken jaw bones), a pā on the

A map showing Māori place names in Auckland. AUCKLAND LIBRARIES HERITAGE COLLECTIONS, MAP 9502

26 | The Near West

# TAMAKI-MAKAU-RAU

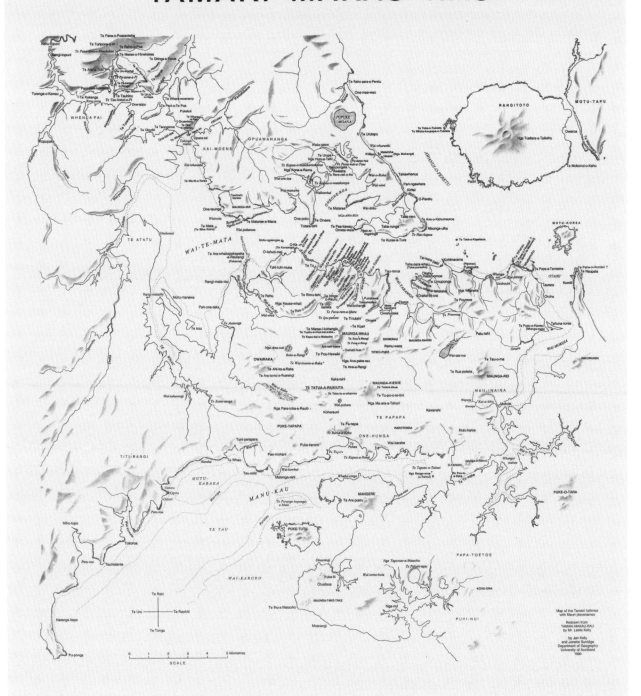

ridge above Western Springs.[21] Kāwharu rested his head on the Surrey Crescent ridge nearby, and the place became known as Te Rae o Kāwharu (Kāwharu's brow).[22] Grey Lynn School now bears this name and the students connect with this history through their patere (chant), which functions as a school song.[23]

In the mid-eighteenth century a series of conflicts between the people of Tāmaki and Kaipara culminated in a battle at Paruroa, west of Titirangi. Here the great Te Wai-o-Hua chief Kiwi Tāmaki was killed, along with many other Te Wai-o-Hua leaders, in a battle known as Te Rangihinganga Tahi (the day when all fell together).[24] Te Taoū, part of the Ngāti Whātua confederation of Kaipara, were now in a position to take Te Wai-o-Hua's great pā, Maungakiekie One Tree Hill, which they found deserted.[25] Te Taoū became the occupants of the central isthmus. The remaining people of Te Wai-o-Hua were taken in as part of the confederation under the hapū names Ngā Oho and Te Uringutu.[26]

The 1820s was a time of unrest across the isthmus as the musket-armed Ngāpuhi came from the north waging a campaign of terror on their way south. Te Taoū and others escaped to the Waitākere Ranges where they were taken in by Te Kawerau. The heavy bush cover of the ranges made this a good place to hide, but food was limited.[27] As soon as they considered it safe to leave, Te Taoū of Tāmaki left the Waitākere Ranges to stay with Te Taoū at Oneonenui, South Kaipara, where they established gardens sufficient to feed them in their exile.[28]

By around August 1822 things had settled. Āpihai Te Kawau, grandson of the great Te Taoū chief Tūperiri who led the occupation of Tāmaki following the defeat of Te Wai-o-Hua, considered it safe to return to Tāmaki. Te Kawau's mother was of Te Wai-o-Hua descent, and through her and his paternal uncle he was related to both Ngā Oho and Te Uringutu. Te Kawau brought Te Taoū, Ngā Oho and Te Uringutu with him to settle on the southern shores of the Waitematā. With them came refugees from South Waikato, who had also sought shelter in Waitākere and South Kaipara and who were invited to stay temporarily on the Waitematā.[29]

Archaeologist Agnes Sullivan's study of Māori gardening in Auckland provides a picture of life at this time for the South Waikato hapū Ngāti Tipa on the Waitematā. Around October 1822, it appears that Ngāti Tipa were clearing and planting gardens and gathering fernroot in the Ōrākei–Ōkahu Bay area. Fish, shellfish and fernroot provided sustenance while they prepared their gardens. The following month these activities were repeated at Te Rehu, on the banks of Waiateao (Motions Creek). Early in 1823 they were fishing at Ōkahu Bay and probably harvesting crops planted the previous year. They then moved again to Te Rehu, likely continuing their harvesting and fishing.

These cycles of planting, fishing and harvesting continued over the next two years. Te Rehu provided the main winter base and the Ōrākei–Ōkahu Bay area the summer base. Periods of planting and harvesting at Te Rehu were interspersed with fishing on the harbour. Eels could be caught in Te Wai Ōrea and pigs were hunted nearby. There were also sojourns to Kaipara to work in the large gardens there for supply to Ngāti Whātua, who were preparing for a regional confederation meeting for which additional supplies of food would be needed.[30] By the end of 1824 Te Taoū and Ngā Oho were living at Te Rehu, Wai Horotiu (Queen Street, Auckland) and Ōkahu.[31] Their seasonal movements were probably similar to those of the other hapū who settled the southern shores of the Waitematā.

In 1825 the pattern of life at Waitematā was broken when Te Kawau's people were called in to support Ngāti Whātua o Kaipara in the battle against Ngāpuhi at Kaiwaka. The battle was named Te Ika-a-ranganui (the great array of fish laid out), a reference to the many Ngāti Whātua warriors who died and were laid out in lines.[32] Te Kawau and his people arrived too late to take part. Fearing a Ngāpuhi attack, they left the Tāmaki isthmus but returned regularly to fish, plant crops and harvest.[33] In the late 1830s they re-established themselves gradually on the southern shore of the Waitematā.[34] By the beginning of 1840, Te Kawau's main base was at Ōrākei, where gardens had earlier been planted and habitations built.[35] The three hapū — Te Taoū, Ngā Oho and Te Uringutu — became known as Ngāti Whātua Ōrākei.[36]

The wars of the 1820s and 1830s had decimated the local population. Now there was an appetite for peace, something that Ngāti Whātua Ōrākei sought to promote by settling the governor on their land, thereby dissuading rival tribes from launching an attack.[37] Te Kawau's nephew Te Rewiti was sent to the Bay of Islands to meet with Governor William Hobson and invite him to make his capital on the southern Waitematā.[38] Māori recognised other advantages in having Pākehā nearby: as well as the prestige of having someone as important as the governor living close by, there were increased opportunities for trade and employment.[39]

The southern shore of the Waitematā Harbour would soon become the capital of the fledgling colony, chosen for its natural advantages of fertile soils, a warm climate, a safe harbour, and rivers that provided easy access to other parts of the country — features that earlier attracted Māori and earned the isthmus the name Tāmaki-makau-rau (translations include 'Tāmaki desired by hundreds' and 'the bride sought by a hundred suitors').[40]

On 20 October 1840, the deed for the first 3000-acre block of land gifted by Ngāti Whātua Ōrākei for the new capital was signed, paving the way for the development of Auckland.[41] Colonial settlers flooded in to build homes and lives for themselves. Most lived in communities separate from Māori. Contact between the races occurred in the centre of town where Māori were frequent visitors, arriving in waka laden with produce to feed the growing population. By the mid-1860s, trade with Māori had decreased dramatically, due in part to the outbreak of war in Waikato and Taranaki. Settlers had established farms and gardens, and there was now less need and willingness to engage with Māori traders.[42]

Māori presence in the city increased from the 1930s, and gathered pace after the Second World War. The Māori population was growing, and the rural communities where many iwi lived had insufficient land, housing, schooling opportunities and jobs for the expanding population. These factors led many to seek new opportunities in the cities, and Auckland, as New Zealand's largest, drew more of the rural Māori population than any other.

Māori initially settled mainly in the city centre and the inner suburbs — particularly Freemans Bay, where cheap rental housing was available close to city workplaces.[43] In 1951, 12 per cent of residents in Freemans Bay and 9 per cent in Newton were Māori. But changes to the city fringe led to a rise in Māori population in other areas. Auckland City Council's slum clearance programme, for example, instigated in the 1950s, saw the demolition of a significant area of cheap rental housing to the south of Franklin Road, as did the construction of the motorway through Newton Gully. Over the next two decades the Freemans Bay Māori population more than halved, and in the suburb of Newton the number fell by almost 90 per cent.[44]

Māori moved to other suburbs, including Grey Lynn, Arch Hill and Westmere. In 1951, just 1 per cent of the 10,997 people living in Grey Lynn were Māori; by 1971 this had grown to around 11 per cent. Arch Hill exhibited a similar pattern of growth: from a Māori population of 72 of the 2402 residents in 1951 (around 3 per cent), by 1971, 14 per cent were Māori. Westmere had a smaller Māori presence: in 1951 just 11 Māori lived among a population of 4818; two decades later the overall population of the area had shrunk to 3917, of whom 147 were Māori.[45]

Early urban migrants paved the way for chain migration as whānau left their rural homes to join family or friends who were already established in the city. Māori households often experienced a succession of arrivals and departures as family and friends stayed temporarily while getting themselves settled in the city. Some younger migrants boarded at Auckland schools, while others lived in hostels provided to meet the needs of new arrivals to the city. Māori hostels

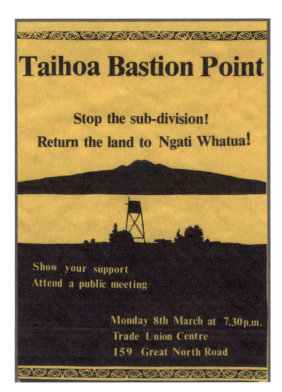 

**ABOVE LEFT:** The Polynesian Resource Centre at the Auckland Trade Union Centre (Auckland Trades Hall) on Great North Road was a gathering place for Māori activist groups.
AUCKLAND WAR MEMORIAL MUSEUM TĀMAKI PAENGA HIRA, EPH-2008-1-31

**ABOVE RIGHT:** Whina Cooper lived at the top of Cockburn Street during the 1950s and 1960s, and was a guiding light for many Māori relocating to the city.
AUCKLAND WAR MEMORIAL MUSEUM TĀMAKI PAENGA HIRA, PH-NEG-C45423

were nothing new — the government built Auckland's first Maori Hostelry in Mechanics Bay in 1850 to provide accommodation for Māori who were visiting to trade produce and wares.[46]

But now Māori needed more long term accommodation. From the 1940s many city hostels were established by church organisations with the aid of funding from the Department of Maori Affairs (known as the Department of Native Affairs until the 1940s). The earliest were close to the central city, but by the 1950s they were also appearing in suburbs further out. A Presbyterian Māori girls hostel was established in the mid-1950s in the grand residence that still stands at the corner of Crummer Road and Ponsonby Road.[47]

One particular Grey Lynn resident became a guiding light for many Māori who were new to the city. Twice widowed and aged in her mid-fifties, Whina Cooper was an established leader in her home community of Panguru in the remote Hokianga region. Her move to the city was prompted partly by the departure of a number of her eldest children and grandchildren to Auckland.[48] Her younger children were either leaving school or needed to attend boarding school to receive a secondary education, just as she had done as a child. Cooper was seeking new challenges, and had been invited to come to Auckland by the Bishop of the Catholic Church, James Liston, who hoped she could do some good for the increasing numbers of Māori relocating to the city.[49]

Geological and Māori history | 31

While most Māori migrants to Auckland were living in hostels or crowded rental accommodation, Cooper had the wherewithal to purchase a home, having successfully run a farming operation and shop in Panguru before moving to the city. In 1951 she bought a villa at 1 Cockburn Street, Grey Lynn, close to the inner-city suburbs of Newton and Freemans Bay where many Māori lived at the time. That year, Cooper became the founding president of the Maori Women's Welfare League, a position she held for the next six years. This nationwide organisation sought to improve the health and wellbeing of Māori women and children.[50]

Cooper and other league members quickly got to work, surveying Māori households in Auckland to gauge the need for government housing assistance, and revealing poor conditions and overcrowding. The results of the survey were typed up in Cooper's home, and league members helped those in need to apply for state-sponsored housing. Within a decade most Māori families in Auckland had adequate housing, and many had moved from the inner city to the burgeoning state-housing suburbs in west and south Auckland.[51]

Cooper lived in Grey Lynn for 13 years during a pivotal time when Māori were arriving in Auckland in increasing numbers. People frequently sought her help and advice and her home was always busy. She devoted considerable energy to providing facilities for Catholic Māori in the city, resulting in the opening of St Anne's Hostel for girls in Herne Bay and Te Unga Waka, the Māori Catholic centre in Epsom. As a result of her work she was appointed a Member of the British Empire in 1953. Further awards were made in recognition of her leadership and work among Māori, culminating in her being made a member of the Order of New Zealand in 1991.[52]

Cooper fought for a better deal for Māori urban migrants, but in the 1970s new issues were raised by young Māori. These Auckland-born rangatahi had grown up in a Pākehā world, and many had little connection to their language and culture. Ngā Tamatoa (the young warriors), a university-based group, formed in the early 1970s to fight racism and injustice and promote Māori language and culture. The group petitioned Parliament to have te reo Māori taught in schools, and as a result Maori Language Day was instigated in 1972; three years later this became Te Wiki o Te Reo Māori — Māori Language Week.[53]

Members of Ngā Tamatoa also worked with and joined the Polynesian Panthers, a group inspired by the American Black Panthers. The group was formed in 1971 at a meeting at the Schmidt family home in Keppell Street, Arch Hill, with the aim of supporting Polynesian people and fighting racial prejudice.[54] Many of their members and activities were based in Ponsonby, Grey Lynn and Arch Hill, where the Panthers established homework clubs, food banks and provided legal advice.[55]

32  |  **The Near West**

In 1980 the Auckland Trade Union Centre (Auckland Trades Hall) in Great North Road, Grey Lynn, became a focal point for Māori activist groups when the Polynesian Resource Centre was opened there, established by Māori trade unionists to educate unionists on the impact of racism.[56]

By the 1970s and early 1980s, race issues in New Zealand and other parts of the world were coming to a head. Groups including Ngā Tamatoa and the Polynesian Panthers took part in protests relating to Māori land rights. The Māori Land March of 1975, led by Whina Cooper, drew attention to the continued alienation of Māori land, enabled through government legislation. These issues were the impetus for the 1977–78 occupation of Bastion Point that sought redress for the loss of Ngāti Whātua land over generations. The Springbok tour of 1981 also brought out many protesters, including Māori.[57]

Diverse Māori activist groups emerged with varying perspectives on the relative importance of race, gender and class in the struggle against oppression. Many of them met at the Polynesian Resource Centre in the early 1980s.[58]

Events that targeted other ethnic groups sometimes spilled over to affect Māori. In the mid-1970s, with the economy faltering, the government cracked down on Tongan and Samoan immigrants who had overstayed their visas. No similar search was carried out for European overstayers. Some Māori were caught up in a police crackdown in October 1976 when hundreds of people in the city were stopped and asked to present evidence of their right to live in New Zealand. If any good came of it, it was that these turbulent times resulted in increased awareness of the importance of Māori language and culture.

In response to community demand, schools in the inner-west suburbs of Auckland began to develop bilingual and immersion language units. Richmond Road School established a Māori bilingual unit in the mid-1980s, with other local schools following. Many of the schools now serving the Grey Lynn, Arch Hill and Westmere communities have Māori bilingual and immersion units that also attract students from outside the area. These schools and others like them have played a part in the revival of Māori language, and today around 2.5 per cent of the population of Grey Lynn, Arch Hill and Westmere has some proficiency in te reo Māori.[59]

Gentrification of the suburbs close to the city, including Grey Lynn, Arch Hill and Westmere, has brought changes to their populations. Where once unskilled and semi-skilled workers and students made up a substantial part of the population, educated professionals are now well represented among the relatively affluent population of this part of Auckland. Today 12.5 per cent of the populations of Arch Hill, Grey Lynn and Westmere are of Māori descent — less than the national average of 18.5 per cent.[60] The story of the Māori who have called these suburbs home is continued through the remaining chapters of this book.

# Farming

**PREVIOUS PAGES:** Cows grazing under trees near Surrey Crescent, early 1900s. AUCKLAND LIBRARIES HERITAGE COLLECTIONS, 80-BIN080

In 1841 the embryonic capital of the new colony was growing, its expansion centred around the eastern slope of the Queen Street valley, on the edge of Commercial Bay. The town's growth required a farming hinterland to support and supply it, and so the focus turned to land neighbouring the town, including the great untamed expanse to the west.

Each month more immigrants arrived from half a world away to make a new life for themselves from the land. Even for those who came from a farming background, there was a steep learning curve. In Aotearoa they were faced with unfamiliar plants, strange soils and altogether different climatic conditions. Not only did crops and pasture not grow the way they did at home, but much of the land that would form the future farms of New Zealand was waterlogged swamp, heavily wooded or covered in scrub.

On 19 April 1841 the first government sale of land at Auckland took place as the overworked colonial surveyor, Felton Mathew, busily drew up the next sections for sale.[1] Mathew's progress was hampered by a lack of staff and the tangle of scrub that cloaked the district, and it would be some years before the surveyor's pegs reached the area west of the fledgling township.[2]

Settler John Cox was keen to establish himself on land beyond the surveyor's reach. Cox had come from Australia and would have been aware of the financial gains made by squatters there: squatting provided an immediate opportunity to establish a farm with little financial outlay. In late 1841 he applied for a squatter's licence to occupy a tract beside the bay and creek that would soon bear his name but which was then known as Opou — a shortened version of its Māori name Opoutukeha.[3] He set to work to clear the land and establish a market garden, and erected a makeshift dwelling for his wife and young sons.[4]

Once his crops had matured, Cox loaded them into a homemade wheelbarrow and headed for town. It was an arduous trip over pig tracks. He headed southeast through what is modern-day Grey Lynn and Newton, before curving around through the Albert Barracks (now occupied by Albert Park and the eastern part of the University of Auckland) and down Princes and

**Farming** | 37

Shortland streets. This meandering route was the easiest — the more direct route through Freemans Bay was covered in dense scrub and blocked by an impassable swamp.[5] The coastal route by boat to Commercial Bay at the foot of Queen Street was the easiest way to get to town, but perhaps the wheelbarrow allowed Cox to sell his produce along the way and then door-to-door once he reached the town.

The survey lines that divided one plot from the next advanced westward, and in late 1844 the government offered for sale the land Cox had tilled. The Cox family was gone, but their name endured.[6]

Many early purchasers of land in the area were speculators and primarily interested in profiting from what they believed would be rising land values. Others sought to make a living from their land. With its freshwater creeks and streams and relative proximity to the growing town, the area was well suited to farming. It was common for these properties to be run initially as mixed farms, growing crops and running a few cows, pigs and chickens, but as the city grew and transport links improved, dairying came to dominate.

**ABOVE LEFT:** A drawing of a bucolic Coxs Creek by an unknown artist, 1863.
STATE LIBRARY OF NEW SOUTH WALES

**ABOVE RIGHT:** John Cox's application for a squatter's licence at Coxs Creek, 1841.
ARCHIVES NEW ZEALAND TE RUA MAHARA O TE KĀWANATANGA, R22804084

Auckland's Court House was the scene of spirited bidding in 1844 and 1845 when land at Coxs Creek, in the area now known as Westmere and the western part of Grey Lynn was offered for sale by the government at auction.[7] The purchasers of the 16 blocks that comprised section 9 in the suburbs of Auckland were not Aucklanders keen to establish themselves in the capital of the new colony; rather, most of them lived in New South Wales or Hokianga, and they were allowed to acquire their suburban

38 | The Near West

land at Auckland without any money changing hands.[8] Few, if any of them would ever see or set foot on it. This peculiar situation stemmed from earlier land sales in Northland transacted in the pre-Treaty era.

Jacky (John) Marmon, who purchased lots 4 and 15 on the western edge of Grey Lynn, was one such purchaser. The Sydney-born son of Irish convict parents, Marmon arrived in the Hokianga as a young man in the 1820s and died there in 1880. He lived as a Māori in Hokianga, marrying a Māori woman and taking part in Ngāpuhi raids led by Hongi Hika in the 1820s. Fluent in te reo Māori, he became an interpreter and negotiated land purchases between Māori and Europeans. He also worked as a sawyer and builder and ran a grog shop. By the time the auctions of 1844 were under way, Marmon was in straitened circumstances: the timber trade which had been the mainstay of the Hokianga economy was in decline and Marmon's skills as an interpreter were no longer in such high demand.[9]

Marmon laid claim to land in the Hokianga that he had acquired directly from Māori in the pre-Treaty era. Known as old land claims, these transactions were to be investigated by the colonial government, and if found to be legitimate, the Crown would award the land to the purchaser. However, the task of surveying and investigating these land claims was immense, and consequently the process of settling the old land claims went on for decades.[10]

Claimants were given the option of swapping their old land claims for surveyed land sold off by the government in and around the main areas of settlement. It was hoped that this would decrease friction between Māori and Pākehā by concentrating settler numbers in and around developing towns, including Auckland, while removing them from areas of interracial tension.[11] Being able to buy land in this way was fantastic news for claimants like Marmon.

Others with old land claims included Matthew Whytlaw, whose land claim was at Kapowai Peninsula in the Bay of Islands, which had been a major centre of trade, but was rapidly usurped when Auckland became the capital of the colony. The outbreak of the Northern War in 1845 further damaged its fortunes. In 1844, when he was living in Sydney, Whytlaw made three purchases in the Coxs Bay/Westmere area.[12]

It appears that immediately after the old land claimants had had their fill of town and suburban land purchases, the government land sales went 'unnoticed and unattended'.[13] Many of the new owners quickly divested themselves of their investments. They had served their purpose: old land claims had been converted into cash when required.

Both Marmon and Whytlaw sold off their landholdings within a few years, and Whytlaw's land later became the Richmond Village subdivision of 1859. Although Whytlaw, Marmon and the other old land claimants would have only

**Farming** | **39**

a fleeting connection with the area, they were by no means the only absentee landowners to buy land in the Grey Lynn/Westmere area in the hope of making money.

In 1849 Peter McNair purchased 35 acres (14 hectares) of land in what is now the western side of Garnet Road (then known as Wolseley Road) between Old Mill and Meola roads in Westmere.[14] The McNair family had been recruited from the struggling Scottish textile town of Paisley as part of the first organised emigration scheme to Auckland, instigated by the Colonial Land and Emigration Commission. They had arrived in the Waitematā Harbour on the *Duchess of Argyle* on the same day in 1842 as the *Jane Gifford*.

The two ships carried over 500 people, many of them members of the Paisley New Zealand Emigration Society. For hand-loom weaver Peter McNair, his wife Jane (née Russell), son Archibald and baby Margaret, it was an opportunity to leave behind the economic depression of their home and forge a brighter future in New Zealand.[15] Margaret died six weeks before they reached their destination, one of 17 deaths on board the *Duchess of Argyle*. An equal number failed to survive the voyage on the *Jane Gifford*. The high death rate was attributed to passengers being in a weakened state due to the poverty they had been living in prior to leaving Scotland.[16]

By 1849 the McNair family had two more daughters and a son, and a third son soon followed.[17] Peter and Archibald, the latter barely in his teens, worked as sawyers at a saw pit on Mill Creek (Motions Creek) to supplement the family's income while they broke in their land — a task that involved cutting and burning the scrub before ploughing and sowing.[18] The view west from the Old Mill Road ridge in late summer would have taken in Low and Motion's flour mill surrounded by William Motion's luxuriant fields of wheat undulating in the breeze.[19] No doubt the success of this neighbouring Western Springs farm encouraged Peter McNair to bring his own property, which he named Bloomfield, into a similar state of production.[20]

In 1858 Peter bought a 4-acre section adjoining the northern boundary of Bloomfield Farm in the area now occupied by Meola Road. Here Archibald built a house where he and his wife Elizabeth (née Weadson) raised their four sons. Around 1880 Archibald bought a farm at Dairy Flat, north of Auckland, and over the next two decades he divided his time between farming this property and tilling a market garden in Garnet Road, his sons no doubt providing considerable assistance. By the start of the twentieth century he had moved permanently to Dairy Flat, where he died in 1929.[21]

Peter gifted his son James a 27-acre portion of Bloomfield Farm in 1884.

James ran a dairy herd there, delivering milk to the emerging residential area of Surrey Hills.[22] Peter retained a 3-acre portion on the northern side of Old Mill Road above Motions Creek for himself, though he later sold this to Archibald. He had earlier sold the neighbouring 4 acres to the north to Gittos and Sons, who established the Bridgenorth Tannery on the site in the mid-1880s.[23] James lived nearby in Wellpark Avenue, where his father had bought land in the 1860s, then later in Garnet Road where he died in 1909, a decade after his wife Eliza (née Crouch). He was survived by three sons and three daughters.[24]

Some third-generation McNairs remained in the area. James and Eliza's daughter Martha lived on in Wellpark Avenue after the death of her parents, and later moved to Garnet Road, where her brother John joined her. Most of the former McNair land had been sold by this stage, but Martha had enough space to raise chickens and supply eggs. Both Martha and John lived in Westmere until the 1950s.[25]

The area between Coxs Creek and the McNairs' land attracted the eye of Archibald Wilson, who was the highest bidder for 40 acres (16 hectares) on the western side of Coxs Creek that today is bounded by Garnet Road to the west and Dorset Street to the south, with the northern boundary extending just beyond William Denny Avenue.[26]

Wilson had arrived in New Zealand from Fifeshire, Scotland, in the early 1840s, and in the mid-1850s was joined by his brother George and his wife and children. Having a relative already established in New Zealand was a significant advantage for an intending settler, and letters home acted as an additional advertisement for the benefits of colonial life. Consequently, chain migration, where members of the same family would follow each other out to the colonies, was common. Like Archibald Wilson's neighbour Peter McNair, George Wilson had also worked in the Scottish textile trade. The industry's declining fortunes no doubt provided the impetus for George and his family to seek new opportunities in the colonies.[27]

George and his wife, Euphemia, had already tried their luck in Australia and were living in Melbourne when their seventh child was born in 1855.[28] Soon after, they relocated to Auckland, where their last child was born in 1858.[29] By this time George was leasing his brother Archibald's property, then known as Wilson Bay Farm.[30]

In the early 1860s, at the age of 59, Archibald Wilson married Christiana Porter, a young widow with two children, and they had a daughter together, Sarah.[31] But before long Wilson was taken to court for failing to support his wife and dependants. Known as 'Miser Wilson', he lived for a time in a

**Farming | 41**

Mary Jane Wilson, wife of Thomas Wilson, feeding chickens on the Wilson farm. Thomas and Mary Jane later built the fine residence Lynton Lodge. It still stands on William Denny Avenue. AUCKLAND WAR MEMORIAL MUSEUM TĀMAKI PAENGA HIRA, PH-NEG-G27665

makeshift hut, built with salvaged material, on the side of a cliff in town. He was regularly seen looking unkempt, his boots laced up with wire.[32]

In 1869 George Wilson secured his own landholding when he bought a neighbouring block of land to the south of Wilson Bay Farm, in the area today delineated by Warwick Avenue, Garnet Road and Dorset Street.[33] George continued to farm his brother's land as well as his own, living with his family in a villa at 28 Dorset Street that still stands today; members of the Wilson family lived there until the 1930s. (The house predates the 1923 road layout and faces side-on to the street.)[34]

Archibald did make arrangements to ensure that his daughter and nieces would not go without. He signed over ownership of his farm at Wilson Bay, at the time leased to his brother and sister-in-law, to his brother's three daughters and his own daughter, Sarah, with the stipulation that the land would be for their sole use 'free from the debts, liabilities or control of any husband or husbands with whom any of them may from time to time intermarry'.[35] He lived in his later years at Wilson Bay Farm, where he died in 1883; George died a few months later.[36]

In the late 1880s and early 1890s, Sarah sold her part of Wilson Bay Farm to her cousin Thomas Wilson for £1560.[37] In 1893 Thomas added to this holding by purchasing land immediately to the north.[38] Thomas ran a baker's shop — the trade practised by his paternal grandfather in Scotland — in the city, and

42 | **The Near West**

David Wilson, son of George and Euphemia, ploughing on the Wilson farm. AUCKLAND WAR MEMORIAL MUSEUM TĀMAKI PAENGA HIRA, PH-NEG-C27674

it appears he combined this with farming. The family lived in a fine residence known as Lynton Lodge that still stands, albeit considerably altered, in William Denny Avenue.[39]

The McNairs and Wilsons made a comfortable life for themselves and enmeshed themselves in local affairs, with members of both families serving on the Newton Highway Board. The McNairs were also pivotal in the establishment of the local Baptist Church.[40]

Over in Arch Hill, Irishman Joseph Young broke in his land on the western slope below Great North Road, where his cows later grazed beneath a belt of blue gums and native trees that he planted.[41] The son of a farmer, Young left his home at 'Archill' (sic), County Tyrone, and arrived in New Zealand in the early 1840s with his wife Jane and three children.[42] The family lived first in Shortland Street, where Joseph was employed as a builder. In 1846 he bought land below the Great North Road ridge on the southern side of what is now Tuarangi Road, and this became part of an extensive 80-acre (32 hectare) farm that extended to Morningside.[43] He named the farm Arch Hill after his home town in Ireland.[44]

Life in Auckland clearly suited Young well. In 1854 he wrote:

> I long to see others of my native land, whose industrious efforts are so scantily rewarded at home, placed in such favourable circumstances as we enjoy in New Zealand . . . to relieve themselves from rack-rent agents, tithe proctors and tenant-right agitation, and hasten to a country where such plagues have never

Farming | 43

yet, nor are likely hereafter to make their appearance — but where all enjoy rights as free as the air we breathe, and where the humblest individual may aspire to occupy the highest stations of honour and emolument our happy land can afford.[45]

In 1861 Young, then in his late fifties, decided to subdivide his Arch Hill land for sale. The large, flat meadow below the ridge was offered for sale as a single lot, while the elevated land above was divided into 14 lots, ranging in size from 2 to 6 acres, and marketed as suburban residence sites. The land did not sell, however, and Young instead offered it for lease.[46]

On the city side of Young's farm was Meadow Farm, the property of George McElwain.[47] McElwain hailed from Killin in Ballymascanlan, County Louth, Ireland, and had travelled to New Zealand via Sydney. He had been recruited to the staff of Captain William Hobson, who was appointed British Consul to New Zealand in 1839 and who later became the first governor of the colony.[48] The Hobson and McElwain families were connected through Hobson's brother, Reverend Henry Theophilus Hobson, minister of the Ballymascanlan Parish Church where the McElwains worshipped.[49]

The Hobsons had lived at Kororāreka Russell until the seat of government was transferred to Auckland in 1841. Preparations for the move to Auckland included the erection of the prefabricated Government House that had been imported from England. McElwain was tasked with converting the scrub-covered land surrounding Government House into a productive farm.[50] Indeed, he was one of the few settlers who had a job to go to when he reached New Zealand. In January 1841 Hobson's wife Eliza noted that, 'MacElwin [sic] has been there for some time, getting the farm in order, and we have two French gardeners employed in making a flower garden for me.'[51]

Hobson clearly valued McElwain as an employee and in 1841 appointed him governor of Auckland's first gaol.[52] The gaol was housed in a makeshift lock-up made of raupō (rushes) that was later replaced by a timber building at the corner of Queen and Victoria streets. The area was marshy at best — the Waihorotiu Stream at the rear of the gaol sometimes flooded and overflowed into the cells. McElwain had his hands full. As the town's population increased, so too did the number of prisoners — in 1842 the two small cells contained so many inmates that they could not all lie down at once. The gaol remained insufficient despite continual enlargements, and the creek that had provided fresh water for the prison, sometimes all too abundantly, gradually became a pestiferous open sewer.[53]

In 1845 McElwain bought 36 acres (14.5 hectares) of land on the southern

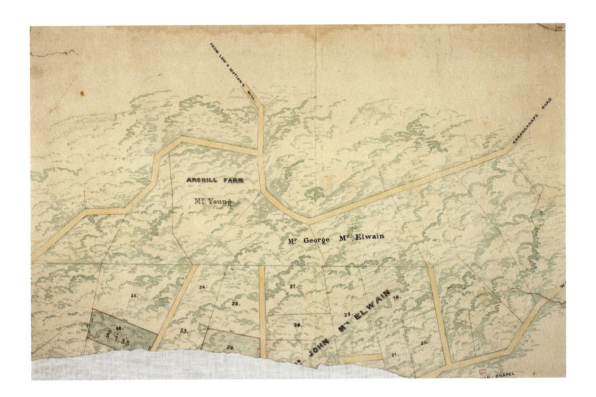

A map showing the location of Joseph Young's Arch Hill farm and George McElwain's Meadow Farm. The road that marks the northern boundary of Young's farm is the original line of Great North Road (now known as Tuarangi Road). AUCKLAND LIBRARIES HERITAGE COLLECTIONS, MAP 4121

side of Great North Road, which he named Meadow Farm. It was part of a larger landholding that straddled both sides of the Arch Hill–Kingsland gully.[54] McElwain then enticed his younger brother John to emigrate in 1849 to assist him with turning the land into a paying farm. He gifted John land on the Kingsland side of the gully, to which John added the purchase of further lots.[55] It appears likely that John helped to establish the farm while George kept Auckland's wayward citizens and animals safely incarcerated, having added the role of pound-keeper to his responsibilities in 1848.[56]

George McElwain married Louisa Conway (née Tucker) in 1848.[57] In 1856 they travelled to Ireland, returning the following year with George's widowed father and another brother, Walter. In 1857 George had a substantial stone house, Glenmore, erected on his Kingsland farm within a few miles of the new Mount Eden gaol for which he also had responsibility.[58]

In the early 1860s, now in his late fifties and in poor health, he retired and sought a pension from the Auckland Provincial Council. At the time, pensions were given to retired military personnel but not to public servants, and McElwain's application was declined. It was noted that he had been well paid while employed at the gaol and was 'as wealthy as any man in the province'.[59] However, the loss of his health and employment no doubt raised financial concerns and he sold the northern part of his Arch Hill estate just before his

Farming | 45

death in 1866.⁶⁰ He willed the remaining part of Meadow Farm to Louisa. She sold it in 1867 to her brother-in-law John, who farmed it along with his adjoining land at Kingsland until its eventual sale in 1883.⁶¹

Besides these early farmers, there were others in the area who arrived later, or whose farming enterprises were smaller or less long-lived. In the 1870s there were still opportunities to buy land held by speculators that had either been leased or lain idle. In 1872 John Billington bought land on Surrey Crescent, now traversed by Stanmore Road and Sherwood Avenue. Here his family established a farm while also running a busy grocer's shop in Freemans Bay, something made possible by having a wife, as well as children old enough to work on the farm or in the shop.⁶²

On the opposite side of Surrey Crescent from the Billington farm was West House Farm, established by Thomas Faulder in 1870. Originally from Cumberland, England, Faulder had come to New Zealand via the Victoria goldfields in Australia. Like Billington, he had a large family. Faulder raised prize-winning dark Brahmaputra and Polish chickens on his farm and was a cartage contractor.⁶³

Unlike the owner-operated farms of Arch Hill and Richmond, the neighbouring Surrey Hills Estate provided leasehold land for those without the wherewithal or inclination to purchase their own land. Originally 198 acres (80 hectares), Surrey Hills encompassed much of the land from Ponsonby Road to Richmond Road in the north and west and Great North Road in the south. This vast expanse had been secured in a series of transactions by John Montefiore, son of a London Jewish aristocrat, who arrived in New Zealand as a young man in 1831. Montefiore established himself as a trader, became fluent in te reo Māori, and spent the next decade on both sides of the Tasman.

By early 1840 he was running a ship chandlery and general store at Kororāreka but he relocated to Auckland in time for the first land sale in 1841. Here he set up a land agency and general merchants in Queen Street and became one of the key business identities in the new settlement. In 1846 he and 17 other businessmen founded the Auckland Savings Bank, initially run from Montefiore's store, which primarily provided banking facilities for Māori and Pākehā workers.⁶⁴

Montefiore would have been well aware of the profits to be made from speculating in suburban land surrounding the new capital. He bought three adjoining lots from the Crown. The 94-acre (38-hectare) property was bounded to the south by Great North Road and to the north by the creek that ran through the Grey Lynn gully to Coxs Bay; the eastern and western boundaries were in the area where Sussex Street and Prime Road are today.[65] Montefiore quickly purchased an additional four lots to the north and east — his estate now included all the land on the Ponsonby Road frontage between Great North and Richmond roads, and much of the land on the southern side of Richmond Road to where Farrar Street is today.[66]

Most of these additional lots were owned by Hokianga settlers who had likely never seen the land they bought in Auckland. As with other purchasers at the sale of Crown land, they had used scrip (a form of credit) to pay for their Auckland lots. This allowed them to swap low-value Hokianga land, which they had bought directly from Māori prior to the establishment of the colony, for land in the new capital.

The Crown land auction netted wildly different amounts for the various lots — Montefiore paid £46 in scrip for a 23-acre lot fronting Great North Road, while John Kelly bought the neighbouring 38-acre lot at the corner of Great North and Ponsonby Roads for £242/11 in scrip. Kelly quickly on-sold his lot to Montefiore for £242/11, effectively swapping his low-value land for cash.[67] Other sellers were content to sell for sums below the value of scrip: George Russell and William Young both sold their lots to Montefiore for a fraction of the scrip value they had paid for them.[68]

Montefiore had now amassed a substantial suburban estate, which he advertised for lease in the *Daily Southern Cross* in 1844:

> To Butchers Graziers and Dairymen. The undersigned is prepared to lease for seven years on an improving Lease, that highly valuable Estate, known as the 'Surry [sic] Hills Estate' comprising one hundred and ninety-eight acres of capital Grazing Land, adjoining the Town, with a beautiful stream of water running through the whole of the ground. For the fattening of cattle or sheep to supply the Auckland district, this estate is invaluable and will be let on highly eligible terms.[69]

To describe the estate as 'capital grazing land' was a little wishful at this time, but the 'improving' leases meant that the land had to be returned in a condition better suited to farming than it had been at the beginning.

In 1847 Montefiore sold the estate to James Williamson and Thomas Crummer for £500, considerably less than the value of scrip and cash he had purchased it with.[70] Williamson was from Belfast. In 1840, while still in his mid-twenties, he settled in New Zealand and established a store on the beach at Kororāreka. The following year he moved to Auckland and went into business with Crummer, running a hotel and the first general store in the new settlement.

Little is known of the early life of Thomas Crummer, but like Williamson

**Farming** | **47**

he was a young man when they established the business of Williamson and Crummer in 1841.[71]

As Montefiore had done before them, Williamson and Crummer added to the Surrey Hills Estate, investing a further £115 to purchase three additional lots, thus extending the property to encompass almost all of the land bounded by Ponsonby, Great North and Richmond roads, only excepting three blocks at the northern end where Tutanekai, Hakanoa and Sackville streets run today.[72] At 314 acres (127 hectares), it was probably one of the largest suburban landholdings at the time and its value would climb exponentially over the next few decades. Crummer and Williamson also owned adjoining farms at Epsom where they bred stock and racehorses.[73]

Part of the Surrey Hills Estate was let to Edward Mayne, who established a model farm on it. Although this was short-lived, his period of occupation was marked by a range of improvements, including 10 acres of fenced land with a cottage, stable and outbuildings.[74] With the departure of Mayne, the estate was again offered for lease in 1855. After being advertised unsuccessfully from January to September, the leasing agent was beginning to sound desperate:

> Mr Hansard cannot close this advertisement without strongly recommending it to the earnest attention of parties in the neighbouring Colonies, affording as it does an ample scope for profitable investment of capital, and a most desirable opportunity for any one intending to settle in this Colony.[75]

By the mid-1860s the Surrey Hills Estate had been leased for two decades, and for at least part of that time it served as a sheep run.[76] Improvements had been made, but much remained in a wild condition. Crummer had died, and Williamson now became the sole owner after buying the share of the estate inherited by Crummer's sons for £11,000. Williamson had done well from his business enterprises, making significant profits from government contracts to supply troops during the Waikato war, and his investments in city and suburban land had been lucrative: he was a wealthy man.[77]

Williamson began to invest in improvements to his Surrey Hills Estate; tenders for clearing, burning and ploughing sections of the property were called and work was soon under way.[78] Grass was sown and circular plantations, protected by ditches and fences, were planted, providing a habitat for the pheasants that had been recently introduced to New Zealand and no doubt provided some sport for Williamson.[79]

Frank Lawry leased part of the Surrey Hills Estate from the late 1860s. Lawry had worked on his father's farm before coming to New Zealand in 1863, where he was soon engaged on the substantial Auckland estates of Thomas

Macky and James Dilworth. He then established his own farm at Epsom, and soon after took the lease on the Surrey Hills Estate so he could expand his operation. He went on to become a stock agent and member of Parliament for North Franklin (1887–90) and Parnell (1890–1911).[80]

At Surrey Hills Lawry created a first-class dairy farm. In 1871 farm buildings went up, and in July Surrey Hills Dairy formally opened for business. Soon queues of up to 100 people, billies in hand, could be seen daily at milking time. Lawry believed in personal service and allowed customers to request milk from their cow of choice.[81]

Proximity to the city was part of the farm's success. The *Daily Southern Cross* noted:

> [M]ilk can be brought from a distance by means of carts and spring-traps, but milk so conveyed over miles of rough roads cannot be expected to equal that which has not been subjected to such rough usage . . . it not unfrequently happens that milk so conveyed is made sour before it is distributed to the consumers.[82]

In the mid-1870s Lawry relinquished the lease to New Zealand Wars veteran and racehorse breeder Major James Walmsley, who carried on with the farm and dairy and added milk delivery in the Newton district.[83] Walmsley advertised in the *Auckland Star*: 'Special Cows kept for Infants and Invalids . . . Contracts made to supply Milk at a fixed rate for the year.'[84]

But not every lessee was able to make a good living from the Surrey Hills Estate. In the late 1870s a farmer with the rather remarkable name of Ponsonby Peacocke purchased Walmsley's lease for the princely sum of £650, borrowing to do so.[85]

Peacocke had been born in Devon into a military family on his father's side and with royal connections on his mother's. In 1857, as a teenager, he emigrated with his family to New Zealand. Theirs was a comfortable journey, made in the company of the family governess and two servants. After a false start in Canterbury, the family settled on a farm in Howick. His father had no agricultural knowledge, was not interested in doing any physical work and had little interest in the day-to-day operation of his estate. Ponsonby, by then aged 19, and his mother, Isabella, took control, learning what they could from neighbouring farmers and employing local labourers to clear, fence and plough the land, which consisted mainly of unpromising clay.

The farm failed to pay, and with the outbreak of the Waikato War in 1863 Ponsonby Peacocke joined the militia, no doubt seeking some welcome income and a diversion from running the farm. Ponsonby later followed his father into politics, serving on the Auckland Provincial Council from 1874 until the abolition of the provinces two years later.[86] Despite gaining considerable farming experience as a young man, he could not turn a profit at Surrey Hills

**Farming | 49**

and was struck a final blow when epidemic disease spread through his stock. Heavily in debt, Peacocke was forced to relinquish the farm and to sell off his remaining assets.[87]

Businesses utilising the by-products of farming soon established themselves at Richmond, many relocated from the more congested parts of the city. Local abattoirs despatched skins to nearby fellmongers, who scraped them of their hair before sending them to tanners for curing and finishing. Wool scourers cleaned the grease and dirt from fleeces. Boiling-down works rendered animal fat into tallow to make soap, candles and Dubbin boot polish, and ground up bones to make fertiliser. All these industries operated within the otherwise bucolic landscape, drawing their raw materials from local and more distant farms.[88]

From the 1870s another set of farmers came to Arch Hill and Richmond. At a time of poverty in their homeland, men from the Pearl River delta area of Guangdong province in Southern China journeyed to Sum Gum Shan or New Gold Mountain, as New Zealand was known, to earn money for their families back home. New Zealand had earlier drawn Chinese men to the goldfields, but these new arrivals sought to earn a living from tilling the soil.[89] Their eventual aim was to return home to a better life.

In February 1878 the *New Zealand Herald* reported that 30 Chinese men had recently arrived in Auckland and had leased property in Khyber Pass, Remuera and Arch Hill, where they had established market gardens. The Arch Hill land measured 10 acres (4 hectares) and was in an area now known as Grey Lynn, east of the Bullock Track between Surrey Crescent and Tuarangi Road, part of Thomas Faulder's farm.[90]

The clay-laden soils of the Arch Hill and Grey Lynn districts provided raw materials for several brickworks, but they required considerable improvement in order to grow vegetables; a Mr Cole who had formerly leased the property to grow willow for basket-making had not met with success. By early 1878, however, the Chinese had trenched and drained the land and gradually increased its fertility by adding manure brought from city stables on the return journey from delivering vegetables. Ah Guit's 'extensive and well stocked kitchen garden' in Richmond Road near Coxs Creek was operating in the early 1880s on land that had 'lain desolate while in the hands of European proprietors'.[91] The Chinese market gardeners' methods allowed them to farm their land more intensively than their Pākehā counterparts.[92]

In the late 1870s Ah Kew was living and working at the market garden on Faulder's farm along with two of his countrymen, tending their vegetables from

Three gardeners standing in the Chinese market gardens on Great North Road, opposite the foot of the Bullock Track, with Arch Hill in the background, early 1900s. AUCKLAND LIBRARIES HERITAGE COLLECTIONS, 80-BIN185

dawn till dusk, and in 1882 Kew Hing, Ah Sing, Ah Chee, Ah Cheok and Ching Fou were all gardening on part of the Young family's farm on the southern side of Tuarangi Road. The success of these gardens brought more Chinese to the area.[93]

The Fong Brothers leased the Billington property on Surrey Crescent before it was taken over by Ming Quong, who gardened there from the late 1880s until the early 1890s. Quong went on to establish a fruiterer and grocery shop in the city as well as a new market garden at Epsom.[94]

Thomas Wong Doo established his garden on the southern side of Surrey Crescent. In 1898 he returned home to Ging Bui Heung in Sun Wui, where he married Chan Unui, later returning to New Zealand with three children. A further two children were born in Auckland. Thomas Wong Doo went on to become a founder of Produce Markets Limited, a Chinese growers' collective that was established in 1930 and continued for decades.[95]

The quiet-living, hard-working gardeners of the area generally attracted little attention, but their peaceful existence was sometimes interrupted by vandals who threw stones, broke windows, destroyed their crops and harassed them.[96] There were occasional disputes with neighbouring farmers who allowed their stock to enter the market gardens, where they destroyed crops of turnips and cabbages. In 1883 Kow Hing (also referred to as Kew Hing) got so annoyed at seeing yet another cow in the garden that he shot the offending animal, landing himself in court.[97]

A similar incident in 1889 landed Ah Chew, Ah Yum, Ah Choy and Ah Soy in court, where a dozen Chinese witnesses were called.[98] The charge was dismissed, but it sparked conflict between some members of the local Chinese market-gardening community, resulting in further court appearances.[99]

The long depression that began in the mid-1880s had a considerable effect on local market gardeners, who were reported as being 'in a very bad state . . . They are not earning tucker.'[100] Where before their efforts had earned them £2–3 per week, they were now earning less than 10 shillings weekly.[101]

In 1890 the gardeners were dealt another blow when one of their number, Ah Goon, was diagnosed with leprosy and put into isolation in his Arch Hill dwelling. As fear of the disease spread through the community, the public appetite for crops grown by the Chinese dwindled.[102] Other health concerns were also aired. There was no water supply to the gardens, so the Chinese had dammed the stream that ran through Newton, Eden Terrace and Arch Hill and used this to wash vegetables. But it was contaminated with sewage and dead dogs, and the practice soon drew the attention of the Newton Borough Council. The council also objected to an 'abominable smell' arising from a market garden in Surrey Crescent where fish refuse had been used to fertilise the land.[103]

Despite their small numbers, Auckland's Chinese residents dominated market gardening in the late nineteenth century. This did not go unnoticed within the wider Auckland community. When the first Chinese market gardeners thrust their spades into the soils of Grey Lynn and Arch Hill in the 1870s, immigration to New Zealand had been unregulated, but in the following decade there was considerable debate about who should be allowed to come to New Zealand. This culminated in the passing of the Chinese Immigrants Act 1881, which sought to reduce the number of Chinese immigrants by applying a £10 tax — known as a poll tax — to be paid upon first entry to the country, and setting a maximum quota of Chinese immigrants per ships' tonnage.[104]

These measures initially had little effect on Chinese immigration; after all, the tax represented around four to five weeks' income for a Chinese market gardener at the time.[105] But an 1896 amendment to the Act altered the ratio: now only one Chinese immigrant was allowed whereas 20 would have been accepted 15 years earlier. The poll tax increased tenfold to an astonishing £100 and the numbers arriving fell considerably.[106]

Chinese market gardeners worked hard to make a profit, and this untiring diligence made Pākehā market gardeners feel particularly threatened. In 1878 Pākehā Auckland market gardeners met to 'consider various matters affecting trade interests, and Chinese labour in connection therewith'.[107] Though opinion was somewhat divided, the meeting elected to petition the Auckland City Council to pass a by-law preventing growers from hawking their produce in the streets — a method common among Chinese growers.[108] Some Chinese market gardeners were also convicted for working on a Sunday after Pākehā farmers complained that 'Celestials were in the habit of getting in seven working days per week, against the six of their white competitors.'[109]

From the 1880s farming in Grey Lynn and Arch Hill began to contract, partly prompted by the financial difficulties in which James Williamson, owner of the Surrey Hills Estate, found himself. Williamson had invested heavily in swampy Waikato land that required considerable investment in drainage to farm and he was enmeshed in other companies with similarly wretched investments. He led a lavish lifestyle at his elaborate Italianate homestead The Pah in Hillsborough, which was surrounded by manicured gardens and staffed with numerous servants. The wealth and power he had accrued as a director of leading companies, including the Bank of New Zealand and the New Zealand Insurance Company, and being elected Member

A mob of sheep near Low and Motion's old mill at Western Springs, 1904. AUCKLAND LIBRARIES HERITAGE COLLECTIONS, 1729-018

of the House of Representatives (1862–67) and serving on the Legislative Council (1870–88), was a long way from his humble beginnings as a ship's mate. But by the early 1880s he was on the brink of financial ruin and the sale of Surrey Hills was imperative. The estate was bought by the Auckland Agricultural Company, of which he was a director.

Surrey Hills was laid out for residential purposes, but the process of conversion from farm to residential suburb was protracted.[110] Houses replaced livestock in the area closest to Ponsonby, but a vast area to the west remained undeveloped for many years. Here cows continued to graze, unfazed by the invisible survey lines that defined the residential plots and paper roads beneath their hooves.

The proximity of agricultural and suburban residential land uses caused some problems. In early 1884 the *Auckland Star* reported that horses, cattle and goats were being driven by their owners to Surrey Hills, where they were cast out onto the estate to graze. The fences that had formerly enclosed the livestock had presumably come down as the estate was surveyed for sale and, as a result, the streets opposite the estate in the Arch Hill district were being frequented by 'nomadic quadrupeds'.[111]

By the turn of the twentieth century Isaac McNair, grandson of Peter McNair who had established a farm at Richmond half a century earlier, was

54 | The Near West

still working the land and George Wilson's sons were also farming nearby. Farms and market gardens on rented land made up much of the rest of the local farming community. The industrial counterparts of farming, including the city abattoirs, Hellaby's meatworks and the Warnock soap and candle works continued to belch pollution into the waterways and atmosphere. These land uses would gradually become anathema to the increasingly residential locale.

As the country emerged from the long depression of the 1890s, suburban advance, encouraged by the extension of tram services from 1903, gradually swallowed up the land at Surrey Hills and beyond. From 1915 the new suburb of Westmere, formerly part of Richmond, began to take shape.

As the intending purchasers of land at Westmere arrived to inspect sections and builders set to work on those already purchased, a few cows still chewed their cud in the vicinity of Faulder Avenue where James Boyd's dairy herd supplied milk to locals.[112] But by the 1930s the farms were all but gone, and the new households of Grey Lynn and Westmere were supplied with vegetables, milk and other farm produce from more distant parts.

# Residential development

**PREVIOUS PAGES:** The Binns' family home at 13 Francis Street, Grey Lynn. Lucy Doris Binns is sitting with a doll's pram by the front door, c. 1905. AUCKLAND LIBRARIES HERITAGE COLLECTIONS, 80-BIN290

It was inevitable that fields and livestock on the gentle slopes west of Ponsonby would eventually be replaced by people seeking a quiet residential area within easy reach of the city. It would take decades for this process to become complete, but many of the original houses remain to tell the story of the suburban growth in this part of the city.

The first residential subdivision in the Grey Lynn/Westmere area was advertised in the press prior to auction in 1858:

> The Village of Richmond . . . comprising about 200 beautifully situated allotments, many of them having frontage to the water . . . from its position, soil, and climate promises to become a favourite resort for the Citizens of Auckland.[1]

At this time Auckland was the capital of New Zealand, a title it relinquished in 1865, but its role as the centre of government in its first decade and a half gave it a boost in investment that helped raise the value of land within the town and beyond it. The Village of Richmond subdivision offered roughly quarter-acre sections, each suitable for a modest dwelling with space for a vegetable garden, fruit trees and a chicken run.[2] Maps of the proposed village showed the northern border gently lapped by the waters of the Waitematā at Coxs Bay, while a government road (Richmond Road) on the southern border provided access to the city. Pretty Coxs Creek and its tributaries meandered on the eastern side and offered a valuable freshwater source.[3]

But the main appeal lay in the potential return for those willing and able to invest. It had already proven a sound investment for Matthew Whytlaw of Sydney, who had purchased the original two blocks. Whytlaw sold off his Coxs Creek properties in 1855, netting £261 in the process.[4] Michael Wood, who was now subdividing the land, also stood to make a good profit.[5]

Wood's subdivision opened up the land at Coxs Bay to people of slender means, allowing them to invest in a small section of suburban land. Hopeful purchasers flocked to Connell and Ridings' auction mart in Queen Street on 13 December 1858. Bidding was keen, and virtually all allotments were quickly

snapped up for prices ranging from £3 to £11/5 per acre.[6]

So who were the purchasers of the Village of Richmond, and what did they do with their land? Brickmaker John Leckie, who was seeking a place to live and work, was well outnumbered by speculators. Buyers were able to secure their lots on payment of a quarter of the purchase price with the remaining amount due four months later.[7] Most bidders secured more than one allotment, and many bought a number of adjoining sites. Some of these were rapidly resold: bricklayer George Arber purchased three and sold them a few months later, making a 42 per cent profit.[8]

Among the investors were several members of the 65th Regiment of Foot, a British infantry unit that arrived in New Zealand in 1846 to serve in the New Zealand Wars. Of all the imperial forces, they served in New Zealand the longest, finally departing in 1865. These men were provided with living accommodation at the various places at which they were stationed, so it appears that their Richmond Village landholdings were not intended for their own use. John Williams Marshall, paymaster of the 65th Regiment, bought two Richmond Village sections in 1859 and sold them six years later for twice the price to another member of the regiment, quartermaster George Collins.[9]

Windle Hill St Hill, aide-de-camp and ensign of the regiment, was one of many absentee owners. He purchased a number of lots at the Richmond Village auction, selling a few of these in the 1860s, when he left New Zealand for India, but retaining the major portion of his land until the early twentieth century, by which time he had been living in Tasmania for decades.[10] Some of the longer-term investors no doubt leased their otherwise vacant land to turn a profit.

Some of these investors made good returns, but Michael Wood, who subdivided Richmond Village, found himself in financial difficulty and in 1866 his remaining property was sold at auction. Included were several lots at Richmond Village that had no doubt reverted to his ownership when the purchasers failed to complete their payments.[11]

Some Richmond land was purchased for industrial purposes, including William Edgar's dye works, which were established by the creek that bears his name. In 1872 a visitor to the dye works described the area:

> The hamlet of Richmond is a beautiful and romantic spot. It is exceedingly rich in old ruins. Decayed brickmaking establishments stand out in pleasing relief, the hills at the rear subdued into a pencilling of magnificent outline. There is an old sheepwash erection worthy of the brush and palette of a Turner or Gibson, and I gazed with rapture upon a ruined two-roomed weatherboard cottage.[12]

Clearly Richmond had so far failed to develop into anything resembling a village. It would retain its bucolic character for years to come.

A map showing the 1858 Village of Richmond subdivision on the north side of Richmond Road between Coxs Creek (top right) and the creek that would soon be known as Leckie's and then Edgars Creek (top left) with the adjoining Richmond Hill subdivision of 1859 (below). Richmond Hill's larger lots were advertised as suitable for vineyards, dairy farms or market gardens and included Wellpark and Greenwood (later renamed Larchwood) avenues. This area was later further subdivided into house lots. AUCKLAND LIBRARIES HERITAGE COLLECTIONS, MAP 4159

**Residential development** | **61**

eanwhile, land further to the south was marked out into residential sites accessed by a grid of streets. Arch Hill, located conveniently close to the city on the south side of Great North Road, was subdivided and offered for sale as far west as Commercial Road in the late 1850s.[13] The 1865 auction of the Newton West subdivision bounded by Bond Street in the east and Commercial Road in the west attracted a large crowd and all lots were sold.[14] Unlike the Village of Richmond, Arch Hill offered easy access to the centre of Auckland, and its smaller lots made it more affordable.

Soon the sound of hammers rang out across the valley and neat little timber cottages sprang up. By the late 1870s Arch Hill boasted a population of 651 — the Newton Highway District (which included Richmond Village) had just 157.[15] Residential development at Arch Hill continued through the rest of the nineteenth century and into the twentieth.

Dramatic population growth in the early 1880s spurred demand for residential building sites close to the city. In just five years the population of Auckland Borough doubled to reach 33,161 in 1886.[16] The time appeared to be ripe for cutting up farms close to the city for residential purposes. In 1883 the Auckland Agricultural Association invited competitive designs for the layout of the 314-acre Surrey Hills Estate as a residential suburb.[17] The subdivision garnered much public interest, as the largest residential subdivision of its day. The *Auckland Star* noted:

> Surrey Hills is the finest estate around Auckland, and many persons in the
> crowded parts of the city have been looking forward to the cutting up of the
> property as a means of escape from crowded neighbourhoods.[18]

The winner of the design competition, Theodore Hickson, pitched a tent on the estate in March 1883 and proceeded to survey the area in preparation for marking out streets and site boundaries for over 2000 sections.[19]

His layout included a rear right-of-way to provide a tradesman's entrance to each property. This triggered an avalanche of criticism. The Newton Highway Board rejected the plan because it would encourage site owners to place two dwellings on each property: one facing the street and another accessed by the right-of-way.[20] The *Auckland Star* was also critical, calling the plan 'one of the worst designs of a new town ever presented to a modern civilised community'[21] and suggesting that it would become 'hedged by fever-breeding slums, in association with which the health of the residents and property values would dwindle away together'.[22]

There were other reasons to condemn the plan:

> A want of liberality and public spirit is most manifestly displayed . . . In an
> area which . . . is intended to carry a population of at least 10,000 persons

The Newton West subdivision to the west of Bond Street, including Commercial Road, Russell Street (now known as Cooper Street), Cheapside (now Seddon Street), and Dale End, which now lies under the northwestern motorway, 1865. LAND INFORMATION NEW ZEALAND, DEED BLUE 26

# NEWTON WEST.
## 170 CHOICE BUILDING ALLOTMENTS.

**BLUE 26**

NORTH

For Auckland City Councils approval
of resubdn. of Lots 159,160+161 see
K 31023
For Local Bodies Consent as to subdn of Lots
36, 37, +38 see K 5.1374

TO BE SOLD BY AUCTION,

TUESDAY, MAY 2nd, 1865,

AT THE LAND MART, FORT STREET,

AT TWELVE O'CLOCK,

SAMUEL COCHRANE,

most eligibly situate on the Great North
mits of the City of Auckland, and deserves par
attention on its healthy and commanding position, possess
ing a prospect which for extent and variety cannot be surpassed, as
from nearly the whole of the Allotments there is a splendid view
of the WAITEMATA, and the distant Ranges of the KAIPARA,
MAHURANGI, WAIHEKE, and the intervening country, comprising
Mount Albert, Three Kings, Mount Eden, and rapidly improving
Newton.

There is a substantial Brick Cottage on Allotment No. 71,
having 50 feet frontage to the Great North Road.

### TERMS:
**ONE-THIRD, CASH;**
Balance by Promissory Notes at Six and Twelve Months, bearing
Ten per cent per annum.

CREIGHTON AND SCALES, PRINTERS, AUCKLAND.

Newton Hotel.

Boyd's Brick-yard.

D  A  L  B  E  N  D  A

Seddon  St.

Cooper  St.

Excepted from subdivisions

G  R  E  A  T   N  O  R  T  H   R  O  A  D

**BLUE 26**

closely packed together, there is not a single breathing space, not a site for a public school.[23]

The Newton Highway Board held a special meeting to discuss the plan just days before the sale of the first sections, and resolved that roads within the district should be at least 66 feet (20 metres) wide. The service lanes would have to go.[24] Though it had no jurisdiction over Surrey Hills, Auckland City Council also entered the fray, concerned that the city's parks, churches and schools would become overtaxed as thousands of new Surrey Hills residents travelled to the city for education, recreation and religious services.[25] The sale was postponed and the plans redrawn, this time without the offending service lanes, but the estate remained devoid of sites reserved for community purposes.[26]

**Well Park Estate plan, 1880.** LAND INFORMATION NEW ZEALAND, DP 254

While this work was under way, several smaller subdivisions of neighbouring areas were brought to the market.[27] Well Park Estate, a subdivision that included Maxwell Avenue and parts of Wellpark and Larchwood avenues (the latter then known as Greenwood Street) was offered for sale in 1883. The following year, Mr Jones subdivided his small farm 'The Pines' west of Richmond Road to form residential sites on Francis, Wilton and Castle (then known as Salisbury) streets. The plans for these small estates were not subjected to the same criticisms as Surrey Hills; they had no back alleys and were not a sufficient size to warrant the provision of reserves.[28]

Well Park Estate was promoted as suited to 'that large and important class of the community known as the Artisan Class'.[29] Like other suburban subdivisions of the day, it attracted speculative investors as well as those wishing to build a home.[30] Of the nine purchasers at the second auction of the estate, four purchased multiple allotments.[31]

In October 1883 the long-awaited auction of part of the Surrey Hills Estate was held. The blocks closest to the city were offered for sale and realised high prices.[32] The terms were attractive: one-fifth cash upon purchase and the remainder payable within five years with interest of 7 per cent per annum.[33] For subsequent sales in the estate, buyers were invited to visit the land agent to purchase lots at set prices.[34]

The first half of the 1880s saw a boom in Auckland's suburban real estate, spurred by speculative purchasers, population growth and the availability of cheap credit. In mid-1885 as the depression set in, the suburban land market collapsed. Credit dried up and some speculators who had paid only deposits on their properties found themselves in financial trouble. Unemployment rose and many men left town in search of work. By 1888 the building industry had come

64 | The Near West

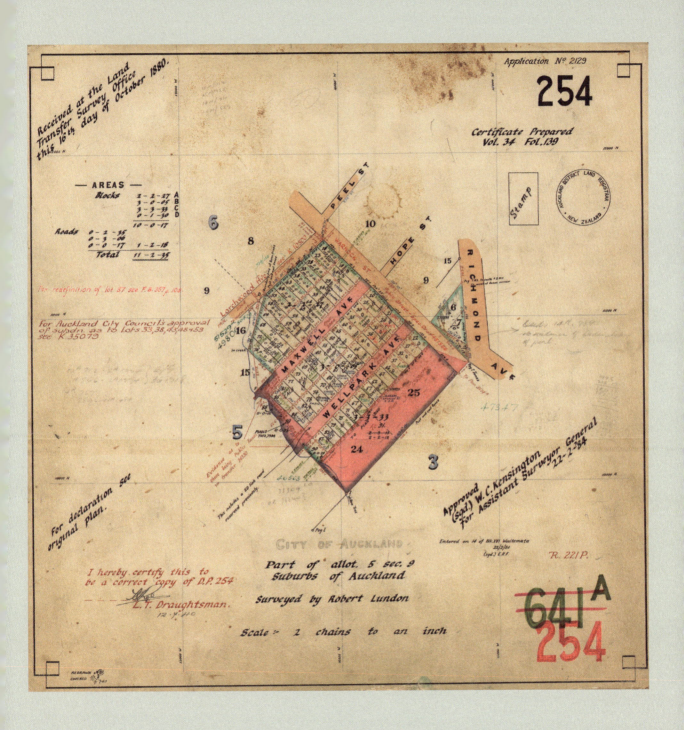

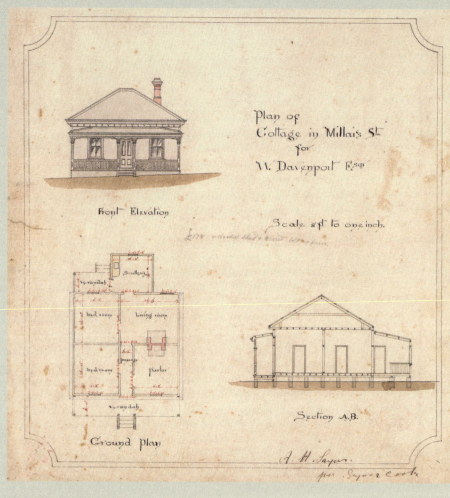

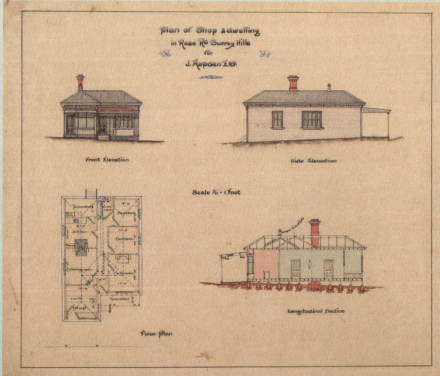

**LEFT:** W. A. Holman was one of the many Auckland architects who designed houses and commercial buildings in the late nineteenth and early twentieth centuries. His residential work included both humble cottages and elaborate villas. The simple two-bedroom dwelling shown at left was built at the northern end of Millais Street in 1897.

**BELOW LEFT:** A smart-looking three-bedroom home with a small shop at the front designed by W. A. Holman and built at 26 Rose Road in 1897.

**OPPOSITE ABOVE:** A more elaborate corner villa designed by W. A. Holman and built at 55 Rose Road in 1900.

**OPPOSITE BELOW:** Many two-storey shops included family accommodation behind the shop and on the upper floor, as shown in this plan of four shops designed by W. A. Holman and built on the corner of Great North Road and Pollen Street in 1910–11. ARCHITECTURE ARCHIVE, UNIVERSITY OF AUCKLAND, HOLMAN MOSES ARCHITECTURAL DRAWINGS, MSS-ARCHIVES-ARCH-2020/17

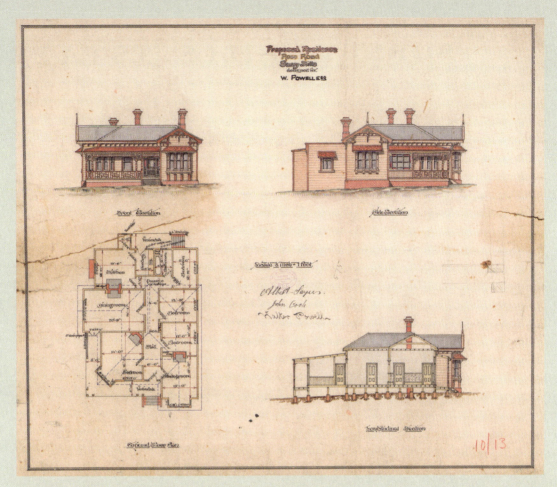
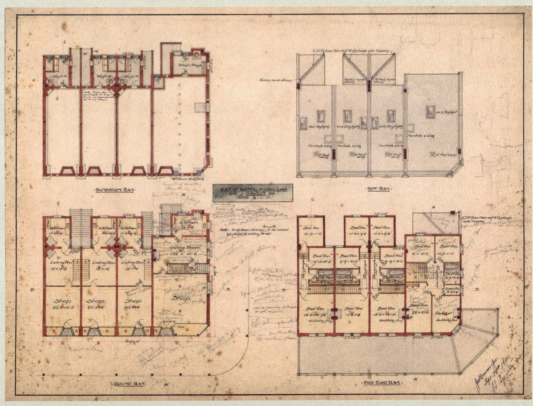

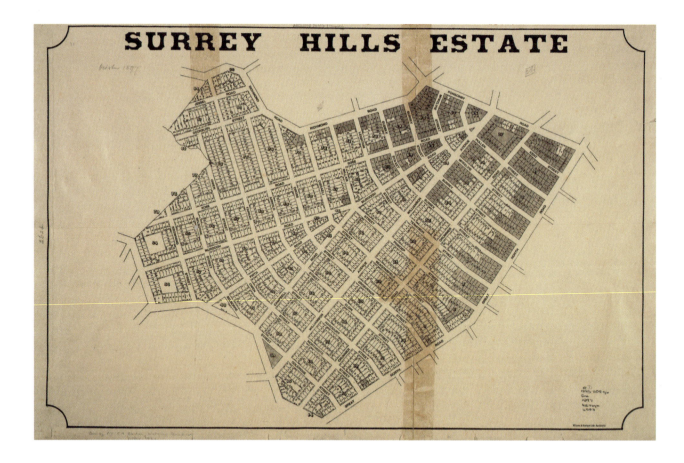

to a standstill.[35] Owners whose land adjoined Surrey Hills complained that council valuations were based on earlier, more buoyant sales figures.[36]

Properties were passed in at auction, and the *New Zealand Herald* noted that high rents during the property boom had resulted in an oversupply of houses that was expected to last many years.[37] Land agents, including Robert Greenwood who had marketed the Well Park Estate, were bankrupted.[38] Prominent businessmen James Williamson and Thomas Russell, directors and major shareholders of the Auckland Agricultural Association, were in considerable difficulty.[39] Commission agent William McKinstry committed suicide on the Surrey Hills Estate.[40] Tales of woe abounded.

As summer arrived, cracks opened in the parched clay of empty sections in Surrey Hills Estate. In 1893 unsold sections of Surrey Hills were leased for grazing, as there was no immediate prospect of buyers for the land.[41] Many seasons would pass before building work resumed with any vigour.

As the economy recovered, residential building gradually resumed in Arch Hill, Surrey Hills and Richmond. The population of Auckland was growing, and by the start of the twentieth century the residential housing

A plan of the Surrey Hills subdivision, without the offending rear lanes that had been part of the original plan. The first sale took place in October 1883, when blocks at the city end of the estate were sold at auction. Although it was the largest suburban subdivision of its day, it had no reserves for sport and recreation. In the early twentieth century low-lying, unsold parts of the estate were vested in the Grey Lynn Borough Council as a public domain. AUCKLAND LIBRARIES HERITAGE COLLECTIONS, MAP 4553

68 | The Near West

market had bounced back.[42] By 1903 there were 1040 dwellings in Grey Lynn Borough (formerly known as Newton Borough and including Surrey Hills and Richmond).[43]

Some people engaged architects, while others utilised designs from architectural plan books that could be purchased for the purpose. Corner sections, prized for their size and double street frontage, often had grander homes. In 1905 Edward Mahoney and Sons called for tenders for a house at the corner of Elgin Street and Crummer Road. Arthur White, one of a number of architects working in the area, sought a builder for a house he had designed in Sussex Street.[44]

Other homes were constructed by speculative builders who purchased a series of sections and built a number of dwellings, often using the same plan. Between 1914 and 1921, for example, builder George Halford purchased sections in Surrey Hills and built a number of houses for sale, including some in Crummer Road in 1911, Williamson Avenue and Millais Street in 1912 and Selbourne Street in 1913. In 1914 he was busy building three near-identical villas in Firth Road.[45] John McCauley, similarly, bought sections in both Grey Lynn and Arch Hill, where he built a number of houses for sale in the 1920s.[46]

A few second-hand buildings were brought to the area as well. When Auckland City Council sold off 18 buildings in Ponsonby Road, Hopetoun Street and Karangahape Road for removal, many were moved to sections on the Surrey Hills Estate.[47] The process resulted in blocked streets and complaints of 'peregrinating old shanties . . . wandering about the streets in all directions'.[48]

Some investors erected dwellings for rental purposes. In 1903 prominent businessman James Mennie, owner of the biscuit, confectionery and jam manufacturing firm Mennie and Dey, engaged architect Richard Keals to design eight cottages at the city end of Arch Hill.[49] By 1919 there were 16 dwellings on a private street known as Mennie's Reserve or Mennie Street (now part of Monmouth Street).[50] The street was made public when the neighbouring part of Mennie's land was purchased for the establishment of the Newton Central School in 1920.[51]

Some clusters of buildings of similar design had nothing to do with speculative builders or investors. The Workers Dwelling Act 1905 provided a mechanism for the government to build houses for workers to combat the nationwide housing shortage. The first state houses were built in the four main centres. Early examples in Auckland were in Ellerslie and Ōtāhuhu. In 1914 tenders were called for six workers' dwellings in Kingsley Street (then known as King Street).[52]

**Residential development | 69**

# Cottages, villas and bungalows

The period houses that define the suburbs of Arch Hill, Grey Lynn and Westmere were built from the 1860s through to the 1930s. These buildings, set in line along the local streets, are representative of this period of suburban growth in Auckland, when this area transformed from paddocks and scrub to neatly set-out suburbs. Most of these relatively modest houses survive intact, and their form and style and the relationship of each to its neighbours and to the street creates the distinct historic character of the area, a character that expresses the waves of residential development that have occurred. Repeating patterns of proportion, scale and setback to the street remain defining features of Grey Lynn, Arch Hill and Westmere.

Most of this early housing was for working people and tradespeople, and these areas remained 'workers' suburbs' up until gentrification began in the 1980s. In Auckland it was possible for working class immigrants to purchase a plot of suburban land on which to build a free-standing home, a dream come true relative to their former lives in Great Britain.

Timber construction is one of the defining elements of these houses. Very few were built of brick — timber was king. The timber industry was well established by the mid-nineteenth century, and grew in size and sophistication as more and more native forest was milled over these decades. At first kauri was freely available, with pūriri and tōtara used for piles or joinery. By the time of the bungalow, kauri had been replaced by rimu as the kauri resource had diminished and milling of the central North Island had begun.[53]

By the 1860s timber merchants in Auckland were selling not only cut timber but also pre-made components such as windows and doors as well as decorative embellishments.[54] The quality and natural durability of kauri and other native timbers has contributed to the long life of these houses. The majority are now over a century old.

Simple workers' cottages generally had little embellishment and were either single-storey with one or more rooms, or double-storey gabled cottages with two or more rooms. These houses could be easily added to and many featured a modest verandah at the front.[55]

The first 'villa' type houses in the area were larger versions of the workers' cottages, a prototype of the 'bay villa' in its many manifestations. These early villas tended to have steeply pitched roofs, and were plainer than late-nineteenth-century villas, without so many mass-produced components. These houses have been described as 'pre-industrial vernacular', a vernacular that was a response to the materials available in New Zealand as well as referencing the contemporary style of housing in Britain.[56]

Stylistically the New Zealand villa drew on British architectural fashions of the nineteenth century. Revivals of Greek and Roman architectural forms, as well as Medieval gothic architecture, included bay windows and numerous decorative features such as Classical columns and friezes, all in miniature to fit the scale of suburban domestic architecture.[57]

The villa, which arose from this experimentation, is the archetypal Victorian house in New Zealand, a result not only of the aspirations

70 | The Near West

and desires of the people of that time but also a consequence of the industrial power of the period. They were built using mass-produced componentry, set in a line with their neighbours, with their finest features facing the street.[58]

The villa style evolved over time and gradually became more heavily ornamented through the Victorian era. Regional variations emerged in response to topography, climate and fashion. In Auckland, villas with faceted bays were particularly common and entire streets of them were built.[59] Whether with square fronts, double bays or corner bays, they share a vocabulary of materials and form, but have a complex grammar of variations on what was a clearly understood structure.[60]

In plan the villa form is simple: a central hall facing the street with rooms either side. The rooms facing the street were for entertaining, with bedrooms behind and private living and services at the back. The street frontages are formal, and all had some form of porch or verandah facing the street.[61]

The death of Queen Victoria in 1901 led to a change in fashion: the villa became lighter and simpler, with larger windows and less ornamentation. In the years that followed, the new bungalow style was increasingly influential.

The earliest versions of the less formal 'bungalow style' emerged in the first decade of the twentieth century — derived in part from an English seaside resort house-type built after 1860, which in turn were influenced by the plantation houses of India and the British Arts and Crafts movement (which championed functional design).[62]

New Zealand's first bungalow type houses were designed by local architects Samuel Hurst Seager, George Selwyn Goldsbro' and Basil Hooper. Seager and Goldsbro' had trained under British architects and all three had worked overseas. Initially these bungalow type homes were designed for wealthy clients, but the style was given a significant boost as a type of humble home for workers when bungalow designs by Seager and Cecil Wood were among the successful entries in the 1905 competition for the first state houses in New Zealand. Several of these houses were built at Petone in Wellington, and they attracted considerable attention.[63]

This new way of thinking about the home had an effect on the villa. From 1900 through until the years of the First World War simplicity became favoured, and the decorative elements fell away. Shingled bow-form bays and casement windows were incorporated and elements of bungalow planning were also adopted, to the degree that by 1910 some villa-type houses had side porches and no central hall. This period of hybrid house style has been called the transitional period, marking the transition of the villa style into the bungalow style.[64]

Following the First World War builders and architects embraced the full bungalow style. These houses were very simple in form, with the Californian bungalow distinguished from the cottage bungalow by its roof form. The Californian bungalow is gable roofed, generally with a projecting stepped gable to form a porch or sunroom. The cottage bungalow is hip roofed. Both have less formal planning than the villa, and are more compact in form with lower ceilings and often a smaller plan area, partly reflecting the austerity of that post war period.

Bungalows were also built as groupings, with a formal relationship to one another that gave pleasing consistency of form and scale to the suburban streets of Westmere, and filled the gaps between the villas of Grey Lynn and Arch Hill.

**RIGHT:** Andrew and Christina Jensen and their daughter on the verandah of their home at 11 Francis Street, Grey Lynn, early 1900s. AUCKLAND LIBRARIES HERITAGE COLLECTIONS, 80-BIN225

---

**BELOW:** The Binns house at 13 Francis Street was built in the mid-1880s as a humble villa, but was extended twice, first with a bay at the front and then with another on the western side. These extensive additions were unusual at the time and reflected the growing prosperity of the Binns family. AUCKLAND LIBRARIES HERITAGE COLLECTIONS, 80-BIN047

---

**ABOVE LEFT:** The natural contour of several sections in Millais Street by the corner of Rose Road did not make for easy building, but building products manufacturer Winstone's filled a substantial hole and by 1933 had built several bungalows using their own products. They employed leading architects Horace Massey, Reginald Hammond and H. W. L. Bates to design the houses. AUCKLAND COUNCIL ARCHIVES, ACC 064 92

**ABOVE:** The Davis family home in Richmond Road (then known as Richmond Avenue) on part of the former Jones property 'The Pines', c. 1890s. ANCESTRY.COM

**LEFT:** The humble home of the Beaney family adjoining its foundry on Great North Road, early 1900s. AUCKLAND LIBRARIES HERITAGE COLLECTIONS, 7-A10489

Some areas remained untouched by this flurry of progress. Cows continued to graze on the subdivided but unsold Surrey Hills land, crops still grew on the western slopes of Arch Hill, and the Hellaby estate west of Coxs Bay remained in use for grazing. In one part of Surrey Hills Estate there was little hope of progress. The 1880s subdivision plan had ignored the part of Coxs Creek that ran through the valley to the north of Williamson Avenue and on to Coxs Bay. The sections in these low-lying areas failed to sell and were ultimately gifted to the city to form the strangely shaped Grey Lynn Park.[65]

With the improvement of the economy in the early twentieth century, further small subdivisions were offered for sale. In 1904 the Grey Lynn Park Estate, comprising Hakanoa Street (then known as Hinemoa Road) and Tutanekai Street, was marketed.[66]

The extension of tramlines along Richmond Road to the West Lynn terminus in 1910 provided ready transport to homes in the area and encouraged a new wave of subdivision west of Richmond Road.[67] In anticipation of this improvement in public transport, the Sherwood Estate, centred around Sherwood Avenue, was offfered for sale at auction in 1909.[68] The Lynnhirst Estate, laid out on the wedge of land bounded by Old Mill Road and Garnet Road (then known as Wolseley Road) was also offered for sale, the locality having become much more appealing since the nearby municipal slaughterhouse (where West View Road is today) closed in 1908.[69]

The sections in the original late-1850s plan for the Village of Richmond were around twice the size of those in neighbouring Surrey Hills, and the tram service encouraged some landowners in this area to subdivide these larger lots. Mary Ryan, who had purchased two lots at the corner of Hope and Warnock streets in 1882, now subdivided her property and gifted three sections to her daughters.[70]

While house building continued on the subdivisions, a vast area to the west, gently sloping towards the water, awaited the surveyors. In the 1910s and 1920s much of the remaining farmland in the Westmere and western Grey Lynn area was subdivided, including the Hellaby Brothers' landholding, where stock was held before being brought to the slaughterhouse at the edge of Coxs Bay. Hellaby's substantial processing plant had been operating for decades, and its removal to Westfield in 1911 freed up a considerable amount of land for other purposes.

In 1914 work began on laying out streets in the West End Seaside Estate, centred around the northern part of the Westmere headland. The appeal of this estate lay in its sunny aspect and seaside location, not to mention proposed improvements at Coxs Bay that included a boat harbour and baths.[71]

Further subdivisions followed in the 1920s and completed a major part of the residential subdivision of Westmere. Many former farms were now being

A 1924 map showing the unsold lots of the Surrey Hills Estate. Grey Lynn Park, made up of lots of which there was little hope of selling, was gifted to the Grey Lynn Borough Council in 1909 by the Bank of New Zealand, which then owned the residue of the Surrey Hills Estate. AUCKLAND LIBRARIES HERITAGE COLLECTIONS, MAP 729

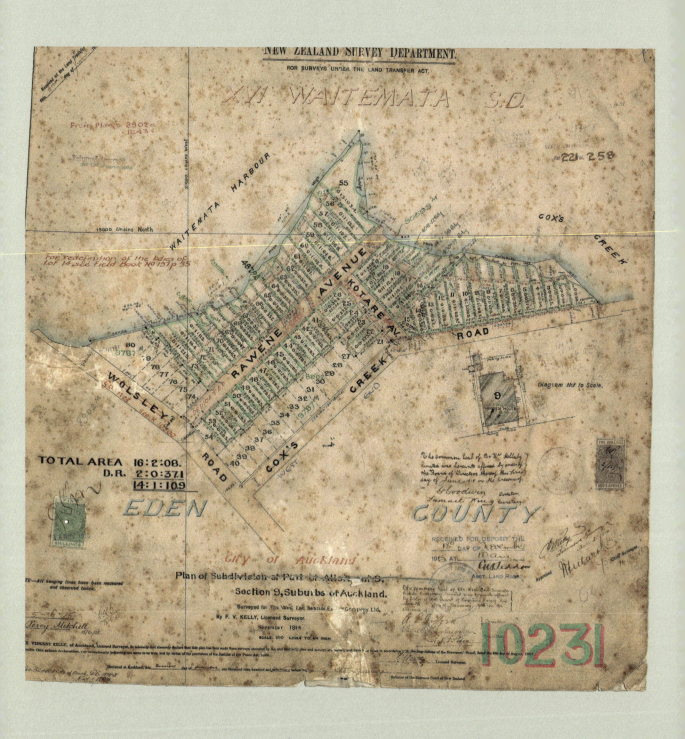

subdivided for residential use and buyers were spoilt for choice. Gone were the days when auction houses heaved with eager bidders wanting to snap up suburban sections. These early twentieth-century estates were sold over a period of months or years.

The 1923 advertisements for the Westmere Estate stressed the amenities, pleasant surrounds and future ease of access to the city:

Westmere Estate
The harbour views are exceptional?
Yes
Electric light poles are down Garnet Road?
Yes
Garnet Street tram service will be within three minutes' walk of estate by Christmas?
Yes[72]

The advertisers also foresaw a happy, friendly community on the estate:

Your friends are building there?
Yes[73]

Most of the 320 sections had sold by late 1923, just a few months after they were offered for sale.[74] Deliveries of sawn timber, roofing iron, chimney bricks and kitchen sinks began to arrive and builders set to work turning the materials into cosy bungalows fronted by neat picket fences.

Like Surrey Hills Estate, Westmere attracted many speculative builders. McNair and Stephens, for example, advertised in 1923 that they had secured 30 sections on Westmere Estate and were ready to build for those wanting a house and land package.[75] In Warwick Avenue on the southern edge, nearly all the houses were built in 1924 and 1925, 38 per cent of them by speculative builders.[76] The successful sales in Westmere Estate prompted further subdivisions. Westmere Estate Extension and Westmere Park Estate hit the market in 1925 and 1926.[77] Purchasers could secure their sections for just £10 deposit with the remainder payable over four years. But although Westmere Estate had been sold under the same terms, the uptake of sections within these later estates was not as rapid.

Depression conditions in the 1930s caused another downturn in building. In 1931 some beachfront sections on Westmere Park Estate remained unsold, and many purchased earlier remained unimproved. Unsold sections in the Westmere Estate Extension were discounted by 25 per cent in 1933 and the best laid plans of some prospective housebuilders faltered.[78] In 1935, for example, Thomas Hodgkinson and Claude Hewitt, who owned undeveloped allotments in Leamington Road, defaulted on their payments and ownership of their land

The West End Seaside Estate subdivision, 1914.
LAND INFORMATION NEW ZEALAND, DP 10231

**Residential development** | 77

# Auckland's Rapid Growth Westward!
## Demand for WESTMERE Sections Unprecedented

### 210 Sections Sold in 10 days

So rapidly are Westmere Sections being taken up that we anticipate the entire estate will be disposed of by the end of the coming week.

Note the glorious attractions of
**WESTMERE**
Nearly all Sections lie to the sun.
Handy to two Tram Routes.
Gas, Water, Electric Light pass the Estate.
City Drainage connected as roads dedicated.
40 to 45 foot Frontages.
Secured by only £10 deposit.

Get all Further particulars from the Sole Agents:
**GRAY & COCKROFT**
Winstone Buildings (2nd Floor), Queen St., Auckland.

**An Ideal Location.**
All Auckland Lies Before You.

**320 Sunny Sections**

The wonderful demand for Westmere Sections can readily be accounted for, because they are the ideal sites for which so many have long been searching. As shown by the plan above, they are handy to two tram routes, and nearly all the sections lie to the sun. Another feature which makes these sites so attractive is that magnificent panoramic views of the harbour or the city are obtained. And it is also important to remember that, together with these distinct advantages, homes built on these sections will have

**All Advantages of City Area**
—gas, electricity, water supply, and drainage. Westmere is in every sense the ideal residential area, and these sections must become in value again and again as Auckland continues to grow westward.

This is an unusual opportunity for securing a section handy to town at a really low price. At £5 per foot and upwards, Westmere lots are exceptionally fine value. Those who have been in search of sections in other localities know too well that most suburbs are already closely built in, and that, where land is available, the prices are much higher than is asked for the Westmere Sections.

**Westmere Solves the Problem**
of where to get a section. This subdivision provides a wide choice of sites at such a bedrock price, because it is virgin land, now offered for selection for the first time. Act promptly! 210 sections have been sold in 10 days, and the remainder are going rapidly. Call or write only for details.

**The Best Land Investment in Auckland To-day.**

Pick out your Location and apply for a Section before it is too late.

**£10 Deposit**
only required.

No further outlay for three months and no interest to pay until dedication of roads.

**NOTE:**
All Sections marked X have already been sold.

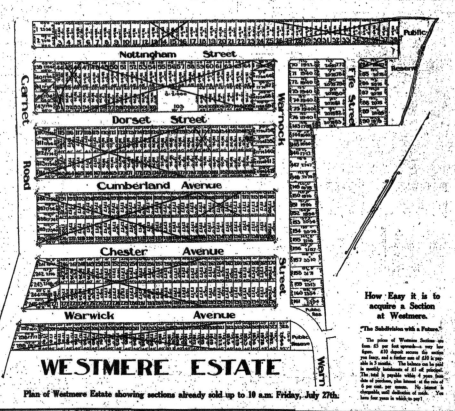

**WESTMERE ESTATE**

Plan of Westmere Estate showing sections already sold up to 10 a.m. Friday, July 27th.

**How Easy it is to acquire a Section at Westmere.**

"The Subdivision with a Future."

The prices of Westmere Sections are from £5 per foot upwards—a very low figure. £10 deposit secures the section you fancy, and a further sum of £10 is payable in 3 months. The balance can be paid in monthly instalments of £1 off principal. The total is payable within 4 years from date of purchase, plus interest at the rate of 6 per cent. per annum. No interest is chargeable until dedication of roads. You have four years in which to pay!

**OPPOSITE:** An advertisement for the Westmere Estate published in the *New Zealand Herald* in July 1923. PAPERSPAST

---

**RIGHT:** The Westmere Estate Extension, 1933. AUCKLAND WAR MEMORIAL MUSEUM TĀMAKI PAENGA HIRA, G9081.G46W1

---

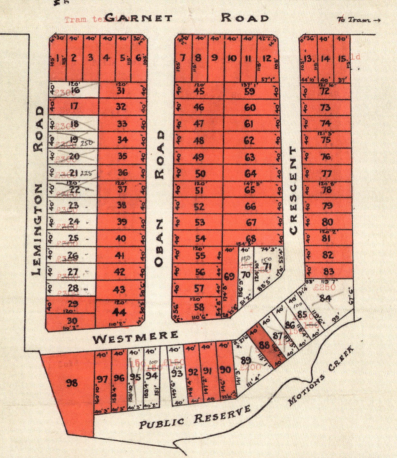

reverted to the Westmere Estate Company Limited.[79] Many of these unimproved sections would have to wait until the late 1930s or early 1940s to be developed.

State flats from the 1940s on the corner of Larchwood Avenue and Garnet Road photographed in 1989. An identical block was built on Great North Road. AUCKLAND LIBRARIES HERITAGE COLLECTIONS, 273-HAR011-03

Bungalows were the predominant form of housing erected in the Westmere area, but another style of house was also built in parts of Westmere and adjoining Grey Lynn. The familiar state rental houses, built from the 1930s, are a recognisable part of many New Zealand towns and cities, but there were also earlier examples of state-funded housing for workers, and some of these were built in Grey Lynn and Westmere. The first state houses in the area were built in Kingsley Street in 1914 to ease the growing housing shortage. These neat timber houses were available for purchase by workers.[80]

In the 1920s the Auckland City Council began building workers' homes funded by a government loan. The council's first foray into public housing had been the erection of six houses in Clarence Street, Ponsonby, which were completed in 1916.[81] The Grey Lynn workers housing project was far larger: 60 concrete houses in Old Mill and West View roads were completed in the early 1920s on land part of which had been the site of the municipal abattoirs.

80 | The Near West

In 1956 several blocks of Demonstration Flats were built on Great North Road west of Tuarangi Road to meet the needs of the 31 per cent of Auckland households made up of just one or two people. The government hoped to encourage local bodies and the private sector to build high-density rental housing and the Demonstration Flats were intended to show how this could be done. However, the flats were not as popular as expected and became an embarrassment for the government. Balconies were later added to the flats. AUCKLAND LIBRARIES HERITAGE COLLECTIONS, 273-HAR038A-06

The New Zealand Institute of Architects criticised their design as 'banal and mediocre', but this was immaterial to the appreciative first residents, who were thankful for the opportunity to move out of cramped and unsanitary housing.[82]

Despite the efforts of the government and municipal authorities, however, the housing crisis continued to grow and was particularly acute in the cities. In 1936 the First Labour Government was elected on its promise to tackle the problem by embarking on a major state housing programme. Their plan was to build high-quality rental houses for better-off workers, thereby raising the overall standard of New Zealand housing, giving the private landlord something to aspire to, and freeing up private rental housing for the poor.[83]

Some of the earliest houses built in Auckland under Labour's scheme were located on the Casey Estate north of Richmond Road between Coxs Creek and St Paul's College just beyond the edge of Grey Lynn. The first of these 127 houses was completed in May 1938, just a few months after the Labour Government completed its first Auckland state houses in Ōrākei.[84] Another group was built soon after in Westmere, west of Garnet Road, more appeared on scattered empty sections in other parts of the district that had been purchased after the government invited offers of land for its housing scheme.[85]

The area had almost no multi-unit housing until the 1940s, when some early

Residential development | 81

state-owned pensioner units were constructed in a U-shaped development in Great North Road and a two-storey pensioner block was built on Surrey Crescent at the corner of Gilbert Avenue.[86] Auckland City Council added to the stock years later with pensioner villages in Great North Road and Surrey Crescent. Other state multi-units were erected on Great North, Ivanhoe, Turangi and Garnet roads in the 1940s and 1950s.

The original housing stock built in Grey Lynn, Arch Hill and Westmere has remained largely unchanged, although naturally there has been some modernisation along the way. Older houses built before electricity and indoor flushing toilets were equipped with these newfangled conveniences in the early twentieth century.

As the years wore on, the original residents of the area sold up and shuffled off, or departed in wooden boxes destined for a permanent resting place. Grey Lynn and Arch Hill became rundown neighbourhoods where most owners had little inclination or money to invest in redevelopment or major renovations. The proportion of rental houses increased dramatically from 1961 to 1981: the percentage of households that rented their homes in 1961 was 31 per cent in Grey Lynn and Arch Hill and 20 per cent in Westmere. In 1981 this had risen

**ABOVE:** This U-shaped state housing development in Great North Road was completed in 1942.
PATRICK REYNOLDS

**OPPOSITE ABOVE:** The home of Richard and Mary Warnock, built in 1887 at 350 Richmond Road, was the second of four houses built for the Warnock family using Wilson's Portland Cement, an experimental New Zealand product. As manufacturers of soap, the Warnock family were well aware of the need to support local manufacturers.
PATRICK REYNOLDS

**OPPOSITE BELOW:** A typical Grey Lynn bay villa on Selbourne Street.
PATRICK REYNOLDS

82 | The Near West

An aerial view of Westmere in 1940 showing newly built state houses in the area west of Garnet Road including Meola Road and Notley Street, with some still under construction. Meola Road (the Westmere end of which was known as Phelan Street) had not yet stretched its way across to link Westmere with Point Chevalier. Older houses on the wedge-shaped 1909 Lynnhirst Estate, bounded by Old Mill Road and the southern end of Garnet Road, would soon be joined on the west by Westmere's newest road, Savage Street, named after the much-loved Labour prime minister Michael Joseph Savage, who died in office in 1940.
RETROLENS

**ABOVE:** In the early 1920s, Auckland City Council built 60 concrete houses on Old Mill Road and West View Road on land formerly occupied by the city abattoirs. The New Zealand Institute of Architects criticised their design as 'banal and mediocre', but this was immaterial to the appreciative first residents, who were thankful for the opportunity to move out of cramped and unsanitary housing. AUCKLAND LIBRARIES HERITAGE COLLECTIONS, 589-0013

**BELOW:** Auckland City Council pensioner flats under construction on Surrey Crescent in 1964. AUCKLAND LIBRARIES HERITAGE COLLECTIONS, A5702

to 45 per cent in Grey Lynn, 48 per cent in Arch Hill and 26 per cent in Westmere. With high demand for rental houses in these areas, landlords were under no pressure to make improvements.[87] A few residents modernised their homes by recladding the weatherboard exterior with faux brick or stone, or by replacing double-hung windows with aluminium joinery. During the 1960s, 1970s and 1980s, some dwellings originally built to house a single family were reconfigured to form two or more flats, but for the most part the houses remained much as they were, though increasingly showing signs of age.

From the 1980s, however, people who appreciated the original features of these houses began to restore the villas, bungalows and cottages. In 1990, parts of Grey Lynn and Arch Hill were recognised as having heritage value. Streetscapes in the area had retained their original housing to a remarkable degree, and the heritage zoning of certain streets offered a level of protection against unsympathetic change.

Of course, not everything has been retained. In the north-facing seaside streets, well-heeled owners have replaced some original houses with newer and grander dwellings. In Grey Lynn and Arch Hill over the past two decades, many townhouses and apartments have appeared on former industrial or commercial sites. A few original houses have been moved off-site, replaced by homes that feature those modern status symbols: multiple living areas, a designer kitchen with state-of-the-art scullery, multiple bedrooms and bathrooms, a double garage and a swimming pool.

86 | The Near West

Some of the varied housing styles of Grey Lynn and Westmere, clockwise from top left: The Isaac on Surrey Crescent (completed in 2013) was one of the earlier high-density apartments to be built; architect Richard Naish's award-winning E-Type house; a tiny worker's cottage on Sackville Street; bungalows on Dorset Street. PATRICK REYNOLDS

# Infrastructure and local government

**PREVIOUS PAGES:** A trolley bus heads towards the city on the Garnet Road route formerly plied by trams, 1953. The redundant tram tracks are being dug up alongside. MUSEUM OF TRANSPORT AND TECHNOLOGY, PHO-2020-19.26

'**D**eplorably neglected . . . impassable . . . disgusting tracks of miry sludge . . . diversified with many a yawning gulph.'[1]

This description of Auckland's main thoroughfares, written in 1848 by a correspondent calling himself Jeremiah Stuck I'-The-Mud of Bog Hall, is but one of a plethora of criticisms that appeared in local newspapers during Auckland's early decades.[2] The roads further out were in an even more primitive condition. But roads were just one problem in the new and growing town.

As the capital of the new colony, Auckland had an advantage over other settlements by being home to the governor and his staff, who were intimately acquainted with local needs and had the power to make improvements — albeit on a limited budget.[3] By 1845 the colonial government, religious groups and local businesses had made significant progress towards establishing the facilities expected of a new town: there were schools, newspapers, a church, a printing office, a customhouse and a cemetery, and in Princes Street there were various government offices, including the treasury, the survey office and the colonial secretary's office.[4] There was also a gaol, a courthouse, a post office and a substantial military barracks.[5]

Beyond the Queen Street valley, however, settler numbers were small and progress was slow. There would be several false starts before an effective form of local government could begin to satisfy demands for improvements.[6]

In 1848 maps and proclamations gazetted and defined the boundaries of the enormous 'Hundred of Auckland', which stretched from Remuera in the east to Whau Creek in the west, and included the areas we now know as Arch Hill, Grey Lynn and Westmere. Crown land within the Hundred was leased for grazing and the somewhat meagre revenue spent on local improvements.[7]

In 1851 a new and extensive Borough of Auckland was proclaimed — Arch Hill, Grey Lynn and Westmere formed part of its Suburban West ward. But the borough proved a complete flop. Rating revenue was needed for improvement works, but the needs of urban and rural-hinterland ratepayers differed. The populace was not enamoured with the idea of local government and could see no reason why the colonial government should not provide what was needed.[8] Many years passed before those living west of the town willingly submitted to being rated for local improvements.

With the establishment of the provincial system in 1852, Auckland gained a provincial council responsible not only for providing many of the town's needs but also for the development of the vast Auckland Province, which stretched from Gisborne to Northland.[9]

As with all settlements, roading was a major issue. Great North Road was the key overland route to the western farming districts, but through the nineteenth and early twentieth centuries it took a steeper route to Western Springs than it does today, following the line of what is now known as Tuarangi Road. In early 1860 there were complaints about the gradient of this stretch of road, but the provincial council lacked the wherewithal for the work required to ease the slope.[10]

Two years later just £318 was set aside for improvements to Great North Road between Arch Hill and Swanson — a woefully inadequate sum.[11] Over the next few years, public meetings and petitions to the provincial council argued for more to be spent. In 1865 the steepest parts of the slope were cut down and a heavy coating of metal was laid — no doubt a significant improvement.[12]

The Auckland Provincial Council struggled to cope with the demands for public works throughout the province, and in 1866 it passed the Turnpike Act, which allowed tolls to be charged for the upkeep of roads in Auckland Province. Travellers on all major roads out of the city, including Great North Road, would be required to pay a fee.[13]

The Great North Road toll booth had an inauspicious start when a storm destroyed it during construction, scattering timber across the road.[14] Once it was completed the turnpike collected sixpence from each passing vehicle. The fee was higher for those pulled by more than one horse or those with large items on board.[15]

In 1868, after a meeting of residents voted to manage local affairs, a more local form of government came to the area with the proclamation of the Newton Highway District, which included all of the area we now know as Westmere, Grey Lynn, Ponsonby, St Marys Bay, Freemans Bay and parts of Herne Bay.[16] Within a few months, residents in the settled areas nearer downtown had decided to look after their own interests, and the city end of the district was carved off to become the Dedwood Highway District (later renamed Ponsonby).[17]

The southern boundary of Newton Highway District ran along Great North Road and turned down what is now Tuarangi Road before taking a crooked line through Western Springs to Motions Creek. From 1871 much of the area to the

**94** | **The Near West**

south of this was administered by the Arch Hill Highway Board, which took its name from Joseph Young's Arch Hill farm on the southern side of Tuarangi Road.[18] Initially the Arch Hill Highway District took in a large area to the west extending all the way to Point Chevalier, but in 1874 the district was split in two, providing Point Chevalier with its own highway district. With this boundary change, Arch Hill became one of the smallest, and poorest, local bodies in Auckland — it had a small population of modest means and lacked reserves that could be leased for grazing livestock to provide additional income.[19]

The Arch Hill Highway District adjoined the Karangahape Highway District, just west of Nixon Street. This seemingly arbitrary boundary was likely the result a desire by John Probert, who owned the 10-acre block at the corner of Great North Road and Newton Road (where Nixon, Burgoyne and Chapman streets are today), to join the small but relatively populous Karangahape Highway District when it formed in 1868. In 1882 the residents of the Karangahape Highway District voted to amalgamate with Auckland City Council, allowing the residents quicker access to the range of services enjoyed by the city residents, including a piped water supply and a fire brigade service.[20] But for the residents of neighbouring Arch Hill and Newton Highway Districts, the pace of progress would be much slower.

As the busiest thoroughfare in the area, Great North Road received a significant amount of attention, but other roads also needed to be properly formed and maintained. In 1874 the Newton Highway Board appealed to the Auckland Provincial Council for assistance:

> We the undersigned having been appointed the Trustees of the Newton Highway Board to wait upon your Honour in reference to the roads and bridges in our district more especially the Richmond road leading from the Ponsonby road to Richmond, the same never having received any attention from the Provincial Government . . . and having become utterly impassable for vehicles of any description.[21]

The sum of £100 was provided for improvement works that were carried out by early 1875, but within a year the road had reverted to a deplorable condition. A dray belonging to the Warnock brothers was stuck for two days in the middle of the road, bogged down in a sea of mud.[22]

Richmond and Great North roads posed particular problems as they were on the boundaries of two separate districts, and spats broke out between neighbouring public bodies over who should be responsible for them. In the 1890s a dispute between the Arch Hill Road Board and

**Infrastructure and local government | 95**

Newton Borough Council (previously the Newton Highway Board) over the maintenance of Great North Road ended up in court after Newton Borough arbitrarily changed a long-standing agreement over the allocation of costs.[23] The different approaches of the Arch Hill and Newton local bodies were apparent when one traversed the road. One road user was Mr Phipps with his horse bus. In 1884 the *Auckland Star* noted:

> The road from Karangahape Road to the Arch Hill pub is peculiar . . . It is under the management of two road boards, and their dividing parts, in their opposite features, like the sun and the moon, have bright and shadowy complexions: the Newton part is bright and level, and in excellent condition (on which the omnibus runs smoothly), but immediately the Arch Hill side is entered, Mr Phipps's passengers begin to talk about 'The Rocky Road to Dublin'.[24]

The Arch Hill board had a more cooperative relationship with the local bodies to the south. In the early twentieth century the Arch Hill and Mount Albert boards planned and shared the cost of bridges across Bond Street and Commercial Road, and the Arch Hill and Eden Terrace boards jointly erected footbridges across the gully that divided them.[25]

Ensuring Auckland residents had access to essential services required a certain amount of cooperation between the various local bodies. With a population of 12,700 in 1871, Auckland City Council was the wealthiest local body in Auckland, and could provide services for its inhabitants that the smaller local bodies could only dream of. Auckland City Council's boundary skirted the Waitematā from Mechanics Bay to Freemans Bay before heading along Franklin Road, Ponsonby Road, Karangahape Road, Symonds Street and back down to Mechanics Bay.[26]

Some needs could not be accommodated within the built-up city area, including the disposal of human waste and household rubbish. Farmer and contractor Thomas Faulder, whose land stretched between Surrey Crescent and Tuarangi Road, in the area now traversed by Sefton Avenue and part of Great North Road, saw a business opportunity and offered waste removal services in 1870, and was appointed the night soil contractor to the city in 1871.[27]

Faulder and his men would set out in the dead of night, carts rattling with empty tins as their horses plodded down Great North Road to the city, where they ventured down the sides of houses and along rear lanes to the outhouses whose sanitary arrangements ranged from cesspits and earth closets to pans and boxes. A week or more's worth of festering excrement was heaved onto the carts, and taken in the early hours to Faulder's farm.[28] At first the night soil was simply spread on his paddocks, but with up to 50 tons arriving weekly there was soon a considerable accumulation.[29] The area's clay soil prevented liquid waste soaking into the ground and excrement oozed down the hillside. An unholy stench hung over the area.[30]

In 1873 a petition signed by 130 residents and the chairmen of the Arch Hill, Newton and Karangahape road boards prompted an inspection by the district health officer, Dr Nicholson.[31] He noted the ditch at the bottom of the gully was 'an elongated cesspool, open to the air, and closely adjoining to the main public road' where it was 'discharging foetid gases'.[32]

The popular theories of sickness and contagion of the period held that certain illnesses could be caused by breathing bad air, so it was no surprise when Faulder's neighbour Francis Jones, who had recently replaced Faulder as chairman of the Newton Road Board, attributed his family's ill health to the night soil depot.[33] He wrote:

> I have seen members of our family prostrated by sickness caused by the abominable stenches of this place, the chief symptoms being acute pains in the stomach, accompanied by parched lips and nostrils, and for days together we have scarcely been able to take food within doors. We have had to wander in search of a mouthful of fresh air, the whole neighbourhood being alive with flies.[34]

There was another problem that threatened to bring Auckland's sewage back to its citizens:[35] the depot oozings were close to Western Springs, where the council's waterworks were under construction, and it was feared that 'the people of Auckland would soon have to drink a very fine decoction'.[36] Something had to be done about Faulder's incontinent depot which, according to the provincial surgeon and medical officer Dr Philson, was the 'worst nuisance in the entire Auckland Province'.[37]

Forcing Faulder to improve standards was a vexed legal issue that was grappled with again and again. He had already been charged, in 1870, with breaching the Municipal Police Act by depositing night soil on his farm, thereby creating a nuisance.[38] In 1874 he was again before the courts after John Williamson, superintendent of the Auckland Provincial Council, directed that charges be brought.[39]

There was some confusion over the relevant legislation, and it was even suggested that Faulder was breaching the law simply by putting the waste in his cart. The judge found that Auckland City Council had no right to designate Faulder's farm as a night soil depot, despite it having been gazetted as such in 1873, and that Faulder's use of his land for this purpose was also illegal owing to its position abutting a main highway. Faulder was duly fined by the court. A new solution for the city's night soil was urgently needed.[40]

Meanwhile, the Board of Health had instructed Faulder to improve his practices. Instead of spreading raw excrement on the surface, the contents of the night carts were now dumped in pits and covered in soil and lime. These measures failed to resolve the problems, however, and in 1875 the depot was relocated to Avondale — a move that added considerably to the cost of Faulder's services.[41]

By the mid-1870s the provincial council was in its death throes. Central government was about to abolish the provincial system and hand various functions to central government and local bodies. Auckland City Council would soon inherit the responsibility for supplying water to its residents, and with this in mind it began to investigate a replacement for the Domain Springs (near the Auckland Domain duck ponds), which had supplied the city's water since 1866. A supply from Western Springs appeared practical. The council bought the springs property from Low and Motion, who had run a flour mill from the site since the late 1840s, and work was soon under way. In 1877, the first fresh, clean water was pumped to city residents and businesses from Western Springs.[42]

Although the springs were just a stone's throw from the western boundary of the Newton Highway District, residents in this area had no access to this water supply. Nor did those living at the city end of the district, where the boundary of Newton was just across from the city water reservoir near the corner of Ponsonby and Karangahape roads.[43] Residents of Newton and neighbouring Arch Hill had to continue to make do with wells, streams and rainwater until the local bodies formed agreements with Auckland City Council to supply the districts with water.

A piped water supply eventually arrived in the late 1880s after a six-foot-long petition signed by over 150 ratepayers was presented to the borough council, which had recently succeeded the Newton Road Board (formerly the Newton Highway Board).[44] At first the pipes served only the Surrey and Sussex wards of Newton Borough. Residents of the extensive Richmond Ward, which encompassed the rest of the borough to the west, voted in 1901 to raise a loan to extend the water supply to their own area. Arch Hill had a piped water supply in 1897.[45]

Auckland City Council also needed land on which to build a public slaughterhouse to replace the ageing Newmarket public abattoir, which had been in service since the early 1850s. The supposedly sanitary Newmarket facility was at times anything but, and an abominable stench emanated into the increasingly residential area.[46] A potential site on the escarpment on Old Mill Road where West View Road runs today offered multiple advantages: it

**ABOVE:** Elizabeth Brown in her backyard on Richmond Avenue (now Richmond Road) before the area was reticulated with water and sewerage. The privy can be seen at right and the pump over the well is shown at centre left. AUCKLAND WAR MEMORIAL MUSEUM TĀMAKI PAENGA HIRA, PH X30-73

**BELOW:** Auckland City Council's Western Springs waterworks, 1890, with the pumping station at left, on the edge of Western Springs lake. AUCKLAND LIBRARIES HERITAGE COLLECTIONS, 7-A5596

The Auckland municipal abattoirs on Old Mill Road in the early twentieth century.
AUCKLAND LIBRARIES HERITAGE COLLECTIONS, AWNS-19031008-04-02

was some distance from any established residential areas and in a locale where a number of noxious trades were already established. An abattoir here was less likely to cause offence.

Despite the proximity of this to the Western Springs water supply, the council pushed ahead and the slaughterhouse opened in late 1877.[47] The buildings were designed by leading Auckland architect Edward Mahoney, who beat five others in a design competition with an entry he called 'Utility'.[48] On a late spring morning over 60 guests travelled from the city to attend the opening. They were shown around the buildings, and before lunch was served in the pig house they received a demonstration of the workings of the slaughterhouse when the mayor ordered that a bullock be killed in front of them.[49] The *Auckland Star* reported the process by which the animal was dispatched:

> A man furnished with a spear stands on a platform above the animals as they are driven in, and selecting his victim, delivers a well-aimed blow to the back of his neck, which, piercing the spinal marrow, kills him at once.[50]

The cattle beast was then 'expeditiously decapitated, denuded of its hide, and hung up'.[51]

Four of the six abattoir houses were leased and the remaining two were available to the public. Some 112 acres (45 hectares) of adjoining land was available for use as holding pens for animals awaiting their final journey to the

100 | The Near West

abattoir.[52] Once the animals had been processed, their meat was transported to the city for sale.

The increased traffic caused by all this activity added to the burden for local ratepayers. In 1882 the Arch Hill Road Board (formerly the highway board) applied for funds to assist with repairs to Great North Road, arguing that £500 was needed to metal the road owing to the wear and tear caused by the slaughterhouse and waterworks traffic.[53] The hill section of the road (then known as Tuarangi Road) was in a particularly bad state, and Mr Phipps's horse bus service from the city down Great North Road to the lunatic asylum was unable to proceed.[54] Henry Walker, a doctor called to attend a patient near the waterworks on a wet winter's evening, described his own treacherous journey:

> After passing the Arch Hill Hotel, about 200 yards down the road, I suddenly dropped into a large hole in the centre of the road, nearly up to the knee in water and a quagmire of clay. I pulled myself out with no little difficulty and tried again in another direction, when I walked into another gulf.[55]

Following the success of a petition to Parliament requesting the abolition of the toll-house, which had been moved from the eastern end of Great North Road

**Infrastructure and local government** | 101

to the top of the hill section (now known as Tuarangi Road) in the mid-1870s, there was no longer any revenue from that source.[56] Money to shovel the road into a more navigable shape had to found elsewhere.

The Arch Hill Road Board was operating under considerable financial difficulties by the mid-1880s, and struggled to meet its other obligations. In 1886 Mr Dines, secretary and inspector of the Arch Hill Road Board, explained to the secretary of the Auckland District Hospital Board that the road board was unable to pay the hospital board rate:

> Our predecessors having run the district into liabilities amounting to between £700 and £1000 and our rates last year only £287 and subsidy of £280 you can see that we are in a nice fix, and therefore ask you to extend your charity out towards the Arch Hill Road Board and as soon as funds are available, we will be glad to contribute our portion.[57]

The board's financial woes were not helped by the secretary, Thomas Morrow, who embezzled board funds over several years before making his escape to Fiji in 1889.[58]

But matters improved for the Arch Hill Road Board in the 1890s. Careful management of revenue had allowed it to extinguish its debts and by 1895, under the Government Loans to Local Bodies Act 1886, it was in a position to borrow funds from the government for improvement works. These loans were for specific purposes: in the case of the Arch Hill board they would finance drainage, the installation of a water supply and roading improvements. Before loans could be approved, though, a majority of ratepayers had to vote in favour

Making improvements to Richmond Road at West Lynn, 1905. AUCKLAND LIBRARIES HERITAGE COLLECTIONS, 226-9278

102 | The Near West

of raising the loan while also agreeing to the levying of a special rate to service the loan.[59]

Other matters caused annoyance. In 1886 Dines wrote to Mr Robinson of Kingsland requesting that he remove or bury his dead horse, which was lying west of Commercial Road.[60] Another letter, to Mr Thomas of King Street, requested that he cease depositing his stable manure on the street.[61]

Before local by-laws required the people of Newton Borough and Arch Hill to engage a night soil collector, locals often simply dug a hole some distance from their back door and erected an outhouse over it. It was less than ideal: liquid seeped into the surrounding land, and in steep areas such as parts of Arch Hill, heavy rain flooded cesspits and caused the contents to overflow — to the detriment of downhill neighbours. Other options for disposal included pails that had to be emptied into a hole, or earth closets that relied on soil and sometimes lime to cover and deodorise the waste.[62]

As late as 1910 an inspection by the sanitary officer revealed that 10 households in Arch Hill were still burying their own night soil; a further 12 had defective privies.[63] A considerable amount of human detritus found its way into the open sewer at the bottom of the Arch Hill gully, which received not only whatever flowed down the hillside or was thrown into it, but also waste from the city upstream.

Over in Newton Borough, a night soil contractor was engaged in the 1880s to deal with the borough's feculent matter, but some residents preferred to make their own arrangements. In 1894, 15 per cent of households in the borough were not using the service.[64] The numerous swamps of Surrey Hills collected whatever seeped down into them.[65] In the 1890s Newton Borough Council attempted to drain these swamps by forming open ditches that fed into permanent drains, but farmers leasing the unsold parts of the Surrey Hills Estate sometimes confounded this by damming the ditches to collect water for their cattle.[66]

Along with the work of installing drains, water pipes and other street services came the need to define permanent street levels. Development in the past had occurred in a haphazard manner. Houses were erected on poorly formed streets that followed straight lines on maps, but in reality often traversed steep inclines, gullies and lumps and bumps. Considerable work was required to cut and fill uneven ground and bridge gullies and waterways to allow residents to get from one part of the street to another.

In 1886 the Newton Borough Council established permanent street levels for the Surrey Hills Estate. For existing dwellings the street levels could be a blessing or a curse.[67] Residents sometimes found they no longer had access to their property once the levelling work was complete; others were now perched precariously above a cutting or sat well below fillings. The height differentials on roads such as Scanlan Street and Tuarangi Road were ultimately solved by forming each lane of the road on its own level, or by providing a separate access lane for houses on the high side.

Through the many decades when farming and residential development coexisted, hard-won roading improvements were prone to damage from stock. In 1888, Argyle Street in Arch Hill (now part of the motorway) was cut up by cattle being driven along the footpath.[68] The situation was not helped by people who allowed their horses, cows and goats to roam free on Surrey Hills Estate soon after it was laid out. The animals frequently strayed onto the streets of Arch Hill, where they were a danger to pedestrians at night.[69] From the late 1870s a ranger and pound-keeper was employed at Arch Hill and in 1886 the newly formed Newton Borough made a similar appointment and erected a public pound.[70]

Newton Borough's mix of farms and suburban streets caused natural tensions. Drainage, water supply and lighting were coveted, but such luxuries were too expensive to be extended to the sparsely settled farming areas of Newton.[71] In order to better cater to the needs of their various ratepayers, Newton divided the borough into three wards in the late 1880s, with the plan that the rating revenue collected in each ward would be expended within it.

Surrey Ward was the most built up and encompassed the area to the south of Williamson Avenue, while Sussex Ward, which included the rest of the former Surrey Hills Estate and extended a little further to the west of Richmond Road, had the next largest population. Richmond Ward, which included the areas we now know as Westmere along with adjoining parts of Grey Lynn, was largely rural.[72]

By early 1886 gas had come some way into the district. Some 20 years after the central city was first lit with gas, three street lamps were installed on Great North Road. The cost of lighting and extinguishing the lamps, carried out by a lamplighter armed with a long crooked pole who traversed streets within the gas area at dusk and then again before midnight, fell upon the local bodies, but in the mid-1880s the cash-strapped Arch Hill Highway Board refused to pay its share.[73] It was best if those travelling through the district by night were familiar with the pattern of the potholes and other hazards that were enough of a threat to safety by day, let alone in the gloom of night.

With so few lights functioning, it was common practice to schedule evening events to coincide with a full moon in the hope that a cloudless night would allow celestial illumination to guide the way.[74] In 1886 gas mains were laid down in Williamson Avenue, marking the beginning of gas reticulation for

The Grey Lynn (formerly Newton) Fire Brigade, ready to proceed to the scene of a fire — on foot.
AUCKLAND WAR MEMORIAL MUSEUM TĀMAKI PAENGA HIRA, PH-NEG-C19954

the houses that were springing up at the city end of the Surrey Hills Estate.[75] Manufactured in coal-fired gasworks, the gas was mainly used for lighting and provided a cleaner, brighter glow than the kerosene lamps and candles previously used for domestic lighting.[76]

With candles, kerosene lamps, open fires and more, there was always a risk of fire. The provision of a piped water supply allowed fires to be fought more effectively than before, and local bodies began to establish fire brigades. In 1886 the need for a brigade was brought home to the Newton Borough Council when St George's Hall on Great North Road near the corner of Ponsonby Road, home to the Newton Borough Council offices, was destroyed by fire, along with five adjacent shops. This disaster was close to the boundary of the Auckland City Council area and the city fire brigade provided welcome assistance.[77]

Newton Borough Council still lacked a water supply, but once this was available in 1889 six men volunteered to form a fire brigade for the district. The council provided uniforms and equipment and agreed to pay the men on the occasion of a callout.[78] Arch Hill established a fire service in 1899, but when fire broke out in Arch Hill sometimes the Newton fire bell was rung and vice versa, resulting in the wrong brigade turning out. Arch Hill's sensible suggestion that the two brigades work together was rejected by Newton Borough and there were numerous instances of one local body attempting to charge the other for the attendance of its fire brigade.[79]

**Infrastructure and local government | 105**

# Law enforcement

In the early afternoon of 13 July 1878 Constable Jonas Abrams, sole officer of the Newton police station, located in a rented dwelling in West Street, was alerted to trouble in a house he was well familiar with near the bottom of a gully in Oxford Street (now known as Waima Street) in Arch Hill — a notorious brothel run by William Crowe. Crowe, who was in his sixties, had 15 previous convictions for drunkenness, larceny and other crimes for which he had spent nearly half his life in prison.[80]

Inside the brothel Abrams found a man known variously as Henry Black, Harry Broome and Yankee Harry. His face, clothes and boots were saturated in blood that had gushed from a skull fracture just above his left ear. Black was loaded onto a borrowed cart and sent to the hospital, in Grafton, where the doctor advised that he was unlikely to survive. Superintendent John Thompson and a Justice of the Peace were dispatched to take Black's deposition at his bedside.[81]

Statements were also taken from other witnesses and a picture of the day's events emerged. At around two that morning, Black and two companions had arrived at the brothel seeking the company of Kate McManus, who was described as 'possessed of considerable personal attractions' in one of many reports of her all-too-frequent court appearances.[82] Twenty-something McManus was probably the oldest of the four working girls at the house at the time; Fanny Spayne, who was aged 16 or 17, was probably the youngest.[83] Crowe had refused the men entry, at which Black verbally abused Crowe and threatened to break the door down. The men eventually left, Black threatening to return in the morning and physically harm Crowe.[84]

The next morning Black was back, this time with another man. They entered the house, sat down by the fire and Crowe insulted Black and challenged him to a fight. Emboldened by alcohol, Black and Crowe went outside, took off their shirts and began to brawl. Black landed a couple of punches and Crowe fell to the ground. But Crowe wasn't finished. Both men went back into the house and after Black sat down, Crowe grabbed a billhook (a large knife with a hooked end) and struck Black on the back of the head.[85]

Crowe was eventually sentenced to two years' imprisonment with hard labour for wounding with intent to cause grievous bodily harm.[86] This was no doubt a good outcome for the neighbourhood: with Crowe in prison, the young women who paid him for the use of a bed in which to conduct their business went elsewhere, taking their rowdy clients with them.[87]

The assault at Crowe's brothel came at a time when the police force in Auckland was in a state of flux. The system of provincial government had recently been abolished and central government now had the responsibility for policing, and had taken over the Auckland Armed Constabulary, a body formed in 1870 when the Auckland Provincial Police and Armed Constabulary were amalgamated, merging police and military functions in an effort to gain efficiencies and bolster the police presence.[88] But the new

106 | The Near West

nationwide New Zealand Constabulary Force that emerged in 1877 struggled with the age-old problem of underfunding and a force that was too thin on the ground.[89]

Nine years later, military and policing functions were separated when New Zealand's first national civil police force was formed. Officers were routinely unarmed and the service evolved from a coercive force into a more benign presence, tasked with maintaining rather than imposing order. New Zealand society was shaking off its frontier character, gradually becoming a more settled society that was less rowdy and more law-abiding.[90]

At the time of Crowe's attack on Black, the city and inner suburbs were served by a staff of 39 police officers, 35 of whom were based in the city station, along with their two horses. The inner suburbs were served by two officers based at the Parnell station, and one each at the Newton and Freemans Bay stations.[91]

The Auckland policeman's lot was a busy one. As well as dealing with serious crime, the public demanded that police relieve the city streets of vagrants, drunks and prostitutes, and suppress the rising problem of larrikinism as gangs of youths disturbed the peace, hurling insults, throwing stones and causing minor damage to property. But some problems were more easily dealt with than others. Local police turned a blind eye to prostitution so long as it was discreet and caused no offence to neighbours.[92]

In the 1880s population growth at Arch Hill and on the newly subdivided Surrey Hills Estate prompted the establishment of a local police station, and in early 1887 the new Surrey Hills station was opened on the northern side of Great North Road, between Turakina and Ariki streets (then known as Tennyson and Princeps streets).[93] It was initially a sole-charge station and, like many suburban stations of the day, it was housed in a rented dwelling which also served as the family home of the police constable stationed there.[94] A series of staff served at the Surrey Hills station over the next two decades, as it was common for police rank and file to be transferred every few years.[95]

Along with occasional murders and serious assaults, there were many other matters to deal with, some mundane, others peculiar, and some that were just plain sad. Children who had died unexpectedly in the district were commonly brought to the Surrey Hills station, where inquests, attended by the coroner, the police and a jury, were held.[96] If an adult died unexpectedly, the local police constable would be summoned and if the deceased was at home then the inquest would often take place on-site.[97] But such events didn't happen every day. Much of the work of the local cop revolved around minor crimes and keeping order.

Most of the policemen stationed at Surrey Hills appear to have been married and their wives were often able to help in the discharge of their duties. In January 1898 an infant, just a few weeks old, was abandoned on the verandah of Mrs Allen's home near the corner of Great North Road and Cooper Street (then known as Russell Street), Arch Hill. An unsigned note requested that Mrs Allen take care of the baby girl as the parents were unable to. Unfortunately there was no one home, but a passerby heard the baby's cries and took her to the police station just across Great North Road. Constable McLellan's wife took care of the baby until she was handed over to the Charitable Aid Board, which boarded her out.[98] Meanwhile the police sought the baby's mother but to no avail. The baby soon became ill and was seen

**Infrastructure and local government** | 107

by a doctor, but died just two weeks after being abandoned.[99]

In the early twentieth century the Surrey Hills police station moved to another rented house on the corner of Commercial Road and Seddon Street (then known as Cheapside). The house was in a poor state of repair and Constable McGilp, who was transferred there in 1904, described it as 'uninhabitable'.[100]

But the days of the Surrey Hills station were numbered. In early 1906 the station was closed and policing the district was carried out from the fine new Newton police station and barracks at 1 Ponsonby Road.[101] As suburban development spread further through Grey Lynn, a more local station was again needed, particularly in the area at the far end of Richmond Road, where the population had expanded with the extension of the tramline to this part of the district in 1910.

A house in Castle Street (then known as Salisbury Street) was rented and converted into a police station and residence with cells.[102] In August 1911 the new station was opened, manned by Constable Patrick Dunne, who had transferred from the Ponsonby station.[103] Dunne's wife no doubt took on the role of assistant to her husband, answering inquiries, searching female prisoners and feeding and caring for any prisoners temporarily held in the cells — all services that the wives of sole-charge constables were expected to undertake.[104]

Living in the communities they served, sole-charge policemen got to know the local people. Constable Thomas Mahoney, who was stationed at Grey Lynn during the 1920s and 1930s, was a common sight riding his bicycle around the streets, cycling being the way many suburban constables got about.[105]

In the late 1930s working conditions improved when working hours were reduced from 56 to 48 hours per week, and officers got a day off each week. But the reality for sole-charge police

108 | The Near West

The fine new Newton Police Station and Barracks on Ponsonby Road served the district after the closure of the Surrey Hills station in 1906. AUCKLAND LIBRARIES HERITAGE COLLECTIONS, AWNS-19060705-13-02

was that they were always on call.[106] In the early 1940s the Crown bought the Castle Street property and in 1946 plans were drawn up for a new police station and residence, which was subsequently built.[107]

In the mid-1950s a nationwide programme began to provide an additional 300 police residences over a five-year period. The Ministry of Works prepared standard plans for police houses, two of which were built next door to the Grey Lynn station at 16 and 18 Castle Street, making a little police village in the street.[108] However, not all the police living in Castle Street were stationed at Grey Lynn; at least one resident worked from the Ponsonby station.[109]

In 1969 the Grey Lynn police station was closed and policing of the district was carried out from the central station in Cook Street as part of a nationwide centralisation of police, resulting in a more impersonal relationship between the police and locals.[110] This came at a time when there was rising tension between the police and people concerned with social justice, many of whom called the inner-west suburbs home. Racial prejudice issues came to the fore in the 1970s and 1980s, particularly with the notorious police dawn raids of the mid-1970s, where police targeted Tongan and Samoan migrants who had overstayed visitor visas, despite the numbers of European overstayers being far greater.

In one of many such incidents, police with dogs charged into a church service in Crummer

Road and asked everyone to present their passports. The priest was one of 18 people who were imprisoned for not having their passport on them. This event, and others in homes across the district in the early hours of the morning, were terrifying.[111] The dawn raids were heavy-handed, discriminatory, horrifying for the community, and a public relations disaster for the police. In 2021 Prime Minister Jacinda Ardern formally apologised on behalf of the government for the dawn raids.[112]

There were major clashes with police during protest action over the occupation of Bastion Point in the 1970s and the Springbok tour in 1981, further damaging relations between the police and the people of Grey Lynn, Arch Hill and Westmere, many of whom took part in the protests or had sympathy with the protesters.

✕

By the mid-1980s, as part of a drive to connect with communities, a community constable was appointed for Grey Lynn. The community constable was available during the working week and operated from rented premises, initially in the Surrey Crescent shops.[113]

In 2013 community policing was reorganised so that the Grey Lynn area no longer had a dedicated community constable, but was instead served by a team of six constables based at the Ponsonby police station, serving a much wider area stretching from Ponsonby to Mount Albert and Mount Eden.[114] When the Ponsonby station closed in 2019 its services were moved to the central police station, which relocated from Cook Street in the city to the corner of College Hill and Gudgeon Street.[115] Today this is the closest police station to Grey Lynn, Arch Hill and Westmere.

**Infrastructure and local government | 109**

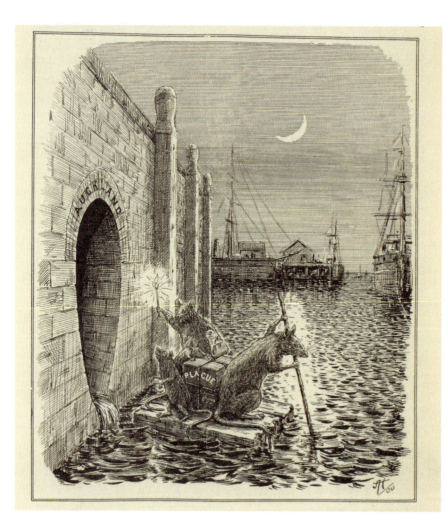

During the 1900 bubonic plague outbreak in Sydney there were fears that ship rats would bring the disease to Auckland, prompting the Grey Lynn Borough Council to declare another war on rats. The caption reads: 'Rough on rats. "Now, Rodie, my love, be quick and get the kids ashore, and I'll look after the baggage".'
AUCKLAND LIBRARIES HERITAGE COLLECTIONS, NZG-19000324-0529-01

In 1900 an outbreak of bubonic plague in Sydney that claimed over 100 lives raised fears of a local outbreak and focused attention on the health risks present in Auckland and the increasingly populous Borough of Grey Lynn (formerly known as Newton). Inspectors were despatched to investigate, serve notices and condemn various public health nuisances and hazards in the city. Incoming ships were quarantined and fumigated, and a war on rats commenced. In June 1900 when the plague made landfall in Auckland it claimed just one life, that of Hugh Kelly from Upper Queen Street in the city. Arch Hill and Grey Lynn Borough escaped the plague despite the area being home to more than its fair share of substantial nuisances.[116]

In 1901, just 14 years after the municipal slaughterhouse had been built on Old Mill Road, the facility was condemned by the Department of Agriculture, which was given responsibility for inspecting and approving plans for new municipal abattoirs under the Slaughtering and Inspection Act of 1900.[117] The department's inspector deemed the facility 'unfit for the purpose of preparing meat for human consumption under proper sanitary conditions'.[118] He suggested that it would be better to have the abattoirs located closer to the saleyards, which at the time were sited at Newmarket and Remuera, but with increasing suburban development in these areas it appeared likely that they would be relocated to a more rural area on the southern railway line.[119]

Auckland City Council considered a number of sites for new abattoirs and initially favoured one near the existing slaughterhouse. Thomas Faulder's widow Dinah offered to sell West House Farm on the eastern side of the Bullock Track between Surrey Crescent and Tuarangi Road, where her husband had established his night soil depot many years earlier. The council considered the site suitable as it 'adjoins the Council's own estate, and offers complete facilities for drainage and water supply, and will be most readily adapted to the requirements of the trade'.[120] The Faulders' property also met with the approval of the Master Butchers' Association. However, it was vehemently opposed by the people of Grey Lynn and Arch Hill, who presented a petition to the Auckland City Council:

> The distance from the market and the dangers attendant upon driving cattle, etc., through a closely-populated district should be of itself sufficient reason, but your petitioners respectfully protest against the continued effort to make this district a receptacle for everything that is unpleasant and detrimental to the health and comfort of residents.[121]

The Health Department, established under the Public Health Act 1900, also had a say in the matter. Abattoirs were considered a noxious trade under the Act and any new facility had to be approved. The Health Department considered Grey Lynn an unsuitable location and preferred Penrose or Ōtāhuhu, which were well served by the railway and closer to the principal farming districts.[122] The city council did not agree, however, and the unwholesome slaughterhouse continued where it was for several more years.[123]

Built of timber, the old city abattoirs were not the most hygienic structures. A visiting reporter offered a graphic description of the facilities in 1903: interior walls were 'from 5ft to 6ft upwards caked with a heavy, dark coating of coagulated blood and other animal matter, lacquered with fat and hair, and polished by the friction of the butchers and their victims'.[124] When the floorboards were walked on 'putrid muck squirted up between the cracks . . . a rich vandyke brown in colour, and smelling pungently'.[125] The local rats apparently had the pick of a magnificent feast and felt so safe in their abundant numbers that they paraded about fearlessly.[126]

In 1908 the vermin were finally deprived of the smorgasbord they

**Infrastructure and local government | 111**

had enjoyed at the municipal slaughterhouse when the new city abattoirs at Westfield replaced the facility.[127] But it was not so easy to rid the area permanently of all its health hazards. The rubbish tip on part of the McNair farm in Garnet Road, where the city refuse had been dumped since the mid-1890s, continued to assault the neighbourhood's senses.[128] In 1900 inspectors had found the place swarming with flies, while 50 fat pigs rooted about in a rotting mess two foot deep.[129]

The stench was so bad that one of the inspectors remarked, 'Although I do not smoke I had to have a cigar to try and stay on the ground.'[130] With the threat of bubonic plague hanging over the settlement, the rubbish was destroyed by digging trenches that were then filled with tar and kerosene and the whole lot set alight.[131] Within two months, however, it had returned to its former condition.[132]

In 1905 local residents had a brief respite from the stench when the city destructor (now Victoria Park Market) began incinerating all the rubbish from Auckland city as well as from Grey Lynn Borough.[133] But the destructor was soon overwhelmed, and the borough reverted to the tip, which continued to be used after Grey Lynn Borough amalgamated with the city.[134] In 1921 the colony of rats that called the dump home was in excellent health and had no fear of people; one resident noted that 'they sit up and say how do you do'.[135]

The dump remained a presence in the area, and though it did move slightly further west to the sites now occupied by Western Springs College, MOTAT, Seddon Fields and Meola Reef Reserve, it continued to trouble nearby residents until its eventual closure in 1976.[136]

**ABOVE:** Laying tram tracks in Surrey Crescent, 1910. The house on the right is on the corner of Browning Street. AUCKLAND LIBRARIES HERITAGE COLLECTIONS, 266-9283

**BELOW:** Laying tram tracks in Richmond Avenue (now Richmond Road). AUCKLAND LIBRARIES HERITAGE COLLECTIONS, 226-7637

The twentieth century brought significant transport improvements to the district. As the farms at the western edge of the Surrey Hills Estate began to be subdivided and developed for housing, the increased rating revenue for the local bodies enabled further improvements to existing infrastructure.

Other new services were on their way. The first car arrived in Auckland in 1900, but it was many years before this mode of transport became affordable for the masses. In the meantime, electric trams improved matters greatly for locals who had hitherto relied on their own two feet or slow and expensive horse buses to get them to the city.

The electric tram era in New Zealand began in Dunedin in 1900 with the Roslyn–Māori Hill line.[137] Seeing the potential for profit, companies vied for the right to lay tramlines in other cities. In Auckland, the Electric Tramways Company secured a licence, negotiating first with Auckland City Council

and then with other local bodies, including the Grey Lynn Borough Council. As a subsidiary of the British Electric Traction Company, which owned and operated tramways throughout Britain and also in India, British Columbia and Venezuela, the company had a wealth of experience.[138]

In November 1902 crowds gathered to watch the first electric tram wend its way up Queen Street. Within days the trams were running from the city to the northern end of Ponsonby Road via Queen Street, Wellesley Street West, Hobson Street, Pitt Street, Karangahape Road and Ponsonby Road.[139] This route skirted the eastern edge of Grey Lynn, and services soon extended into the Grey Lynn and Arch Hill area. In 1902 tramlines were laid down Great North Road, and in 1903 the line ran far as the corner of Tuarangi Road.[140] The Grey Lynn Borough Council worked hard to ensure that locals could afford to use this newfangled mode of transport, and did its best to secure discounted fares for workers and apprentices and half-fares for children.[141]

The residents of Richmond were keen to have tram services, too, and in 1906 the Richmond Tramways League lobbied the tramways company to extend the service to the area.[142] By mid-1910 the lines ran from Tuarangi Road along Surrey Crescent and down Richmond Road to Francis Street. Further extensions had to wait a few more years, but in 1923 the public could travel by tram to the Auckland Zoo when the line from Surrey Crescent was extended down Old Mill Road.

A branch line extending from Old Mill Road down the length of Garnet Road opened in 1931, as did a line down Richmond Road that connected Ponsonby Road with the Francis Street tram terminus. Trams eventually ran down Great North Road to Point Chevalier, but posed a very steep gradient, and one regular passenger recalled her relief each time the tram reached the top.[143]

The trams were a boon for people in the suburbs who worked in the city. On weekday mornings, suburban front doors opened and a procession of workers made their way to the nearest stop to catch a tram to the city; the process was reversed at the end of the day when the dash to catch the tram heralded the beginning of Auckland's rush hour.[144]

The system was not without its problems. Congestion soon became an issue on the Great North Road line, where at first only a single set of tracks was installed. When trams travelling in opposite directions met, one would have to wait for the other to pass, and if the line was busy the wait could be lengthy.[145] Delays on the line eventually resulted in it being double-tracked.

In summer the trams stirred up dust that infiltrated houses and shops and caused a nuisance to pedestrians. In 1906 residents of Arch Hill and Grey Lynn signed a petition requesting that steps be taken to resolve the issue.[146] As a result, three electric road sprinklers were commissioned to water the tracks to keep the dust at bay.[147]

**Crowds gather around the first tram to West Lynn, 1910.** AUCKLAND LIBRARIES HERITAGE COLLECTIONS, 226-9289

It was several years before householders were able to flick a switch and enjoy the benefits of electricity. Auckland lagged well behind other New Zealand cities in providing residents with electric power.[148] The small South Island town of Reefton was the first to have a public electricity supply when a hydroelectric power station built to crush rock at the Reefton coalmine began supplying the settlement in 1888. In Auckland a few private electric generating plants operated in the late nineteenth and early twentieth centuries, including one at Josiah Firth's flour milling operation that powered a public display of electric light in the city over Christmas 1887; the Chelsea Sugar Refinery was lit with electricity in 1896.[149]

The electric tram era sparked the development of a substantial generating plant in the city. Under an agreement between Auckland City Council and the tramways company, Queen Street was lit with electric light from 1903.[150] Pressure grew for a public electricity supply, and on 10 February 1908, power finally ran through lines from the Auckland City Council's generating plant at the city destructor to eight lucky households. Demand was huge, and an additional generating plant was soon needed.[151]

In 1909 the council was keen to extend electricity to the suburbs. Initially, the city sought permission to install lines and sell electricity to suburban

Infrastructure and local government | 115

The charming Newton (later Grey Lynn) Borough Council offices and fire station building, c. 1880s, which remains today on the wedge of land bounded by Williamson Avenue, Rose Road and Pollen Street. Built in 1889 to the design of architect John Mitchell, it was a prominent statement of solidity and progress for the young borough.
ALEXANDER TURNBULL LIBRARY, 1/2-096198-G

consumers at the same price that city residents paid. Arch Hill Road Board agreed immediately, but there was considerable mistrust between the city and many other suburban local bodies.[152] Grey Lynn Borough rejected the city council's offer; instead it requested that in addition to providing the electrical infrastructure and supplying power at city rates, the city also pay 25 per cent of the profits to the borough council — something the city would not entertain.[153]

Despite a number of meetings on the subject, and a premature approach to the government with a view to having the borough supplied by the Horahora hydroelectric power station on the Waikato River, the Grey Lynn Borough Council flip-flopped on the issue. At the time, Auckland City Council had a monopoly on generating and supplying electricity to the suburbs; if the borough council signed an electricity supply agreement with the city it wouldn't be able to take advantage of alternative, cheaper power supplies that might become available in the future. Some also felt the borough council should have a say in where and when the supply lines were laid.[154]

A small area was connected with the city supply by 1913, when underground lines were installed along Richmond Road and Great North Road as far as Pollen Street, but the Grey Lynn Borough Council continued to debate the matter of further extension. It opposed the installation of overhead wires, citing safety concerns, but that didn't stop the owners of the Arch Clark and Sons' shirt factory in Williamson Avenue connecting to the city supply via a temporary overhead wire without the council's consent.[155] The Grey Lynn Borough Council and the city council finally agreed on an electricity supply in January 1914.[156]

Despite Arch Hill giving the Auckland City Council free rein to supply the area with electricity in 1909, material shortages occasioned by the First World War hindered progress. Parts of Arch Hill and Grey Lynn were still waiting for electricity to arrive well into the 1920s.[157]

✕

One of the issues that had plagued local bodies for decades was the hygienic and efficient disposal of human waste. The provision of public water supplies in Grey Lynn and Arch Hill in the 1880s and 1890s made it possible for houses to have flushing toilets, but it was a long time before every house was fitted with these modern conveniences.

There had been considerable public pressure to rid the borough not only of its night soil but also anything connected with the removal services. In 1903 a petition signed by 848 people was presented to the Grey Lynn Borough Council, complaining of the presence of depots in Surrey Crescent, on the city side of Thomas Faulder's earlier depot, where the night soil contractors stored their equipment and stabled their horses. Night soil was not buried at these depots but was instead taken to Avondale and Point Chevalier for burial.[158] On the recommendation of the district health officer, Dr Robert Makgill, the Grey Lynn Borough Council considered building a large septic tank at Coxs Creek that would allow the night soil service to be replaced with modern water closets in each home.

Auckland City Council was also considering a sewerage system and hoped to involve other local bodies, and this had the effect of stalling any immediate progress for the Grey Lynn Borough.[159] In 1906 Grey Lynn mayor John Farrell noted with some frustration that 'the Council had been trying to get a proper drainage system, but were bound to follow in the footsteps of the Auckland City Council and await the decision of that body as to what scheme to adopt'.[160]

Around this time night soil deposits made an unwelcome return to the district when a burial site was used in Garnet Road. It was a constant battle to find and retain suitable places to dispose of the collected waste beyond the district boundaries.[161] Night soil was still being deposited at Garnet Road as late as 1913, at which time the Grey Lynn Borough Council was presented with another petition, this one with over 800 signatures, requesting its closure.[162]

In 1908 Grey Lynn and Arch Hill both became part of the Auckland

**Infrastructure and local government** | 117

Suburban Drainage Board district, a body established to coordinate drainage of the area stretching from Point Chevalier to Remuera.[163] One of its early projects was to pipe the long-decried open sewer in the Arch Hill gully.[164] It was part of a larger scheme in which trunk sewers conveyed sewage to a pumping station and outfall at Ōkahu Bay, a small beach close to Bastion Point on the edge of the Waitematā Harbour; this project was completed in 1914.[165]

In the meantime, the Grey Lynn and Arch Hill night soil collectors continued to make their rounds and the drainage of the districts made its way down to Arch Hill gully or any of the various waterways leading to the harbour. At Coxs Creek no fewer than five sewers disgorged their pestiferous contents onto the mud flats.[166] The area had been set aside as a recreation reserve, but the presence of the sewer outfalls made it a leisure ground not for humans but for flies, typhoid and other pestilential organisms. In 1908 a long-feared typhoid outbreak at Coxs Creek occurred. Twelve residents contracted the illness, including three members of one family. Government health officer Dr Purdy praised the Grey Lynn Borough Council for its efforts to contain the outbreak by supplying disinfectant to residents free of charge.[167]

With the completion in 1914 of the Auckland Drainage Board works that conveyed Arch Hill and Grey Lynn waste to the Ōkahu Bay outfall, it was possible to have effluent removed quickly and cleanly from one's household and sent far, far away. However, the replacement of the night soil collection by the piped system was not as rapid as hoped. Although many home owners did install flushing toilets, landlords were not as keen to invest in such improvements. For several years, those with modern toilet facilities were still woken at night by the rattle of pans as the night soil contractor dealt with their neighbours' doings.[168]

Eventually every resident in Grey Lynn, Arch Hill and the burgeoning suburb of Westmere was able to pull the chain and release their waste into subterranean sewers where it then oozed its way to Ōkahu Bay. Several decades later, a flushing station on Motions Road by Auckland Zoo was still receiving the remaining city night soil from other districts, and it was 1969 before the conversion to flush toilets across Auckland's suburbs was finally complete and the now-motorised night carts had made the final collections from their few remaining householders.[169]

In 1913 and 1914 the Arch Hill and Grey Lynn boroughs became part of Auckland City, ending over four decades of independent local government. This was the culmination of a strange and lengthy courtship. Auckland mayor James McCosh Clark had raised the idea of incorporating

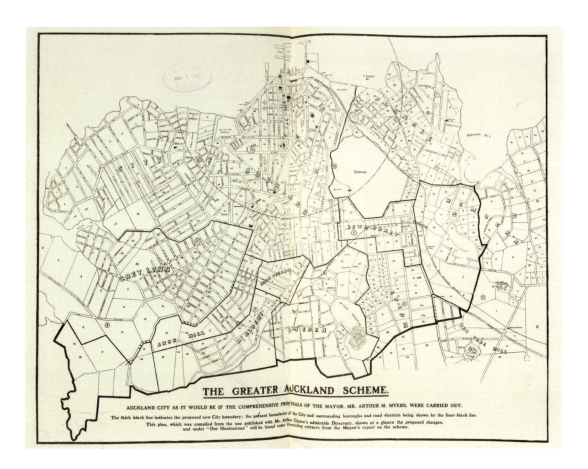

A 1906 map of Arthur Myers' Greater Auckland Scheme. Many of the local bodies shown on this map amalgamated with Auckland City Council in the following decade: Arch Hill (1913), Parnell (1913), Grey Lynn (1914), Eden Terrace (1915), Remuera (1915) and Epsom (1917).
AUCKLAND LIBRARIES HERITAGE COLLECTIONS, NZG-19060303-0033-01

nearby local bodies with Auckland City in 1882. The residents of Ponsonby, Karangahape and Grafton, all suburbs that had been run by their own local bodies, voted in favour of becoming part of the city and soon gained fire and telephone services and extensions to existing water connections and drainage. Newton and Arch Hill could not be incorporated at this time, as the city could legally only merge areas immediately adjoining its boundaries.[170]

In 1891 the Arch Hill Road Board wrote to the city council seeking clarification of what amalgamation would mean for residents.[171] At the time, the board was still recovering from the financial crisis of the 1880s prompted by expensive roading contracts and exacerbated by the embezzlement of rating revenue. Relations with Newton Borough Council were also fractious due to the ongoing saga of apportionment of costs for improvements to the Great North Road, among other things.

Opinions on whether or not to join the city were divided. Some, like long-term resident William MacDermott, favoured amalgamation: Arch Hill, he said, 'was a narrow strip of land with a main road that was too much for it to maintain'.[172] Others were unwilling to pay the substantial increase in rates that

Infrastructure and local government | 119

amalgamation would incur, or thought the benefits insufficient. The matter was allowed to drop.[173] This was probably something of a relief for Auckland City Council, which was under financial stress, in part because of the cost of providing services and infrastructure for the suburbs it had absorbed.[174]

By the early twentieth century Auckland City Council was courting the suburban districts, and invited Arch Hill and Grey Lynn (as Newton was now known), Eden Terrace, Mount Eden, Parnell, Newmarket and Remuera to a conference to discuss the possibility of amalgamation. At the time there were 23 local bodies across the Auckland isthmus and reducing this number would simplify administration, enable more efficient delivery of services and bolster the city's ability to raise loans for costly improvements.[175]

Grey Lynn Borough Council favoured amalgamation and approached the city in early 1904 in an effort to progress the matter — a meeting in Arch Hill of just 12 ratepayers resolved to take steps toward amalgamating with the city.[176] However, this ardour for the city was not something shared at the right time by all the right people. Conferences were attended by enthusiastic representatives of Grey Lynn and Arch Hill, but the city dithered.

In 1905 Arthur Myers was elected mayor on a policy of forming a 'Greater Auckland' by absorbing many suburban boroughs and road boards. But it did not follow that ratepayers of smaller local bodies would simply acquiesce. After much discussion, several of the boroughs and road boards, including Parnell and Eden Terrace, decided to stick with the status quo.[177]

The elected members for Grey Lynn, Arch Hill and Newmarket were still keen to amalgamate.[178] The Arch Hill Road Board felt amalgamation would offer the district better value for money — if they joined the city they would gain a rubbish removal service, something the road board had been unable to provide, and would benefit from a cheaper water supply and a more modern fire service. Merging with the city also promised a speedier solution to the problem of the open sewer in the Arch Hill gully that had plagued the area with its smells.[179]

The Grey Lynn Borough Council invited its ratepayers to vote on the subject in 1906. Around a quarter of ratepayers voted, and of these, 54 per cent opposed amalgamation.[180] Two days earlier the Newmarket Borough Council had considered whether to poll its own ratepayers, but the council decided instead to let the matter drop.[181] Arch Hill was now the only interested party of the 11 local bodies originally included in Myers' Greater Auckland proposal.[182] With the others gone, there seemed no good reason to proceed.[183]

The Greater Auckland scheme was revived in 1912 by Mayor James Parr, who was determined to woo the suburbs, attending meetings of local bodies and their ratepayers to entice them to join the city.[184] He offered Arch Hill a guarantee that its rates would not increase, and with this the members of

Arch Hill Road Board and their ratepayers voted to join.[185] The board held its final meeting on 31 March 1913. It thanked the clerk Mr Franklin, foreman Mr Corden and his assistant Mr Laurence, the registrar Mr Skeen and the volunteer fire brigade for their work, and passed the final accounts for payment. One of the oldest local bodies in Auckland was now extinct.[186]

Grey Lynn Borough followed Arch Hill's lead, though the terms of the merger took some time to settle as Grey Lynn was determined to negotiate a favourable agreement for its ratepayers. One of the sticking points was Grey Lynn's desire to retain its method of determining rates based on unimproved values rather than adopting the city's system. Eventually an agreement was reached whereby the city guaranteed that rates would remain the same for a period of seven years, and with this over 70 per cent of voters supported amalgamation with the city. In July 1914, Grey Lynn Borough Council held its final meeting and the area joined the city just as the First World War broke out.[187]

Under the terms of the amalgamation agreement between Grey Lynn Borough and Auckland City Council, the council had agreed to take a poll within Grey Lynn Borough seeking approval to raise a £100,000 loan for street improvements and extensions to the water supply and drainage network. The council was able to proceed with raising a £10,000 loan that funded the extension of the municipal water supply, but the remaining projects had to wait until the war ended.[188]

Hot on the heels of the war came the devastating influenza pandemic of 1918, which spread rapidly after arriving in Auckland with returning troops. Auckland mayor James Gunson called a meeting on 31 October at which a citizens' committee was established to organise help for those in need. In Grey Lynn, St Joseph's School on Great North Road became a temporary hospital where 30 Catholic sisters nursed the sick.[189] There were scenes of despair around the city. Maurice O'Callaghan, a volunteer with the St John Ambulance, visited a house in Grey Lynn where he found the decomposing body of a man in the bed on which he had died three days earlier. Sharing the bed with him was his grief-stricken wife, who was so ill that she was unable to get up.[190]

Rose Road was particularly hard hit, with one in 12 households suffering a death from influenza.[191] Included in the local toll were two members of the Henderson family of Scanlan Street (then known as Surrey Street). Their mother, Elizabeth, had been widowed in 1913, when her husband died of miner's phthisis, but she suffered yet more losses in 1917 and 1918.[192] A memorial notice in the *New Zealand Herald* expressed her grief:

**Infrastructure and local government** | 121

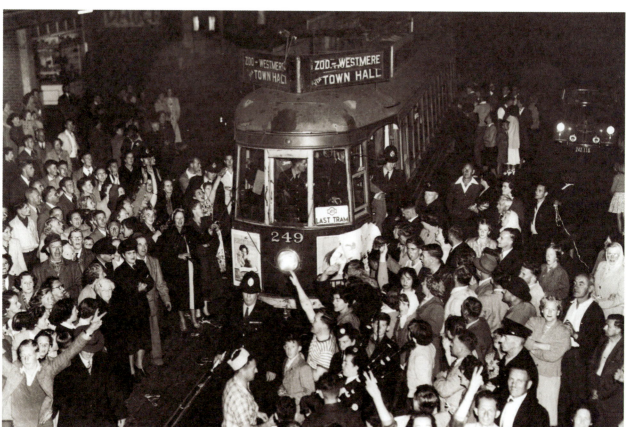

In affectionate remembrance of L Corp Wallace Henderson. Ninth Reinforcements, died of wounds received at Passchendaele, October 30, 1917; also Harry L Ninth Reinforcements (returned); died of influenza November 3, 1918, and William, died of influenza November 12, 1918 . . . Inserted by their sorrowing mother, Elizabeth Henderson.[193]

In the space of just over a year, Elizabeth had lost three of her six children.

The illness or resulting complications claimed the lives of possibly as many as 9000 people throughout the country and 1200 in Auckland alone.[194] In the wake of the pandemic Auckland City Council instigated one of its campaigns to clean up the city with the usual inspections by sanitary staff, burning of rubbish, closing of rubbish tips and yet another declaration of war on rats. These measures had become the standard response to the various epidemics that swept the city and suburbs, and while they may have improved the environment, their effectiveness in curtailing the spread or severity of any future outbreak of disease was limited.[195]

ABOVE: Two trams travelling along Richmond Road near the corner of Lincoln Street, 1952. MUSEUM OF TRANSPORT AND TECHNOLOGY, PHO-2020-19.5

BELOW: Crowds gather around the last tram to Westmere, 13 March 1953. MUSEUM OF TRANSPORT AND TECHNOLOGY, PHO-2020-19.26

As residential development stretched beyond Grey Lynn and through the new suburb of Westmere in the 1920s and 1930s, streets were formed with domestic connections to water, drainage and power supplies. Trams plied the Westmere route down Garnet Road. Arch Hill, Grey Lynn and Westmere had well-kept streets, modern services and reliable public transport as well as a branch library and a lecture hall — all of which were mere dreams a few decades earlier. The challenge for Auckland City Council was to maintain the existing infrastructure while keeping pace with developments and demands from the community.

The 1950s marked the demise of trams that had served the people of Arch Hill, Grey Lynn and Westmere for decades. At the beginning of the Second World War Auckland's tramway network was in excellent condition and well patronised, but labour and material shortages occasioned by the war led to deterioration of the infrastructure. Around the world tramways were being replaced by buses, and the Auckland Transport Board, which was responsible for the city trams, looked to follow the trend.[196] Between 1949 and 1956 buses replaced trams across the city and by the end of 1953 all routes west of the city, including those serving the Arch Hill, Grey Lynn and Westmere areas, had been converted from tram to bus.[197]

The post-war economic boom brought car ownership within reach for many, and with wartime petrol rationing now at an end private cars became a popular mode of transport. Patronage of the new bus services suffered and city planners began to develop a motorway network to serve the city in the

Infrastructure and local government | 123

automobile age. Part of this network was the Northwestern Motorway, which cut a swathe through the Arch Hill gully and reached as far as Western Springs in 1979.[198] Cedric Street, Bute Street and Dale End near the bottom of the gully disappeared, and several streets further west were bisected by the motorway. The Mountain View Road underpass provided access from the western end of Grey Lynn to the southern part of the Western Springs district. The quiet gully was no more, replaced instead by the hum of car engines and rubber on tarseal.

In 1961 Auckland City Council adopted the first district plan. This embodied the existing land-use pattern in Arch Hill, Grey Lynn and Westmere and designated most existing industrial, residential and reserve areas for continued use, thus ensuring that industry would not be further dispersed across the area.[199]

As the years passed, council functions expanded. In 1972 the people of Grey Lynn requested that Auckland City Council provide a community centre for the area, and three years later Grey Lynn gained one of Auckland's first such centres when two prefabricated buildings were erected on Richmond Road. The buildings were replaced in 2000 with a purpose-built structure that today hosts numerous community groups and events, including Plunket, the Citizens Advice Bureau and the Grey Lynn farmers market.[200]

Local bodies also have a role to play in preserving the heritage of their districts. Arch Hill and Grey Lynn have some of the most intact collections of late-nineteenth and early-twentieth-century timber houses in the world. Auckland City Council recognised the collective heritage value of many villa- and bungalow-lined streets in Grey Lynn and Arch Hill, and these heritage streetscapes were protected in the Auckland City Council district plan from the 1990s.

Nearly a century after the Arch Hill Road Board and Grey Lynn Borough joined Auckland City Council, there was another wave of local body amalgamation. In 2010, 12 local bodies were merged to form the Auckland Super City. In 2013 the new council began public consultation on its Unitary Plan, the planning rule book that would replace the various district plans that governed everything from residential building developments, heritage protection and the use of public parks to industrial and commercial development within the area now governed by Auckland Council.

The draft plan proposed rezoning large swathes of Grey Lynn for high-density housing. It was an unsophisticated approach to replanning the suburb and took little account of the topography, existing housing stock and amenity

After Grey Lynn Borough amalgamated with the Auckland City Council, much work was done to improve services and streets, including beautifying streets with trees. London plane trees were planted along Hakanoa Street in the 1920s. They were known as the 'town-loving plane' because they thrived in the polluted air of London. PATRICK REYNOLDS

values. What was immediately clear was that Arch Hill, Grey Lynn and Westmere were different to other parts of Auckland. Many people had lovingly restored decrepit villas and bungalows that, in other suburbs, would have been demolished in the blink of an eye. Locals wanted intensification to happen in appropriate places — they did not want Grey Lynn to lose its character.

Auckland Council received numerous submissions on the plan from the residents of Arch Hill, Grey Lynn and Westmere. In the end, while other parts of Auckland lost heritage protection of streetscapes and places, much of the heritage of Grey Lynn and Arch Hill remained protected under the Unitary Plan; areas like the Great North Road Ridge and the commercial zones close to Ponsonby Road were zoned for high-density development. The ongoing challenge for Auckland Council will be to retain what is good about the neighbourhoods while allowing growth and development in appropriate areas.

**Infrastructure and local government** | 125

# Party politics

In the 1890s the voice of the working-class residents of Newton electorate (including Grey Lynn, Arch Hill and Westmere) was bolstered by the introduction of a single vote for all eligible voters, removing additional votes given to men who owned property in more than one electorate. In 1893 female suffrage vastly increased the number of eligible voters, and broke new ground internationally. These reforms created a fairer electoral system and paved the way for increased working-class participation in government.[201]

Population growth in the inner west suburbs, including Arch Hill and Grey Lynn, led to a redistribution of electorates in the area. The Newton electorate, which had included the areas we know as Grey Lynn, Arch Hill and Westmere, was abolished, and in 1893 local electors found themselves either in the small urban City of Auckland (Grey Lynn and Westmere) or the vast and largely rural Eden (Arch Hill). A decade later a new electorate, Grey Lynn, emerged and included Grey Lynn, Arch Hill and Westmere.

The New Zealand Labour Party would not be formed until 1916, but in the intervening years the electorate was served by local candidates who understood the needs of working-class people. George Fowlds, the Member of Parliament for City of Auckland and then Grey Lynn from 1899 to 1911, came from a humble background. He was the son of a hand-loom weaver in the small Scottish village of Fenwick, where his family's cottage often hosted liberal and radical politicians. He left school at 12 to be apprenticed to a tailor, and later attended night school in Glasgow to improve his prospects.

By the time he emigrated to New Zealand in 1885, after a stint in South Africa, he was married and about to start a family. Within a few years he was running his own menswear business, living in Mount Albert and becoming involved in local affairs, including serving on the Mount Albert School Committee and Road Board.

By the time he entered Parliament in 1899 he was a crusader for a single tax as a simple and fair means of eliminating poverty and improving the lives of ordinary people. He was a champion of progressive ideas, including temperance, equality for women, state banks and proportional representation. As minister of education, public health, and immigration and customs, he grew frustrated at the lack of progress and the discord that had crept into the Liberal cabinet. He resigned from Cabinet in 1911 and stayed on in Parliament as an independent.[202]

Fowlds stood again for election to the Grey Lynn seat in 1914, this time under the United Labour Party banner, but he narrowly lost to John Payne, the self-proclaimed 'People's Popular Labour candidate'. Payne campaigned on 45 proposals, including an expanded range of pensions to cover sickness and other misfortunes, a 40-hour working week, free tertiary education for working-class children, and a state bank. Payne was an eloquent and forceful speaker, but he was also mercurial, and made few friends in government. He ultimately failed to deliver.[203]

In 1919 the passing of the Women's Parliamentary Act allowed women to stand for election, and Ellen Melville became the first woman to run as a candidate for the Grey Lynn

126 | The Near West

**LEFT:** Member of Parliament for Grey Lynn, John A. Lee. ALEXANDER TURNBULL LIBRARY, 1/2-043306-F

**FOLLOWING PAGE:** Grey Lynn artist Mervyn Williams' poster *Take a hand against racism*, 1985, was one of a number of artworks created by members of Auckland Artists Action for the exhibition *JustArt*, which raised funds for the campaign to stop the planned New Zealand rugby tour of South Africa. TE PAPA TONGAREWA MUSEUM OF NEW ZEALAND, GH026413

seat that year. Melville, who stood for the Reform Party, came second to Labour's Fred Bartram, the first Labour candidate to win the seat.[204]

In 1931 Grey Lynn voters chose war hero and writer John A. Lee to represent them in Parliament. One of the most controversial of a string of Labour MPs in what had become a safe Labour seat, Lee had risen from a life of poverty. Raised mainly by his dressmaker mother and maternal grandmother in Dunedin, he left school with only a basic education. He was soon in trouble with the law and was sent to the Burnham Industrial School and then later to Mount Eden Prison, where he served a year for smuggling liquor and breaking and entering. In prison he was influenced by socialist ideas. After working in Northland and Auckland, in 1916 he joined the New Zealand Expeditionary Force and served on the Western Front. He met like-minded soldiers with whom he swapped socialist books and journals, and became known as Bolshie Lee. Lee was awarded a Distinguished Conduct Medal following the Battle of Messines in 1917 and returned home in 1918 after he was wounded and his arm was amputated.

His passion for politics grew and he became an active member of the Labour Party and the New Zealand Returned Soldiers Association. In

**Infrastructure and local government | 127**

the early 1920s he won the Labour nomination for the East Auckland by-election but was defeated. He won the Grey Lynn seat in 1931, a time of economic hardship, particularly for the working class. His electorate office was on the first floor of the Richmond Buildings on the corner of Richmond Road and Francis Street. On the Opposition benches Lee was a vocal opponent of the United–Reform Coalition government and played an important role in encouraging demonstrations to oppose its cost-cutting policies. Lee wrote his first novel, *Children of the Poor*, during this time.

In 1935 Labour swept into power and Lee further increased his majority in Grey Lynn. He was a member of Parliament's finance and defence committee and in 1936 was given responsibility for housing — a role in which he revelled. With the Director of Housing Construction Arthur Tyndall, he established a new government department which, by March 1939, had built around 3440 state houses, including 120 on the Casey Estate on the northern side of Richmond Road, east of Coxs Creek, and several in Westmere.[205] Many more were soon under way in Grey Lynn and Westmere.

Lee became increasingly critical of Labour's economic policies, which he believed were not radical enough, and he clashed with Prime Minister Michael Joseph Savage and Finance Minister Walter Nash. His open criticism led to his expulsion from the Labour Party in 1940. Lee went on to establish his own party, the Democratic Labour Party, for which he contested the Grey Lynn seat in 1943. He was defeated by Labour's Fred Hackett, who held the seat for the next two decades.[206]

But there were others who were more radical than Bolshie Lee. In 1935 Grey Lynn electors were offered a new choice of party. That year Communist Party candidate Henry Mornington Smith, an English seaman who lived in Mackelvie Street, stood in Grey Lynn. He polled poorly but the party, whose headquarters were on Newton Road, continued to contest the Grey Lynn seat.[207]

Meanwhile Arch Hill and the eastern part of Grey Lynn became part of the new Arch Hill electorate in 1946. Through the 1940s, 1950s and 1960s, electoral boundaries in the area went through major changes, and Grey Lynn was particularly fractured. For example, residents of Dryden Street voted in Grey Lynn electorate in 1943, the Arch Hill electorate from 1946 and then the Ponsonby electorate from 1954 before returning to the Grey Lynn electorate in 1963. In 1978 the Grey Lynn electorate was abolished and Grey Lynn, Arch Hill and Westmere became part of the Auckland Central electorate.

Grey Lynn had long been a centre of agitation for the rights of workers and the fight against prejudice. Back in the 1930s there was an active Grey Lynn Unemployed Workers Association and in the 1960s the *Grey Lynn Live Wire* newsletter was published by the Communist Party. In the early 1970s the Polynesian Panthers organisation had its first meetings in Arch Hill and the Auckland Trade Union Centre building, a meeting place for a variety of unionist and activist groups including Halt All Racist Tours (HART), Black Unity and many others, was opened on Great North Road.[208]

The area that has sometimes been referred to as 'the People's Republic of Grey Lynn' has been part of the Mount Albert electorate since 2014. A solidly left seat for decades, at the 2023 election the sitting member, Labour's Helen White, held it by a tiny majority, demonstrating a real sea change in voter sentiment.

**Infrastructure and local government**

# Industry and business

**PREVIOUS PAGES:** Low and Motion's mill at Western Springs, 1870s, with William Motion's house at left and stables with hay lofts beyond the mill, and a worker's cottage beyond the mill at right. The waterwheel can be seen in the centre of the image beside the mill. Old Mill Road runs between the mill and Motion's house. AUCKLAND LIBRARIES HERITAGE COLLECTIONS, 5-0305

**P**lentiful fresh water was one of the earliest commercial advantages of the Grey Lynn area. In the pleasant area we now know as Western Springs Lakeside Park, to the west of Grey Lynn and just south of Westmere, an abundant natural spring fed a creek that ran to the Waitematā Harbour. It was the ideal location for a water-powered flour mill, much needed in Auckland to mill local wheat crops and provide an alternative to expensive imported flour.[1]

Joseph Low and William Motion's Western Springs mill, which opened in 1846, was the third to be built in Auckland, and Low, a millwright from Fifeshire, had a connection with all three.

In 1844 Low was engaged by William Mason to build Auckland's first flour mill, the wind-powered Eden Flour Mill, and such was the demand for milling that within a few months Low and Motion had also built their own water-powered mill in Mechanics Bay, driven by a tributary of the Domain Springs. Its harbour-edge location had a considerable advantage over Mason's mill, as wheat could be brought in by boat. But soon the Domain water supply began to prove insufficient, and Low and Motion turned their eyes to Western Springs, a site also accessible by water up Waiateao, soon to be renamed Motions Creek.[2]

By September 1846 they had established their New Mills on Waiateao on the northern side of Old Mill Road, with stables and housing opposite.[3] Motion's extensive wheatfields stretched between Western Springs and Point Chevalier, and at harvest time workers could be seen rhythmically swinging their scythes to bring in the crop.[4]

The mill was a substantial enterprise, equipped with two large waterwheels that powered six sets of grinding stones. Two dams regulated by floodgates ensured a steady supply of water that ran through wooden races to turn the waterwheels. A steam plant kept the mill in production if the water supply was insufficient.[5]

The mill was housed in a large three-storey building with spacious storerooms and a tall chimney.[6] Workers were accommodated in two large stone buildings.[7] When it was empty, the grain store was used for dances to

**Industry and business** | 133

which the elite of Auckland society were invited. These were timed to coincide with a full moon so everyone could see their way home.[8]

The firm owned three cutters, the *Jolly Miller*, the *Dusty Miller* and the *Watchman*, which plied the waters between the city and the mill. On a high tide the crews pulled the cutters up Motions Creek by plunging long poles into the creek bed to propel them forward.[9] As well as buying wheat from farmers, the mill also ground wheat on contract, taking in the grain and returning fine flour.[10] Flour from the mill went not only to Auckland but also further afield, and in 1849 the firm opened a store in Queen Street that sold flour and bran.[11]

Māori were growing increasing amounts of wheat and selling any surplus to settlers. Some iwi built substantial mills of their own in the 1840s and 1850s, particularly in inland areas where wheat from nearby cultivations could be processed, saving transportation costs. Māori wheat growers on the east coast of the North Island invested in ships to convey their crop to Auckland, where it could be milled at Low and Motion's or other Auckland mills.[12] In 1851 a sample of flour milled at Low and Motion's using Māori-grown wheat was shown at the Great Exhibition at London's Crystal Palace.[13]

But the growth of the city soon caught up with Low and Motion's milling operation. The water supply was needed for other purposes, and in the mid-1870s the mill and surrounding property were sold to Auckland City Council and the grindstones ceased to turn.[14] The council then decided to lease the parts of the estate not needed for waterworks purposes, and from 1880 the mill was leased by Edward and Charles Partington, who had run a wind-powered flour mill established by their father at the corner of Karangahape Road and Symonds Street in the early 1850s.[15] They ran the Western Springs mill successfully for several years, but in 1886 found themselves in financial difficulties and were declared bankrupt.[16] In the late 1880s the mill was converted to process flax by the Western Springs Flax Company.[17]

Low and Motion's mill, which appears to have been the first industrial enterprise in the locality, was soon joined by a range of industries at Coxs Creek and Arch Hill. One of the first of these attracted the attention of the *Daily Southern Cross* in September 1862:

> It is with no small degree of pleasure we notice the fact that a manufactory for the making of sulphuric acid — the first, we believe, ever erected in the colony — is now in working condition, on Messrs. Willis, Morris & Co.'s premises, Richmond Hill.[18]

Established by entrepreneurs Frederick Willis and Francis Morris, the

Willesden Works at Richmond Hill by Coxs Creek was no small enterprise. The 4-acre (1.6-hectare) site had two large factory buildings, stables and a house with grounds planted in gum trees.[19] The works produced a patented pesticide for crops, sulphuric acid which was used to manufacture phosphate fertiliser, and artificial stone that appears to have been made in a similar way to concrete and was cast into various items including pavers, architectural details for buildings, flower pots and grinding stones.[20]

The site was appealing for such an industry. Plenty of land was available at a reasonable price, and it was located up what was then a wide, deep creek that offered easy access to the city by boat. But despite these advantages, the Willesden Works closed after only a year, possibly because of a lack of demand for its products.[21] It could be difficult to market new and unproven goods in a developing economy, and it is not hard to see how their 'artificial stone' would have struggled to find a market in a city blessed with an abundance of volcanic rock.

Further industrial enterprises arrived during the 1860s. In 1865 Scotsman John Leckie, a mechanical engineer who brought a good understanding of brickmaking with him from his homeland, established the Caledonian Brickworks by a substantial seam of clay in the Coxs Bay area.[22] Leckie had spent four years testing clay at various sites before finding his ideal site, likely to the west of Kingsley Street near the waterway that was known as Leckie's Creek (it was later renamed Edgar's Creek after resident and businessman William Edgar).[23] Unlike other brickworks in Auckland at the time, this was a technologically advanced operation that cost more than £4000, an enormous sum at the time.[24]

Leckie's brickworks were an impressive sight. Beneath the 34-foot (10-metre) chimney was a considerable array of buildings and machinery, central to which was a Ralston's brickmaking machine from Glasgow powered by a coal-fired 12-horsepower engine with a 22-foot (7-metre) boiler. Clay was fed into the motorised pug mill and combined with pulverised scoria from Mount Eden.[25]

Once mixed to an even consistency, the clay was extruded and compacted under high pressure into four-brick moulds, thereby expelling much of the water content. The bricks were proudly stamped 'Caledonian Brickworks, Richmond, Auckland' and were collected by a team of six boys, who loaded them onto barrows at a rate of 20 bricks a minute. Labourers then wheeled the laden barrows to drying sheds.[26] Mechanisation of the brickmaking process meant that Leckie needed a large expanse of drying space — his drying sheds measuring 120 × 24 feet (270 square metres).[27]

An Anderson's tile-making machine, also imported from Glasgow, was connected to the engine by a rubber belt and could churn out 12,000 tiles

**Industry and business** | 135

per day.[28] Leckie planned to build a tramway to transport his products to the harbour's edge, from where they could be taken by punt to the city.[29]

Leckie's Caledonian Brickworks appears to have been the most highly mechanised brick- and tileworks in Auckland at the time; many others relied on horses that walked in a circle around a pug mill, driving its rotation. Clay was then thrown or pressed into brick moulds by hand, although some works utilised simple extrusion and wire-cutting machinery.[30] The quality of handmade bricks relied on the skill of the brickmaker, but Leckie's machinery allowed him to produce bricks of uniform size and consistency with just a few employees, many of whom were boys or unskilled labourers and therefore cheap to hire.[31] His labour-saving machinery evidently met with some opposition, and he noted that there had been two attempts to damage his equipment.[32]

Evidently Leckie's finances had been stretched by the heavy outlay in setting up the works, and he hoped to attract investors and have the enterprise run by a company.[33] Within months of opening he had leased the brickworks to Frederick Mills and William Slater, who were well acquainted with the operation, having helped Leckie to set it up. There were other connections, too: Slater was Leckie's son-in-law from his second marriage.[34]

The following year Leckie advertised the enterprise for sale, but finding no immediate buyer, he offered the premises for sale or lease.[35] It appears that the brickworks were no longer working by 1868, when some of the equipment was moved to Moanataiari Hill, above Thames, where the Royal Blue Gold Mining Company used it to crush ore.[36] Gold had been discovered in the area the previous year, but unlike the South Island goldfields, where much free gold could be found by the lucky and determined, that at Thames was embedded in rock and required expensive crushing machinery to release it. Equipment like Leckie's that could be adapted to crush ore was in demand.

In 1869 George Element and Marmaduke Constable of the Monte Christo Smelting Company converted Leckie's old brickworks to extract gold from rock using a smelting process that they patented themselves.[37] The location might seem surprising given that it required tons of ore to be transported from the Thames goldfields for processing, but there were advantages to being close to the city. Much of the capital required for the development of the goldmining industry at Thames came from Auckland, and a new means of extracting more gold from the rock in which it was embedded would undoubtedly require investment from moneyed Aucklanders. A smelting works close to the city might also act as a good advertisement for investors, and could be visited by the local press as well as curious potential backers.

For a few months in 1869 Element and Constable carried out smelting experiments that evidently met with some success, and in June 1869 shares

**The Warnock Brothers works on the edge of Coxs Creek, 1890s.**
AUCKLAND WAR MEMORIAL MUSEUM TĀMAKI PAENGA HIRA, PH-PR-DU436-1264-C87-1

were sold in the newly formed Thames Gold Smelting Company Limited, established to erect smelting furnaces in Thames utilising the Element and Constable patented process. The works at Coxs Creek were subsequently closed.[38]

New and more successful businesses moved into the area in the 1870s, including William Edgar's Alpha Dye Works, which relocated from Grey Street (now Greys Avenue) in the city to the banks of Leckie's Creek, now known as Edgars Creek, in 1872.[39] Edgar had established his business in the mid-1860s following a trade he had practised in Scotland.[40] The creek offered plenty of water and ample room for drying.[41] Edgar evidently had a sense of humour — his business slogan was 'Still Dyeing to Live and Living to Dye'.[42] The business continued into the twentieth century, carried on after William Edgar's death in 1893 by his son John.[43]

Irish brothers James, Robert and William Warnock arrived in Auckland aboard the *Indian Empire* in October 1862, and within a few weeks had purchased John Goodfellow's soap and candle factory in Parnell Road, on the site where the Blind Foundation building would later be erected.[44] They were joined by their brother Richard and their parents, Mary and James senior; the latter was a soap and candle manufacturer.

**Industry and business | 137**

Unfortunately for the brothers, their Warnock Soap and Candle Works factory and adjoining house on Parnell Road were destroyed by fire in November 1864.[45] Soon afterwards they purchased land in Brown Street, Ponsonby, where they set up a new factory. They then re-established themselves in Chapel Street (now known as Federal Street) in the central city, where they took over an existing soap and candle factory — probably that of John Higgins, whose Chapel Street enterprise near the corner of Wellesley Street was disposed of in a mortgagee sale in 1867.[46]

The expansion of residential development on the edge of the city had brought people into closer proximity with polluting industries established there in earlier years, and it was an unhappy mix. In 1873 Chapel Street locals, offended by the smell of rendering fat and concerned about the effects on their health, appealed to the Auckland City Council, 'praying for an abatement to the nuisance'.[47] The council ordered the Warnock brothers to remove their offending manufactory from the city within six months.[48]

Richmond provided an ideal locality — close enough to the city trade and labour markets but far enough away so as not to cause a nuisance — and by the end of 1874 the new factory was up and running on the southern side of Richmond Road, on the edge of Coxs Creek.[49] After the expense of moving, however, the business was dealt a further blow in late 1876 when the factory was severely damaged by a tornado, then struck by lightning a fortnight later.[50] Undaunted, the brothers repaired the damage and were soon back in production.

They started out at Richmond with a site of just 1.5 acres, but two decades later had extended their landholding to 20 acres (8 hectares), and had created a substantial lake created by damming Coxs Creek. They also expanded their range of products. Large brick buildings had replaced many earlier timber structures that were destroyed in yet another catastrophic fire in 1893. Fuelled by flammable materials it took hold quickly; with no piped water supply on site, the Newton and Auckland firefighters could only throw buckets of creek water at the inferno.[51] The only buildings to escape were the tannery, the four-storey woolsheds and the 90-foot (27-metre) brick chimney, which stood forlornly in the middle of the charred remains of the engine house that had surrounded it.[52]

The brothers rebuilt quickly, and within a year a staff of over 60 were producing leather, scoured wool for export, tallow, soap, fertiliser made from rendered bones, and coconut oil from imported copra.[53]

The Warnock Brothers relied on good supplies of animal fat, bones and hides for many of their products, and soon after moving to Richmond they found this was very much closer at hand: during the 1880s the area had become a centre of meat processing for Auckland.

Electricity was a sign of modernity, efficiency and health, and from the nineteenth century all manner of 'electric' products were marketed, including belts and corsets which promised to cure many ailments. Electric soap was much more mundane. Dingman's electric soap (an American laundry and household soap) was available in New Zealand from the late 1880s and Warnock Brothers later marketed their own electric pumice sand soap and electric soap powder. MUSEUM OF TRANSPORT AND TECHNOLOGY, 2010.680; AUCKLAND LIBRARIES HERITAGE COLLECTIONS, AS-19330225-14-10

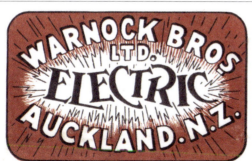

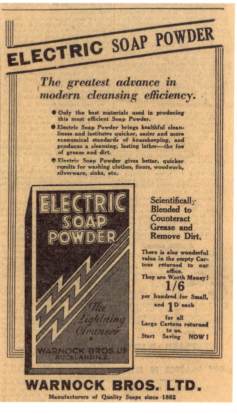

In 1850, prompted by the risk to public health of meat slaughtered in unregulated private slaughterhouses with varying hygiene standards, a public abattoir had been erected in Newmarket conveniently close to the cattle saleyards.[54] From the earliest days there were complaints about the state of the Newmarket facility. At one stage the stench from rotting matter beneath the floor could be smelt a mile off.[55] By the mid-1870s the extension of suburban development in the Newmarket area had brought more residents within the whiff of the abattoir and a new and more suitable location needed to be found.[56]

When the Auckland Provincial Council was wound up in 1876, Auckland City Council was given the responsibility of providing a public abattoir and opted to move the problem outside their boundaries. This was the abattoirs erected above Western Springs in 1877 (see Chapter 4), where West View Road is today.[57]

Seeing the advantages of the area for meat processing, Hellaby Brothers, which had grown significantly since its establishment on a small scale in 1873, began buying coastal land between Coxs and Meola creeks in the 1880s.[58] By mid-1882 they had 50 acres (20 hectares) of land, some of it leased, where they could hold animals before processing them in the onsite slaughterhouse.[59]

Although the area was sparsely populated, there were still complaints about both abattoirs from residents, particularly those from the Bayfield area to the east of Coxs Bay, who had to endure the putrid smell of rotting flesh when the wind blew in their direction. The lingering odours of the Hellaby's plant were also transported in the clothes of workers who caught the horse-drawn tram that ran between the top of College Hill in Ponsonby and the city, prompting a petition from fellow tram users to exclude the Hellaby staff.[60]

Frequent articles in the newspapers reported the complaints about both

Sheep awaiting their fate at Hellaby's tannery and fellmongery on the lower slopes of their Richmond property, 1898. AUCKLAND LIBRARIES HERITAGE COLLECTIONS, 7-A5875

Hellaby's staff at the Richmond works. Richard Hellaby, wearing a bowler hat, is at middle right and James 'Ikity' Pike, the Richmond works manager, is in a bowler hat at middle left. The four boys in school uniform at the rear are the sons of Richard and William Hellaby. Richard was known as a hard-working but kindly employer who often helped financially if there was sickness or a misfortune in the family of an employee. He was also well respected by the farming community.
DICK SCOTT, *STOCK IN TRADE*, P.29

plants. In 1888 Hellaby Brothers was charged with offences under the Public Health Act relating to 'large quantities of offal, manure, decaying animal matter and blood spread over a two-acre paddock, and the odour arising therefrom . . . being "abominable and terrible", and . . . decidedly injurious to health'.[61] The municipal abattoirs were no less malodorous. In fact, the Hellaby slaughterhouse was described as 'well kept' in comparison.[62]

Over time Hellaby Brothers added a fellmongery, tannery, boiling-down works, bone mill, manure works and wool scour to its slaughterhouse. The bone mill and manure works produced fertiliser, while the boiling-down works produced tallow from animal fat. Bones and scrap meat from city butchers and hotels were also taken in and processed.[63] At the fellmongery, skins were scraped of hair to prepare them for tanning. In the 1890s the works employed 150 men and each week processed around 250 cattle and calves, 1000 sheep and lambs and a number of pigs.[64] By 1898, Hellaby was the largest butchering firm in New Zealand.[65]

Hellaby provided a comprehensive nose-to-tail processing plant, but there was plenty of room for other businesses specialising in one or other of the animal product trades, and from the 1880s these proliferated along the coast and the creeks and streams of the district. In 1884 Auckland Tallow and Blood Manure Company (also known as the Auckland Tallow Company) was operating at Mount Pleasant, the former farm of Archibald Cochrane, located near Hellaby's works in the area now traversed by Sunny Brae and Winsomere crescents in Westmere.[66] The company processed bones, fat, blood and offal collected from the abattoirs and city butchers and fed it into steam digestors, converting it all into rendered fat and fertiliser. In 1886 the company built its own slaughterhouse.[67]

**Industry and business** | 141

The company had started out on the south side of Great North Road, just west of Western Springs Road and not far from the Auckland City Council water supply at Western Springs, but had met with opposition from the council, which feared the factory would contaminate the city's water supply. This prompted the move to Westmere.[68]

In 1884 Bridgenorth Tannery was built on Old Mill Road overlooking Motions Creek, near where Savage Street runs today. Unlike some other local firms, including Warnock Bros and Edgar's Dye Works, which had started out in the city before being forced out, the new tannery at Richmond was relocated from where it was first established by Benjamin Gittos on Oakley Creek in Avondale in the 1860s, where his sons joined him in the enterprise. The creek's ample water flow had both supplied the tannery and taken away its waste, leading to complaints from farmers downstream.[69] The new location by Motions Creek had the advantage of being closer to the harbour, where waste would be rapidly removed by the tide.

Bridgenorth Tannery was a substantial enterprise with structures of one, two and three storeys built to a design based on 'the best American tanneries'.[70] A visiting reporter from the *New Zealand Herald* described the processing of skins. This began in the spacious beam shed, which could accommodate between 5000 and 6000 hides:

> Here the raw hides are salted, and sorted as required. They are then taken to the water pits . . . they are cleansed, and from these pits they are removed to the limepits . . . [where they are left] sufficiently long to remove the hair, they are unhaired and fleshed, and cleansed according to requirements.[71]

After this, some of the skins went into colour pits, where soaked bark produced the tanning liquid. Sole leather was rolled and finished in one part of the factory; other parts were devoted to the production of leather for saddlery and shoe and bootmaking. Dubbin, made from oil and tallow, was also produced.[72]

The Gittos Brothers, who continued the firm after the death of their father, ran into financial troubles as the local economy fell into depression, and in August 1889 Frank Jagger and William Parker, successful Auckland businessmen and directors of a number of companies, bought them out. The 1898 Auckland Industrial and Mining Exhibition catalogue commented, 'Any business with which [Jagger] is connected has to "hum", and the association of his name with a concern is a guarantee of push and enterprise.'[73] At this time the company was humming along nicely, employing 31 men and processing over 15,000 hides a year.[74]

Jagger and Parker's tannery on Old Mill Road, below where Savage Street runs today, 1900. It was originally known as the Bridgenorth Tannery and was established by the Gittos Brothers in 1884. In 1889 it became one of several successful businesses run by Frank Jagger and William Parker. AUCKLAND LIBRARIES HERITAGE COLLECTIONS, 226-9279

There was further development of the meat by-product trades in the 1890s with the establishment of a number of smaller enterprises, including Alexander Donald's tannery and fellmongery at Livingstone Street. Donald had come to New Zealand around the early 1870s, and after working as a foreman for Warnock Bros for several years he established his own fellmongery, which was up and running by the early 1890s.[75] Some of his sons also entered the business, which by the late 1890s was operating as A. Donald and Sons. The firm soon expanded into tanning.[76]

John Redshaw took over the former works of the Auckland Tallow Company in 1891.[77] He had learned the trade from his father, Joseph, who ran a boiling-down works and tripe-dressing establishment at Cabbage Tree Swamp (now known as Sandringham).[78]

Work at these enterprises was physical and dangerous. In 1910 Donald's son Robert lost part of his arm in the fleshing machine.[79] This was not an isolated incident. A few months earlier, 17-year-old Frederick Burgess was injured in a similar accident at Warnock Bros nearby.[80] Local factories were apparently also hazardous to inquisitive children. In one instance, three-year-old George Bedingfield drowned in a vat of tanning liquid at Warnock Bros after squeezing under a broken door at the back of the factory.[81]

In parts of the district with a piped water supply there was at least some

**Industry and business** | 143

prospect of fighting fires. But the far end of the district remained beyond the reach of the water pipes into the twentieth century. John Redshaw's bone and tallow works were completely destroyed by fire in 1906. Efforts to extinguish the fire with water from a well were no match for the ferocious tallow-fuelled blaze.[82]

※

Gradual residential expansion brought public pressure to minimise the pollution from these industries, known collectively as the 'offensive trades'. Following considerable pressure, in 1908 Auckland City Council relocated its municipal abattoirs to Westfield, at the head of the Manukau Harbour near Ōtāhuhu.[83] Increasing land prices also encouraged business owners to seek cheaper locations further from the city in order to realise the capital gain on their land. Hellaby Brothers had been working towards a move to Westfield since 1899, and had been buying land in the area.

The Department of Agriculture forced the issue when it refused to renew Hellaby's licence, and the company moved production to its new Westfield works in 1911. Hellaby subsequently sold its considerable Richmond landholding, which was marketed as the Westend Seaside Estate.[84] Local residents were probably relieved that they no longer had to seek safety behind fences when mobs of unruly cattle passed through the streets on the way to the slaughterhouse, cutting up the roads as they went.[85]

Other business relocations were prompted by calamitous events. In 1920 the timber mill established by the Cashmore brothers on the eastern side of Coxs Creek in 1899 was destroyed by fire. By this stage it was clear that residential development would continue to spread throughout the district and, as well, the mill had been the subject of complaints from the people of Herne Bay, who objected to its smoke and noise. Cashmore's opted not to build a new mill, and instead opened a timber yard at Newmarket, selling sawn timber that arrived by rail from mills elsewhere. In its two decades of operation from Coxs Bay, the mill had produced much of the timber required to build the houses in the vicinity as well as others further afield.[86]

Although meat and animal by-product trades dominated the industrial landscape in Coxs Creek and Westmere, in the late nineteenth and early twentieth centuries an altogether different industrial character developed around Arch Hill and Great North Road. Great North Road provided the main access from the city to the west, and a number of brickyards were established there. The first of these belonged to builder George Boyd who,

144 | The Near West

Sheep grazing in Hellaby's extensive paddocks on the edge of Coxs Creek, early 1900s. They would soon be heading to the works.
AUCKLAND LIBRARIES HERITAGE COLLECTIONS, AWNS-19050810-05-01

frustrated by the inferior quality and high prices of bricks in Auckland, decided to manufacture his own.

Initially Boyd hired some brickmakers and established a brickyard in Symonds Street.[87] He later moved to a large block of land on Great North Road on the eastern side of Burns Street.[88] By mid-1862 his Newton Brick and Tile Works (later known as Newton Potteries) was producing drainage tiles and bricks for sale.[89]

Boyd's works started out relying on horse- and manpower and gradually incorporated more technology.[90] By the mid-1860s the works were extensive, with a kiln capable of firing 40,000 bricks at once and a drying shed measuring 300 × 22 feet (90 × 7 metres). The machinery included a 'Clayton's well-known patent machine from the Atlas Works, Dorset-square, London'.[91] This device could produce 350 bricks an hour, but even that was insufficient to meet demand. Handmade bricks were also produced at the works, but were inferior in quality. Drainage pipes and tiles were made in various sizes by another patent machine.[92]

Boyd also produced ornamental products, including vases, water bottles and flower pots, for which he won awards, and his works expanded as he added new products to his range.[93] By late 1878 steam power had been harnessed. The factory occupied around 5 acres and was churning out everything from doorsteps to kitchen sinks.[94] Boyd was a considerate employer and provided cottages 'built expressly for the occupation of the employees of the works, and comprising every convenience for the homes of working men'.[95]

Industry and business | 145

**OPPOSITE ABOVE:** Timber workers at Cashmore's Coxs Creek mill, with stacks of sawn timber behind. AUCKLAND WAR MEMORIAL MUSEUM TĀMAKI PAENGA HIRA, PH-NEG-B8882

**OPPOSITE BELOW:** Looking across from Westmere to Herne Bay, showing West End Road crossing Coxs Creek, 1907. Cashmore's Mill is at upper right. AUCKLAND LIBRARIES HERITAGE COLLECTIONS, 7-A1836

**BELOW:** Two men standing in the vicinity of Fife Street with Coxs Creek and Cashmore's Mill behind them. The bridge across the creek can be seen at left. AUCKLAND WAR MEMORIAL MUSEUM TĀMAKI PAENGA HIRA, BROWN LANTERN SLIDE 83

Boyd's success prompted other business ventures. In July 1865 the *Daily Southern Cross* noted:

> Encouraged by the success of the Newton brickworks . . . several small capitalists have erected their plant and begun the work of making bricks on a humble scale, encouraged by the natural facilities of the soil and the reputation of the Newton Works.[96]

One of these may have been Joseph Johnson's brickyard, which was operating near Commercial Road in the early 1870s, probably in the area immediately west of Commercial Road — known at the time as the brickfield.[97] Further down Great North Road, close to the corner of Tuarangi Road on part of the Young family's farm, the Arch Hill Brick and Pottery Works, established in the mid-1870s by William Sloane and Thomas Murray, offered a range of products from the artistic to the utilitarian.[98]

The firm hired Moses Exler, a skilled potter from Nettlebed in Oxfordshire who had earlier worked for George Boyd.[99] Following a public share issue, in 1881 the company became known as the Arch Hill Brick and Tile Company. New kilns were built and equipment purchased that would enable the

**LEFT:** A fish jug made at George Boyd's Newton Potteries. AUCKLAND WAR MEMORIAL MUSEUM TĀMAKI PAENGA HIRA, 1998.56.1

**RIGHT:** A planter stand made at George Boyd's Newton Potteries, 1885. TE PAPA TONGAREWA MUSEUM OF NEW ZEALAND, CG000639

Looking across from Eden Terrace to Arch Hill, c. 1880. The Newton Potteries drying sheds are visible in the distance. AUCKLAND LIBRARIES HERITAGE COLLECTIONS, 4-254

production of 20,000 bricks per day.[100] But the firm was unlucky — heavy rains hindered completion of the kiln and a landslip caused considerable damage. Within a few years the firm was once again borrowing to relocate to a more convenient position.[101]

But the timing was terrible — the Auckland building boom of the early 1880s that had no doubt encouraged the company to invest so heavily came to a rapid end in the mid-1880s, and in 1890 the company closed and sold the remaining equipment and stock.[102] The *Auckland Star* described it as 'an unfortunate affair from beginning to end'.[103] Residents of the area would have appreciated its closure, having long complained of 'soot eruptions' from its chimney.[104]

By the late 1890s the only brickworks still in operation on Great North Road was Alfred Dolphin's enterprise on the site of the former Arch Hill Brick and Tile Company. It was later run by Holden and Moon but had closed by the start of the First World War.[105] With residential development extending through the district, the brickmaking industry of Arch Hill had completed its decades-long march along the Great North Road ridge and was now gone from the district. Another Great North Road business was the iron founders Beaney

**Industry and business** | 149

and Sons, established in Arch Hill in 1881 by Adam Beaney, who had learned his trade in London before coming to New Zealand in 1862.[106] The family firm was ultimately run by three generations of Beaneys and remained part of the Arch Hill industrial landscape until the late 1960s, by which time its long buildings were flanked on the west by St Joseph's Convent and on the east by a group of state-housing units.[107]

The firm took on all manner of works, but was well known in the late nineteenth century for producing sawmilling machinery and the iron lighthouses that stand on Repanga Cuvier Island and Takapourewa Stephens Island.[108] The works were divided into different departments: a moulding shop, a pattern department, a fitting shop and a blacksmith's shop equipped with 'the usual anvils and furnaces, and two travelling cranes, also a . . . steam hammer'.[109] In 1898 it employed around 25 men.[110]

Around the turn of the century a range of light manufacturing industries

Bricks made at the Caledonian Brickworks, George Boyd's Newton Brick and Tile Works, and the Arch Hill Brick and Tile Company, 1860s. The brick stamped 'NONSUCH' was made in George Boyd's Clayton's patent brick machine, while the brick marked 'G. Boyd' was handmade.
TE TOI UKU, CROWN LYNN AND CLAYWORKS MUSEUM, 2016.44.24, 2016.44.62, 2016.44.36, 2016.44.159

sprang up, which better suited the developing suburban identity of the area. They generated less pollution and they offered jobs for locals.

James Tattersfield established a mattress factory on the corner of Sackville Street and Richmond Road (then known as Richmond Avenue) around the turn of the century. Tattersfield had a background in textile manufacturing in his native Yorkshire, where his family had a blanket-making business in Heckmondwike.[111] After his arrival in Auckland in 1899 he was employed by a wool-buying firm where he learned about New Zealand wool, which was different in character to the wool in England.

Early in the new century he established a drapery shop on Great North Road near the corner of Turakina Street (then known as Tennyson Street), before moving into a spacious new shop that still stands at the eastern corner of Karangahape Road and Pitt Street.[112] James's wife Evelyn ran the shop while he travelled the country taking orders and selling a range of products. On one

**Industry and business** | 151

of his business trips he stayed at a boarding house, where the owner asked him to supply a new mattress. Tattersfield ordered this from a firm in Wellington, but when the mattress arrived Evelyn was dismayed by its poor quality and suggested to James that they could make a better product themselves.[113]

And so the Tattersfields branched out into manufacturing. They bought land at the corner of Sackville Street and Richmond Road and borrowed to establish a factory. They erected a substantial shed and a family home on the site, and relocated their Karangahape Road shop to the Richmond Buildings on the corner of Francis Street. Using equipment bought from the Onehunga Woollen Mills, in 1906 James made New Zealand's first commercially produced mattress. This marked the beginning of the Tattersfield manufacturing business, in which James and Evelyn were joined by Evelyn's brother Howard Abbott. Their mattresses found a ready market and the firm grew to have a staff of 200 by 1920, rising to 300 a decade later.[114]

Tattersfield made use of waste products from other industries. In 1920 it advertised for cuttings from tailors and clothing manufacturers which were then used in manufacturing the mattress stuffing or flock — fibres were teased apart by feeding fabric scraps into the teeth of a rapidly spinning carding drum.[115] The flock-making plant allowed the firm to expand its range of mattresses. The 'Peerless' model was available in various sizes and grades, and for those with deeper pockets there was a mattress with a horse-hair centre surrounded by silver-down. One cheaper model was made from coir fibre from coconut husks and a lower-grade flock.[116]

In the 1920s the firm began making reversible wool rugs from grades of wool that often went to waste. Through the family connection with Heckmondwike it sourced the equipment and specialist skills needed to establish its new Tattersfield Textiles factory. Rug- and carpet-making machinery arrived in 1922, followed by Mr Marsden, who would install it, and Mr Eccles, formerly in charge of the Axminster department at Heckmondwike, who would take charge of the Auckland factory, which was soon operational.[117] Evelyn designed many of the company's patterned rugs, examples of which were exhibited in 1924 at the British Empire Exhibition at Wembley. Queen Mary requested that one be sent to Buckingham Palace.[118]

The factory buildings gradually expanded to fill the corner site, and the firm purchased a property over the road where it built a garage for its fleet of vehicles.[119] In 1930 the firm added a spinning and dyeing plant and adjoining wool scour on the edge of Coxs Creek near the end of Livingstone Street. Tattersfield responded to changes in floor-covering fashions, making wall-to-wall carpets from 1947 and later establishing a subsidiary company, Tattersfield Brinton Carpets Limited, in partnership with British firm Brintons Limited. Axminster and Broadloom carpets were manufactured on

**ABOVE:** The Beaney and Sons exhibit of agricultural equipment at the Auckland Metropolitan Spring Show, 1909. AUCKLAND LIBRARIES HERITAGE COLLECTIONS, AWNS-19091202-13-04

**BELOW:** A view up Sackville Street showing the imposing Tattersfield factory, 1978. AUCKLAND COUNCIL ARCHIVES, ACC 064, IMAGE 163

the company's Coxs Creek site. Both sites had a tall chimney, one of which still stands on what is now the Richmond Road Woolworths supermarket carpark.[120]

✕

Some firms reliant on a female workforce established themselves at the Ponsonby end of Grey Lynn. In 1899 in the block bounded by Ponsonby Road, Williamson Avenue, Pollen Street and Crummer Road, premises were built for Arch. Clark and Sons, 'one of the largest shirt manufacturers in the Colony'.[121] In 1900 the factory had just under 300 workers producing Zealandia-brand shirts and collars. The firm later made tents as well.[122]

The company was good to its workers and provided a lunch room for staff in 1907. The *New Zealand Herald* noted: 'The majority of the employees at the factory are girls, and the firm has generously fitted the hall with a piano for their use.'[123] At the time it was hard to get workers, particularly young women who, with pay rates well below those of men, were an affordable labour force. In January 1908 the firm advertised for 50 staff, including 'young girls leaving school', who would be taught all branches of the work at the Zealandia factory.[124] The school leaving age at the time was 14.[125]

Nearby in Mackelvie Street, Macky Logan and Caldwell opened a clothing factory in 1906 to make women's Classic-brand undergarments, aprons and glory gowns, the latter designed to provide a smart appearance at short notice in the event of an unexpected visitor.[126] By mid-1919 the factory was just one of six Macky Logan and Caldwell premises in Auckland, each producing a different line of garments and bedding.[127] In 1925 the firm moved out of the Mackelvie Street factory and was replaced by Robert T. Woods, a clothing enterprise that was upgrading from smaller premises in Ponsonby.[128]

Arch. Clark and Sons' shirt factory was destroyed by fire in 1920, although the lunch room was spared, allowing the firm to continue some production on the site while moving the shirtmakers to a new factory elsewhere.[129]

In 1925 the Dominion Compressed Yeast Company, first established in Christchurch in 1915, opened a North Island branch on the site, producing compressed yeast and vinegar. The four-storey concrete and brick factory had louvre windows to provide ventilation for the pungent manufacturing process.[130] Only two factories produced baker's yeast in New Zealand — the other was the firm's Christchurch works — and products from Grey Lynn supplied bakers and retailers throughout the North Island.[131]

Smaller factories proliferated, too, some near the large factories and others in residential streets. Charles Augustus Brown's brush and broom manufacturing business opened in Surrey Crescent in the mid-1890s.[132] Within a decade his

**ABOVE:** Men cutting fabric for white shirts at Arch. Clark and Sons' Grey Lynn factory. Women and girls work in the background, 1900. AUCKLAND LIBRARIES HERITAGE COLLECTIONS, AWNS-19000406-12-02

**BELOW:** Girls and women working in the laundry department of Arch. Clark and Sons, Grey Lynn, in 1900. AUCKLAND LIBRARIES HERITAGE COLLECTIONS, AWNS-19000406-11-03

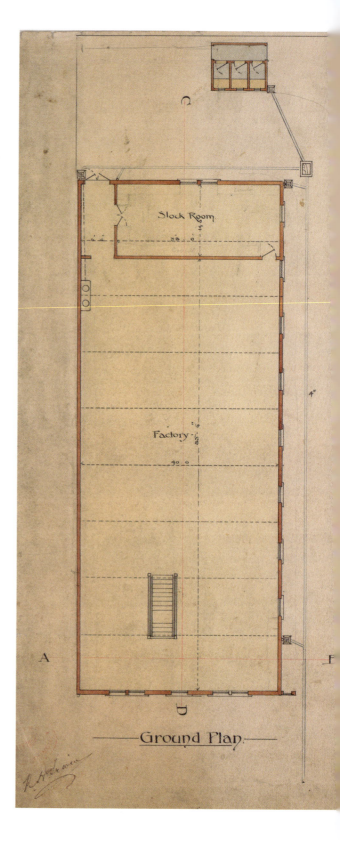

A plan of the Macky, Logan and Caldwell clothing factory in Mackelvie Street, designed by W. A. Holman, 1906. Electricity had not yet reached Grey Lynn so the large skylight would have been an important light source. ARCHITECTURE ARCHIVE, UNIVERSITY OF AUCKLAND, MSS-ARCHIVES-ARCH-2020/13

son, Charles Augustus Brown junior, was living in Richmond Avenue (now part of Richmond Road) and working as a brush finisher. The firm moved to Wilton Street, where a substantial factory was built on the northern side near the corner of Richmond Road.[133] Down the road was Benjamin Davis's boot factory, a small family business established on Richmond Avenue around 1909 that later moved to Wilton Street.[134] At the other end of Wilton Street, Hosken Bros made ornamental fibrous plaster ceilings and wallboards in their new factory from 1923. The firm was run by William and Joseph Hosken and had earlier operated from smaller premises at 1 Sherwood Avenue.[135]

Several of these smaller factories established in residential streets have remained in use. The corrugated-iron building on the corner of Williamson Avenue and Ariki Street was Shenkin's Cabinet Factory, which produced dining, bedroom and Chesterfield suites from 1920.[136] From the mid-1930s Torrens and Son Cabinetmakers occupied the building. In the 1990s the building became the home of He Taonga Films, founded by Māori actor, director and producer Don Selwyn to produce the work of Māori writers. The building has more recently been occupied by Karma Drinks, a fair-trade soft drink company.[137]

Marsden & Co was one of the few industries established in Westmere at the time when the area was developing a more residential character. The bedding and mattress manufacturing company had been founded in 1929 by Israel (Jack) Marsden, who came to New Zealand with his wife Lily in 1922.[138] The firm later moved into manufacturing furniture.

156 | The Near West

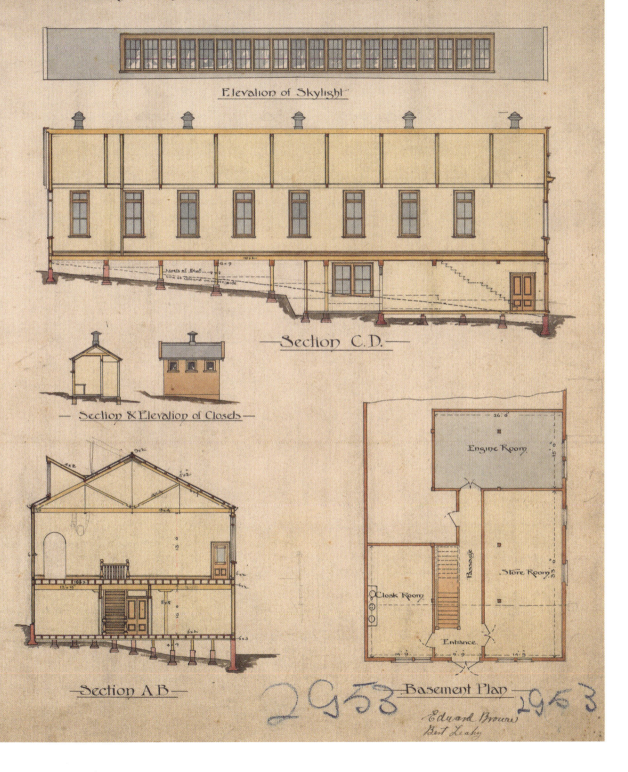

**ABOVE:** Workers bottling vinegar in the DYC factory in Grey Lynn, c. 1950s. AUCKLAND WAR MEMORIAL MUSEUM TĀMAKI PAENGA HIRA, PH-NEG-SIP-2-315 F

**RIGHT:** Packing malt vinegar into boxes for dispatch at the DYC factory, Grey Lynn, c. 1950s. AUCKLAND WAR MEMORIAL MUSEUM TĀMAKI PAENGA HIRA, PH-NEG-SIP-2-315E

**BELOW:** The staff of Marsden & Co. outside their factory on Garnet Road, c. 1930s. AUCKLAND LIBRARIES HERITAGE COLLECTIONS, 1372-1

**LEFT:** Elizabeth Brown and a horse at the back of Brown's brush factory, c. 1905. AUCKLAND LIBRARIES HERITAGE COLLECTIONS, 226-7640; ;

**ABOVE:** A man carrying brushes outside Brown's brush factory on Wilton Street. AUCKLAND WAR MEMORIAL MUSEUM TĀMAKI PAENGA HIRA, PH-X30, LANTERN SLIDE LS15-40

Larger enterprises established from the early twentieth century tended to be located on the main roads, and Surrey Crescent was no exception. In 1929 the vast Auckland Laundry Company building opened on land to the west of Grey Lynn School after the company took over the Auckland Steam Laundry, which had been established in the city 25 years earlier and was running at almost full capacity.[139] In the days when washing, drying and ironing clothing and linen in the home was an arduous and time-consuming task that started with chopping wood to fuel a fire beneath a copper, many people outsourced their laundry chores. Washing machines were expensive and out of reach for many until the 1950s and 1960s.[140]

Auckland Laundry Company provided services to hotels, ships and some households, and was keen to expand further into the domestic market. Increased capacity at the Surrey Crescent laundry allowed it to offer a new service. Its 10 motorised vans, decked out in blue and silver livery, made a constant circuit of the city and suburbs, picking up and delivering laundry.[141] Such services were common overseas, but Auckland Laundry Company was the first to offer it in Auckland.[142]

As the building neared completion, the firm advertised for a 'smart woman' to work at the factory, and was besieged by applicants.[143] Local unemployment was on the rise as the Great Depression began to bite. It also bit the company's bottom line: many households had to make do with less and reduced spending where they could. Having just invested heavily in its new premises, the firm now found itself in financial trouble and went into liquidation. It was subsequently reconstructed as the New Auckland Laundry Company, and within a few years had turned its fortunes around.[144] Growing demand saw the premises extended to double capacity in the late 1930s.[145]

Some business enterprises developed a symbiotic relationship with others. Auckland Laundry Company had space to lease in its Surrey Crescent premises in the 1950s and was joined by Stebbings record-pressing plant. Eldred Stebbing and his wife Margaret had established a recording studio in their Avondale home in 1946 and were ready to expand.[146] They had opened a studio in Queen Street in 1950, and now sought to press records, both of their own material and under licence for international companies.[147] A good supply of steam and water was necessary to heat the record presses and shellac dough, as was space for electroplating masters, pressing records and the finishing work of trimming edges and affixing labels. The spacious upper floor of the Auckland Laundry Company building was perfect.[148]

The presses were kept busy and many local artists were immortalised on records despatched from the factory. The local recording industry took advantage of the lengthy delays in getting the latest hit records by artists from the United States and Britain, which arrived by ship, so Stebbings would

**ABOVE:** The extensive Auckland Laundry Company site on Surrey Crescent (centre), with Grey Lynn School and the Surrey Tennis Club courts above (top middle), 1930s. The new factory of hosiery manufacturer Korma Mills can be seen on Surrey Crescent between the Auckland Laundry Company and St Columba Church, with the Grey Lynn Bowling Club at far right. The Cereal Foods factory on Surrey Crescent is opposite Korma Mills. ALEXANDER TURNBULL LIBRARY, WA-55948-G

**BELOW:** A rear view of the Auckland Laundry Company showing its delivery vans ready to take freshly starched laundry to customers and bring in new loads for laundering, c. 1940s. St Columba Church can be seen at left. AUCKLAND LIBRARIES HERITAGE COLLECTIONS, 580-00304

have the sheet music flown in and select local artists to record it.¹⁴⁹ As well as pressing their own recordings under the Stebbing and Zodiac labels, the firm pressed records under licence from American and British firms. Labels included Mercury, Fidelity, Bosworth, Esquire and Hallmark.¹⁵⁰

In 1953 the pressing plant was sold to Fred Green and Tony Hall, who equipped it with presses for the new long-playing format. Among the early pressings was the Howard Morrison Quartet's hit song 'My Old Man's an All Black', a song about the 1960 All Black tour of South Africa from which Māori players were excluded under South African apartheid laws. Over 60,000 copies were pressed, labelled and packaged at the Surrey Crescent plant.¹⁵¹ Green and Hall was taken over by HMV in the mid 1960s and the record-pressing plant appears to have closed down at this time.¹⁵²

✕

Several of Auckland's early aerated water and cordial manufacturers had been located in Eden Crescent, where they had access to the abundant Waiariki Springs, but as the city's reticulated water supply developed they were free to move elsewhere.

The Grey Lynn electorate had voted to become dry early in the twentieth century, and in the 1920s it was Auckland's soft-drink manufacturing centre. Simmonds and Osborne were located on Crummer Road, Sharpe Brothers in Millais and then Dickens Street (then known as Disraeli Street), Blockley & Co. in Mackelvie Street, Francis Foley in Surrey Crescent, and Waiwai Ltd and Hollis, Walls and Co. on Great North Road.¹⁵³ Factory sites were plentiful and the area was close to the most heavily populated parts of the city.¹⁵⁴

Sharpe Brothers was the first to move to Grey Lynn.¹⁵⁵ The Sharpes had begun a mineral water and cordial business in their hometown in Cumberland as a sideline while working in the mines. Three brothers emigrated and

**BELOW LEFT:** One of the refreshing beverages made by Purity Products, which started out in the former George Blockley and Son factory on Mackelvie Street before moving in 1937 to the Dickens Street factory established by Sharpe Brothers and later run by George Puddle. MURRAY R. FROST, *CORDIALLY YOURS: LIFE STORIES FROM THE SOFT DRINK INDUSTRY*, P.78

**BELOW RIGHT:** Foley's lemonade was produced at Francis P. Foley's Surrey Crescent factory during the 1920s and 1930s. PETER E. W. ROBSON, *A HISTORY OF THE AERATED WATER INDUSTRY IN NEW ZEALAND 1845–1986*, P.39

162 | The Near West

**BELOW LEFT:** Sharpe Brothers stoneware jars, with their metal handles for ease of lifting, were delivered to households throughout New Zealand and Australia from the many Sharpe Brothers factories, including one in Grey Lynn. COLLECTION OF KATHERINE MANSFIELD HOUSE AND GARDEN

**BELOW RIGHT:** Robinson's ice-cream truck number 10, pictured here at the seaside holiday spot Long Bay in the 1920s. By 1941 Robinson's had a fleet of 14 refrigerated trucks and was churning out almost 5000 litres a day at its Arch Hill factory. AUCKLAND LIBRARIES HERITAGE COLLECTIONS, EF0250

established their first factory in Dunedin in 1903 before rapidly opening branches in other centres, including Auckland and Sydney.[156] In 1910 their labels bore the slogan 'Largest Manufacturers of Non-intoxicating Beverages in Australasia'.[157]

Their brews, bottled in heavy stoneware gallon jars, were loaded onto horse-drawn vehicles that made the rounds of Auckland; the delivery men called at back doors, depositing the jars in a cool place.[158] Refrigerators did not become a common feature in New Zealand homes until the 1950s, by which stage the gallon jars had been replaced by glass bottles, an amendment to the Sale of Food and Drugs regulations having prohibited the sale of aerated waters in stoneware jars in 1941.[159]

By the mid-1920s there were 35 Sharpe Brothers factories in Australia and New Zealand, although many New Zealand branches, including the Auckland operation, were sold off to their managers as the Sharpe family moved its focus to Australia and England.[160] From 1915 the Millais Street operation was owned by John Tietjens, who had managed the Auckland branch since 1911. Tietjens sold the business to George Puddle in 1920, and three years later the enterprise moved to a larger factory in Dickens Street.[161] Puddle and his staff brewed a variety of drinks, including Sharpe Brothers' famous ginger beer, non-alcoholic

Industry and business | 163

hop beer, horehound beer, lemonade and fruit cordials.[162] Puddle later opened branches in Devonport and Pukekohe.[163]

Not all drinks manufacturers were as successful. Hollis Walls and Co. operated from the Arch Hill side of Great North Road for just six years from 1915, using recipes handed down to John Hollis by his stepfather, Cyprian Nicholls, who had earlier run a soft drink factory in Ponsonby Road at the corner of Brown Street.[164]

Many of these enterprises were family affairs, but the younger generation did not always wish to take on the family business. In 1932 Lance and Esther Moses and Freda Nicholson bought George Blockley and Son, a cordial factory in Mackelvie Street near the junction with Williamson Avenue. They renamed it Purity Products and began to produce fruit-flavoured aerated waters in orange, passionfruit, grapefruit and lemon varieties. In 1937 they moved to the former Sharpe Brothers factory on Dickens Street. Lance and Esther's son Ron recalled that demand was enormous in the summer months, during which the family worked up to 15 hours a day, seven days a week — Christmas Day was their only day off over the summer, and they were often too tired to celebrate.[165] This was enough to put Ron off a life in the family business, and it closed in 1952 when his parents retired.[166]

Some of the soft drinks produced in Grey Lynn went out of fashion and others took their place. In the late 1950s the Waiwai factory on the corner of Great North Road and Bond Street, in operation since 1924, was sold to rival soft-drink manufacturer C. L. Innes & Co., which had been manufacturing Coca-Cola at its Gillies Avenue factory in Newmarket. New Zealanders had developed a taste for Coca-Cola after it was made locally under licence to supply American soldiers stationed at camps around the country, including at Western Springs. The Great North Road factory allowed for expansion and had more convenient access for the company's new fleet of large delivery trucks.[167] Along with soft drinks, various foodstuffs were produced in quantity in Grey Lynn and Arch Hill.

Robinson's Ice Cream factory began production on Putiki Street (then known as James Street) in Arch Hill in 1912. Founded by Edwin Robinson, the firm had started out in Victoria Street in the city around 1910 with just one ice-cream churn and a handcart.[168] By 1930 Robinson's had the largest turnover of any ice-cream manufacturer in New Zealand and was the sole Auckland manufacturer of the Eskimo Pie (recently renamed Polar Pie), a popular American chocolate-coated ice-cream bar.[169]

As well as eating ice cream, many Aucklanders breakfasted on Vita Brits, Weeties and Kornies produced at the Cereal Foods factory that opened in 1931 in Surrey Crescent opposite the Auckland Laundry Company.[170] Collector's cards included in each packet boosted sales, and the firm offered a free book of recipes featuring Weeties to interested cooks.[171]

**164 | The Near West**

A. B. Wright and Sons transported a record shipment of East Indian kapok that arrived at Auckland in 1913. It's shown here on the Auckland wharves, loaded up and ready to be conveyed to Tattersfield's bedding factory on Richmond Road by a team that includes Wright's famous greys. AUCKLAND LIBRARIES HERITAGE COLLECTIONS, AWNS-19130206-16-05

There was plenty of work in the city and suburbs for carters, and Grey Lynn and Arch Hill were home to several carters' stables. In 1897 A. B. Wright and Sons built stables in Great North Road on the corner of Nixon Street. Their grey horses were a familiar sight in the streets of Auckland, working in pairs to move goods to and from the wharves, the railway station, city warehouses and the suburbs.[172] By the early twentieth century the company was also running a coal and firewood yard from its depot and had offices in Customs Street and at the city wharves. In 1910 it built a fine five-storey head office and warehouse building, which still stands on the Commerce Street corner of Fort Street near the railway station, which at the time was located above today's Britomart Station.[173]

Further north, the carrying firm Rich and Dimery had stables in Millais Street, near the intersection with Richmond Road, from the late nineteenth century, but as more dwellings sprang up on the Surrey Hills Estate the presence of stables, with their noise and smells, became a source of irritation. In 1901 Rich and Dimery applied to Grey Lynn Borough Council for a permit to build a brick addition, but a petition from 22 local residents opposed it on the grounds that it was inappropriate in a residential neighbourhood. Nevertheless, the council approved the application — with the proviso that the stables floor have proper drainage.[174] When John Rich and William Dimery retired from business in 1911, among other things they sold were 21 horses, seven lorries and a 40-stall stable.[175]

**Industry and business** | 165

**ABOVE:** Carr and Haslam's freight depot on Dickens Street, around 1915. The company's first motor vehicle leads the way and its horse fleet follows. Grey Lynn Park, part of which was leased to the company for grazing, can be seen in the distance at right. In the 1990s the stables were converted to apartments, accessed from Wallingford Street.
JENNY HAWORTH, *ROAD'S THE MODE: THE STORY OF NEW ZEALAND'S ROAD TRANSPORT INDUSTRY*, P.11

**RIGHT:** A. B. Wright and Sons staff with the company's horse-drawn carts and motorised lorries, c. 1920s.
AUCKLAND LIBRARIES HERITAGE COLLECTIONS, 1102-01

- GREAT · NORTH · ROAD · ELEVATION ·

In 1911, just as Rich and Dimery were winding up, Carr and Haslam moved into new brick stables in Dickens Street on the edge of Grey Lynn Park, which had recently been designated a domain, and where land for grazing for horses was available for a small fee payable to the Grey Lynn Borough Council.[176] Here they had fewer neighbours and less likelihood of complaints.

Carr and Haslam remains in business today and is now based in Mount Wellington and run by members of the Carr family. The firm's history stretches back to the early days of Auckland, when Robert Pollock set himself up as a carter in the fledgling town in the 1840s.[177] Two years after his death in 1872, his widow sold the business to James Ballantine and George Cammell.[178] In 1882 Ballantine sold his share to John Nearing, who departed within two years.[179] Cammell died in 1902 and management passed to his son William and son-in-law Edwin Carr. The following year Carr purchased the firm with William Haslam.[180]

When Carr and Haslam moved to Dickens Street, motorised transport was still in its infancy. The transition from horses was a gradual process, but Carr and Haslam had an eye to the future when they built a benzine store alongside the Dickens Street stables in 1915 to supply their first motorised truck.[181] In 1919 the firm sold off its wagons, carts and drays, as well as its horses, harnesses and saddlery.[182] The motor age was here to stay.

✕

**T**he first shops in the area were located at the city end of the district along Ponsonby Road and at the eastern end of Great North Road. Butcher George McElwain was running one of the earliest in the 1880s at the intersection of Great North Road and Nixon Street.[183] Further shops were built opposite, and by 1886 they extended as far as Pollen Street.[184] In 1907 a few shops and houses on the south side of Great North Road by the corner of Newton Road were replaced with a block of 10 shops with accommodation above, known as the Probert's Buildings.[185]

Another cluster of shops developed at the present junction of Williamson Avenue and Tuarangi Road. The Arch Hill Hotel on the southern corner of Great North and Tuarangi roads provided alcoholic refreshments to locals and visitors from 1880 and was a stopping place for the horse buses that carried the paying public west of the city. After losing its liquor licence in 1903, the hotel was used as a boarding house and then converted to shops in 1912.[186]

By this stage a few other small retail outlets had opened, and more would follow, including the substantial blocks of brick and concrete shops built in the 1920s and 1930s. In 1938 two prominent corners were redeveloped; the existing single-storey timber dwellings with shopfronts at the corner of

**ABOVE:** This 1910s image taken from the end of Karangahape Road shows the considerable commercial development at the city end of Great North Road. Probert's Buildings, erected in 1906, can be seen on the left and Robert Rew's grocery shop is on the right. Probert's block was demolished in the 1970s and is now a car sales yard. AUCKLAND LIBRARIES HERITAGE COLLECTIONS, 1703-ALB342-01

———

**BELOW:** Blocks of shops, including this one, were built as investments and offered for rent. This attractive design by architect W. A. Holman was designed for a site on Great North Road and included living accommodation above. It was one of two similar blocks that Holman called tenders for in 1911. The other still stands on the corner of Ponsonby and Franklin roads. ARCHITECTURE ARCHIVE, UNIVERSITY OF AUCKLAND, MSS- ARCHIVES-ARCH-2020/17

———

**Industry and business** | **169**

**RIGHT:** A shop on the corner of Great North Road and Williamson Avenue. The post office would later be built on this site in 1938–39. AUCKLAND WAR MEMORIAL MUSEUM TĀMAKI PAENGA HIRA, PH-NEG-B6343

**MIDDLE:** A tram approaches the Grey Lynn shops at Surrey Crescent, around 1910. The two-storey former Arch Hill Hotel is on the right and a single-storey building advertising American Dental Parlors is seen in the foreground. It was replaced by the brick ASB Bank building in 1938. AUCKLAND WAR MEMORIAL MUSEUM TĀMAKI PAENGA HIRA, PH-NEG-C17481

**BELOW:** Richmond Buildings on the corner of Richmond Road and Francis Street, 1912. AUCKLAND LIBRARIES HERITAGE COLLECTIONS, 1-W1549

**LEFT:** Harry Burrage's grocery store, which included the Arch Hill Post Office and Telephone Bureau, Great North Road, early 1900s.
AUCKLAND WAR MEMORIAL MUSEUM TĀMAKI PAENGA HIRA, PH-NEG-C19929

**BELOW:** Charles Norgrove's fine brick shop on the corner of Richmond Road and Hakanoa Street. Its window is well-stocked and its staff are ready to serve, c. 1910. The shop floor would have been covered in sawdust to soak up blood.
AUCKLAND LIBRARIES HERITAGE COLLECTIONS, 226-7639

Williamson Avenue were replaced with the two-storey Grey Lynn Post Office, and the single-storey brick ASB bank was built diagonally opposite.[187]

Shops had also appeared in West Lynn, drawn to the growing population in this part of the district.[188] Butcher Charles Norgrove moved from Ponsonby to Richmond Road (then known as Richmond Avenue) in 1905, and soon added another floor to his shop.[189] Builder Thomas Short erected a brick block of seven shops just across from Norgrove at the corner of Richmond Road and Francis Street.[190] Alfred Bryan built a shop at the southern corner of Tutanekai Street and later added a second store in Dryden Street at the corner of Baildon Road.[191] These early buildings were soon joined by further blocks erected in the 1920s and 1930s.[192]

Premises also sprang up further down Richmond Road, at the bend where Lincoln Street intersects it and by the Chamberlain Street corner. By 1908 Alfred Murray had established the two-storey wooden grocer's shop that still stands at the corner of Richmond Road and Lincoln Street, and butcher Henry Kimber had built the two-storey wedge-shaped shop that can be seen on the corner of Norfolk Street.[193] Others followed — some after the tramline had been extended from the Ponsonby Road end of Richmond Road, reaching Lincoln Street in 1930 and extending to West Lynn the following year.[194]

The extension of residential development and the opening of Auckland Zoo in 1922 prompted Charles Crosby to open a grocer's shop at the intersection of Garnet and Old Mill roads, and other shops were built opposite this.[195] Several appeared in the late 1920s at the other end of Garnet Road as residential development increased. In 1927 Frank Brinsmead's Westmere Bakery opened in the art deco building at the corner of Garnet Road and Lemington Road, and it was soon joined by others clustered at the intersection of Garnet Road and West End Road, a convenient location for users of the trams that ran down Garnet Road to the West End Road corner from 1931.[196] Other shops, often on the street frontage of an otherwise conventional villa or bungalow, provided goods to locals who didn't wish to venture far.

Many purveyors of food also offered home deliveries. The Arch Hill and Grey Lynn Chinese market gardeners, for example, went door to door offering vegetables for sale. Newdicks on the Arch Hill side of Great North Road delivered butter, cheese and eggs.[197] This firm appears to have grown out of a grocery store established in 1907 by Herbert Newdick on Great North Road, halfway between Mackelvie and Scanlan streets; by 1913 Newdick had established himself as a butter merchant at the corner of Hadlow Terrace. His sons later took over the business, trading as Newdick Brothers.[198] Their horse-drawn delivery vans, replaced with motorised vans in 1927, were a regular sight in suburban streets. The salesmen wore white aprons and jackets and arrived at the back door twice a week to supply household needs.[199]

**172** | **The Near West**

Ambury's Ltd, the dairy firm of former Newton borough mayor Stephen Ambury, also offered home deliveries. The company built a dairy at the junction of Richmond Road and Surrey Crescent in 1911, one of nine Auckland branches where milk, butter and cream were sent from the Ambury factories in the city and in Māngere to be sold and delivered. The firm, originally known as Ambury and English, started out in 1882 in Māngere, where it built a substantial factory using the latest machinery from Europe, processing milk from its own cows and from local farms. It was by far the largest dairy factory in Auckland at the time, and not only supplied the local market but also exported butter to England from the mid-1880s.[200]

In 1898 Ambury's established a second factory close to Grey Lynn on Hopetoun Street at the corner of Hereford Street. Equipped with an imported De Laval pasteuriser, it supplied Auckland consumers with fresh pasteurised milk, free of harmful bacteria and with a longer shelf life than the raw milk generally available.[201] It also provided cream, butter, and a variety of soft cheeses as well as humanised milk — a mix of cow's milk with additives including whey and lactose, to provide a more nutritious form of milk for infants who were not able to be breastfed.[202]

In the late 1920s, prompted by the Town Planning Act 1926, Auckland City Council began compiling land-use maps showing the existing pattern of industrial, commercial and residential development. The first of these was drawn soon after the Town Planning Act was passed in 1926.

The maps showed little surviving industry in the west of the district. The former site of the Hellaby meatworks and holding yards was now traversed by streets that were gradually filling with houses. The municipal abattoirs had been replaced by workers' houses built in the 1920s; the disused tannery on Old Mill Road remained (but would soon be gone). Other industrial buildings, including Cashmore's Timber Mill and Edgar's Dye Works, were already consigned to the past.[203]

The pattern of industrial and commercial development through the nineteenth century had been largely unregulated — only the most polluting and noxious industries had been subject to controls. The Town Planning Act 1926 required the preparation of plans to define what types of development could occur and where. But with no clear deadline for the adoption of the plans, progress was slow. By the mid-1930s a tentative scheme for Grey Lynn, Arch Hill and part of Ponsonby had been developed that envisaged most of the industrial development being focused on the area closest to Ponsonby and also in the vicinity of Coxs Creek, where there were already significant pockets of industry.

**Industry and business** | 173

**ABOVE:** Elliot's Four Square at the junction of Old Mill and Garnet roads. AUCKLAND WAR MEMORIAL MUSEUM TĀMAKI PAENGA HIRA, PH-NEG-SIP-3641P

**BELOW:** Shops at the end of Garnet Road, near the intersection with West End Road, where the trams stopped, in 1953. MUSEUM OF TRANSPORT AND TECHNOLOGY, PHO-2020-19.167

**RIGHT:** The interior of Pawson's well-stocked Four Square at 64 Warnock Street in 1947. AUCKLAND WAR MEMORIAL MUSEUM TĀMAKI PAENGA HIRA, 3641Q, 3641O

**LEFT:** Pawson's Four Square, 1947. Located at 64 Warnock Street, it was one of a number of shops scattered throughout the district on the street frontage of an otherwise conventional villa or bungalow, providing goods to locals who didn't wish to venture as far as the local shopping centre. AUCKLAND WAR MEMORIAL MUSEUM TAMAKI PAENGA HIRA, PH-NEG-SIP-3641N

**BELOW:** Plans for the Surrey Bakery, designed by architect W. A. Holman. Andrew Robertson's Surrey Bakery, on the corner of Great North Road and Elgin Street, was up and running by 1900. Baking in a backyard baker's oven, Robertson probably sold bread from a shop in the front room of his house as well as delivering it throughout the district. This building is now part of the Elgin Street Historic Heritage area. ARCHITECTURE ARCHIVE, UNIVERSITY OF AUCKLAND, MSS-ARCHIVES-ARCH-2020/17;

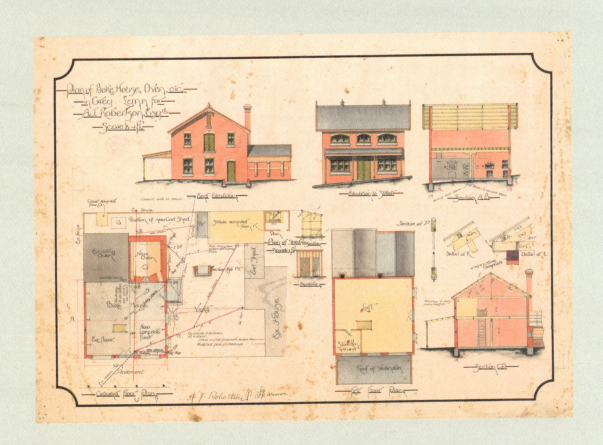

Commercial zoning was proposed for Great North Road as far west as Northland Street and on Ponsonby Road and parts of Richmond Road, Surrey Crescent and Garnet Road, where shops were already part of the landscape.[204] This general pattern of industrial and commercial zoning was later embodied in the first Auckland District Plan that was adopted in 1961 under the provisions of the Town and Country Planning Act 1953.[205]

×

The late 1920s and 1930s were a tough time to be in business. Business failures were common as the economy faltered and people were forced to make do with less. It was not the time for buying what one could do without, and the philosophy of recycling and reusing, already ingrained in working-class households, became more entrenched during the 1930s. William Rodwell, who ran a joinery and furniture factory at the corner of Crummer Road and Mackelvie Street, was able to weather the storm but only by letting all of his employees go, apart from his three sons.[206]

Joshua Carder's boot and shoe factory at the corner of Williamson Avenue and Mackelvie Street was unable to survive the plummeting demand for footwear. His factory became a depot for bottles, rags and bones collected by the men who traipsed the streets singing 'bottle-oh' to alert residents to bring out their empties.[207] Almost nothing that could be reused or converted into some other useful product was wasted.

The Second World War brought considerable challenges for many industries. Those with a predominantly male workforce were especially hard hit as men left to join the war effort. The staff of non-essential services could be diverted into essential work through the manpower regulations that came into force in early 1942. International shipping was also disrupted by the war and many materials were in short supply. Products like butter and meat were rationed so that supplies could be sent to feed the British and also the allied forces in the Pacific.[208]

As the war ended and servicemen and -women returned home, there was considerable pent-up demand for consumer goods. Couples whose plans to get married, set up a home and begin a family had been deferred by the war would soon start a baby boom, and household goods were in hot demand.

New Zealand's manufacturing businesses were set to grow. Not only was local demand for consumer products high but imports were heavily restricted. With little competition from imported goods, local manufacturing and assembly industries flourished.

In the decades immediately following the war, Auckland was an ideal location for any budding manufacturer wanting to establish a consumer goods

**176** | **The Near West**

**ABOVE:** Ambury's dairy at the junction of Richmond Road and Surrey Crescent, c. 1920s–1930s. AUCKLAND WAR MEMORIAL MUSEUM TĀMAKI PAENGA HIRA, B6340

**FOLLOWING PAGES:** Plans for the Grey Lynn district. AUCKLAND COUNCIL ARCHIVES, TP 005/76

factory because it had the greatest number of consumers and the largest labour market.[209]

With labour in high demand, businesses had to find new ways to attract and retain staff. In the 1950s Tattersfield converted its former motor garage in Richmond Road into a hostel for young women working at its two Grey Lynn factories, providing accommodation at a time when the nationwide housing shortage that had plagued the country since the 1930s was still being felt. Single women were particularly disadvantaged in the housing market, and so it made good sense for the company to offer accommodation for them.[210]

Upholstery manufacturers Renwicks encouraged staff to work hard by offering employees shares in the company. The firm had been started in an old shed in Home Street, Arch Hill, in 1948 by newly qualified upholsterer Ces Renwick. Initially working alone, Renwick funded the growth of his business by living frugally and ploughing profits back into firm, enabling him to take on staff and expand.[211] In 1955 he formed a limited company, holding half the shares and distributing the remainder to his staff.

The following year the firm moved to the Richmond Road and Surrey Crescent properties adjoining the former Ambury's dairy building, and in 1961 purchased the corner building also.[212] By 1966 the firm had a workforce of 60. Renwick sponsored his more promising staff to attend courses to improve their skills, and some lucky ones accompanied Renwick on his annual research trips

**Industry and business | 177**

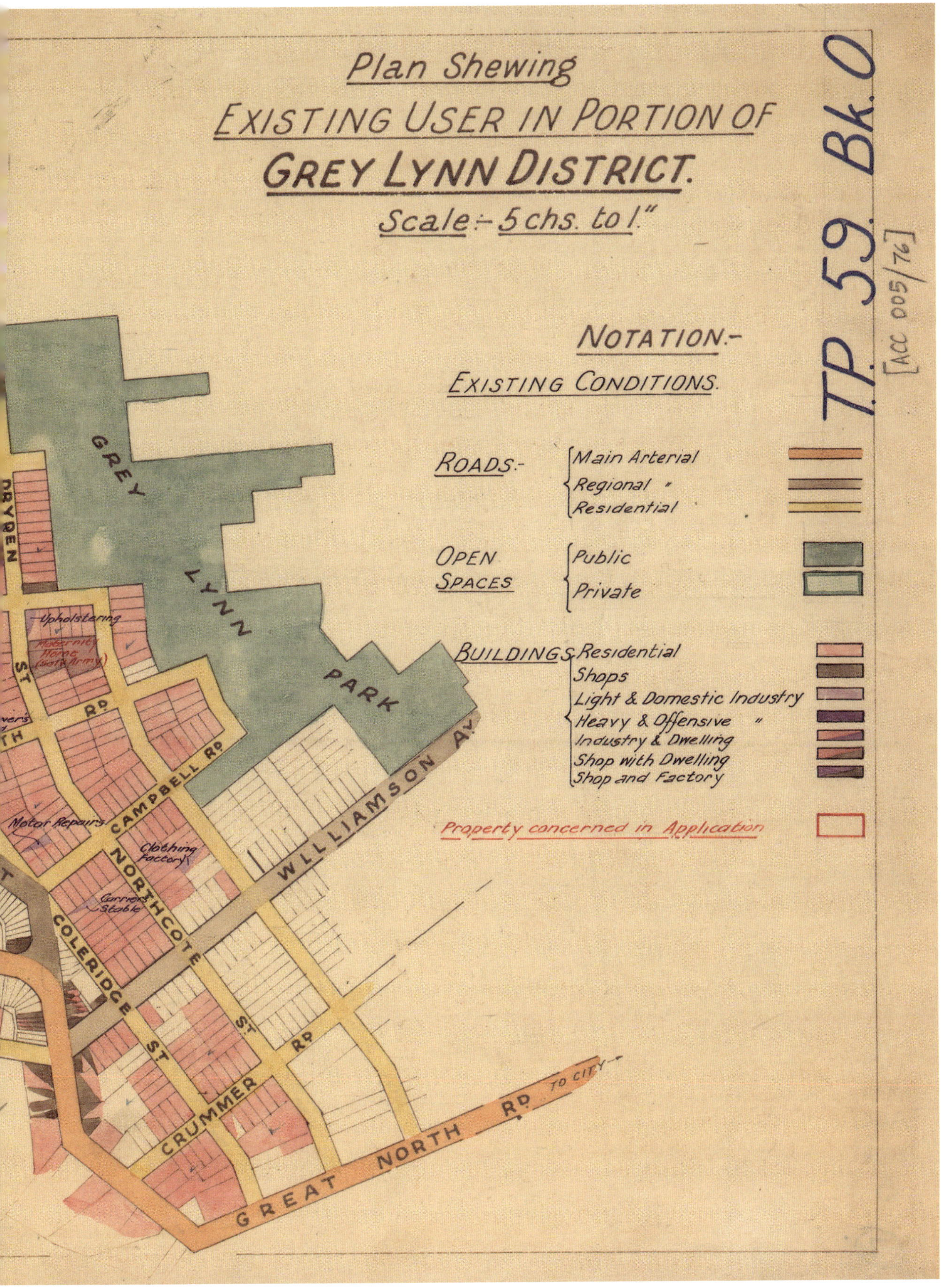

# Plan Shewing
## EXISTING USER IN PORTION OF
## GREY LYNN DISTRICT.
### Scale :– 5 chs. to 1."

TP. 59. Bk. O

[ACC 005/76]

### NOTATION:–

#### EXISTING CONDITIONS.

ROADS:–
- Main Arterial
- Regional "
- Residential

OPEN SPACES
- Public
- Private

BUILDINGS
- Residential
- Shops
- Light & Domestic Industry
- Heavy & Offensive "
- Industry & Dwelling
- Shop with Dwelling
- Shop and Factory

Property concerned in Application

GREY LYNN PARK

DRYDEN ST

Upholstering

Maternity Home (Salv. Army)

RD

Motor Repairs

CAMPBELL RD

Clothing Factory

NORTHCOTE ST

Corner Stable

COLERIDGE ST

ST

CRUMMER RD

WILLIAMSON AV.

GREAT NORTH RD TO CITY

overseas to keep up with the latest designs and manufacturing techniques.[213]

C. Renwick Ltd set up a new company with two other Auckland firms with which Renwick had business ties: cabinetmaking firm R. G. Norris Ltd and furniture frame manufacturers J. Flower Ltd. Together they formed Airest Industries, soon to be Auckland's largest furniture manufacturer, with Ces Renwick as managing director. The company produced stylish furniture, influenced by Danish mid-century modernist design, and made with local materials and timbers. Needing a much larger factory, Airest left Grey Lynn and moved to a new industrial zone in Rosebank Road in the late 1960s.[214]

Clothing manufacturer Ambler and Co., famous for its Summit shirts, offered a different incentive to employees. Recognising that a lack of childcare was a barrier to employment for mothers, the company opened its first on-site crèche at its Browns Bay factory in 1969. A new factory, built in Great North Road at the corner of King Street in 1976, also had a crèche, located at the corner of King and Dean streets in the building now occupied by Kindercare Grey Lynn.[215] The mothers who sewed, pressed and packaged shirts could focus on their work, safe in the knowledge that their children were in good hands across the street from their workplace. Summit House, as Ambler and Co.'s Grey Lynn factory was known, remained part of the Great North Road landscape until 2012, when the firm relocated to the industrial area in Rosebank Road. The building has since been demolished and replaced with a branch of Australian hardware retail giant Bunnings Warehouse.

In the post-war era the factories of Grey Lynn and Arch Hill were fortunate to be close to a good labour supply at a time when labour shortages threatened to hinder the growth of manufacturing. Help for understaffed industries was soon at hand as the government sought immigrants from Britain, Europe and the Pacific Islands to supply much needed labour, with many new migrants from the Pacific Islands coming to live in the inner-west suburbs of the city, including Grey Lynn and Arch Hill.

One of the many firms to benefit from this new labour supply was the Sheffield Radio Company, which was established in 1936 and by 1940 was operating from 48 Mackelvie Street.[216] The company produced stylish radio sets at its Grey Lynn factory until the 1980s, when it moved to Gudgeon Street in Freemans Bay.[217]

Some of the immigrant workers had higher aspirations than factory work, but family responsibilities and other factors could halt their ambitions. Vaitulutulusinaolemoana Purcell, for example, came to New Zealand from Sāmoa in the 1950s to train to be a teacher, but money was needed to pay for school fees for her brothers and sisters back in Sāmoa, so she got a job as a machinist in the Modelux Factory on Maidstone Street, which made, among other things, shower curtains. In the 1960s she was living in Williamson

An aerial view of Richmond Road taken in 1957. Sackville Street runs diagonally from lower right to top right. Tattersfield's bedding factory can be seen on the corner of Richmond Road and Sackville Street, where the original Tattersfield residence now houses the company office. The Warnock factory is on the right of Richmond Road near the centre of the image and Tattersfield's rug and wool scouring plant is across the road. The new Wilton Motor Body Company premises in Westmoreland Street can be seen near the top right. ALEXANDER TURNBULL LIBRARY, WA-43904

Avenue with her husband, Iosefa Sofi Pua, who had been a teacher back home in Sāmoa, but who worked at the central post office in the city as his teaching qualifications were not recognised here.[218]

New factories were established in Richmond Road from 1953, when the Warnock Brothers sold off land on the eastern side of Coxs Creek.[219] The first was the Wilton Motor Body Company premises at 18 Westmoreland Street, which provided panelbeating, painting and other vehicle repairs. Battered vehicles, from small passenger cars to buses and petrol

**Industry and business | 181**

Coxs Creek industries, 1949. The extensive Warnock Brothers works are on the south side of Richmond Road (top) and Tattersfield's gleaming new carpet factory is opposite. Below is Tattersfield's wool scour and dyeing plant with the tall chimney that remains today. A. Donald and Sons' former tannery and fellmongery buildings are at bottom left. ALEXANDER TURNBULL LIBRARY, WA-20941-F

tankers, arrived daily and departed looking shiny and new.[220]

The company had started out in Wilton Street in 1945 before moving to Tutanekai Street and then to its new premises in Westmoreland Street.[221] From 1949 until 1954 the company also built buses. Most were designed by Wiltons, but some Australian Ansair designs were built under licence. One of their early buses, a 32-seater built for the Weymouth Bus Company, was considered the smartest bus in town when it hit the road in the early 1950s — passengers enjoyed luxurious seating and electric heaters on the long Auckland–Weymouth route.[222]

The company also pressed motor-body panels for clients, and in 1957 created the largest panels yet made in New Zealand for Dominion Motors.[223] In the early 1960s Wilton Motor Body Company held the franchise for Datsun cars, and imported 300 fully assembled Datsun Bluebirds from Japan. These arrived in May 1962 and marked the beginning of commercial Japanese car imports to New Zealand. The firm also imported unassembled Bluebirds that were put together in Ōtāhuhu at the local Volkswagen assembly plant and sold by J. Gardner Motors in Newmarket. Nissan Motor Distributors (NZ) Ltd. continued the local assembly of Datsun cars, and took over the Wilton Motor Body

Company in 1965.[224] The former Wiltons building was subsequently used by carrying firm Carr and Haslam, which already had premises in Dickens Street.[225]

The Warnocks also sold land on the western side of their factory, and in the early 1960s a large factory was built for Leighton's Packaging, the paper bag division of the United Empire Box Company.[226] It still stands, at 300 Richmond Road.

In Arch Hill, the area east of Kirk Street between Monmouth Street and Great North Road, as well as the land east of Newton Central School, was zoned for industry under the Auckland City district scheme, which became operative in June 1961. The Ponsonby end of Grey Lynn, including much of the land east of Scanlan Street, was similarly zoned. In the latter half of the twentieth century, houses that had lined Putiki Street, the northern side of Monmouth Street and the lower parts of Nixon and Burgoyne streets in the 1950s were replaced by small factories, as were most of the houses between Scanlan Street and Ponsonby Road.[227]

The 1980s was a time of change in central Auckland. Older buildings in the city were being demolished with alarming regularity. Some had provided space for artists' studios, music studios and galleries — many of whom now looked west for new premises. Real Pictures Gallery, for example, moved to 300 Richmond Road in 1988 after its former home in His Majesty's Arcade on Queen Street was reduced to rubble.[228]

Other people started businesses in creative fields in Grey Lynn. Belgian couple Frans Baetens and Magda Van Gils, who arrived in New Zealand with their two daughters in 1983, had a background in teaching and a passion for the arts. They brought with them two small lithography presses with the aim of making prints with local artists.[229] The couple established a lithographic studio in Brown Street in Ponsonby and named it Muka, the te reo Māori word for prepared flax fibre, which can be used to make paper.[230]

Their friend, the artist Tony Fomison, sold them his home in Chamberlain Street, Grey Lynn, when he took up an artist's residency in Wellington in 1985.[231] Fomison supported the couple by creating prints that were sold to pay the deposit on the house. They moved in, renovated the property and relocated their studio from Brown Street to Chamberlain Street. In 1986 they imported a 9-ton, century-old French lithography press, which they installed in the basement.[232]

Muka worked with local artists to produce lithographic prints, and overseas artists were invited to stay while they created and exhibited work at the Muka studio and gallery.[233] Baetens and Van Gils' daughters Saskia and Dominiek

**Industry and business** | 183

began the annual Muka Youth Prints exhibition, where children could buy small, signed, limited-edition prints, produced at the studio by notable local and overseas artists, at affordable prices.[234] The success of Muka Studio led to the opening of a separate exhibition space in nearby Brown Street in the mid-1990s, in the building where the studio had first been established a decade earlier.[235]

Some established galleries had already moved west from the city: Aberhart North Gallery had shifted to Freemans Bay, and the Auckland Society of Arts Gallery was in Ponsonby. Art dealer Gary Langsford could see that Grey Lynn was well positioned to form the western edge of an art gallery circuit. In 1987 Langsford and John Gow set up an art gallery in a former mechanic's garage on Richmond Road at the intersection of Warnock Street. They converted the building, though some vestiges of its former use remained — including the pervasive smell of engine oil and the car hoist, which was repurposed as a table.[236]

The opening show in August 1987 featured work by Allen Maddox and Mervyn Williams, both of whom had a connection to the area. But the buoyant mood of the opening was soon crushed by the sharemarket crash of October that year. The Gow Langsford Gallery survived, however, and within a few years was going so well that larger premises were needed. In 1990 the gallery

Frans Baetens and Magda Van Gils of Muka Studio, working at their 9-ton French lithography press they imported in 1986. PATRICK REYNOLDS

184 | The Near West

The first premises of Gow Langsford Gallery on the corner of Richmond Road and Warnock Street, 1987.
COURTESY GOW LANGSFORD GALLERY

moved to a former warehouse in Parnell; they sold the Richmond Road gallery to the Friends of the Western Buddhist Order, who established a meditation and education centre there.[237]

As older businesses shut up shop or moved elsewhere, their premises became available for a new generation of businesses. From the 1980s several of these have been associated with the music industry, including studios, radio stations and print media, and have found a natural home in Grey Lynn and Arch Hill. *Rip It Up* was New Zealand's only local popular music magazine when it was established in 1977 by Murray Cammick and Alastair Dougal. It was run from various premises in the city over the years, and in the mid-1980s it called Crummer Road home.[238]

Crummer Road was the first permanent home of Mai FM, a radio station founded in 1992 by Grey Lynn musician Taura Eruera with Vivien Sutherland Bridgwater and Ngāti Whātua Rūnanga to promote Māori language and culture to the youth market. It had a meteoric rise, becoming the most popular station in Auckland in 1996.[239] Popular radio station George FM, now located in Hargreaves Street in Freemans Bay, started as a pirate radio station in Grey Lynn in 1998.[240]

One of the early music studios established in the area, Montage Studios, was established by Michael Donnelly and Eion Brown at 49 Murdoch Road in the

Industry and business | 185

 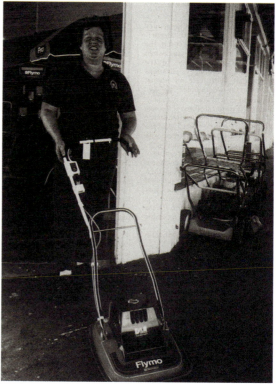

early 1980s.[241] Studio Two, later known as Arch Hill Studios, was established by sound engineer Ed Case in an old shop on Great North Road near the corner of Elgin Street. Case and musician Ben Howe started the record label Arch Hill Recordings from the premises in 1998.[242] Bob Frisbee (Mahoney) moved his studio to the Legion of Frontiersmen Hall at the bottom of Bond Street, Arch Hill, in the late 1990s after the Symonds Street building he rented was demolished as part of a road widening project. Frisbee Studio later moved to Great North Road, occupying the premises vacated by Arch Hill Studios, and in 2003 relocated to the former Auckland Laundry Company building. In the building were several large makeshift flats and art studios where filmmakers, artists and other creatives lived, worked and partied.[243] In 1998 Peter van der Fluit and Michael O'Neill, former members of the 1980s band The Screaming Meemees, established Liquid Studios, a composition and audio post-production studio on Richmond Road. Many soundtracks for the advertising, television and film industry are still created here.[244] And just down the road from Liquid Studios, at the top of Hakanoa Street, are the offices of Recorded Music New Zealand, which promotes and licenses New Zealand music, advocates for musicians, compiles the official top-40 music charts and produces the annual Aotearoa Music Awards.[245]

LEFT: *Rip it Up* co-founder Murray Cammick in the stairwell of the magazine's office on Crummer Road, 1987. PHOTO BY KERRY BROWN, COURTESY MURRAY CAMMICK

RIGHT: Myra Nicols of Luv Ya Mowar, one of several businesses run solely by women in West Lynn in the late 1980s. *BROADSHEET*, APRIL 1988

186 | The Near West

Inside the women's clothing store Moa, in 1988, at West Lynn. Tracy from Pagan Prints stands at the counter. From the late 1980s West Lynn was developing quite an alternative feel. Several of the shops commonly found in suburban shopping centres had been replaced by those run on cooperative lines, including Moa and the Women's Co-operative Bakery. *BROADSHEET, JANUARY/FEBRUARY 1988*

Some local businesses started in the 1980s were established as a way of creating employment for their founders. Unemployment had been a problem since the 1970s and by the 1980s was on the rise, particularly for those under 25.[246]

In 1983 Myra Nicols was unemployed. She had previously worked in a lawnmowing repair business and had run her own domestic cleaning business. With support from her friends and a loan from a neighbour, she took a lease on an empty shop at the corner of Richmond Road and Hakanoa Street (where Malt bar is today) and opened Auckland's only female-owned and -operated lawnmower servicing shop, Luv Ya Mowar.[247]

Other locals banded together to set up business. In 1983 six unemployed women secured financial support and advice from the government through SCOPE (the Small Co-Operative Enterprise Scheme) to establish a business in a disused bakery.[248] The West Lynn Bakery had provided fresh bread to locals from 1907 but was in a dilapidated state.[249] The women set to work restoring the premises and, after 18 months of hard work, loaves of fresh bread were brought out of the ovens and sold to the public. The business later became known as Mamata Bakehouse.[250]

A collective of eight women, many of whom had been designing and printing textiles and making clothes, established Moa Unlimited in an empty shop on Richmond Road in the 1980s. They wanted to market their products

**Industry and business** | 187

while avoiding the high mark-ups that existing retail shops charged, and felt that a collectively run shop could be the answer. Before long the collective had grown to 13 and moved to a larger shop at the corner of Francis Street, where it remains today.[251]

Further along Richmond Road, another business working on collective lines was formed when business partners Nick Stanish and Russell Withers, along with Chris Fox and Stuart Scott, formed Archangels Architects Collective in a former shop at the corner of Richmond Road and Lincoln Street. They wanted to work in a more supportive and cooperative environment where they could explore and share their individual interests. There were partnerships and sole traders within the collective, but the office was run collectively and they worked together on large projects and competitions as well as on individual projects. In the early 1990s the Archangels building was sold by the owner and the collective moved across Richmond Road to the former Preest's store near the corner of Chamberlain Street.[252] The collective continued for decades, with new architects joining as others left. Archangels was one of a number of architecture studios that would call Grey Lynn home over the next few decades, many of them started by local architects.

**The founding members of the Archangels Architects Collective outside their first premises at 138 Richmond Road, 1970s. From left: Stuart Scott, Chris Fox, Russell Withers and Nick Stanish.** AUCKLAND WAR MEMORIAL MUSEUM TĀMAKI PAENGA HIRA, PH-1992-5-RM-N2-F9-19

The types of shops operating in Grey Lynn and Westmere also began to change from around the 1990s. Some new enterprises catered to residents who were keen to make improvements to their homes and gardens. Tippett Nurseries on the corner of Williamson Avenue and Northland Street provided garden plants and advice, while Burrell Demolition, which had moved from Mount Eden to the former Wilton Motor Body factory in Westmoreland Street, was a rich hunting ground for renovators. Café culture came to Grey Lynn in the 1990s with the opening of Gerhard's Café on Great North Road.[253]

In the late twentieth century, some long-established local industries declined, unable to adapt to the economic reforms that stripped back the import controls which had protected the local market from overseas competition. Other existing businesses sold their premises and closed or moved elsewhere. Some of these were adapted to other purposes or provided homes for different enterprises, while others met with the wrecking ball. Marsden and Co.'s bed and furniture factory, which had operated on Garnet Road since the 1920s, closed in the 1960s and was later occupied by furniture manufacturer Karl Katte.[254]

Some factories were demolished to provide land for terrace houses. In the early 2000s the former Marsden and Co. site was developed into terraced

**Industry and business** | 189

David Tippett and Simon Stiles of Tippett Nurseries. COURTESY DAVID TIPPETT

housing, just as the former Tattersfield factory at the corner of Sackville Street and Richmond Road had been a decade earlier.

Other substantial business premises, including Leighton's Packaging factory at 300 Richmond Road and the Auckland Laundry Company buildings, became home to numerous small businesses. The Warnock factory site on Richmond Road was redeveloped as a retail precinct.

The former DYC (Dominion Yeast Company, formerly known as Dominion Compressed Yeast) factory was demolished in the early twenty-first century, taking its fragrant fumes with it. Work soon began on a massive excavation of the site for the proposed Soho Square development, an imposing mall-style mix of retail and entertainment venues. It met with considerable opposition from the community because of its scale, which threatened to dominate the small-scale heritage buildings nearby. Auckland City Council refused to grant planning permission, and by 2011 all that had been achieved was the demolition of the DYC factory and the excavation of a deep hole for a five-storey underground carpark. The 'So Hole', as it became known locally, was eventually sold and a new, more modest development was drawn up with a supermarket and business premises on the Williamson Avenue frontage. The sites on the Crummer Road side were sold off and developed as a mix of retail and apartments. The new street that ran through the site from Crummer Road to Pollen Street was named Vinegar Lane in reference to the former use of the site.

Apartment buildings have since sprung up on a large number of old commercial sites on Great North Road, and other sites have made way for retail on a grand scale in the form of high-end vehicle sales.

Car yards have been a feature of the Great North Road ridge for several decades, with the types of cars on offer reflecting the changing fortunes of Grey Lynn and Arch Hill. Cheap second-hand cars once stood for sale on asphalt-covered sites, but these days a better class of second-hand vehicle is on offer as well as shiny new luxury vehicles, including Lamborghinis and McLarens, housed in spacious, air-conditioned showrooms.

The industries of the Grey Lynn, Arch Hill and Westmere areas today bear little resemblance to those of former times. Once, many high chimneys dotted the skyline of the Grey Lynn area. The sole survivor of these is the Tattersfield chimney in the carpark of the Woolworths supermarket on Richmond Road, saved at the request of locals when the site was redeveloped. The large-scale and polluting industries that were part of the landscape are now located in broad industrial zones in places like Westfield. Today's local industries are comparatively small, and cater for a niche market.

# Grey Lynn and the demon drink

In 1902 imbibing at the local pub became a thing of the past for the people of the Grey Lynn electorate when they voted to reduce the number of liquor licences in the electorate. Three years later they voted the area completely 'dry'.

But it had not always been that way. Before 1902, getting a drink was relatively straightforward. For over two decades the Arch Hill Hotel had been serving thirsty patrons. Locally produced beer was the drink of choice for many; spirit drinkers mostly favoured whisky, which was imported; and local and imported wines were less popular.[255] The Arch Hill Hotel, which opened in 1880, stood on the corner of Great North Road and what is now known as Tuarangi Road (then it was the original route of Great North Road). It was a handy location, equidistant between the Great Northern Hotel (later known as the Old Stone Jug), further down Great North Road opposite Western Springs, and the Star Hotel on Karangahape Road. It was also the stopping place of the new horse bus service. There was considerable local support for the establishment of a hotel on the site: in 1880, 110 of the 360 adult residents of the area signed a petition in favour of granting a licence; only five objected.[256]

Other applications for hotel licences had been rejected. In the late 1870s the Auckland licensing commissioners, comprising the resident magistrate and members appointed by the governor under the Licensing Act 1873, refused repeated applications by Auckland brewer Samuel Jagger for a licence for the Surrey Hotel that stood on the corner of Great North Road and Cracroft Street (now Kirk Street).[257] Even

before Jagger lodged his licence application, a meeting of locals resolved to fight the establishment of a hotel in the Arch Hill district.

The chair of the meeting was John Graham, who lived in Arch Hill and was employed as the relief officer to the Auckland Charitable Aid Board. He frequently saw the effects of alcohol on the lives of Aucklanders and believed it was the principal cause of much poverty and deprivation.[258] His sentiments were echoed by Reverend Willis, of the Church of England Temperance Society, who stated: 'If the hotels were abolished, people would have more money and be able to spend it to improve their cottages and property, and provide proper food and clothing for their families.'[259]

Jagger was not without his supporters. Petitions with hundreds of signatures backing Jagger were presented to the licensing committee. Only a fraction of the signatories were local, however, and others were invalid, having been signed by wives on behalf of their husbands.

By 1880 Jagger had leased his property to Henry Leon, who also applied for a licence and was refused. Leon then tried to circumvent the licensing regulations by opening the Arch Hill Workingmen's Club, which allowed him to sell liquor to members of the club. Leon was accused of serving liquor to non-members, and evidence emerged that the club was frequented not only by men but also by women and children.[260]

The goings-on at Leon's establishment provided further fuel to the rising temperance movement, which was particularly active in cities, where social problems associated with

A temperance demonstration making its way down Pitt Street on election day 1902, the day the Grey Lynn electorate voted to reduce the number of hotels in the district, resulting in the closure of the Arch Hill Hotel. At the following election Grey Lynn became the first North Island electorate to vote dry, and it would remain so until 1996. AUCKLAND LIBRARIES HERITAGE COLLECTIONS, AWNS-19021204-01-02

alcohol consumption were particularly visible.[261]

Arch Hill was home to William J. MacDermott, one of the leaders of the temperance crusade in Auckland. His wife Hanna also took a prominent role in the movement.[262] By 1878 Arch Hill had its own branch of the Band of Hope, an organisation that encouraged children to take a vow of abstinence from alcohol in the hope that they would be lifelong teetotallers.[263] At the time it was not uncommon for parents to send their children to purchase alcohol on their behalf.[264] The Band held fortnightly meetings at Newton West School, and its concerts featured children performing recitations and songs, including 'The lips that touch liquor', 'How Frank saved £600' and 'Hark the temperance trumpet'.[265] The organisation was so successful that in early 1883 it was decided to form an adult branch at Arch Hill.[266]

Liquor was an increasingly divisive and political issue. With the passing of the Licensing Act 1881, the appointed licensing commissioners were replaced with a licensing committee elected by ratepayers.[267] In 1886 the candidates for the Arch Hill committee were in two camps: those who were determined to close the district's only hotel, and those who supported its continued existence.[268] It was a fairly close contest, but a majority of electors supported the status quo and the Arch Hill Hotel continued serving beer, wine and spirits.[269] Through the 1880s and early 1890s it was evidently a well-run hotel, and long-serving publican Thomas Long received a number of positive reports on its operation.[270]

In 1895 Arthur Dempsey took over the licence. Within a few years his own life had become a salutary tale of the dangers posed by liquor. On the morning of 4 September 1901 Dempsey's body was found floating in the Waitematā Harbour. He had taken his own life at the age of 49, leaving a wife and five children.[271] The inquest into his death revealed that for several years he had been drinking to excess, and this had resulted in delusions and a 'softening of the brain'.[272]

A few weeks before his death Dempsey had flown into a paranoid drunken rage at the hotel, swearing, making accusations against his wife and pushing her out of the building. He was subsequently given notice to leave the hotel by the building's owners.[273] One of Dempsey's last acts was to write a public apology to his wife,

Industry and business | 193

The former Arch Hill Hotel some time between 1920 and 1930. A hardware shop is on the ground floor and a dentist's premises are above. The building still stands today, although considerably altered, at the corner of Great North Road and Tuarangi Road. AUCKLAND WAR MEMORIAL MUSEUM TĀMAKI PAENGA HIRA, B6345

which was published in the *New Zealand Herald* on the day his body was discovered.[274] Dempsey's widow took over as licensee and the Arch Hill Hotel survived for another couple of years.[275]

The Arch Hill Hotel was one of two in the Grey Lynn electorate, which not only took in Grey Lynn, Arch Hill and the area we now know as Westmere but also parts of Newton, Eden Terrace, Mount Eden and Western Springs. The other was the Eden Vine Hotel, on the eastern side of the electorate on the corner of Symonds Street and Mount Eden Road. This was an unusually small number of hotels for the size of the area and population — perhaps other prospective hoteliers were frightened off by the opposition to Jagger's Surrey Hotel.

The Alcoholic Liquors Sale Control Act of 1893 gave voters the option to prohibit the sale of liquor altogether, reduce the number of liquor licences, or keep the status quo. In 1902 a majority of voters in the Grey Lynn electorate supported reduction, which required the number of licensed premises to be reduced by between 5 per cent and 25 per cent.

This was something of an impossibility given that there were only two pubs in the Grey Lynn electorate. In the end the issue was resolved when the owner of the Eden Vine Hotel purchased the Arch Hill Hotel and closed it.[276] At the next election the electorate decided to go further and voted no licence, resulting in the closure of the Eden Vine Hotel. With nothing more for its members to do, the licensing committee disbanded.[277]

Grey Lynn was the first North Island electorate to vote no licence. In the South Island, Clutha and Mataura in Southland and Ashburton in Canterbury had already voted dry.[278] Others followed suit and by the end of 1908 Grey Lynn was one of 12 electorates that had voted to close their liquor outlets, representing around a sixth of the country's electorates.[279]

In elections from 1911 until 1989 voters had the option of voting for complete nationwide prohibition. National prohibition had its strongest support in 1911, and was narrowly defeated in 1919 after the prohibition threshold was lowered from 60 per cent to a bare majority.[280]

The temperance vote, made up of the no licence and prohibition votes, was unusually strong. From 1911 to 1925 a majority of Grey Lynn voters supported the whole country going dry.[281] Richard Newman's study of the distribution of the temperance vote to 1911 reveals that Grey Lynn had the highest proportion of temperance voters of any electorate in the country in 1908 and 1911 and the results for 1902 and 1905 were also unusually high. Relatively strong support for no licence and prohibition was also seen in other electorates populated by working-class families.[282]

Voters who lived in both the poorest and richest parts of New Zealand cities were least likely to support no licence and prohibition.[283] The social elite were not known for their abstinence, and wealthy businessmen with links to the trade were more likely to live in affluent suburbs. The poorest areas of cities generally had a more transient population, which would have made them more difficult to recruit to the temperance cause. In between these two extremes were the people of the Grey Lynn electorate, whose support for temperance was strong.

Grey Lynn may have been dry, but residents were not far from the city pubs that remained open in the neighbouring wet district. The law allowed alcohol to be purchased in wet areas and brought home to dry areas for consumption by residents and their guests, but no liquor could be sold within the electorate until legislative changes in the 1960s and 1980s allowed restaurants and clubs to sell liquor to diners or members and their guests.[284]

Every three years voters were offered the option of voting for a return of bars, hotels and other licensed premises. The majority of Grey Lynn Licensing District electorate voters continued to support the no-licence option until 1935, when just over half voted to restore liquor licensing.[285] However, until 1990 a three-fifths majority was needed in order to overturn the no-licence vote of 1905; in 1990 the Local Restoration Polls Act altered this to a simple majority.[286] Grey Lynn electors voted wet in 1996, becoming one of the last areas to do so, and thus ending one of the longest dry spells in the country.[287]

Grey Lynn's thirsty decades were a time of major changes in licensing regulations, including the imposition of six o'clock closing in 1917 as a temporary war measure, and its repeal by public vote in 1967. Early closing encouraged those wanting a drink after work to dash to the pub and guzzle their drinks before 6pm. In order to accommodate the rush before closing, hotels moved furniture out and bars began to resemble sheep pens where patrons jostled their way to the bar and stood about drinking.

On the stroke of six the hotels disgorged their patrons, with some walking or catching the tram home to the suburbs, including Arch Hill, Grey Lynn and Westmere. By staying dry for the 50 years of early closing, the Grey Lynn area avoided some of the worst effects of the binge-drinking culture that six o'clock closing encouraged.

The return of longer opening hours in 1967 provided a less hurried atmosphere, and licensed premises began to attract patronage by offering comfortable surroundings for those who wished to socialise and enjoy a drink or two.[288] In the years since 1996, small neighbourhood bars have opened in Grey Lynn and Westmere. The Returned Services Club in Francis Street, one of the few premises to hold a club licence during the latter part of the dry era, continues to serve members and their guests.

**Industry and business** | 195

# Education

**PREVIOUS PAGES:**
Newton West School
in the early 1900s. The
buildings multiplied
to accommodate the
growing school roll.
AUCKLAND WAR MEMORIAL
MUSEUM TĀMAKI PAENGA
HIRA, PH-NEG-B2840

We sang two songs so repeatedly and so metronomically that they are irremovable in my memory: 'Po Kare Kare Ana' and 'Deep In a Forest I Know a Fairy Glade' . . . there were no fairy glades in Grey Lynn. The music that the class really liked . . . was the chanting of the times table, an arithmetical plainsong that we rendered with the precise rhythms and cadences of a well-trained group of monks.[1]

These are the memories of the historian Russell Stone, who grew up on Williamson Avenue and attended Richmond Road School in the 1920s and 1930s. Elements of his school experiences — rote-learning times tables and songs that were hard to relate to — will be familiar to many who attended New Zealand schools in the decades before and after Stone. But as well as continuity, there has been enormous change and variance in education. The schools that opened in Arch Hill, Grey Lynn and Westmere through the later decades of the nineteenth century and into the twentieth drew on educational traditions that settlers brought with them.

The earliest schools in New Zealand were missionary schools, established from the mid-1810s to teach Māori children and adults to read and write. They were based on British schools that had been established for the poor.[2] With the arrival of settler ships from the 1840s came the need for schools for settler children.

Not all settlers had received schooling in their homeland. In the Auckland Province in 1861, 89 per cent of European males and 84 per cent of European females aged 16 and over were able to read and write, considerably below the national average of 93 per cent and 87 per cent respectively.[3] Most parents no doubt hoped their children would at least learn to read and write, and for some children, the immigrant journey provided an opportunity to attend lessons onboard ship.[4]

Schools in the new settlement of Auckland were established by the churches, following the British tradition of providing charity schools for the

**Education | 199**

poor, or by settlers, some of whom established private schools in their own homes.[5] There was no public funding for these early schools. However, given that in Britain public money had been granted for educational purposes since 1833, settlers would have had some expectation that schools in New Zealand would eventually receive government support.[6]

In 1857 Auckland Provincial Council passed the Education Act, the first legislation to provide funding for schools within Auckland Province.[7] Initially just 13 schools received financial assistance. Around half of these were in the town of Auckland, while others were beyond the urban fringe, including at the Fencible settlements of Onehunga, Ōtāhuhu, Howick and Panmure — where military pensioners had received land in return for miliary duties — as well as the North Shore, West Tāmaki and Mount Albert.[8] The funding was to augment teachers' salaries rather than pay for buildings and resources, and had some oversight from the provincial government.[9] Numerous private schools operated without any provincial council funding.[10]

Few children lived in the predominantly farming districts of Arch Hill, Grey Lynn and Westmere at this time, and certainly not enough to support a local school of any size, particularly given that attendance was not compulsory. Jane Motion, who lived with her family opposite Low and Motion's flour mill on Old Mill Road in the 1840s and 1850s, attended school in Newton, riding there and back on a pony.[11] Other children lived far from their nearest school, including the McNair and Wilson children, who grew up in the area we now call Westmere. Family members may have provided education for some of these children.

As suburban settlement expanded, so too did the school-aged population. In the mid-1870 the nearest schools were a mix of private and public establishments in Ponsonby, the city, and on the ridge above the south side of Newton Gully. Legislation was passed that allowed householders from areas with no school to form an education district where an education rate could be levied and a school provided.[12] Rating for educational purposes was unpopular, however, particularly among those with no children.[13]

The Auckland Board of Education, responsible for administering schooling in the Auckland province, struggled on with woefully inadequate income, given that many households refused to pay.[14] But changes were on the horizon. Nationwide, provincial councils had been hampered by insufficient revenue to meet expanding needs, and access to schooling was far from universal. The situation was particularly acute in the cash-strapped Auckland province, where large numbers of children were growing up 'ignorant and illiterate'.[15]

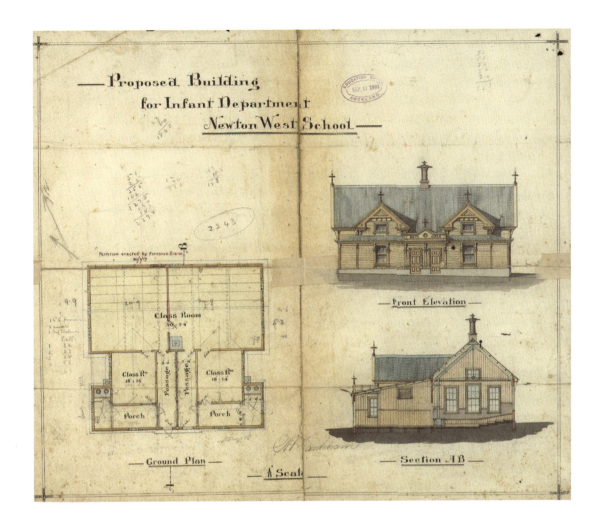

**Plans drawn in 1901 for the Infant Block at Newton West School.**
ARCHIVES NEW ZEALAND TE RUA MAHARA O TE KĀWANATANGA, YCBD A688 19843, BOX 1657D

In the mid-1870s provincial councils were replaced with national administration, and in 1877 the government passed the Education Act, which provided free and compulsory education for Pākehā children aged between 7 and 13 who lived within 2 miles of a school.[16] Those aged 5 to 7, or 13 to 15, were provided with free non-compulsory primary school education.[17] School attendance became compulsory for Māori children seven years later.[18] Native Schools were built predominantly in rural areas with large Māori populations, but both Māori and settler children were accepted into all government-supported schools.[19]

The education legislation had a big effect on the cities. Existing schools became overstretched and new schools were required in the suburbs. In early 1877, when the Education Bill was still being formulated, the need for a school in Arch Hill was raised at a meeting of the Newton School District.[20] At the time, the Newton School District Committee, an elected body of local residents who oversaw schools in the area, had two schools under its charge, the unimaginatively named Newton No. 1 and Newton No. 2, which were housed in St David's schoolroom at the junction of Symonds Street and Khyber Pass, and at the Newton Academy building in Karangahape Road, respectively.[21] By the mid-1870s both buildings were overcrowded and dilapidated, so it was a relief when funding was finally provided to erect two schools, one of which would be built in Arch Hill.[22]

On 22 August 1877, 155 children, many from Arch Hill, headed up the road to their new school, Newton West, which stood proudly on the south side of Great North Road between Brisbane and Potatau (then known as Codrington) streets. To mark the opening, the Newton School District Committee treated the children to an ample lunch of buns, oranges and lollies, followed by running races in the school playground.[23]

The new school had just one room that measured 70 × 25 feet (21 × 8 metres). While not large, it was no doubt a considerable improvement for the staff and pupils transferred from Newton No. 1, which was now closed.[24] The roll grew quickly, and in 1880 two large classrooms with adjoining cloakrooms were added to the building, doubling its size.[25] Newton West School continued to grow, and by the end of 1883 the headmaster, Herbert Mason, had six teaching staff under his charge and a roll of 286, with an average attendance of 206.[26]

The residents of Richmond were still without a local school, the nearest ones being Newton West and Ponsonby School in Cowan Street (then known as Church Street). In 1883 the Ponsonby District School Committee impressed upon the Auckland Education Board the need to acquire sites for schools at the Ponsonby end of the Surrey Hills Estate and at Richmond.[27] The existing Ponsonby School was at capacity with well over 600 pupils in daily attendance, and many pupils who should have been attending there were enrolled at schools in the city instead.[28]

Meanwhile, the residents of Bayfield and Home Bay (to the east of Herne Bay) wrote to the Education Board and the Ponsonby District School Committee, requesting that a school be established in their district.[29] Evidently the committee considered that there was a greater need in the Richmond area, which had a growing population and was on the northern edge of the newly subdivided Surrey Hills Estate, which promised to soon become a populous district.

In January 1884 a school was opened in the Primitive Methodist Chapel located on the bend of Richmond Road opposite where Mokau Street runs today.[30] Known variously as the Richmond, Richmond Road or Coxs Creek School, the building could accommodate just 60 pupils.[31] By early 1888 it had a roll of 100 with an average of 80 pupils attending each day, and new premises were needed. In mid-1888 the Ponsonby District School Committee advised

**ABOVE:** Richmond Road School cadets with their wooden rifles, 1901. In 1909 legislation was passed to require 52 hours annually of military training for boys aged 12 to 18. Prior to this some schools, including Richmond Road and Newton West, had established their own cadets. Numbers grew during the wave of imperial pride when New Zealand offered troops to fight in the South African War, the first overseas war to involve New Zealanders. Schools were supplied with flags from 1901. AUCKLAND LIBRARIES HERITAGE COLLECTIONS, NZG-19010831-0401-02

———

**BELOW:** Unfurling the flag at Richmond Road School as the children sing: 'For we're "Sons of the Empire" and united we will stand, for the honour of Old England the dear old Motherland; the fern, the rose, the thistle, and the shamrock shall entwine, all closely bound together by the thin red line.' AUCKLAND LIBRARIES HERITAGE COLLECTIONS, NZG-19000825-0349-03

———

202 | The Near West

that they had found a suitable, though small, site at the lower end of Brown Street, running through to Douglas Street.

The land was subsequently purchased from the owner, Mr McKinstry, and in late 1888 a former girls' high school building was moved from Queen Street in the city to the new site on Brown Street in Ponsonby, where it opened on 5 November 1888.[32]

The second-hand school building featured rows of double desks arranged on a stepped floor that rose to the back of the room, much like a lecture theatre, an arrangement seen in some of the British charity schools of the nineteenth century.[33] The small site and the use of a second-hand building were an economical response to an urgent need, and a number of additions to both the site and buildings were made over the coming years.[34]

✕

Meanwhile, a third school had opened on the edge of Grey Lynn, but as this was not a state school it received no money from the public purse. The Catholic Church was opposed to the secular education offered by the public schools and elected to expand the number of Catholic schools — the aim was one in every parish — to provide an alternative system for children of the faith.[35]

In the early 1880s the nearest Catholic schools were some distance away at St Marys Bay, Hobson Street and Pitt Street.[36] These would soon be joined by a school established by the Sisters of St Joseph of the Sacred Heart, an Australian religious order called on to establish schools for Catholic children in

**LEFT:** The imposing edifice of Sacred Heart College on the northern side of Richmond Road, **1904.** AUCKLAND LIBRARIES HERITAGE COLLECTIONS, NZG-19040130-0041-01

**MIDDLE:** Dormitories for boarders on the top floor of Sacred Heart College, **1904.** AUCKLAND LIBRARIES HERITAGE COLLECTIONS, NZG-19040130-0042-02

**RIGHT:** A maths class taught by Brother Benignus at Sacred Heart College, **1903.** TONY WATERS, CONFORTARE: A HISTORY OF SACRED HEART COLLEGE, AUCKLAND, 1903–2003, P.30

204 | The Near West

New Zealand. The order had made a start in the South Island in 1883, before Bishop Luck of the Auckland diocese invited them to establish a school in the city.[37]

In 1884 the sisters opened a school in a shop in Karangahape Road, and within a few months the roll had grown from 55 to more than 200.[38] Clearly a new school building was needed, and in 1885 several sites fronting Sussex and Turakina (then known as Tennyson) streets near Great North Road were purchased for the purpose. There was great interest in the new convent school, and some 2000 people watched Bishop Luck lay the foundation stone in November 1885.[39] By early March the school was open. The building also served as a church for the people of the district, with the pews stored in a house nearby during the week.[40]

In 1903 a second Catholic school was erected in the area. Located on the northern side of Richmond Road, just beyond the Grey Lynn boundary, Sacred Heart College was established by the Marist Brothers for Catholic boys.[41] The French Marist Brothers first came to New Zealand as missionaries, but from 1876 teaching brothers began arriving to establish schools in New Zealand. In 1885 four brothers arrived in Auckland to take over the running of a Catholic boys' school located at the junction of Pitt and Wellington streets, which they named Sacred Heart Boys' School.[42] A secondary department was added in 1891, and in 1893 the school began accepting boarders.[43]

The progress of Sacred Heart Boys' School was hindered by its position in a noisy and built-up part of the city. Bishop Lenihan and the school's principal, Brother Basil, both felt the school would do better on a new site. Fortunately the diocese had some suitable land, part of a 48-acre (19.5-hectare) block to

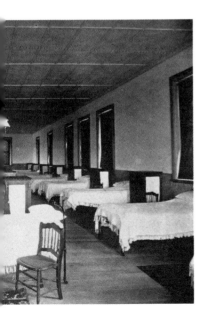

A postcard showing Grey Lynn College sent to student Ida Eise, c. 1906. ARCHIVES NEW ZEALAND TE RUA MAHARA O TE KĀWANATANGA, R928996

the east of Coxs Creek that had been gifted to the diocese by Irish Catholic businessman Hugh Coolahan in 1851. Thirteen and a half acres fronting Richmond Road were leased to the brothers.[44]

In November 1902 Bishop Lenihan laid the foundation stone of the new school, and in June 1903 the Marist Brothers opened their first dedicated secondary school in New Zealand.[45] The main building was an impressive three-storey concrete and brick structure with accommodation for boarders on the top floor. At this time less than 10 per cent of children attended secondary school and, despite the grand premises, the roll was initially small with around 40 boys attending, half of whom were boarders. In the coming years the proportion of boarders increased. Many came from remote areas or had parents with transient jobs that kept them on the move.[46]

But the Catholic schools were not the only religious schools in the area. The Seventh-day Adventists had established a church in Mackelvie Street in the 1880s, and by 1902 a school was being run from the property by Miss Ward.[47] By 1918 it had relocated to the corner of Great North Road and Northland Street and had 19 girls and eight boys on the roll.[48] The school moved back to Mackelvie Street in 1928, but the roll declined and it closed in 1931.[49]

206 | The Near West

Through the late nineteenth and early twentieth centuries the area was also home to some small private schools. The first of these was the Crummer Road School, established in the mid-1880s and taught by Miss F. Hoskins and her sister. It was a short-lived venture and closed soon after it began.[50] In 1897 sisters Edith and Inez Taylor opened a school in Mr Wiseman's residence near the top of Ponsonby Road, and in 1898 a building was erected opposite Western Park and the school moved there. It was known first as Western Park School before being renamed Grey Lynn College.[51] It had a roll of around 50 in 1902. In 1903 it moved again, to the corner of Williamson Avenue and Pollen Street.[52]

The teaching profession was a popular choice for single women from respectable backgrounds who wished, or needed, to support themselves. Edith and Inez Taylor were in their twenties when they opened the school.[53] Teaching was in their blood. Their grandfather, Reverend Richard Taylor, had come to New Zealand in the late 1830s as a missionary and ran the Church Missionary Society school at Waimate North.[54] For women like the Taylor sisters, the establishment of a private school provided an independent income with more freedom than could be found in employment in the public or religious school system.

A postcard sent to senior pupil Ida Eise, who lived nearby in Mackelvie Street and was given responsibility for opening the school one winter's morning, reflects the warm tone between the staff and students at Grey Lynn College:

> Remember dear to bring the key
> And open the door to the GLC
> On June 4th at a quarter to ten
> I think I shall be there by then
> But if I fail the windows raise
> And you will receive my thanks and praise.[55]

Ida Eise graduated as dux of the school in 1907 and received a scholarship and numerous prizes.[56] She went on to become an art teacher and a well-respected artist; several of her works are held in the Auckland City Art Gallery Toi o Tāmaki collection.[57]

Grey Lynn College closed in 1910, and in the same year work began on an impressive state school in Surrey Crescent.[58] Grey Lynn School owed its beginnings to a desperate state of affairs at Newton West and Richmond Road schools. As far back as 1902 a deputation from the Grey Lynn Borough Council had urged the Auckland Education Board to establish a school in Grey Lynn to serve the rapidly increasing population of the borough. Newton West and Richmond Road schools had large rolls, and both were just outside the borough

Education | 207

boundary. A school was needed in the southwestern section of Richmond Road.[59]

The board, however, had already decided to make additions to the existing Richmond Road and Newton West schools to cater for the increasing population of Grey Lynn borough.[60] The new accommodation quickly became overstretched. In late 1906 Richmond Road School had a roll of 830 — 80 more than the maximum allowed — and by early 1907 both Richmond Road and Newton West were turning children away.[61]

For those who did manage to gain admittance, conditions in the classroom were challenging. Classes were often taught by a qualified teacher assisted by pupil teachers. Prospective pupil teachers had to pass an entrance exam and be at least 15 years old — often they were taken on at the school that they had themselves attended.[62] They were apprenticed for around four years, during which time they taught during the day and received teacher training after hours, often from a head teacher at the school.[63]

In 1907 A. S. Webber, the headmaster of Newton West School, bemoaned the fact that the youngest children at the school were taught in a single class of 172 by the infant mistress and two young pupil teachers. The older children fared little better: there were over 100 pupils in each of the standard 1, 2, 3 and 4 classes, each of which was staffed by an assistant teacher and one pupil teacher.[64] Another school was desperately needed.

One hundred and eight people from the area around the southwestern part of Richmond Road signed a petition requesting that the Auckland Education Board build a new school for the district.[65] A site was available for educational purposes in Garnet Road —Westmere School would later be built there — but as this was on the outer edge of residential settlement the board decided that it would be better to start a school in the Richmond Hall (now the Grey Lynn Returned Services Club) at the eastern end of Francis Street. A substantial number of school-aged children lived nearby.[66]

On 8 April 1907 the school was opened with a roll of 50, and it initially operated as a side school administered by Newton West School.[67] Known originally as Richmond School, it grew quickly, and in early 1908 John Campbell, an experienced teacher from Newton West School, was appointed its first headmaster.[68]

In March 1908 Minister of Education George Fowlds visited the school and found the accommodation insufficient for the 197 pupils.[69] Plans were made to build another school, and a site fronting Surrey Crescent was eventually acquired from the St John's College Trust Board, which owned the property as an endowment for the Anglican College of St John the Evangelist at St John's.[70]

**ABOVE:** Children play in a makeshift playground opposite Richmond Hall, where Grey Lynn School was established in 1907. The school moved to its current site in 1911.
AUCKLAND LIBRARIES HERITAGE COLLECTIONS, 226-9274

**BELOW:** Children parading at Westmere School (originally known as Richmond School and then Richmond West). Both Westmere and Grey Lynn schools were designed by a former mayor of Grey Lynn Borough, John Farrell, who served as architect to the Auckland Education Board from 1908 until 1924.
AUCKLAND WAR MEMORIAL MUSEUM TĀMAKI PAENGA HIRA, PH-NEG-C33732

The land had been leased for a variety of purposes and was dotted with houses and commercial buildings.[71] There were long delays in acquiring the site under the Public Works Act, partly because of the status of the land as an endowment, and partly because of the need to compensate leaseholders as well as the owners of the land.

In mid-1909 the school was still housed in the Richmond Hall with nearly 250 pupils on the roll. The overcrowding was temporarily alleviated by renting additional space in the Church of Christ building on the opposite side of Francis Street.[72] It was mid-1910 before work got under way on Grey Lynn School, which would have space for 350 pupils.[73] It was finally opened in February 1911, and within two months the roll was at capacity.[74]

Grey Lynn School was a grand edifice in brick and concrete designed by Auckland Education Board architect John Farrell. It differed markedly from the earliest public school in the area, a one-roomed timber building erected in 1877 at Newton West. Grey Lynn School was divided into a number of classrooms,

The students and staff of Grey Lynn School, 1935. The older children were taught in the main building while the younger children were taught in the building at right, known as the infant block. AUCKLAND WAR MEMORIAL MUSEUM TĀMAKI PAENGA HIRA, PH-TECH-661-69

each equipped with a built-in cupboard and most with a sink. It boasted a headmaster's room with a cloakroom and staffroom above, wide hallways, indoor lavatories and a storeroom.[75]

Within months of the school opening, the primers were being taught in the St Columba Hall at the junction of Surrey Crescent and Selbourne Street, which was rented for the purpose.[76] In 1912 the school building was enlarged with an additional classroom. Meanwhile, Richmond Road School was utilising a hall in the Anglican children's home (the former Costley Training Institute) along Richmond Road for 80 pupils who could not be accommodated in the existing school buildings.[77] At the end of 1912 Newton West had an average attendance of 725 pupils, Richmond Road had 779 and Grey Lynn 474.[78]

The long-term problem with overcrowding at local schools had led to frequent complaints of local children being refused admission.[79] At the end of the nineteenth century 100 children had been refused admission to Richmond Road School within the space of a year.[80] In 1911 all the local schools were

overtaxed, and 70 uneducated waifs had been unable to find a school that would enrol them.[81] Despite numerous extensions and additions, local school buildings failed to keep pace with the expanding school-aged population. There was no option but to build yet another school.

The education reserve in Garnet Road, which had waited patiently for residential development to reach it, was finally put to its intended use.[82] In July 1914 a new brick school building, similar in style to Grey Lynn School, was officially opened. It had three classrooms, a headmaster's room and teachers' room, and was intended to cater for around 180 children.[83] It was originally known as Richmond School, but the Auckland Education Board decided just a few months after it opened to change the name to Richmond West to avoid confusion with Richmond Road School.[84]

Houses continued to spring up in Grey Lynn and Westmere through the early decades of the twentieth century, bringing more families to the district.

In 1918 one of the oldest schools in the district was moved to a new, larger and more prominent location. St Joseph's Convent School in Turakina Street had been growing since its opening in 1886. It had taken over a side room in the convent in 1902, and later converted a stable and hayloft into classrooms to cater for the expanding roll. No more space was available, so a new school was built on Great North Road. The school welcomed 320 students at the beginning of 1918, but it was not long before the school routine was entirely disrupted by the influenza epidemic. Children were kept at home for several months and the school was converted into a temporary hospital staffed partly by the sisters.[85] When the school reopened in 1919 it was without Sister Teresa Norbert, who had contracted influenza while tending to the sick and died in November 1918.[86]

The school continued to take in a few boarders, accommodated in the convent that had been moved to a site alongside the new school in 1917.[87] When fire destroyed the timber convent just before Easter 1921, the boarders and sisters had to make do with temporary living accommodation. Each night until the new convent was opened, two years later, a classroom and cloakroom were converted into sleeping and dining accommodation.[88]

The interwar period brought a number of changes to the educational landscape of the area, including the opening of the first kindergarten in the area. St James Kindergarten (renamed Grey Lynn Kindergarten in 2014) was first established in a church hall in Freemans Bay in 1913 and was the third free kindergarten opened by the Auckland Kindergarten Association. Here young children learned through play according to the philosophy of

**ABOVE:** Children in the sunroom of St James (now Grey Lynn) Kindergarten, 1950s.
AUCKLAND LIBRARIES HERITAGE COLLECTIONS, NZMS1275-2

**BELOW:** Students of the Secondary Department, Forms 3 to 6, of St Joseph's School, on Great North Road, Grey Lynn, in 1954. This section of the school closed at the end of 1960 to make more accommodation available to the full Primary Department, Primer 1 to Form 2.
AUCKLAND LIBRARIES HERITAGE COLLECTIONS, 7_A10715

212 | **The Near West**

**Newton Central School, 1927.** AUCKLAND LIBRARIES HERITAGE COLLECTIONS, 4-05266

Friedrich Froebel, the nineteenth-century German founder of the kindergarten ('children's garden') movement. The long-held desire to erect a purpose-built kindergarten for the children of St James was finally realised in 1924, when the kindergarten was relocated from its increasingly commercial neighbourhood to the residential working-class area of Arch Hill, where it was considered it could do the most good.[89]

But there was also a need for more primary school accommodation, and by the time St James Kindergarten opened in late 1924, another school had opened nearby. As early as 1919 the Newton Schools Committee, which had under its charge Arch Hill's Newton West and Newton East School at the corner of East Street and Belgium Street (formerly known as Upper Queen Street and now under the path of the Northwestern Motorway), was considering future needs.[90]

Both Newton East and Newton West had been built in 1877 and were two of four schools identified in 1918 by the Auckland Education Board's architect John Farrell as being in need of replacement. Farrell noted, however, that with the labour and materials shortages occasioned by the war, the time was inopportune for rebuilding.[91] Both Newton East and Newton West were overcrowded, and the dilapidated condition of the Newton East buildings was blamed for a high rate of sickness among its teaching staff.[92] Rolls continued to rise; Newton West would reach its peak roll of 892 pupils in 1923.[93]

The school, Newton Central, was two storeys high with eight classrooms and was built just a few blocks east of Newton West School on a 7-acre site, the largest of any public school in the district. The site had been owned by John Mennie of the city biscuit manufacturing firm J. M. Mennie (formerly Mennie and Dey), and was part of a larger block of land that stretched to Great North Road. The land had been used to keep the horses that pulled J. M. Mennie's delivery carts, and the old stables still stood in the corner of the playground in the early years after the school opened.[94]

The infant block was the first to be built and received its first pupils at the

214 | **The Near West**

**Folk dancing was a weekly feature of school life at Richmond Road School in 1933.**
ALEXANDER TURNBULL LIBRARY, ARCHIVE PAPER COPY NZ HER

beginning of 1923 when some of the younger pupils from Newton East and Newton West were transferred there.[95] A further five classrooms were added in 1927, which allowed all the remaining pupils from Newton East to be relocated to Newton Central. Newton East School was subsequently closed.[96]

By now the Richmond Road School buildings were showing signs of age. The second-hand school building, moved onto the site in 1888, was still in use, along with a collection of other timber buildings dating from the nineteenth century. From the early twentieth century, facilities that were for the benefit of a number of local schools, as well as trainee teachers, were provided on the site. The Manual Training School erected on the corner of Richmond Road and Douglas Street in 1903 housed cooking, sewing and manual classes for the children of schools in the area. In 1919 Richmond Road School was designated as an auxiliary normal school while a new normal school was under construction, and an open-air classroom was built for the use of teacher trainees.[97]

Education | 215

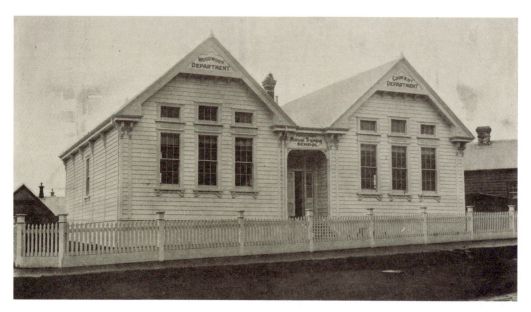

Overcrowding had been an ever-present problem at Richmond Road School, and in March 1919 the roll had reached 782 and children were being turned away.[98] Headmaster T. U. Wells expressed his frustration, stating that the conditions could not be endured any longer: 'In some rooms . . . where there was room for 60 pupils, 120 were crammed in, and it was a common thing in hot weather for children to faint from the heat and oppressiveness.'[99]

Some relief came in 1922 when the new Curran Street School was opened, resulting in a reshuffling of students attending Richmond Road, Ponsonby and Bayfield schools. Richmond Road was the largest with 808 on its roll, and around 200 of these pupils were transferred to Ponsonby School (then located in Cowan Street), while around 350 of Ponsonby's students were transferred to Curran Street School.[100]

In 1922 a meeting of householders urged the Auckland Education Board to erect modern school buildings at Richmond Road as they felt the existing school 'failed in every way to meet up-to-date requirements, and the classrooms were . . . unhygienic and entirely unfitted for their purpose'.[101] The Auckland Education Board responded with the idea of remodelling the existing school buildings, but these plans were scuppered when the board's architect advised that the old buildings, most of which were either second-hand or had been built using reclaimed materials, were not worth repairing.[102] The confined site also compared unfavourably with other schools in the area that had been built on much larger plots, and though additions had been made to the Richmond Road School site in the mid-1890s, in 1912 and again in 1920, the schoolyard was extremely crowded during playtime.[103]

Plans were drawn up for a brick and concrete structure that would bring Richmond Road School up to the standard of the newer schools in the area. However, in 1928 an application to the Education Department for the necessary £14,605 was unsuccessful, and with the economic situation worsening, the school committee could do little but plead for help.[104]

Despite visits to the school by Minister of Education Robert Wright in 1926 and his successor Harry Atmore in 1929, no funding was forthcoming to rebuild the school.[105] The dire state of Education Department finances meant that Richmond Road and Parnell schools, the highest priority for rebuilding in Auckland, had to make do for several more years.[106] The school buildings, described in 1928 as 'shacks and patches, but mostly patches', continued to deteriorate.[107]

Funding was finally granted in 1935, and in March 1937 the new building was opened by Prime Minister Michael Joseph Savage in the presence of 1000 people, including the chairman of the Auckland Education Board, T. U. Wells, who was headmaster of the school from 1898 to 1922.[108] Richmond Road School now boasted a light and airy 10-classroom timber building with rooms

**ABOVE:** The Ponsonby Manual Training School with the woodwork department on the left and the cookery department on the right. Upon entering the building, boys headed left and girls right. AUCKLAND LIBRARIES HERITAGE COLLECTIONS, NZG-19030801-0318-01

**MIDDLE:** Boys learn woodworking skills at the Ponsonby Manual Training School on Richmond Road in 1903. AUCKLAND LIBRARIES HERITAGE COLLECTIONS, NZG-19030801-0322-03

**BELOW:** A cooking class in the kitchen corner at the Ponsonby Manual Training School, 1903. AUCKLAND LIBRARIES HERITAGE COLLECTIONS NZG-19030801-0319-03

**Education | 217**

for the headmaster and staff as well. The school extended across the corner of Brown Street and Richmond Road, and the classrooms surrounded an internal quadrangle that served as the junior playground.[109]

In the early 1930s an established boarding school was transplanted temporarily across the North Island to Grey Lynn. Hukarere School, an Anglican girls' boarding school in Napier, was damaged in the earthquake that struck on 3 February 1931. Fortunately no students were in residence at the time. Archbishop Averill of Auckland visited Napier soon after and offered the use of the former Anglican Children's Home in Richmond Road, originally built as the Costley Training Institute, while the damaged Hukarere School was repaired.[110] Fifty-five girls and their teachers arrived to continue their education and in early 1932 they returned to Napier.[111]

By the 1930s the rapid population growth that had stretched the local school rolls was slowing. Residential development continued in the western parts of Westmere, but much of the rest of the area was now built-up. The national birth rate was declining, and so too were the rolls of many local schools, although Grey Lynn, Newton Central and Richmond Road retained rolls of over 600 pupils through the early 1930s. In 1932 the government raised the school-entry age to six as an economy measure; this brought a further decline in school enrolments, and a number of teachers lost their jobs. But it was also a time of improvement: many school playgrounds benefited from the government relief schemes established to assist the unemployed. Rough play areas were levelled and retaining walls built, making playgrounds more usable and orderly.

In the mid-1930s, when five-year-olds were still excluded from schools (they were readmitted in 1936), Mrs Nash, a former teacher from Warwick Avenue in Westmere, established a kindergarten in her home for her own children as well as those living nearby, which she ran until her own offspring had all passed on to school.[112] In the mid-1940s Miss McCoskrie also ran a kindergarten in the area, assisted by her sprightly 90-year-old father.[113] It was still operating in the early 1950s, but local demand called for an additional kindergarten in the area.

In 1952 Westmere Kindergarten, established under the auspices of the Auckland Kindergarten Association, started up in St Cuthbert's Church. In 1958 it moved into a purpose-built building in Garnet Road.[114] In the years since St James Kindergarten was relocated to Arch Hill in 1924, kindergartens had proliferated and were becoming part of the educational landscape of many suburbs, as more families recognised the value of early childhood education.[115]

Meanwhile, changes had occurred in the schools of Arch Hill. By the late

**218** | **The Near West**

1930s the only school that retained its original nineteenth-century building was Newton West, and plans were afoot to rebuild it. However, with Newton West and Newton Central schools so close to one another, the birth rate in decline and the roll falling, the plans were dropped. In 1943 the main school closed, though three teachers continued to run the infant department as a side school to Newton Central, a temporary measure until classrooms there were freed up by the planned closure of the standard 5 and 6 classes in 1945.[116] Students graduating from standard 4 would then receive intermediate schooling at New Zealand's first intermediate school.

Kowhai Intermediate (initially called Kowhai Junior High School) opened in 1922 in buildings originally planned for a primary school on the south side of Newton Gully.[117] It was based on the junior high schools that had been developed from 1909 in America. At intermediate children were introduced to secondary school subjects, allowing them to develop their interests and aptitudes earlier. Some would complete their education there, while others were encouraged to further their education at a high school.[118]

Kowhai had initially drawn its pupils from primary schools on the south side of Newton Gully, but the development of intermediate schools at Epsom and Balmoral in the mid-1940s allowed it to include Newton Central as a contributing school.[119] By this stage a second intermediate school had been built near Grey Lynn and Westmere, on the west bank of Motions Creek. Opened in March 1942 and designed to cater for 520 children, Pasadena Intermediate initially welcomed 439 enrolled pupils.[120] It was only the third intermediate school to be opened in Auckland, the other one being Northcote.[121] Pasadena Intermediate drew its pupils from four surrounding schools, including Grey Lynn and Westmere, which now closed their standard 5 and 6 classes.[122] Richmond Road retained its standard 5 and 6 classes until 1976, when Ponsonby Intermediate opened.[123]

In 1944 the school leaving age was raised from 14 to 15 and additional high schools were needed.[124] The two local Catholic schools, St Joseph's Convent School and Sacred Heart College, were the only ones catering for secondary students. Arch Hill, Grey Lynn and Westmere had no state high schools of their own, and children had to travel to attend Auckland Girls' Grammar for girls and Mount Albert Grammar for boys. Auckland Grammar, which for some residents was closer than Mount Albert Grammar, took boys from the inner and eastern parts of the city, excluding Arch Hill, Grey Lynn and Westmere.[125] Seddon Technical College in Wellesley Street provided a co-educational option for those seeking a technical secondary education.

Education | 219

There were big changes for Sacred Heart College in the 1950s. The three-storey school building erected in 1903 was originally intended as the first half of a grand Catholic college, but various factors, including concerns about the suitability of the site, led to the abandonment of this plan. Some additional, mainly timber buildings were erected on the Richmond Road site as the roll expanded.[126] The Marist Brothers looked for a new site for the college, and in 1931 leased land at Northcote behind Hato Petera College. During the Second World War, however, the government required the use of the Northcote site, and the brothers eventually swapped it for a property at Glen Innes that adjoined land that the Crown was developing for state housing.[127]

In 1955 the new Sacred Heart College opened in Glen Innes and the former school in Richmond Road was renamed St Paul's College. The Glen Innes college took not only the name, Sacred Heart, but also virtually everything that spoke of the history of the Richmond Road school, including the college crest, honours board and photographs.[128] St Paul's became the poor relation, keeping the less-experienced teaching staff, who took on the challenge of making the school a success.[129] St Paul's opened with just 314 boys but the roll soon expanded and it regained its numbers.[130]

In 1964 Seddon Technical College was relocated from Wellesley Street to land fronting Motions Road, just west of Grey Lynn and Westmere. Seddon Tech, as it was commonly known, was renamed Seddon High School in 1968 and Western Springs College in 1990.

Grey Lynn was also home to a tertiary institution in the 1950s and early 1960s. After fire destroyed Elam Art School's Symonds Street premises in early 1949, the painting and sculpture departments were relocated to the former Newton West School.[131] At this time Elam ceased to be a technical school controlled by the Auckland Education Board and became part of the University of Auckland.[132]

The post-war era brought changes to the inner-west suburbs of Arch Hill, Grey Lynn and Westmere. Many families who had made their homes there decades earlier left the area, and new families moved in.

New Zealand was looking to Britain, Europe and the Pacific Islands for immigrants to stem the labour shortage that threatened to quell economic growth.[133] At the same time there was considerable internal migration as rural Māori moved to the cities. Many migrants made their homes in the inner-west suburbs, including Grey Lynn and Arch Hill, which were centrally located and offered affordable rental housing.

The changing community had a marked impact on schools. In 1964 the

Auckland Education Board surveyed the schools under their charge and found that 18.5 per cent of pupils were Māori, Pasifika, or immigrants from other countries who did not speak English.

At Newton Central these groups accounted for 81 per cent of the 356 children on the roll, the second-highest proportion in the Auckland Education Board area, exceeded only by Napier Street School in Freemans Bay. Fourth highest was Richmond Road School with 68 per cent; Grey Lynn School had 30 per cent and Westmere School just 6 per cent.

The Auckland Education Board recognised that extra help was needed for schools like Newton Central and Richmond Road, where many children spoke little or no English, and so additional teaching staff were hired.[134] This approach was not just confined to schools in the area — the Auckland Kindergarten Association also provided an extra staff member at St James Kindergarten in Arch Hill for the same purpose.[135]

New methods of teaching were also needed. In the late 1960s Richmond Road School became the centre of a project to develop an approach to literacy that was designed to meet the needs of the multicultural community.[136] Part of this was the development of a cooperative reading programme using large-format books that were written, illustrated and produced by staff at the school and sometimes featured illustrations by students. Richmond Road School attracted academics from New Zealand and overseas keen to see the programme in action.[137]

The innovative programme was further developed by Richmond Road School principal Jim Laughton (1972–88), who reorganised classes to include a variety of ages, abilities and ethnic backgrounds. Based on the idea of the family, children learned from and about each other. In 1976 the school established a unit to cater for children for whom English was a new language.[138]

Other schools in the area also adapted to changing needs. In the early 1970s special financial grants allowed Newton Central school to conduct experiments in how best to meet the educational needs of their pupils. By 1972, 95 per cent of the school's pupils were Pasifika, the highest proportion of any school in Auckland. Those who could not speak English attended an English language class each morning before joining regular classes in the afternoon.[139]

Cultural enrichment classes that included woodwork, painting and crafts were provided to help new arrivals adjust to their environment and gain a sense of achievement at school. Parent evenings featuring local speakers, musical entertainment and meals were popular with local families and helped connect the parent community with the school.[140]

Just as Richmond Road and Newton Central schools looked for new ways to teach, so too did the staff of a school established nearby during the 1970s. Auckland Alternative Secondary School opened its doors in early 1973 in

Education | 221

the former Costley Training Institute in Richmond Road. It was one of a number of alternative schools established throughout the country from the 1960s, influenced by overseas examples that took a less structured and more individualised approach to learning, and where children were involved in making decisions about what and how they would learn.[141] The schools sprang from the revolutionary spirit of the era.[142]

Auckland Alternative Secondary School was established partly to cater for children who had graduated from Rosedale School, an alternative primary school that opened on the North Shore in 1969. Rosedale had been started by parents dissatisfied with the established system and offered more freedom of choice and greater links between school and community. Auckland Alternative Secondary School also served students who had dropped out of traditional secondary schools, or whose needs were not being met by them.[143]

In February 1973 the school opened with 45 students. Students were treated as equals by teachers and there were no compulsory subjects.[144] An enrolment fee was charged to begin with, but after six months the school became registered as a private school and was eligible for state funding.[145] As well as more conventional subjects it offered classes in car mechanics, glassblowing and philosophy.

But the building did not comply with Auckland City Council fire regulations and its owner, the Church Army, was unwilling to upgrade it. In 1976 the school reopened in the Maori Community Centre in Fanshawe Street in the city. It subsequently moved around a number of other premises in the city.[146]

Another alternative school, Auckland Metropolitan College (better known as Metro), opened in 1977. As an experimental school, from the outset it had the distinct advantage of being sanctioned and funded by the Education Department.[147] Auckland Alternative Secondary School lost a significant number of its students to this enterprise and in early 1978, yet again without premises and with just 10 pupils, the school closed for good.[148]

There were major physical changes for many schools in the Arch Hill, Grey Lynn and Westmere areas in the 1970s and 1980s. Grey Lynn, Westmere and Newton Central schools' imposing brick and concrete structures were replaced with single-storey buildings arranged around a central court.[149] Richmond Road School was the only state school in the area to escape the wrecking ball. Newton Central had the most disruption when in 1971, the Ministry of Works requisitioned the school field at the bottom of Newton Gully for the Northwestern Motorway. A new playground was formed in 1972, and the school was rebuilt in the early 1980s.[150]

**222** | **The Near West**

St Paul's College Marcellin Champagnat Building, designed by Architectus, opened in 2018. PATRICK REYNOLDS

The Catholic Church firmly believed that there should be a place for all children of the faith at Catholic schools, but they received little government support and were reliant on church communities for funding. This was a heavy burden. Catholic schools had been under increasing financial pressure in the decades after the Second World War, a situation exacerbated by rising rolls occasioned by the post-war baby boom and the raising of the school leaving age.

As well, the nuns and brothers who for decades had been the mainstay of teaching staff at Catholic schools were thinly stretched, and Catholic schools became increasingly reliant on lay teachers who demanded remuneration well beyond the meagre stipend that a nun or brother received. As a result, from 1960 Catholic schools began to charge fees.[151]

At state schools, class sizes were reduced and standards improved. Catholic schools suffered by comparison.[152] In addition, as religious observance declined, so too did the proportion of Catholic children attending schools of the faith. In 1956 nearly 70 per cent of Catholic children attended Catholic schools; by 1969 this number had fallen to just under 50 per cent.[153] The influx of families from the Pacific Islands to Grey Lynn had bolstered Catholic school rolls, but the cost of education was not easily borne by immigrants who were trying to establish themselves in a new country. The Catholic school system was close to collapse and needed considerable financial support to ensure its survival.[154]

This came finally in the late 1970s and early 1980s with the progressive integration of Catholic schools into the state system, a change that relieved parents of some financial pressure.[155] St Paul's College, which had recently

Education | 223

become solely a day school, was integrated in 1982 as a secondary school with an intermediate attached. The roll stood at 50 intermediate and 285 secondary pupils.[156] St Joseph's became a state integrated school in 1983, and in 1990 the school was rebuilt.

In 1989 major changes were made to the governance of schools under the Tomorrow's Schools reforms. Education boards were disestablished and each school community elected a board of trustees to govern their school. In theory, this meant a school could be more responsive and accountable to its community, but it also relied on the community having people with the necessary skills who were willing to serve on the board. Some schools fared very well under the new regime while others did not.

Grey Lynn School ran into problems in the early 1990s when it received a series of damning Education Review Office reports.[157] Local parents began to avoid sending their children there, and the rolls at neighbouring schools, including Westmere and Newton Central, rose as a result.[158] The roll dropped to 85 and the school was threatened with closure.[159] In late 1998 Bill Barker was recruited from the Education Review Office as principal, and the Ministry of Education provided additional funding and training to address numerous issues at the school.[160] It was a mammoth task, but with the support of the staff, community and board of trustees, the failing school was transformed once again into a thriving one.[161]

St Paul's College was also struggling, with poor results in the 1990s and 2000s, particularly in the National Certificate of Educational Achievement (NCEA). Attendance at St Paul's had become a family tradition, and many boys travelled a considerable distance from other parts of Auckland to attend, their families having left the area.[162] In 2015 the school unveiled an ambitious plan to raise the achievement of its students in external exams and become the Catholic school of choice for local boys, many of whom bypassed St Paul's.[163] It used the funds from the sale of a block of land fronting John Street to build a middle-school classroom and administration block.[164] In recent years the school has seen improvements in NCEA results and roll growth.

Two major changes in education in recent years have been the inauguration of bilingual and immersion foreign language units at many schools, and the development of language-immersion preschools. During the 1960s and 1970s there was a strong focus on improving the English

**224** | **The Near West**

language skills of the many immigrant children who had arrived. Now the children and grandchildren of immigrants were growing up with improved English language skills but with declining knowledge of the language of their forebears. Similarly, many Māori tamariki whose parents or grandparents had moved to the city from rural communities where te reo Māori was spoken now sought to reconnect with their Māori heritage.

Schools in the multicultural inner-west suburbs fostered the development of bilingual and immersion language units in response to community demand. At Richmond Road School a Māori bilingual unit was established in the mid-1980s and New Zealand's first Samoan bilingual class was inaugurated soon afterwards. The school also established a Cook Island Māori bilingual unit during the 1980s, and a French bilingual unit followed in 1996.[165]

At Newton Central School a Māori bilingual unit was introduced in 1993, and in 1996 a Māori immersion unit was added.[166] From 2000 to 2012 there was also a Fanau Pasifika unit where Pacific Island languages and cultures were incorporated into classroom learning, but changes in the community saw the number of students with Pacific Island heritage at the school decline — from 95 per cent in 1985 to just 4 per cent in 2014 — and the class was discontinued.[167] In comparison the number of Māori students at the school rose steadily, and by 2014 they made up 43 per cent of the roll. In 2018 buildings were erected to house the Māori immersion unit and the bilingual unit, which had been re-established in 2005.[168]

In 1989 Grey Lynn School established a Māori bilingual unit and a Samoan bilingual class, and later a Tongan bilingual class, but problems with school governance and management caused these to be relatively short-lived: the Māori unit closed in 1994 and the Samoan and Tongan classes followed suit soon afterwards.[169] Westmere School opened its Māori bilingual unit, Ngā Uri o Ngā Iwi, in 1991, and today offers both bilingual and immersion pathways.[170]

Students who graduate from the bilingual and immersion units at local primary schools now have options for continuing their education at intermediate and high schools. Gāfoa le Ata provides Samoan bilingual education at Kōwhai Intermediate School, and both Kōwhai and Pasadena intermediates have Māori immersion units. Ngā Puna o Waiōrea, which opened in 1989, operates as a school within a school at Western Springs College and provides a next step for children from te reo Māori immersion kura (schools). School immersion and bilingual units have become a magnet for students from a wide area, stretching well beyond the suburbs of the inner west.

Hand-in-hand with the development of bilingual and immersion units in local schools has been the inauguration of te kōhanga reo (Māori language nest) and other non-English-language-based preschools. Ritimana Te Kōhanga Reo Centre was established in 1985 at Richmond Road School, three years after

Education | 225

Western Springs College's bold new buildings designed by Jasmax won awards in 2020. DENNIS RADERMACHER

Aotearoa's first kōhanga reo was opened. In 1987 Aʻoga Faʻa Sāmoa, a Samoan immersion early childhood centre, was relocated to Richmond Road from Herne Bay, where it had been established in 1984.[171]

In 1988 Mataʻaga Aʻoga Amata, another Samoan language preschool, was established in Grey Lynn by the Congregational Christian Church of Sāmoa.[172] An Italian language preschool ran from Grey Lynn School in 2000, but later relocated to Freemans Bay.[173]

At the same time there has been a proliferation in other early childhood education and care services, as social change has seen many children growing up in families where both parents work. This has been encouraged by changes in government policy since the late 1980s that have fostered the growth of childcare and education businesses in an area that was earlier dominated by non-profit community providers.[174] The kindergartens established decades earlier by the Auckland Kindergarten Association in Arch Hill (Grey Lynn Kindergarten, formerly known as St James) and Westmere have been joined by many preschool care and education centres offering a range of options for parents.

In the past few years, the state schools of Arch Hill, Grey Lynn and Westmere have adopted Māori names in addition to their English names: Newton Central School Te Kura a Rito o Newton; Richmond Road School Te Kura o Ritimana; Westmere School Te Rehu; and Grey Lynn School Te Rae o Kawharu.

There has been a significant change in the way schools teach their students. Single classrooms are gradually being replaced with what are known as innovative learning environments — larger and more flexible spaces suited to modern learning needs. New buildings have appeared at Richmond Road School, Newton Central School and St Paul's College, and existing buildings at Pasadena Intermediate and Richmond Road School have been adapted to provide modern learning spaces. The biggest changes have been at Grey Lynn School, Westmere School and Western Springs College, which have been entirely rebuilt. The renewal of the Western Springs College campus is the most expensive secondary school rebuild in New Zealand's history.

Today many parents and grandparents of school-aged children marvel at the changes that have taken place in education since they attended school. The blackboards, overhead projectors and film reels that were part of school equipment in the past have been replaced by computer technology. This was a big advantage during the recent Covid-19 pandemic, when schools shut for the first time since the polio epidemic of 1948.

Although so much has changed in children's schooling experience since the first students toddled off to Newton West School in 1877, no doubt the parents of those nineteenth-century learners hoped that school would provide their children with an education that would prepare them for life. That much has not changed.

# The pride of Mrs Emma Rooney

In the late nineteenth century talented and experienced female teachers occupied a precarious position within the state education system, a situation illustrated by the career of Emma Rooney (née Fletcher).

London-trained Fletcher was the first teacher at Richmond Road School and had considerable teaching experience.[175] Originally from Ipswich in England, she travelled to New Zealand with her parents and five siblings in late 1879, when she was in her late twenties.[176] Her teaching career in New Zealand began the following year when she took an assistant teaching position at Kauaeranga Girls' School in Thames under headmistress Frances Haselden.

Fletcher was the second-highest paid of the nine teachers at the school.[177] She moved to Auckland in 1881 and served initially as the sole teacher at Mount Roskill School before she was joined by another teacher the following year.[178] At the start of 1884 she took up the position of headmistress of the new school in Richmond Road.[179]

Soon after taking charge, Fletcher married Andrew Rooney, a music teacher.[180] It was common at the time for women to give up their careers when they married, but Emma Rooney clearly enjoyed her employment and elected to continue. She went on to have four children, three of whom were born during her time at the school.[181]

In 1889 the Ponsonby District School Committee, an elected body of locals who oversaw the running of their school, won a victory for working mothers when the committee rejected the Auckland Education Board's directive that Rooney's employment at Richmond Road School be terminated on the grounds that she was a nursing mother. The committee argued that 'as Mrs Rooney has conducted, and is still conducting, the Richmond School to the complete satisfaction of the Committee, she be now left undisturbed in her position as head-teacher'.[182]

Five years later Rooney's employment as head teacher of Richmond Road School was again under threat, this time from the Ponsonby District School Committee. The school roll had grown substantially, to 300 pupils. Members of the committee believed a male teacher should be in charge of such a large school and urged the board to replace Rooney.[183] William Leys, the chair of the committee, was particularly outspoken on the matter. While claiming that he had nothing against Rooney, he said that only a man could keep discipline in such a large school.[184] He made his view of women clear: 'Women naturally looked to the home as their settlement, and only look upon teaching as a matter of expediency. Whatever a man took up he took up seriously in order to make a living at it.'[185]

Arguments went back and forth, and the Auckland Education Board initially rejected the request. There were deputations, including from the Women's Liberal League and a group of Richmond Road School parents, as well as a letter from the New Zealand Educational Institute in favour of Rooney retaining her position at the school.[186] Inspectors had reported favourably on the school and noted that pass rates were high and discipline and order were good.

The Ponsonby District School Committee had appointed many female teachers at its three schools, something that no doubt had financial appeal, given that female teachers were paid less than males. In 1895 the committee employed 28 female and three male teachers at its three schools. At Richmond Road there were seven female teachers in charge of 305 children, and it was the only public school of its size in the Auckland Education Board district to have no male teachers.[187]

In light of the 1893 decision to give women the vote, the *New Zealand Herald* noted the irony of Rooney's situation:

> It seems curious in these days, when equal rights are claimed for women in all departments, that it should be proposed to discharge a woman who has done as much as any man could have done, and much better than most men.[188]

In the end the only choice given to Rooney was demotion or resignation. She chose the latter. Rooney would be missed; the esteem and affection in which she was held by the school community was expressed at a farewell picnic at Takapuna attended by some 200 of the senior pupils.[189]

Emma Rooney subsequently moved to Wellington, where she became principal of Queen's College girls' school before moving to Stratford in Taranaki, where she opened a boarding and day school for girls in 1901.[190] She died in 1903, aged 51.[191]

Rooney's experience was certainly not isolated, and by the end of the century the small number of headmistresses in the Auckland Education Board area, which included much of the North Island, had dwindled from 11 in 1895 (14 per cent of all head teachers in the board's area), to just six in 1905 (8 per cent).[192] Meanwhile, women made up more than half of all school teachers in New Zealand.[193]

Other headmistresses forced out of their positions in the late nineteenth century included

Frances Haselden, the talented headmistress of Kauaeranga Girls' School, and her sister Mary Harden (née Haselden), the headmistress of Remuera School.[194] Jane Simpson, the headmistress of Bayfield School who, like Rooney, had been in charge of her school since its inception, resigned in 1896. No doubt she could see that the writing was on the wall for her, too.[195]

Discrimination against married female teachers again reared its ugly head in the 1930s, a time when the economic downturn and rising unemployment among newly trained teachers — something that had been building for several years — reached crisis point.[196] The Auckland Education Board lobbied the government to pass legislation giving education boards the power to dismiss married female teachers, no matter how capable, well qualified and experienced they were.[197]

The idea that the dismissal of married female teachers provided a just solution to teacher graduate unemployment was bound up in the notion that married women should be supported by their husbands and that their 'natural' role was that of wife and mother.[198] The Finance Act 1931 was subsequently passed, and in May 1931 the Auckland Education Board required every married female teacher to 'provide sufficient reasons against the termination of her engagement within three months'.[199]

Married female teachers with working husbands were firmly in the crosshairs. Of the 124 married women employed as teachers by the Auckland Education Board, 33 were fired and another 15 resigned while the board considered their circumstances.[200] But not all were prepared go quietly. Mrs Katharine Browne, who taught at Westmere School, was given three months' notice soon after the passing of the Finance Act in 1931. She took the matter to the court of appeal — and won.[201]

Education | 229

# Sport and recreation

**PREVIOUS PAGES:** The opening of the Grey Lynn Bowling Club in 1904 on the former Richmond Tennis Club site on Richmond Road (then known as Richmond Avenue). AUCKLAND LIBRARIES HERITAGE COLLECTIONS, NZG-19041203-0041-02

On New Year's Day 1873, 500 pupils and 50 teachers from the various Wesleyan Sunday schools of the city and suburbs met at the corner of Pitt Street and marched in procession to 'that beautifully retired spot known as the Surrey Hills Estate' for their annual fête.[1] At this regular event children took part in running races and games, and enjoyed lashings of cake and strawberries all washed down with tea.[2]

Other groups of children also enjoyed picnics and games at Surrey Hills through the 1870s and 1880s, including the Sunday school scholars of the Franklin Road Primitive Methodist Church and St Thomas's Church in Union Street, and the pupils of Newton West and Newton East schools.[3] There was ample space for cricket. When the Arch Hill Wesleyan Sunday school held its annual festival there in 1885 the *Auckland Star* reported that 'the usual cricket match — teachers versus students — took place'.[4]

Surrey Hills Estate was just a stone's throw from Western Park, which Auckland City Council had developed in the 1870s. Its easy slopes led to wide open spaces of gentle contour. It was an ideal place for picnics and sports games, and although not in public ownership, the estate was frequently made available to the public for these purposes. Adults used it for sport, and from the late 1870s the loud thwack of leather on willow could regularly be heard.[5] The Surrey Hills Cricket Club met on the pitch in Surrey Hills, one of several places where Auckland teams played.[6] Other teams followed, including the Newton Cricket Club, which was up and running in the early 1880s, and the Richmond Cricket Club soon after.[7]

In 1881 Auckland newspapers published details of James Williamson's offer to sell the Surrey Hills Estate to Auckland City Council for £100,000, with the proviso that only the street frontages were to be sold or leased so that the vast interior could be reserved as a public park.[8] But the council had other priorities, and the estate was sold instead to the Auckland Agricultural Company, which had interests in developing Waikato swamp lands into farms, and of which Williamson was one of four major shareholders. A profitable sale of the estate

**Sport and recreation** | **233**

was needed to prop up the company, which was burdened by its Waikato drainage costs.[9]

A design competition for the subdivision plan of the Surrey Hills Estate was won by Theodore Hickson, though the council roundly criticised his design for its lack of recreation reserves. It no doubt anticipated that the area would amalgamate with the city sooner rather than later.[10] The daily newspapers were also unimpressed and devoted many column inches to criticising the plan.

Just prior to the auction of the first sites on the estate, Hickson drew up an alternative design which he described in detail in a letter published in the *New Zealand Herald*: it provided abundant space for sport and recreation, including a 16-acre cricket oval, a public park with stream-fed gullies that could be dammed to create ponds for ornamental and practical purposes, and a series of semi-private neighbourhood parks.

This idyllic scheme relied on the council purchasing the entire estate from the Agricultural Company and leasing the 750 building sites within it.[11] But this ploy failed, and the vendors soon put parts of the park-less Surrey Hills Estate up for sale.[12] The estate was not all sold at once, however, and some areas continued to be used for sports matches for years to come.

Some sports clubs centred on residential areas while others were formed at workplaces or by those engaged in a particular trade. Arch Hill resident John Mell, for example, was a long-serving foreman at James Holland's city building firm, a cricketer and an enthusiastic supporter of the company's cricket club. He hosted Holland's Cricket Club meetings and social events at his Great North Road residence and continued to be involved even after he left Holland's employment.[13] In 1886 a team of Mell's bricklayers played cricket against Mr Stevenson's carpenters at the Auckland Domain, the best-formed cricket ground in the city.[14]

There was a proliferation of clubs as keen cricketers formed teams wherever they found enough interest. But in the late 1870s and early 1880s some Auckland cricket clubs folded or were merged with others as they struggled to attract players.[15] In the mid-1880s the Newton Cricket Club's senior team was incorporated into Holland's Cricket Club, perhaps because there were insufficient players to support two teams.[16]

Cricket may have been the first sport out of the starting blocks in the area, but winter sports soon followed. In 1874 rugby union was established in Auckland when settlers who had attended public schools in England played the first game under rugby union rules.[17] Football had been played before this, but the rules were something of a movable feast and reflected the varied winter ball

234 | **The Near West**

games played in England that coalesced into the running and kicking games we know today as rugby and soccer.[18]

Like cricket, rugby teams were established in both workplaces and local areas, and matches were played at Surrey Hills from as early as 1883.[19] In late 1883 the Newton Football Club, which had been active since 1881, played a series of matches at the Auckland Domain against teams from the city's boot factories.[20] The Newton team went further afield, too, travelling by steamer to Thames in 1884, 1886 and 1891 to play local teams, and to Whangārei in 1885.[21]

In 1891 Auckland Rugby Union was the first of the major sports to organise teams around places of residence. This no doubt required some reallocation of players to the various teams, including the Newton club, which was now known as the Newton District Football Club.[22] By the early twentieth century Newton had a training shed in East Street, off Karangahape Road; a few years later it built a larger shed at the end of Virginia Avenue (then known as Victoria Avenue) in Eden Terrace, where the motorway now exists. The training shed adjoined Mennie's Reserve, which would later be the site of Newton Central School.[23]

Interclub matches were held at Potters Paddock in Epsom (later known as Alexandra Park) and occasionally at Devonport on the North Shore.[24] At Potters Paddock there was sufficient space for several games to be played at once. On match days the Newton team would travel to Potters Paddock in a horse brake decorated in the team colours, to return either proud winners or crestfallen in defeat.[25]

Schoolboy teams also existed, and some boys went on to join adult teams when they left school. As early as the mid-1890s, a rugby team from Richmond Road School and a soccer team from Newton West School were playing other Auckland schoolboy teams.[26] And in 1907 a Catholic boys' rugby competition was established in which teams from Sacred Heart and Surrey Hills competed.[27] Some adult teams were also school-based, including Marist Old Boys, a team of former pupils of Sacred Heart College (now St Paul's College) in Richmond Road.[28]

Rugby and cricket were the main sports, but others also vied for players. In 1900 the Grey Lynn Lacrosse Club hit the field in a white uniform with a maroon sash and black socks.[29] The team was one of a number that developed in Auckland following the establishment of the New Zealand Lacrosse Association in 1899. The game was played in Auckland as early as 1885, and the association had aspirations to expand.[30]

**ABOVE:** Newton District Football Club, 1890s.
AUCKLAND LIBRARIES HERITAGE COLLECTIONS, AWNS-18990721-01-02

**BELOW:** The Brotherhood Football team, 1918.
AUCKLAND LIBRARIES HERITAGE COLLECTIONS, APL-31-WP828

**RIGHT:** The Richmond Cruising Club clubhouse at Sloanes Beach, Herne Bay, in the 1930s.
AUCKLAND LIBRARIES HERITAGE COLLECTIONS, 7-A15860

**ABOVE:** Bowlers at the Grey Lynn Bowling Club, c. 1904. AUCKLAND WAR MEMORIAL MUSEUM TĀMAKI PAENGA HIRA, PH-NEG-C19952

**BELOW:** An Auckland championship lacrosse game at the Auckland Domain in June 1900. The Grey Lynn lacrosse team was placed last in this championship and folded soon afterwards. AUCKLAND LIBRARIES HERITAGE COLLECTIONS, NZG-19000616-1128-01

Practice matches and competition games were played at the Auckland Domain, since this was the ground best adapted for field sports.[31] The Grey Lynn club was short-lived, however, and folded after coming dead last in the 1901 championship.[32] Lacrosse evidently suffered competition from rugby, which was growing in popularity, and lacrosse was not revived in Grey Lynn.[33]

×

Cricket, rugby and lacrosse needed large grassed areas, but other sports made do with smaller, carefully manicured lawns. In the late nineteenth century, sports teams and facilities began to develop at the western end of Richmond Road (then known as Richmond Avenue), where flat land suitable for lawn sports was available.

From the 1890s Richmond Avenue rang with the sound of tennis balls being whacked across the Richmond Tennis Club court that adjoined Charles I. McMaster's grand two-storey house, The Pines, near where Fisherton Street runs today.[34] Tennis was one of the few games considered sufficiently genteel for women, although playing in the long skirts of the late Victorian era was no doubt something of a challenge.[35]

Richmond Tennis Club folded in 1904 and the facilities were immediately adapted for lawn bowls. By late 1904 the gentle clink of bowls driving to the jack could be heard on the green that had been laid out on the tennis courts by the newly formed Grey Lynn Bowling Club.[36]

Bowls, brought to the country by Scottish settlers who established the first club in Auckland in 1861, was very much at home in the suburbs.[37] Grey Lynn was the eighth Auckland club to be established and began with a membership of 50.[38] On opening day in November 1904, members turned out in their club colours and Miss Donald, daughter of club president Alexander Donald, was given the honour of casting the jack across the green ready for play.[39]

It appears there was some trouble over the lease of the club's green, which was still owned by McMaster. In 1906 McMaster's son, Charles Jnr, and other past members of the Grey Lynn Bowling Club formed the Richmond Bowling Club, which used the greens and pavilion previously leased to the Grey Lynn club.[40] This left Grey Lynn without greens for a season, but they continued to play in other parts of the city and soon secured a 21-year lease on a property on Surrey Crescent, just east of Grey Lynn School.[41]

Here a new green was laid out, a pavilion was erected, and the venue opened in November 1907.[42] The two clubs, located a short distance from each other, continued to draw members, but in 1910 the Richmond club was wound up. McMaster had died three years earlier and the trustees of his estate were unwilling to lease the property on terms agreeable to the club.[43]

**238** | **The Near West**

Lawn bowls was almost exclusively a male sport at the time, but the clubs were well supported by members' wives and daughters, who served refreshments and helped out with the concerts, dances and other fundraising entertainments that were a regular part of the clubs' social calendars. There were ceremonial roles, too: the club president's wife or daughter was generally given the honour of throwing the jack onto the green to open the bowling season each year.[44] Newspaper reports of early bowling club events mention the attendance of 'members and their lady friends' — there being no female members.[45]

In 1910 the facilities at Grey Lynn Bowling Club were extended with additional bowling greens and croquet lawns 'for the ladies'.[46] Attention turned to the formation of a croquet club, and several wives and daughters of bowling club members formed the committee.[47] Grey Lynn was one of a number of bowling clubs that added a croquet lawn around this time, and women were eventually invited onto the bowling green for a ladies' tournament in 1926.[48]

Meanwhile, on the seaward side of the district, another sporting club was finding its feet. With its Waitematā Harbour access and sheltered water, Coxs Bay was an ideal location for water sports. James Donald, of the fellmongery firm A. Donald and Son, had a boat shed on the western edge of Coxs Bay, and here Donald and other local yachtsmen formed the Richmond Cruising Club (later known as the Richmond Yacht Club) in 1903.[49] In its early years the membership remained small — there were just seven members in 1906 — but they still held races in Coxs Bay and went cruising on the harbour. Membership numbers soon swelled, however, and the club became organised on more formal lines.

In 1906 the neighbouring Home Bay Sailing Club, which had been in existence since 1902, folded and its members joined other clubs, including Richmond. By 1906 Richmond Cruising Club had 70 members and was ready to build a clubhouse. Sloanes Beach, just east of Coxs Bay, was considered ideal. However, the club ran into problems with the Marine Department and Auckland City Council over the right to build, and objections from nearby landowners added further complications.

The saga dragged on for several years, but in November 1913 a single-storey clubhouse, which survives today with a second-storey addition, was opened before a large crowd. Although no longer in Coxs Bay the name Richmond was retained, and the club continued to count many sailors from the Richmond area among its members. It later built a clubhouse at Westhaven, where it remains today.

**Sport and recreation | 239**

As the district's population grew new clubs formed and various sporting codes expanded. Some clubs leased paddocks for play, but more playing grounds were needed.

The Auckland Adult School Association Football Club, which formed in 1912, was one of many sports clubs associated with religious and social organisations. Auckland Adult School — based on the Adult Schools established in Britain from 1845 by Quakers to provide non-denominational education — was opened in 1891 by the Quakers (Society of Friends) as a place where adults, from the godless to the devout, could meet to discuss matters of interest and hear invited speakers. Several branches of the Auckland Adult School were active by the early twentieth century, and cricket and soccer clubs formed from their social club meetings.[50]

The Auckland Adult School Association Football Club was one of only a few soccer clubs with a home ground — thanks to the efforts of the club secretary Francis Dance, who lived in Sherwood Avenue.[51] The field was in the vicinity of Garnet Road (then known as Wolseley Avenue) in Richmond.[52] Club members worked hard to improve the field and were given the use of a training shed on the southern stretch of Richmond Road (then known as Richmond Avenue).[53] By 1913 the Richmond ground was considered second only to Victoria Park and the Domain.[54]

The Adult School club shone, but only for a short time.[55] In 1915 it ran afoul of the Auckland Football Association for refusing to play in protest at the suspension of one of its players, and after this the club appears to have folded.[56] It was a challenging time for many sports clubs as players left to fight in the First World War. Despite being formed from a pacifist organisation, the Adult School club had many non-Quaker players who volunteered for active service, including club president and Grey Lynn local William Harrison.[57]

Harrison went on to join the Brotherhood Club, which was formed in 1910 from the members of the Auckland Brotherhood, a Christian men's organisation founded at a meeting in Newton in 1907 by men who sought to 'assist each other spiritually, intellectually, and socially'.[58] At the beginning of the 1915 season the Brotherhood Club secured a home ground at Richmond near the Adult School's ground.[59] To avoid confusion, the two grounds were referred to as Richmond No. 1 (Adult School) and Richmond No. 2 (Brotherhood).[60] Both were used for Auckland Football Association matches, and each weekend during the season teams would walk or catch the tram to Richmond to play, as spectators looked on.

The Brotherhood Club membership was also depleted during the First World War, and in 1916 it suspended play due to the large number of players on active service or about to leave.[61] In June 1918 the club's war record was reported in the *Observer*: 'Forty-five club players on active service. Of these seven have been killed, twenty-two wounded, four have returned to the Dominion, one has re-enlisted and is back again in France, one is on the high seas, and is due back at an early date.'[62]

The club recovered and continued to play, and in 1920 it again secured a private ground, this time adjoining Westmere School (then known as Richmond West School).[63] However, by 1923 it was having trouble finding sufficient senior-grade players and the following year it was decided to change the name from Brotherhood to Newton, possibly to give it wider appeal.[64] The club continued until 1926, but appears to have folded after the resignation of Arch Hill resident and club secretary Edwin Hutson, who had served in the role since the club's establishment in 1910.[65]

Meanwhile, two new soccer clubs had emerged in the Grey Lynn area. The Richmond Association Football Club was formed in 1915 and played until 1917 before going into recess, probably because of the war, but re-emerged in 1919. In 1923 the Grey Lynn Wanderers Football Club was formed.[66]

The soccer clubs were not the only ones to make use of the fields of Westmere. By mid-1915 rugby league, a relative newcomer to the Auckland sporting scene, was being played on Wilson's paddock somewhere in the stretch of land between Warnock Street and Garnet Road.[67]

Rugby league's origins were in the north of England, where working-class rugby players lobbied to be financially compensated for having to take Saturdays off in order to play. In 1895, 22 northern clubs broke away from the English Rugby Football Union to form the Northern Union, which set about changing the rules of the game to make it more exciting and provide better support for its players.[68] In Auckland, local interest in rugby league was sparked after the first tour of England by the New Zealand rugby union team in 1905–06. Although this first All Blacks tour was highly successful, some of the players were unhappy with their meagre tour allowance of 3 shillings a day, especially given that the English and New Zealand rugby unions made large profits from the venture. It was especially galling for players who had to give up jobs in order to take part in the tour and returned to New Zealand broke and unemployed.[69]

But there was another way to run things, and this was illustrated by the 1907–08 rugby tour of Northern England and Australia, organised by Wellington postal employee Albert Baskerville. Known as the Professional All Blacks or the All Golds, the team members paid £50 each toward the cost of the tour and in return received a share of the profits. The team played under the rules adopted by the English Northern Rugby Football Union in the game that

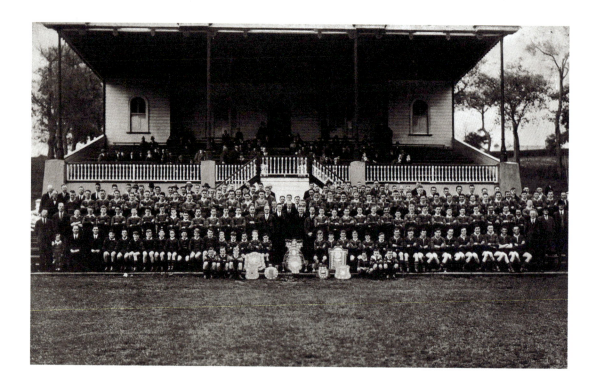

Richmond Rovers Rugby League Club players and officials at the Auckland Domain grandstand in 1935. That year nine New Zealand Rugby League representatives came from the club. AUCKLAND LIBRARIES HERITAGE COLLECTIONS, SDR-19351010-29-01

would become known as rugby league. It was the first international tour played under Northern Rugby Football Union rules, and it attracted considerable talent from local rugby union teams, including from a number of former All Blacks.[70]

When Baskerville's team left New Zealand its members included two former Newton Rugby Union players: Harold Rowe, an accountant who lived in Dean Street, and William Trevarthen, a surface layer from Sussex Street.[71] On their return, both men joined Auckland's first rugby league team in 1908. Both Rowe and Trevarthen represented New Zealand in the 1909 tour of Australia and later returned to England, where Trevarthen played for Huddersfield and Rowe for Leeds.[72]

Rugby league clubs began to make an appearance at this time: Newton Rangers and Ponsonby were among the first four registered in Auckland in 1909.[73] Early games were held at Epsom, but as the number of clubs expanded more grounds came into use.[74]

Rugby league had a particular appeal for working-class men, so it is not surprising that it was popular among the blue-collar workers of Grey Lynn. The Richmond Rovers Rugby League Club had its genesis in 1912 at two boot factories — Benjamin Davis's in Grey Lynn and Elliotts — where the staff became interested in playing and friendly games were arranged.[75] It was soon decided to form a club, and in 1914 the Richmond Rovers affiliated with another club to play in the third grade, and joined the Auckland Rugby League competition in its own right the following year.[76] During the early years, meetings of the Richmond Rovers were held at Benjamin Davis's workshop in Wilton Street.[77] Like the soccer and rugby union teams of the district, Richmond Rovers looked for open land for practices and matches, and in 1915 it arranged the lease of Wilson's paddock in Westmere; the rent was paid by Auckland Rugby League.[78]

The club made good use of the ground for practices and also hosted games between the various rugby league teams.[79] The father of young team member Jack Redwood allowed the team to use his stables in Peel Street, which were converted for use as a training shed. Jack Redwood would later take a leading role in the administration of the sport, serving as president and chairman of New Zealand Rugby League.[80]

The private sports grounds of the area had served several local teams well, but it couldn't last. With residential development advancing through the district it was only a matter of time before streets of shiny new houses encroached on the privately owned fields where sport was played.

The parks and sports grounds that we know as Grey Lynn Park and Coxs Bay Reserve had their roots in the early years of the twentieth century. The Grey Lynn Borough Council was constituted a domain board to manage the Grey Lynn Domain, which would later be known as Coxs Bay Reserve, an area of 22 acres (9 hectares) set aside in the early twentieth century.[81] The board dutifully met for the first time in early March 1904, and at this and the monthly meetings that followed over the next few years, appears to have achieved almost nothing.[82]

Grey Lynn Domain, as it had been rather grandly named, consisted mainly of tidal flats through which the creek oozed, and was quite unsuitable for recreational purposes. The noise of nearby Cashmore's Mill and the heady stench of the adjacent Hellaby meatworks and Donald's boiling-down works, along with several drains that disgorged fetid matter into the creek, did nothing to improve its appeal.

The first improvements to the area were made in 1907 when Cashmore Brothers, with the consent of the Grey Lynn Domain Board, built a bridge from the mill to the foot of Regina Street (then known as Queen Street). The bridge provided easy access between the mill and Grey Lynn, while the creek provided an area in which to dispose of the tons of sawdust generated at the mill.[83] It would be many years before the area was developed into a recreation ground for the public.

Grey Lynn soon gained another reserve, one more immediately suitable for

**Sport and recreation | 243**

recreational purposes. Although the 1880s subdivision plan for the Surrey Hills area had included no reserves for recreation, this had not stopped it from being approved by the borough council, and now the Grey Lynn Borough Council began negotiations to buy 27 acres (11 hectares) of land at the bottom of the gully, where streams and swamps were a deterrent to building, with a view to turning it into a park. However they baulked at the £4000 price tag, and by 1901 the cost had risen to £6000.[84]

There was no progress until 1907, when negotiations recommenced.[85] The council sought a court judgment to clarify which party — the council or vendors — was responsible for the cost of roading in the unsold parts of the estate, and the legal status of existing roads. This prompted a fresh round of negotiations between the Bank of New Zealand, which now owned the remaining unsold parts of the estate, and Grey Lynn Borough Council.[86]

Eventually the two parties came to an agreement. The gully land would be given to the council for a park, and in return the council would delete the paper roads from the park and build the remaining unformed roads in other parts of the Surrey Hills Estate. With the roads in place and water and drainage service laid on, the bank would be better able to find buyers for any remaining sections. As part of the agreement, the bank provided the council with a low-interest loan to fund necessary works in the borough, including around £18,500 for the roading works.[87]

In 1909 the gully land was vested in the Grey Lynn Borough Council by the Grey Lynn Domain Vesting Act, along with the area that would later become the Coxs Bay Reserve. This meant that there was no longer a need for a domain board as the Grey Lynn Borough Council could manage the land itself in accordance with the Act.[88] The Surrey Hills gully was in an untamed state and the council quickly got to work cutting gorse and mānuka, trimming willows and erecting fences and gates.[89] Parts of the reserve could now be let for grazing horses.[90]

Further improvements came soon after Grey Lynn Borough amalgamated with the city. In 1915 a 5-acre section of the park was levelled to form a sports ground.[91] This was a boon for the local schools, which were struggling with high roll numbers and insufficient space — both Richmond Road and Newton West schools had well over 700 children in daily attendance, with Grey Lynn School not far behind.[92]

Adults were also keen to use the newly levelled sports field. Outdoor sports were becoming increasingly popular with both players and spectators, and municipal grounds were in high demand.[93] In 1921 the *New Zealand Herald* decried the lack of playing fields for the thousands of rugby union and rugby league players who turned out each week through the winter.[94]

The main fields were the Domain and Victoria Park and these, along with

**ABOVE:** An aerial view of Coxs Creek in 1953. The courts of the West End Lawn Tennis Club can be seen at bottom left. Note the row of boats lined up to the left of the Regina Street bridge. AUCKLAND LIBRARIES HERITAGE COLLECTIONS, 7A15698

**BELOW:** Rutted ground at the northern end of Grey Lynn Park, 1963. AUCKLAND LIBRARIES HERITAGE COLLECTIONS, 580-04003

244 | **The Near West**

smaller municipal grounds and privately owned fields, made up the sum total of the city's winter sports grounds. In Grey Lynn and Westmere there were three grounds in use for rugby league: a field at Grey Lynn Park and the two private grounds in Westmere.[95]

Each year the city council allocated municipal fields to the various sporting bodies. The field at Grey Lynn Park was allocated to rugby league in 1923, but the following year the land that Auckland Rugby Union used at Richmond was sold and rugby league and rugby union were forced to share a single field.[96] More grounds were needed, and two more were formed at the park.[97] Grey Lynn Park became the main sports field in Grey Lynn.

A panoramic view of the Auckland Zoo, looking west, in 1925. The elephant house, which still stands on Old Mill Road, can be seen at right. AUCKLAND LIBRARIES HERITAGE COLLECTIONS, 1-W0656-PAN

Nearby reserve land was extensively developed for recreational purposes during the 1920s. At this time Western Springs Reserve was an unkempt expanse of wetland and weeds interspersed with scoria outcrops and patches of native vegetation. The large spring-fed pond still had a role as a water reservoir and was the back-up supply for the city after dams in the Waitākere Ranges became the main supply in the early twentieth century. On the northwest corner of the reserve, where Motions Creek meandered through on its way to the sea, a municipal zoo would be built.

The genesis of the zoo was in the private collection established in the early twentieth century by John Boyd at Aramoho, Whanganui, which he transported to Royal Oak in 1911. Boyd's animals had been purchased on trips to Australia, England and Europe.[98] His zoo was popular with the public, although some locals objected to its sounds and smells. Boyd fought a long-running battle with the Onehunga Borough Council over this, but his success in the borough's

mayoral election of 1917 showed that he had supporters as well as detractors.

Boyd's troubles with the local governing body weren't over, however, and in 1918 he tried unsuccessfully to sell his menagerie to the Auckland City Council.[99] At that time municipal authorities around the country were adding zoological gardens to their increasing lists of responsibilities. Wellington Zoo, which opened in 1906, was the first in New Zealand; Auckland was about to get the second.

In 1921 Boyd was in his early seventies. His battle with Onehunga Borough Council had not abated and he again offered his collection to the city council. When this offer was rejected he sold some of the animals to Wellington Zoo and packed the remaining lions, leopards, tigers, baboons and other animals into trucks to form a travelling zoo, which toured various North Island towns. Some of the animals could perform circus tricks, including the lions, which were taught to jump through a ring of fire. When the menagerie returned to Royal Oak in April 1922 the battle with the Onehunga Borough Council resumed.[100]

In June 1922 Boyd made another overture to the Auckland City Council. There was now growing support for his offer, and a deputation of influential citizens, including former Member of Parliament for Grey Lynn George Fowlds and Reverend Jasper Calder, the unconventional Auckland city missioner who had earlier served as vicar of Grey Lynn's St Columba Church, urged the council to establish a municipal zoo. Lions, bears, wolves and two dogs that had survived Sir Ernest Shackleton's failed trans-Antarctic expedition formed the nucleus of the collection.[101] The idea appealed to Mayor James Gunson, and with the support of Grey Lynn local and Auckland city councillor James Warnock, who was chair of the Parks Committee, a report was prepared for council to consider.[102]

The newspapers ran hot with letters on the subject, some in favour of the

Sport and recreation | 247

A family visiting the Auckland Zoo, c. 1920s. The elephant house can be seen at left and Jagger and Parker's tannery with its high chimneys is on the hill behind. AUCKLAND LIBRARIES HERITAGE COLLECTIONS, TAB-P-0425

zoo and others against. Many opponents were concerned about the cost to ratepayers. When Boyd stated that the animals would be destroyed if he could not sell them, animal lovers were moved. In the end the decision was left in the hands of ratepayers, who were asked to vote on the council raising a £10,000 loan to finance the purchase of the animals and development of the zoo on the council-owned reserve at Western Springs.[103]

The location was chosen on the advice of the scientific assistant at Auckland Museum, Louis Griffin, who had worked at Pretoria Zoo in South Africa and received his training at London Zoo and the Royal College of Surgeons.[104] Griffin found the Western Springs site 'excellent in every way, being fairly well sheltered and warm with rich volcanic soil'.[105] It had an abundant water supply and was within easy reach of the city.[106] The animals would thrive and provide a popular excursion for Aucklanders and visitors to the city. Griffin and veterinarian Dr William Ring, a New Zealander who had received his training in veterinary science at the University of Pennsylvania, inspected the animals.[107] Now all that was needed was the go-ahead from ratepayers. In July the votes were cast: 70 per cent favoured the zoo.[108]

Work got under way quickly on cages, paths and enclosures, and in a matter of months the animals were installed. Members of the public were invited to walk through the high stone gateway on Old Mill Road that formed the original entrance, in December 1922.[109] The zoo proved immensely popular and in its first full year of operation almost 190,000 people visited. In 1923 the tramline along Surrey Crescent was extended down Old Mill Road to stop at the zoo gate, easing the trip to the zoo for many visitors.[110]

Improvements at the zoo progressed rapidly and its initial spartan appearance was softened with plantings. New species came thick and fast after Mayor Gunson appealed to Auckland businessmen to seek out animals while on overseas trips. There were many willing helpers, and zoos and animal dealers in London and Australia sent a variety of species, including llamas, black panthers, polar bears, emus, wombats and kangaroos. Others came from local sources, including three sea lions from the Marine Department.

In 1923 one of the bigger attractions, Jamuna the elephant, arrived from Calcutta, a gift from Auckland businessman John Court.[111] The population was boosted significantly when Griffin, now the zoo's curator, travelled to Africa, and in April 1925 a veritable ark of hundreds of African animals arrived in Auckland after a storm-battered sea voyage lasting several weeks. The weary animals included a giraffe, three zebras, many antelopes, marmosets, porcupines and hundreds of birds.[112]

There was the odd unplanned departure. In 1924 a sea lion made a bid for freedom and was spotted heading for deep water by a small boy who attracted the attention of Frank Mullins, one of a group of returned soldiers who were busy working on the sea wall at the end of Garnet Road. Mullins waded in and caught hold of the sea lion by the tail. There was a terrific tussle as the enraged animal protested loudly and tried to bite his captor on the leg, but with the help of another man Mullins dragged the sea lion to shore, where it was loaded onto a dray and returned to the zoo.[113]

The following year a leopard, newly arrived from India, made her escape. Despite the truant animal being a sizeable predator with a 'fierce, snappy temper', Auckland City Council reassured locals that 'little is to be feared from the leopard. Her species . . . are nocturnal animals and do not attack human beings except when driven at bay.'[114] This did little to calm the nerves of anxious parents and children living nearby.[115] Bill Grieve, who lived in Westmere at the time, recalled many people out on the reef looking for the leopard, probably with little idea of what they would do if they encountered her.[116]

Several weeks after her escape, the body of the unfortunate animal was

**Sport and recreation | 249**

Children riding Jamuna the elephant in 1956.
AUCKLAND LIBRARIES HERITAGE COLLECTIONS, 1207-783

found floating in the harbour at St Heliers. Evidently she had ventured to Jagger and Parker's tannery, and paw prints at the site revealed that she had fallen into a vat of tanning liquid, climbed out and then fallen into a second vat. From there she had found her way to the water, possibly at nearby Motions Creek. Weakened from the chemical exposure at the tannery, she had either fallen into the creek and drowned or had become stuck in the mud at low tide, where she would have drowned on the high tide. It was a sad ending.[117]

Beside the zoo on Western Springs Reserve there was plenty of land available for sporting and recreational purposes. As early as 1926 part of the extensive reserve was used as a rugby field and cricket pitch, and it was soon home to a regional facility and more sports fields that catered to a wider variety of disciplines.[118]

Although Auckland was yet to feel the full force of the looming economic depression, unemployment was already on the rise in 1927, and a Citizens' Unemployment Committee was formed to raise funds for local projects to employ those in need.[119] The committee chair, Mayor George Baildon, a keen

250 | The Near West

sportsman and Grey Lynn local, was in a good position to know what work could easily be undertaken.[120] Plans were drawn up for a cinder running track, a banked cycle track and playing fields for football and cricket at Western Springs Reserve.[121] Work began in late 1927, and early the following year 50 men, many of them unused to physical work, were busy with picks and shovels carving out the hollow that would form the stadium for field sports and athletics competitions.[122]

There was also demand for the stadium to be used for motor racing, something that had been gaining in popularity. Soon after the first motorcycles arrived in New Zealand, motorcycle enthusiasts began pitting their machines and riding skills against each other in races held on grass tracks. Many of these events were held on horse-racing tracks, but concerns about damage to the grass meant that by the late 1920s it had become increasingly difficult to secure a grass track for motorcycle racing.[123]

Motor cycles and cars also competed in road races, and from 1921 the annual Muriwai Beach races were popular with both competitors and spectators.[124] Attention turned to the development of dirt tracks, which had been used for motorcycle racing in America since 1909.[125] Dirt tracks offered a different style of event to the reliability trials, hill climbs and beach races that were part of the car and motorcycle enthusiasts' calendars.[126]

Dirt tracks were developed in New Zealand from the late 1920s. In Māngere, motor-racing enthusiast George Henning drained Pūkaki Lagoon and formed Auckland's first dirt track in the natural amphitheatre. Henning's Speedway opened in March 1929 before a huge crowd of 9000 with a programme of car and motorcycle racing and a flyover by planes from the nearby Auckland Aero Club.[127] This private speedway was later joined by the publicly owned venue at Western Springs.

While the stadium was under construction at Western Springs, motor sport enthusiasts Albert (AJ) Roycroft, John Kay and Arthur Jacob negotiated an agreement to lease it each Saturday during the racing season for motorcycle speedway events. Kay and Roycroft travelled to Australia to see how the sport operated there and invited some of the top Australian riders to compete in New Zealand.[128] They subsequently formed Auckland Speedways Limited to promote motor sport and run speedway events at the Western Springs Stadium.[129]

On 30 September 1929 the stadium was opened before a crowd of 15,000, who were treated to a display of daring motorcycle riding. Cinders flew as riders hurtled round the track at speeds that the *New Zealand Herald* reporter noted 'would have given a Queen Street traffic inspector apoplexy'.[130] Speedway was here to stay at Western Springs.

In March 1934 another type of race was held at Western Springs Stadium

**Sport and recreation | 251**

A plan of Western Springs improvements, 1929. AUCKLAND COUNCIL ARCHIVES, ACC 005 0039 4

as part of the St Patrick's Day amateur sports competition organised by the Auckland Amateur Athletic and Cycle Club. The four-legged competitors lined up with their ears back, quivering with excitement. Suddenly, a mechanical hare on a wire set off around the track. The greyhounds chased after it as the crowd cheered them on.[131]

✕

The development of the Western Springs Stadium and adjoining fields added considerably to the sports facilities in the area, but other reserve areas still awaited improvement.

The land that would later become the Coxs Bay Reserve had been proclaimed a recreation domain soon after the turn of the twentieth century. In 1913 Grey Lynn Borough Council gained an extension to its reserve at Coxs Bay under the Reserves and Other Lands Disposal and Public Bodies Empowering Act 1913. This curiously named legislation was known as a 'washing-up' Act, whereby various small legal matters were dealt with in one piece of legislation. The Act vested the waters of Coxs Bay, a 31-acre (12.5-hectare) area north of West End Road (then known as Coxs Bridge Road) that extended to a line drawn northeast from Hellaby's Point to meet the shoreline below Marine Parade.[132]

The council envisaged developing the area to provide swimming baths, a boat harbour and a hauling-out area for repairing and repainting vessels, while the area south of West End Road could be reclaimed to provide sports fields. This idyllic vision of recreational amenities would have

Sport and recreation | 253

to wait, however, and would ultimately be only partly realised — the baths never eventuated.

In the mid-nineteenth century, swimming was regarded as an undignified activity popular only with health fanatics, but by the turn of the century it was gaining acceptance as an invigorating and healthy form of exercise.[133] It was now considered beneficial for the body, and learning to swim helped to reduce incidences of drowning, something so common in the nineteenth century that it was referred to as 'the New Zealand death'.[134]

The nearest public swimming baths were at Shelly Beach, just off Point Erin where the approach to the Auckland Harbour Bridge is today. In the murky saltwater of the baths, the children of Richmond Road School were taught to swim in the 1910s and 1920s by famed swimming instructor Duncan Anderson (known as Professor Anderson) under an arrangement with the Ponsonby Swimming Club.[135]

There were other places to swim that were closer to home. Coxs Bay had become a popular spot in the 1920s, and adults and children alike made use of the sheltered waters. Since the diversion of local drainage to Ōkahu Bay in 1914 and the departure of several polluting industries, including Hellaby's meatworks in 1911 and Cashmore's timber mill in 1920, the creek and the bay were now much cleaner than before. In the mid-1920s Auckland City Council erected dressing rooms for swimmers, and sometimes hundreds of people could be found swimming there on summer evenings when the tide was right.[136]

In 1928 the *Auckland Star* reported (in language that would never be considered today) that swimming at dusk and after dark was not uncommon and particularly appealed to those with ample figures: 'Fat folk don't always care to parade themselves in bathing costume before their slimmer neighbours, and to such night affords a kindly mantle, enveloping a whole world of obesity.'[137]

The bay was also used as a venue for competitive swimming. In February and March 1924 spectators crowded the shores to watch the Richmond Amateur Swimming Club gala, which featured diving and races of 50 and 100 yards, with events for boys, men and women.[138] The Richmond club, one of two Auckland swimming clubs founded during the 1923–24 season, and one of six that held galas, appears to have lasted only one season, possibly because the following year was disrupted by a polio outbreak.[139]

By the late 1920s the area to the south of the West End Road bridge was used as a winter haul-out for around 40 boats belonging to members of the Richmond Cruising Club. Many coastal areas closer to the city that had been used for this purpose were now occupied by commercial enterprises, so on sunny winter weekends Coxs Creek became a hive of activity as boat owners repaired, sanded and painted their boats in readiness for summer.[140]

On the eastern edge of the bay the newly formed Hawke Sea Scouts emerged

**254** | **The Near West**

Midget cars on the Western Springs track in 1940. ALEXANDER TURNBULL LIBRARY, ARCHIVE PAPER COPY NZ HER

to teach youngsters seafaring skills, and erected a boatshed in 1928 to serve as its headquarters.[141] The shed was extensively damaged by fire in the early 1950s and the present structure, known as The Ship, was erected in its place. Hauraki Kayak Club later built a clubhouse next door.

In 1926 West End Road was widened and a concrete bridge replaced the single-lane timber structure that had spanned the creek from the nineteenth century, providing a better connection between Westmere and Herne Bay. However, the area to the south of the bridge remained unimproved.[142]

In 1930 a large deputation of frustrated local residents, headed by Dr Emma Buckley Turkington of Rawene Avenue, made a submission to the Auckland City Council seeking action to improve the reserve. It was, the residents said,

> a breeding place for mosquitos and flies, a tip for dead animals and putrefying rubbish, which washed up and down with the tides, a place of fogs and odours that were a menace to health . . . a fever spot set in picturesque surroundings the causeway harbouring sun bathers that were a menace to passing motorists . . . and a menace to morality.[143]

The deputation presented a 1000-signature petition organised by Tutanekai Street resident Alice Sexton, of the Grey Lynn Women's Political Organisation.[144]

Whether in response to this or not, in the early 1930s the council considered reclaiming the tidal mudflats that covered much of the reserve, and in 1931 drew up a plan that featured an extensive reclamation with five rugby fields —

**Sport and recreation** | 255

two for soccer and three for hockey — along with a croquet lawn, two bowling greens, two basketball courts, 11 tennis courts and two children's playgrounds. To the north of West End Road, a stone seawall stretching from the western extremity of the bay would form a sheltered boat harbour and swimming baths reserve.[145] It was a grand scheme, but in the end the only part to eventuate that decade was the development of the tennis courts at the corner of Fife Street and West End Road.

In February 1932, after much filling and levelling — work carried out by the unemployed — the first two courts were opened, and later that year two more courts and a pavilion had been built. The facilities were leased by local residents who founded the West End Lawn Tennis Club.[146] Tennis was popular, and two years later, at the other end of the district, the Surrey Tennis Club was established on the site of the former Grey Lynn Bowling Club after the bowling club moved west along Surrey Crescent.[147]

Other parks of the district saw some improvement during the 1930s, thanks to government subsidies for unemployment relief projects. At Western Springs the area between the lake and the zoo was developed into a municipal campground with a swimming pool. Equipped with basic facilities, it was one of many such campgrounds established in New Zealand from the late 1920s.[148]

The campground later became a US forces camp during the Second World War as the theatre of war moved ever nearer through the Pacific. Part of what was popularly known as the 'friendly invasion', these US servicemen, on leave from the war effort, provided a local defence presence while New Zealand's military force was overseas, and were housed at camps established on open spaces across Auckland. During their stay, locals were treated to an exhibition match of American football at Western Springs Stadium, played between teams from two army regiments.[149]

After the American servicemen had departed, the facility was converted into a transit camp and used as temporary housing for families as the post-war materials shortages exacerbated the housing shortage that had gripped the nation since before the war.

There were more improvements in Grey Lynn Park in the late 1920s and early 1930s. In 1927 a new dressing shed equipped with three showers and room for 50 players was built in the park. Soon afterwards the gully near Williamson Avenue was filled in to form a children's playground where equipment donated by businessman John Court was installed in 1933.[150]

The development of all these municipal sports facilities provided more opportunities for sport to be played locally, and new teams emerged in response. By the 1930s the Auckland United Friendly Society Cricket Association was organising games between teams formed at the various Friendly Societies in the city and suburbs, including the Grey Lynn Druids

**256 | The Near West**

and the Westmere Independent Order of Oddfellows.[151] This added to other occasional sporting events, including athletics and tugs-of-war, held between Auckland's various Friendly Societies.

The societies were particularly strong in working-class neighbourhoods like Grey Lynn and Westmere in the era before the passing of the 1938 Social Security Act, as they provided financial benefits to members in times of hardship.[152] Friendly Societies offered men yet another avenue to participate in organised sport and it seemed that wherever men gathered, sports teams would materialise.

Women had limited opportunities to play sport. Some clubs, including the West End and Surrey tennis clubs and the short-lived Richmond Swimming Club, welcomed women. Croquet was played exclusively by women at Grey Lynn Croquet Club, which had been established in 1910 alongside the Grey Lynn Bowling Club. Golf was also popular but required expensive equipment and green fees that would have put it out of reach for most women of the working-class suburbs west of the city, which included Arch Hill, Grey Lynn and Westmere. There were no golf courses in the area until the opening of the municipal Chamberlain Park golf course, to the south of Western Springs, in mid-1939.[153]

Many local children were introduced to sport at primary school. Before 1902, when physical drill for boys and girls became part of the curriculum, the amount of physical activity enjoyed by school pupils varied. Although some team sports existed for boys, there were none for girls.[154] Energetic sports had been considered not only unfeminine but also positively harmful for the female sex in the nineteenth century, and medical men warned of the harm that might be caused to the delicate female reproductive system by physical exertion and mental stress.[155]

But by the early twentieth century, new ideas about the benefits of sport for females were emerging. Spurred on by a moral panic over New Zealand's declining birth rate, and couched in the familiar notion that the most important role a woman could have in society was motherhood, girls and women were now encouraged to be fit and healthy so that they might bring forth a robust new generation of children. Meanwhile, as medical men debated what was good for females, girls and women got on with playing sport.[156]

In 1909 Auckland Girls' Grammar appointed Sally Heap as drill mistress, one of the few teachers in New Zealand secondary schools employed to teach physical education, many years before it became a core subject for third and fourth formers in 1945. Heap made the best use of the facilities at her disposal

**ABOVE:** Children enjoying a summer dip at Coxs Creek, December 1928.
ALEXANDER TURNBULL LIBRARY

**BELOW:** Children jumping off the Coxs Creek bridge on a sunny afternoon in 1939.
AUCKLAND LIBRARIES HERITAGE COLLECTIONS, AS-19390203-05-10

**RIGHT:** A view of the canvas town that grew each summer at the Auckland City Council municipal motor camp at Western Springs, looking south from the zoo with Mount Albert in the distance at right.
MUSEUM OF TRANSPORT AND TECHNOLOGY, 14-0190

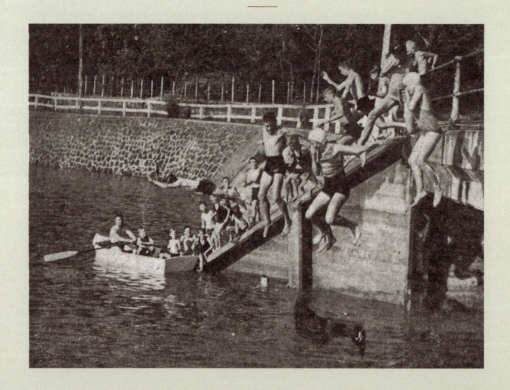

**ABOVE:** Holidaymakers enjoying themselves at the Auckland City Council's municipal motor camp at Western Springs, 1939. AUCKLAND LIBRARIES HERITAGE COLLECTIONS, AWNS-19390118-43-02

**BELOW:** A view of West End Road looking northeast in 1959. 'The Ship', the new Hawke Sea Scouts clubhouse, is on the eastern edge of Coxs Bay at left. AUCKLAND LIBRARIES HERITAGE COLLECTIONS, 580-03999;

Perspective View of
CHILDRENS PLAYGROUND
GREY LYNN PARK

T.P. 21. B.H.
[ACC 005/34]

at the school, including a tennis court that was so confined that its baseline was right up against a wall, which hampered the ability of players to hit any balls that reached that end of the court. It was a common problem: girls' secondary schools were generally on much smaller sites than those attended by their brothers.[157]

In 1911 Auckland Girls' Grammar also introduced the gym tunic, a durable box-pleated serge dress that allowed girls more freedom of movement for sport and other activities.[158] But until the school leaving age was raised to 15 in 1944, few girls went on to secondary school, particularly in working-class neighbourhoods, so many of the girls of Arch Hill, Grey Lynn and Westmere missed out on the opportunities for physical education offered by Heap.[159] The influence of the Auckland Girls' Grammar School drill mistress went far beyond her school, however. Heap also taught the female students at Auckland Teachers' Training College, inspiring a new generation of teachers, and became an authority on physical exercise for girls.[160]

There were a number of barriers to women's participation in team sports. Men were reluctant to share sports grounds, and any women's team affiliated to a men's sports association was bound to be given the worst field in the most far-flung location. In addition, funding for uniforms and travel expenses was hard to come by for working-class women.[161]

A few local girls played team sports at school in the early 1900s. Netball, originally known as basketball due to the placement of a basket under the hoop to catch the ball (it was later replaced with the net that is familiar to today's players), was a new team sport considered suitable for girls and women — and it was less aggressive than hockey, which was also gaining in popularity. It was not yet played by men and boys, so females didn't have to compete with male players for access to courts.[162]

The game had its origins in late nineteenth-century America and was played in the 1890s at Wanganui Girls' College. In Auckland, the young ladies' Bible classes from Presbyterian churches in Remuera and Epsom played basketball in the early twentieth century, and the game was popularised by Herbert Milne, principal of the Auckland Teachers' Training College. The sport required a relatively small space and so could be accommodated at many schools.[163] As early as 1912, Newton West and Richmond Road schools entered teams in the public schools competition with matches played on the courts at Auckland Teachers' Training College in Wellesley Street.[164]

A growing number of adult women's teams also competed in the Auckland Basketball Association competition, including city and suburban teams as well as those formed at workplaces, schools and social organisations. In 1927 women of the district formed the Surrey Hills Basketball Club, and by 1940 a Westmere team was also playing. Their games were held at the courts

**ABOVE:** Children from local schools playing on the new Grey Lynn Park playground after its official opening in November 1932. The playground area was excavated by unemployed workers in 1929 and the equipment was donated by Auckland businessman John Court senior. ALEXANDER TURNBULL LIBRARY, ARCHIVE PAPER COPY NZ HER

**BELOW:** A perspective view of the children's playground in Grey Lynn Park, c. 1930. AUCKLAND COUNCIL ARCHIVES, ACC 005, RECORD ID 103540

**Sport and recreation** | **261**

in Windmill Road, Mount Eden.[165] There was also a Catholic Basketball Association competition in which a team from Grey Lynn competed from the 1930s.[166]

Hockey came to the fore for those girls and women who hankered after a faster field sport. In 1896 a women's hockey club had been established in Kaiapoi, north of Christchurch, and the sport was soon taken up by the women of Wellington and Christchurch, with a match held between the two cities in 1899.[167] In 1907 Auckland Girls' Grammar had a team, but there do not appear to have been any other local hockey teams for girls.[168]

Individual sports tended to be more welcoming of female participants. Girls and women competed at school and club athletics competitions, although distances were often shorter and events required less physical strength than those of their male counterparts. In 1933 adults and children arrived at Western Springs for the athletic and cycling carnival, organised by the Technical Old Boys Athletic Club and the Manukau Cycling Club to raise funds for the relief of distress in Grey Lynn.

Among the competitors that day was Doreen Lumley of Westmere School, who won both the schoolgirls' 75- and 100-yard events.[169] Lumley would go on to have great success as a runner (see pages 268–69). There was no local athletics club until the mid-1940s when the Western Suburbs Amateur Athletics Club was formed, with its headquarters at Grey Lynn Park, but the Auckland Primary Schools Athletic Association annual athletics competition for schoolchildren in the Domain was attended by thousands.[170]

Some women fought hard to be allowed to compete in sports where no women's division existed. One such woman was Irish motorcyclist Fay Taylour, who was a major drawcard when she raced at the Western Springs cinder track in 1930.[171] Locals looked on with delight as she roared around Town Bend and along the straight to Pine Tree Bend 'with smoke and sparks belching from her exhaust'.[172] She raced Bill Herbert, one of the top local riders, beating him in two out of three races before returning a few nights later to claim victory in a race against the Auckland champion, Alf Mattson.[173]

Taylour was back in the 1950s, by which time she was racing in cars, which had taken over as the vehicle of choice at Western Springs Speedway. In the intervening years she had encountered obstacles, including being banned from various international race tracks because of her sex. She had been known to pretend to be a man in order to race.[174]

Fay Taylour in her motorcycling leathers in the 1920s. ALEXANDER TURNBULL LIBRARY, EP-0632-1/2-G

**ABOVE:** Local state schools compete at the annual Auckland public school sports competition at the Auckland Domain in **1901.** AUCKLAND LIBRARIES HERITAGE COLLECTIONS, NZG_19010406_0642_02

**BELOW:** Girls from Auckland Girls' Grammar School playing basketball (later known as netball) against Hamilton Girls' High School, 1930. By this stage sporting attire was much less cumbersome. AUCKLAND LIBRARIES HERITAGE COLLECTIONS, AWNS-19300827-48-01

**LEFT:** Catholic schools held their own annual school sports competitions, including this one on St Patrick's Day 1901 at the Auckland Domain. AUCKLAND LIBRARIES HERITAGE COLLECTIONS, NZG-19040326-0041-01

**BELOW:** Sports attire for girls and women was a considerable impediment for players, particularly those playing athletic games. The Auckland Girls' Grammar School hockey team is shown here in 1905. AUCKLAND LIBRARIES HERITAGE COLLECTIONS, NZG-19050819-0036-03

In 1950 Western Springs Stadium was one of several Auckland sports venues to host international athletes competing in the 1950 British Empire Games (later renamed the Commonwealth Games). The Auckland Games were the fourth to be held since the first British Empire Games in 1930, and the first since 1938, after war interrupted the planned 1942 and 1946 games. It was the biggest international sporting event held in New Zealand at the time, and an exciting time for locals.[175]

A total of 495 men and 95 women competed at the Auckland Games. Events were held at Eden Park (athletics and opening ceremony), the open-air Olympic Pool in Newmarket (swimming, diving and water polo), the town hall (boxing, wrestling and weightlifting), the drill hall in Rutland Street (fencing), Carlton Bowling Club green in Epsom (lawn bowls), Lake Karāpiro (rowing) and Western Springs (track cycling and closing ceremony).[176]

In preparation for the games, the Western Springs Stadium track was steam-cleaned and lights were installed for the night cycling events and closing ceremony.[177] A crowd of 25,000 watched the cycling heats on 7 February, and large numbers of spectators were present on the 9th and 11th when the remaining events were held, ending with an exciting photo-finish in the 10-mile cycling race in which New Zealand's Les Lock was beaten by Australia's Bill Heseltine in an Empire Games record time.[178]

The races were followed by the pageantry of the closing ceremony and speeches from Prime Minister Sidney Holland, who noted that the games had 'in every respect exceeded all that had been hoped for', and the chair of the Empire Games Federation, Arthur Porritt, who was well satisfied: 'I don't think we will ever have a more sporting public than here in Auckland.'[179] The crowd sang 'Auld Lang Syne' and 'Now Is the Hour' and the 1950 British Empire Games were over.[180]

The Empire Games were a sporting highlight in a country recovering from the aftermath of the Second World War. The war had disrupted many local teams as players joined the war effort, but in the following two decades participation in sport grew, particularly in urban areas.[181] In Grey Lynn and Westmere the well-established Grey Lynn Bowling Club continued to flourish, as did the West End Tennis Club, the Richmond Rovers Rugby League Club and the Western Suburbs Amateur Athletics Club, among others. Some older clubs went into abeyance or merged with others.

There was a demographic shift in the post-war era as the country struggled with labour shortages in the cities. Internal migration and immigration brought increasing numbers of rural Māori and immigrants from the Pacific Islands to the city. Many made their homes in Arch Hill and Grey Lynn and joined local and workplace sports teams, or formed their own from church groups. Grey Lynn Park became the venue for the annual Samoan summer

Cyclists competing in the 1950 Empire Games at Western Springs Stadium. AUCKLAND LIBRARIES HERITAGE COLLECTIONS, 1370-0597-01

sports festival, where a variety of events were held, including kilikiti, the Pacific Island variant of cricket played with a long three-sided bat.[182]

By the 1970s an increasing number of the Richmond Rovers players hailed from the Pacific, or were the children of Pasifika migrants, and the club became a focal point for Pacific Islanders. The later inclusion of teams for women and girls in this and other local sports clubs further developed the family and community feel of the club.

For those who preferred to play rugby union, the nearby Ponsonby Rugby Club was welcoming. A fledgling Samoan rugby union team moved to this club in the late 1960s after their original club, Parnell, folded. The team had played rugby in Sāmoa, but there were differences to adapt to, including playing in boots instead of bare feet.[183]

Television began to beam men's major sporting events into New Zealanders' living rooms. Netball was gaining in popularity, and the success of the national team led to their exploits on the international court being televised from the mid-1970s, but men's sport received far more coverage than women's.[184]

Sport and recreation | 267

# Local running stars

Doreen and Bernice Lumley, in matching tracksuits, arrive at Carlaw Park in March 1939 after catching the tram to Parnell to compete against Sydney Empire Games champion Decima Norman (who arrived in a Daimler). The Lumley twins were very close, so when Doreen was selected to compete in the Sydney Empire Games in 1938 her parents were worried about how she would perform without Bernice present. The £70 they had saved for a new verandah for their house was used instead to send Bernice to Sydney to support Doreen. NORMAN HARRIS, *LAP OF HONOUR: THE GREAT MOMENTS OF NEW ZEALAND ATHLETICS*, P.67

In August 1921 William and Annie Lumley welcomed their first children, twin daughters whom they named Bernice and Doreen. The girls attended Westmere School, where they competed in the annual primary schools sports competition and set records for running. They went on to attend Auckland Girls' Grammar School, where their success continued in athletics as well as tennis, basketball (later known as netball) and swimming. But their talents didn't just revolve around sport — they were also skilled artists and musicians, and were known for their cheerful sense of fun.[185]

After leaving school, both girls were employed at city offices but continued their sporting activities. When Doreen was 15 she came second in the national 100-yards championship and competed in the winning 4 x 100 relay team.[186]

In 1938 both girls travelled to Sydney, where Doreen represented New Zealand at the British Empire Games (now known as the Commonwealth Games) with her sister cheering loudly from the sidelines. She came second to Australian Decima Norman in her heat of the 100-yards before being eliminated in the semi-final. Unfortunately, Doreen ran out of her lane in her heat of the 220-yards and was disqualified.[187]

The following year Norman, who had won five medals at the Empire Games, including gold in the 100-yards, toured New Zealand, competing against local athletes. In preparation Doreen received coaching from the men's 100-yards record-holder Allan Elliot, who helped her run with a smoother style and improve her starts. On 11 March at the Auckland Championships, Decima Norman and Doreen Lumley met again on the track. Carlaw Park was a fairly rough ground at this time with a slight upward slope — a challenging track for competitors. To the great surprise of Norman and the crowd, Doreen Lumley beat Norman in the 100-yards race,

equalling the world record time. Bernice came a respectable fourth.[188]

Two weeks later at the National Athletics Championships, Norman beat Doreen in the 100-yards race, but Doreen won the 75-yards and came third in the 220-yards. Soon afterwards both Doreen and Bernice played in the Auckland representative basketball team.[189]

Doreen became something of a local celebrity. She was a guest of honour at the Labour Party's monster charity ball in March 1939 — her presence was advertised in the press in larger type than that for Prime Minister Michael Joseph Savage.[190] She was also selected as the Grey Lynn Returned Services Social and Cricket Club's queen in the Queen Carnival that raised money for ex-servicemen in need. She beat the two other queens and was crowned at an elaborate faux regal ceremony in September 1939, having been a central part of the community effort that raised over £200.[191]

Just three weeks later, the unthinkable happened: Doreen and Bernice were passengers in a car that collided with a truck. Both girls were rushed to hospital. Doreen died soon after arrival and Bernice died a few hours later.[192]

Locals and the wider sports community were devastated by the tragic loss of these two popular young women at the age of just 17. Over a thousand people attended their funeral service, held outside their home at 43 Livingstone Street. The children of Westmere School formed a guard of honour as the funeral cortège of over 130 cars moved along Richmond Road.[193] Doreen and Bernice are buried at Waikumete Cemetery, where their grave is marked with a headstone erected by the Auckland Amateur Athletic and Cycling Club. Each year, the Lumley Sisters Memorial Shield is awarded to the team scoring the most points in the women's competition at the National Amateur Athletics Championship.[194]

**Sport and recreation | 269**

Western Springs Reserve was developed further in the 1960s when an area on the Great North Road frontage was leased for the Museum of Transport and Technology (MOTAT), established by a group of collectors and museum and technology societies. MOTAT opened in 1964, and in 1967 trams that had disappeared from Auckland's streets just over a decade earlier were running on tracks there.[195]

The zoo was expanded in the 1970s and took in an adjoining area of Western Springs Park to increase its size by a third. Redevelopment plans were drawn up to replace cages with more natural-looking habitats in which the animals would be separated from the public using pits and moats rather than large fences. The entrance gate on Old Mill Road was relocated to Motions Road.[196]

Other sports grounds were developed when the tidal mudflats to the south of West End Road were finally reclaimed, a task that began in the 1960s. In 1973 sport could at last be played on part of the area. Further reclamation and improvement works continued, and in 1983 the completed park, with its sports pavilion, children's playground, extensive sports fields and native plantings was ready to be enjoyed. An urban walkway beside the creek linked the park with Richmond Road and was later extended to a greenway that connected with Grey Lynn Park.[197] Out beyond West End Road the clubrooms of the Hawke Sea Scouts and the Hauraki Kayak Group looked out across the bay.

On the edge of Westmere the sports ground known as Seddon Fields was developed in the late 1980s from a rough field and a rubbish dump. It's now home to the Western Springs Association Football Club. WSAFC, which formed in 1989, is one of a number of local clubs that traces its lineage back through the decades as smaller clubs merged. Among its forebears was the Comrades Club, which started life in 1923 as a soccer club based at Victoria Park. By the 1950s most of the club's players hailed from Grey Lynn and Westmere and the club had merged with Grey Lynn United, which had formed in the mid-1930s.

The Grey Lynn United clubhouse in Great North Road opposite Western Springs was a casualty of the motorway that advanced through the site in the 1980s. In 1986, after another merger, the club became Grey Lynn Celtic, and it later amalgamated with the Point Chevalier Association Football Club to become Western Springs Association Football Club, nicknamed 'The Swans' after the residents of the nearby lake.[198]

Even as some sports facilities were developed, others were abandoned. The Western Suburbs Amateur Athletic Club was established in 1945 by Williamson Avenue resident Alf Taylor and Sam Darbyshire, who lived in Westmere. The club was based at Grey Lynn Park, where it initially made use of former Home Guard huts that remained in the park after the Second World War, before a two-storey concrete-block clubhouse was built in 1959.[199] After a number

**ABOVE:** The Niuean stage at the 2016 Pasifika Festival at Western Springs. AUCKLAND LIBRARIES HERITAGE COLLECTIONS, PASF-D-2016-095

**BELOW:** Cook Island dancers performing at the 2016 Pasifika Festival. AUCKLAND LIBRARIES HERITAGE COLLECTIONS, PASF-D-2016-113

270 | **The Near West**

# Fred Ah Kuoi

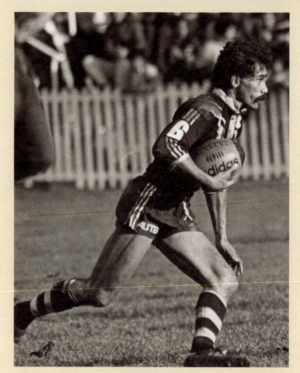

Fred Ah Kuoi was born in Sāmoa and came to New Zealand with his family at the age of two, settling in Grey Lynn. He began playing at the Richmond Rovers Rugby League Club when he was twelve and rose through the grades, eventually becoming captain of the premier side. In 1975, at the age of 18, he played his first international match with the New Zealand Maori Rugby League team, the start of a stellar international career during which he played for the Kiwis for 11 years as well as for North Sydney and Hull. After his retirement he returned to Grey Lynn and coached at the Richmond Rovers.[200]

PHOTOSPORT

# Les Mills

Les Mills, who spent much of his childhood and early married life living in Grey Lynn, was one of the stars of the Western Suburbs Amateur Athletics Club which he joined at the age of 11. He started out as a sprinter and hurdler but took up shotput and discus in his early teens, and in 1955 he became New Zealand champion in both field events. He and his wife Colleen lived at 43 Dickens Street, overlooking Grey Lynn Park. When he trained at the park he took a bucket of warm water with him to clean the mud off his shot after each throw. He competed at four Olympics and five Commonwealth Games, winning five Commonwealth Games medals. Colleen and their children Phillip and Donna were also talented athletes. They were members of the Western Suburbs Amateur Athletics Club and competed at the 1974 Commonwealth Games. Phillip also competed at the 1978 games.[201]

NEW ZEALAND HERALD

# Bryan Williams

Westmere resident Sir Bryan Williams, former All Black — famous for his nimble side-step — and coach, was born in Auckland in 1950 to immigrant parents who met and married in New Zealand. His mother, Eileen Bouchier, was born in Rarotonga to a Samoan mother and a father of Irish descent from Capetown. His father, Arthur Williams, was born in Sāmoa to an English father and Samoan mother.[202]

Williams grew up in Ponsonby and initially played rugby league for Ponsonby, but when his team was disbanded he began playing rugby union for the Ponsonby Rugby Club, where his older brothers played.[203] He attended Richmond Road Primary School and Mount Albert Grammar School, where he excelled in athletics and rugby. He also reconnected with rugby league, which he played for Marist on Saturday afternoons after playing rugby for Mount Albert Grammar in the mornings.[204] After leaving school he enrolled to study law at the University of Auckland University in 1968. That same year he toured Japan and Hong Kong with the Ponsonby Rugby Club and the following year he played rugby for Auckland.[205]

In 1970 Williams was selected to play for the All Blacks in their controversial tour of South Africa, one of four players who toured as 'honorary whites' — a status given them by the South African government to exempt them from apartheid laws. The South African government had required previous teams to be all white and so they were the first non-white All Blacks to tour the country.[206]

Anti-racism groups of the day opposed all sporting contact with South Africa. At university Williams would hear activists rallying students

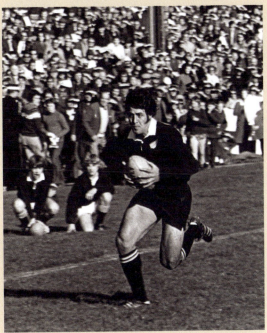

PHOTOSPORT

to protest against the tour in which he was soon to take part. Williams was opposed to apartheid but could see that having Pasifika and Māori players in the touring team was another way of challenging the apartheid system.[207] He went on to tour South Africa again in 1975 as part of the Ponsonby Rugby Club team that also included two Tongans and several Māori players and again the following year with the All Blacks as one of six non-white players.[208]

Williams married Lesley Ensor in 1973 and the couple settled in Westmere, where they were soon joined by fellow All Black Andy Haden and his wife Trecha, who lived with them for four years. This made the long absences of Lesley and Trecha's husbands on international tours easier.[209]

Williams' All Blacks career ended in the late 1970s after playing 113 matches, 34 of them tests.[210] He continued to play locally and had a long career as a coach for local and regional teams as well as Manu Sāmoa.[211]

**Sport and recreation** | 273

**ABOVE:** From small beginnings in 1984, the Grey Lynn Park Festival has grown into a huge annual event attended by up to 100,000 people.
COURTESY GREY LYNN PARK FESTIVAL

of successful years the club struggled with declining membership, possibly because the Pasifika families that now comprised a large proportion of the local population were more attracted to team than individual sports. The clubhouse stood forlornly at the edge of the park for many years until, condemned as a safety risk, it was finally demolished in 2020.

In recent years neighbourhood parks have been enhanced with plantings and paths, and in the 1990s an area of wasteland below the library and at the end of Ivanhoe Road was levelled and grassed. Links between neighbourhood parks provide routes through the district that traverse various green spaces. In recent years cycling has become more popular as a form of transport as well as a recreational activity, and the development of cycle paths has made the route safer and more enjoyable.

Parks are places where people gather, and this is particularly evident in the annual local festivals. For many years, beginning in 1993, the popular Pasifika Festival was held at Western Springs Park and the Grey Lynn Park Festival, which began in 1984, attracts many thousands of people. Western Springs Stadium is still in use for summer speedway and concerts.

Today the attractive parks and reserves of the area are busy places where dog walkers, runners and cyclists can be found enjoying the open spaces. Weekends and early evenings are busy with people playing sport, exercising or enjoying a little bit of nature in the city. These parks, hewn from mudflats, waterlogged wastelands and rubbish dumps, have come a long way to become the green spaces we value today.

Faith

**PREVIOUS PAGES:** The Epiphany Chapel stood on the corner of Arney (now known as Chapman) and Nixon streets from 1874 to 1894. From 1886 it served as the Sunday school for the new Epiphany Church on Karangahape Road, and in 1894 the chapel moved to a site adjoining the new church.
AUCKLAND LIBRARIES HERITAGE COLLECTIONS

On Sunday, 25 January 1874 a procession of the faithful, dressed in their Sunday best, wound its way to the newly completed Anglican Epiphany Chapel at the corner of Nixon Street and Chapman Street (then known as Arney Street) at the city end of Arch Hill. The simple, neat timber chapel looked smart in its fresh lick of paint. Once inside they seated themselves in the pews and listened intently to the first service, delivered by Reverend Benjamin Dudley, the incumbent of Holy Sepulchre Church on Symonds Street, and who would later become the Anglican Archdeacon of Auckland.[1]

The chapel was the first house of God in the Arch Hill–Grey Lynn area and was erected at the request of the people of Newton and Arch Hill, who found it difficult to traverse the deep gully that separated them from the mother church.[2]

It was a humble weatherboard building in humble weatherboard surroundings. The building was funded partly by donations that included £50 each from the Anglican Bishop of Auckland and St Matthew-in-the-City church. In common with most churches of the day, borrowings provided the remainder — in this case a diocesan loan of £100.[3] It took five years before the debt was fully repaid.[4]

As a result, no doubt, of the chapel's somewhat precarious finances, the matter of pew rents was raised in 1883. Pew rents were a source of income for many churches at the time, including Holy Sepulchre. Members of the congregation typically paid an annual fee to reserve the best seats, while the rest were available for visitors and those who either did not wish to pay or could not afford to. But it was felt that pew rentals were 'undesirable in a church like the Epiphany'.[5] Instead the congregation was invited to give a quarterly subscription of 5 shillings. The Epiphany Church appears to be one of the few city churches of the era never to have rented its pews.[6] The system was elitist and discouraged the poor from attending church, and it was abolished in the Auckland diocese in 1917.[7]

For the first decade services at Epiphany Chapel were taken primarily by

Faith | 279

lay preachers, and occasionally by the ordained minister who was shared with other churches in the expanding parish.[8] The congregation was unable to fund a minister's stipend, but in any case there was a shortage of trained clergy available to serve in all the churches that wanted them.[9] The Epiphany flock was lucky to have the services of lay readers until it became an independent parish in 1884.[10]

Church attendance was very much a free choice. Emigration to New Zealand had provided settlers with the opportunity to escape the confines of the religious world of home. Others continued the familiar practices and traditions they brought with them and adapted to suit this topsy-turvy land, where Christmas was in summer and Easter in autumn.

When the *Auckland Star* conducted a survey of church attendance on Easter Sunday in 1882 it found that only around a third of Auckland's population was at church and many services had an abundance of empty seats.[11] In its first year Epiphany Chapel mustered an average of around 50 people at services — eight years later an *Auckland Star* survey revealed that 71 people had attended the morning service and 57 were present for the evening service.[12] Given that the church had seating for 140, these figures were far from impressive, but it was common to erect a large church building in the hope that the congregation would eventually expand to fill it.[13]

Parents were often very keen to send their offspring to Sunday school for a good dose of religious education, even if they didn't go themselves. Sunday schools were among the most successful church institutions: in 1874, 53 per cent of children between the ages of 5 and 15 attended Sunday school. Attendance increased through the rest of the nineteenth century and into the early twentieth.[14] The Epiphany Chapel Sunday School was remarkably successful and its attendance grew from 36 children in the year it opened to 130 children, taught by 11 teachers, in 1882 — by which time the accommodation was stretched to the point that sometimes 30 children were crammed into the little vestry.[15]

Additions were made to the building in 1882 so that the Sunday school could be conducted in less cramped surroundings, but the vestry felt the chapel might have more success attracting adult parishioners if it was enlarged and relocated to a more prominent position. A Church of England-owned site at the corner of Karangahape Road and Gundry Street was secured for the purpose. The initial intention was to move the chapel from Nixon Street and enlarge it, but in the end a much larger church was built on the new site and opened in 1886, its lofty spire visible for miles around.[16] The chapel in Arch Hill continued to serve as the Sunday school, but the distance between the two buildings was far from ideal for parents.[17] In April 1894, 20 years after it was opened, the chapel shuffled off its Nixon Street site and moved two blocks to the west, where it settled at the rear of the Epiphany Church.[18]

**280** | **The Near West**

The Richmond Primitive Methodist Church, shown here on its second site at the corner of Richmond Road and Sackville Street, was built in 1882 and originally stood on the bend of Richmond Road opposite where Mokau Street is today. It served as the Richmond Road School from 1884 until 1888 and was well used by the wider community for non-church purposes. AUCKLAND WAR MEMORIAL MUSEUM TĀMAKI PAENGA HIRA, PH-NEG-C19921

By this time several other churches had been established in the Grey Lynn–Arch Hill area. The first of these, built in 1882, was the Primitive Methodist Church, which stood on the bend of Richmond Road opposite where Mokau Street runs today.[19] It was the only church building in this part of the district until the twentieth century.

Special services were held in a tent near the site on Sunday, 12 November 1882 and the following day the footprint of the Primitive Methodist Church building was marked out with foundation piles. A well-attended public tea and meeting followed.[20] Rapid progress was made, and in just over a month the simple church building with its arched front windows was complete. The first service was delivered by lay preacher Joseph Geary, who was pivotal in the church's establishment.[21]

The Prims, as the Primitive Methodists were known, were the second largest of the Methodist churches that came to New Zealand, and traced their origins to early nineteenth-century rural England. They differed from the more numerous Wesleyan Methodists by their spontaneous and impassioned style of preaching, which earned them the nickname 'the Ranters'. The Prims had a strong sense of social justice and placed a high value on the many enthusiastic lay preachers who were a major part of the movement's success.[22] Their values and simple gospel preaching particularly appealed to working-class people.[23]

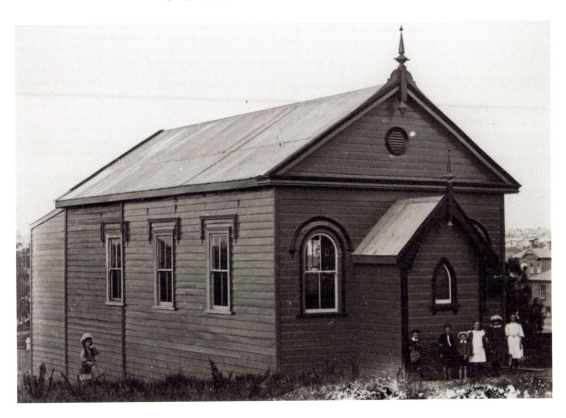

Faith | 281

The Arch Hill Wesleyan Methodist Church on its original site in Cooper Street. In 1910 it moved to Great North Road and later to Sackville Street. In 1993 it was sold and relocated to Schofield Street, where it was converted into a residence. WILLIAM MORELY, *THE HISTORY OF METHODISM IN NEW ZEALAND*, P.266

The Primitive Methodist church building had several other roles. From 1884 to 1888 it housed Richmond Road School and it also hosted a variety of political, religious and social meetings and entertainments.[24] Because of its frequent use for non-church purposes it was sometimes referred to as the 'Richmond Road hall'.[25]

Locals of other faiths attended more distant churches. From the higher points of the district one could see the spires of those on Ponsonby Road and in the city, and when an easterly wind blew their pealing bells could be heard. Keen churchgoers who were not of the Anglican or Primitive Methodist persuasion made a regular Sunday exodus eastward on streets that were muddy and rutted in winter and dry and dusty in summer. But other faiths were soon active in the Great North Road area.

Although they were the first Methodists to build a church, the Primitive Methodists of Richmond were not the first Methodists to begin church services in the Arch Hill–Grey Lynn area. The United Methodist Free Church was established in Auckland in 1872 after Reverend George Henry Turner was sent from London, and they soon purchased a brick chapel in Pitt Street, just north of the corner of Vincent Street, in the city. By September 1878 there was

282 | The Near West

sufficient interest for a suburban branch just west of the city in Arch Hill. It held services within the walls of the newly completed Newton West School, which stood at the corner of Great North Road and Brisbane Street.[26]

It was common at the time for schools to be used for church services, with school buildings making up 13 per cent of New Zealand's places of worship in the late 1870s.[27] The situation was reversed in Richmond Road, where the only church building was used to house the first school. The fortunes of the Arch Hill United Methodists faltered in the early 1880s, but another group of Methodists was already making headway in the area.[28]

John and Isabella Wakerley, a Wesleyan Methodist couple from Darlington in the north of England, began holding prayer meetings for locals at their home on Commercial Road, Arch Hill, in the late 1870s. Before long, Wesleyan Methodist Sunday school and church services were being held in the Newton West School and plans were afoot to build a church.[29] In April 1883 the Arch Hill Wesleyan Methodist Church held its opening service in Cooper Street (then known as Russell Street).[30] Like the Epiphany Chapel, the church was located just down from the Great North Road ridge, probably because sites were cheaper there than on the main thoroughfare.

As housing spread and the population grew following the subdivision of the Surrey Hills Estate in the 1880s, other denominations established themselves in the area. The *New Zealand Herald* reported in November 1883 that several were negotiating the purchase of church sites on the estate.[31] At this time the nearest Presbyterian churches were St Stephen's on Jervois Road and St James in Freemans Bay, and with both nearing capacity Reverend R. W. Runciman of St Stephen's proposed that a site be purchased on or near the Surrey Hills Estate.[32] According to the *Auckland Star*, the church intended to make do with a makeshift building to begin with but had ambitious plans: 'When the congregation has been organised and ascertains its strength, the projected building will be moved back to serve as a schoolhouse, and a more pretentious edifice erected in its stead.'[33] This was a common pattern in the development of parish churches, but not all congregations were able to afford the grand edifice of which they dreamed.

In August 1884 work began on the humble building that would be home to the Presbyterian congregation on a substantial section bounded by Rose Road, Scanlan Street (then known as Surrey Street) and Murdoch Road, but all did not go smoothly. On 25 September with the framing complete and work under way on the weatherboarding, a strong gust of wind caused the partially constructed building to collapse. Gavin Darroch, who had taken on the

contract with his brother George, was crushed and died instantly.[34] Despite this tragic event George continued with the contract, and on 21 December 1884 the first service was held at the church, which was named St Peter's.[35]

It was soon joined by the first Catholic presence in the area. Unlike the other faiths, the Catholic Church's primary motivation in the Surrey Hills area was to establish a school. The state provided a secular school system, and under the Education Act of 1877 Pākehā children between the ages of 7 and 13 were required to attend. Māori children could also attend but their attendance was not compulsory until 1894.[36]

The Catholic Church decided to expand its small network of existing schools to provide an alternative to the secular state schools. As noted in Chapter 6, the Sisters of St Joseph of the Sacred Heart built a school and convent on Sussex Street whose sanctuary served as a school during the week and a place of worship on Sundays, served by clergy from St Benedict's parish in Newton.[37] In 1887 a timber church was erected on the Turakina Street (then known as Tennyson Street) frontage of the site.

Some smaller and newer denominations also established themselves in the area. As early as 1884 the Church of Christ was meeting in the Newton West School on Sundays and in William Vickery's Great North Road home on Wednesday evenings.[38] By 1887 the church had built a Christians Meeting House on Williamson Avenue, opposite the site where the Newton Borough Council Chambers would soon be built.[39] A new Church of Christ was erected on the corner of Ponsonby Road and Pollen Street in 1897 and the meeting house was moved to the site to serve as a Sunday school.[40]

**S**urrey Hills was also the venue of early Seventh-day Adventist services conducted by young American missionary Arthur Daniells, who had been sent out from Des Moines, Iowa, after Auckland was identified by an earlier missionary as a promising location for a mission. Daniells arrived in late 1886 equipped with an enormous blue tent capable of seating 300 people, which he pitched on the western edge of the Surrey Hills Estate by the intersection of Mackelvie Street and Ponsonby Road. It was a convenient location, flat and relatively close to the city.[41]

Daniells drew large audiences to his 'cotton church' to hear his talks on subjects such as 'The Origin, History and Destiny of Satan' and 'Everlasting Fire and the Final Condition of the Impenitent'.[42] His series of illustrated lectures on 'the injurious effects of the use of alcoholic spirits' featured experiments and anatomical diagrams and were particularly well received, echoing as they did the views of the growing local temperance movement.[43]

**ABOVE:** St Peter's Presbyterian Church on its second site, around 1899. Originally built on the wedge of land bounded by Rose Road, Scanlan Street (then known as Surrey Street) and Murdoch Road, the building was moved to a more prominent site on Great North Road next to Newton West School in the late 1890s. The church building was enlarged and embellished and became a prominent feature on the ridge. PRESBYTERIAN ARCHIVES

**BELOW:** Sussex Street in 1917 showing the two-storey St Joseph's Convent on the left, prior to its removal to Great North Road later that year. It was destroyed by fire in 1921. AUCKLAND LIBRARIES HERITAGE COLLECTIONS, 1703-ALB342-04

Faith | 285

A Seventh-day Adventist camp on the corner of Schofield Street and Prime Road, 1912.
AUCKLAND LIBRARIES HERITAGE COLLECTIONS, AWNS-19120208-06-02

Each talk was accompanied by hymns with Daniells' wife Mary providing a tuneful lead on her pedal organ.[44]

Daniells courted the media, and his tent was the location for over 100 lectures that he delivered over a 15-week period with as many as 450 people attending. But as winter approached it was time to pull up the tent pegs and move indoors. Temporary accommodation was found at the nearby St George's Hall at the city end of Great North Road while work began on what would be the first purpose-built Seventh-day Adventist church in the southern hemisphere.[45]

By mid-July the simple timber building stood proudly on the western side of Mackelvie Street, halfway between Ponsonby and Rose roads.[46] It was a considerable achievement in a short space of time for a faith that was so new to the country, and which, in its observance of the sabbath on Saturday, travelled against the tide of the other Christian churches.

St George's Hall was also used by other faiths and belonged to its designer, architect Alexander Lee, who was elected to the Newton Borough Council in 1885 soon after its completion. Built as a hall for rent, it was used on Sundays by the Open Brethren. In 1886 the hall was destroyed by fire, but was soon rebuilt and a baptistry constructed under the stage. The Brethren worshipped at the hall into the 1890s.[47]

In the nineteenth century it was ideal for a church to be just a short walk from the homes of the faithful, so while the small Richmond Road Primitive Methodist Church was convenient for those on the northern side of the Grey Lynn gully, there was also scope for the Primitive Methodists in the Great North Road area to establish their own place of worship. The Primitive Methodists of Arch Hill first met in John Coad's house in Waima Street (then known as Oxford Street) before building a Primitive Methodist hall in 1898 on the north side of Great North Road between Scanlan Street (then known as Surrey Street) and Sussex Street where the Auckland Trade Union Centre (Auckland Trades Hall) now stands.[48] Regular Sunday services and a Sunday school were held in the hall, which had a capacity of 150.[49] It was the first house of worship erected on Great North Road, and over the next few years it would be joined by several more.

In 1894 members of the Ponsonby Baptist Church provided church and Sunday school services in the McNair home in the bucolic area now known as Westmere. When the house became too small to accommodate the numbers attending, Mrs Wilson's home and later her stable loft were used instead.[50] These temporary arrangements served until a small Baptist Sunday school was built on Garnet Road (then known as Wolseley Road) in 1898. The Ponsonby Baptist Church laymen continued to preach to the faithful in the evenings after the children had attended Sunday school.[51]

Faith | 287

By the late nineteenth century nearly all the major denominations, and several of the smaller ones, were established in the area we now know as Arch Hill, Grey Lynn and Westmere. Most of the churches were perched on the slopes on either side of Great North Road, on sections that would have commanded lower prices than those on the main road. Once they had become established with loans paid off and a sizeable and steady congregation in attendance, consideration could be given to future needs. A decision to enlarge a church building was often accompanied by discussions about whether to move to a more prominent site, and in many congregations what followed was a fervent effort to do just that.

In 1888, just four years after St Peter's Presbyterian church had opened, the annual meeting of the congregation resolved 'that as soon as possible the church be removed to a convenient position on the main road'.[52] But although the land and building were advertised for sale in 1889, the church and its congregation remained on the original site until 1898, when a new site was secured and preparations were made for the move. Services were transferred temporarily to Newton West School while the timber building was hauled up the hill on skids to Great North Road and installed at the corner of Brisbane Street near Newton West School.[53] Numerous additions and improvements were made, and on 6 February 1899 St Peter's reopened with a new transept, belfry and porch. The church could now accommodate 350 worshippers — a considerable advance on the original 150.[54]

The Catholic Church chose a prominent site on Great North Road. St Joseph's Convent (now a hotel) is at left, St Joseph's School is at centre left and St Joseph's Church and its presbytery are at right. Grey Lynn Library can be glimpsed at far right. AUCKLAND LIBRARIES HERITAGE COLLECTIONS, 7-A10481

In 1906 the Arch Hill Wesleyan Methodist Church was finding its existing building in Cooper Street (then known as Russell Street) 'generally unsuitable and out of sight'.[55] Later that year it was moved up the hill and repositioned near the corner of Great North Road and Northland Street (then known as Northcote Street).[56] It was intended that a new, more impressive church building would ultimately be built on the Great North Road frontage, but this never eventuated.

By 1914 the Catholic population had grown so much that Grey Lynn was able to split from St Benedict's and become a separate parish. By this stage St Joseph's School was too small and the new parish needed not only to expand the school but also to provide a presbytery. With insufficient space on the existing site a larger section was purchased on the south side of Great North Road, and in 1917 a new school opened there with the old convent relocated alongside. The church that had stood in Turakina Street followed suit in 1920.[57]

Overseeing these changes was Father Henry Holbrook (later Archdeacon and Monsignor), who was appointed parish priest at St Josephs in 1914, a role he held until his death in 1952. Holbrook was active in charitable and social ventures within the parish, diocese and wider community and was legal manager of the Catholic orphanages and spiritual director of the St Vincent de Paul Society. During the depression of the 1930s he served on the Auckland Metropolitan Relief Committee.[58]

The Catholic Church had a large presence in Great North Road, and with

Faith | 289

its Presbyterian and two Methodist churches, the street had become God's highway.

✕

Meanwhile changes were occurring in the West Lynn area of Richmond Road, a part of the district that was growing in importance. Population growth at the southern end of Richmond Road prompted the 1906 relocation of the Baptist Chapel, which was transported from the grassy slopes of Garnet Road to a site in Richmond Road (then known as Richmond Avenue) near the intersection of Tutanekai Street. The Sunday school met in the next-door fire station for several years, and when this was no longer available it was decided to move the building again to a larger site and extend it.[59] It was relocated in 1922 to the corner of Baildon Road where it remains today.[60]

In 1910 the Primitive Methodist Chapel that had stood since 1882 on the bend of Richmond Road opposite Mokau Street was relocated to the southwest

The Richmond Baptist Church on its final site at the corner of Baildon and Richmond roads, where it has been since 1922. COURTESY CAREY BAPTIST COLLEGE

corner of Sackville Street, closer to the growing population centre at West Lynn, where there was greater room for expansion.[61]

Other churches that had established themselves in the Great North Road and Ponsonby Road areas were also keen to have a presence at West Lynn. In 1907 the Church of Christ, which had a church in Ponsonby Road, built a hall on the south side of Francis Street near the corner of Richmond Road.[62]

Two years later St Peter's Presbyterian Church in Great North Road also sought to extend its reach and hired the recently erected Richmond Hall (now the Grey Lynn Returned Services Club in Francis Street) for Sunday school and evening church services.[63] Having established a congregation at West Lynn, attention then turned to building a church of its own, and in October 1910 a foundation stone was laid on the corner of Francis Street and Stanmore Road.[64] The wooden building, opened in November 1910, was named St Mungo's after the sixth-century founder and patron saint of Glasgow.[65]

In 1910 the Anglican Church, which had been absent from the area since the closure and removal of the Epiphany Chapel in 1894, built a Sunday school room known as St Columba Hall at the junction of Selbourne Street and Great North Road (this building remains, albeit considerably altered, at 571 Great North Road). It was named after the sixth-century Irish missionary who spread Christianity through Scotland and founded Iona Abbey.[66] It made sense for the building to be erected at a central location where it could serve the people of the Great North Road area as well as those in West Lynn. It was also close to Grey Lynn Primary School, which was about to open in Surrey Crescent, and was at the end of the second-section tram stop.[67]

James Williamson had gifted the site to the Anglican Church when the Surrey Hills Estate was subdivided.[68] The Church had initially intended to erect a modest building at Grey Lynn, but with the population expanding, plans were redrawn for a large building that would meet future needs and could be hired out as a venue for non-church events to generate income.[69] St Columba served as both church and Sunday school for the next two decades.

By the outbreak of the First World War the people of Arch Hill and Grey Lynn were well supplied with churches, most of which were located on Great North and Richmond roads, the busiest thoroughfares in the district. But the proportion of New Zealanders who attended church was in decline, and by the end of the First World War the country's cinemas attracted more people than its churches.[70]

Some creative efforts were made to entice residents to attend church. The vicar of St Columba, Reverend Jasper Calder, who would later become well known as the first city missioner, was well aware that many working-class men did not attend church. He had grown up in working-class Ponsonby as the son of the vicar of All Saints Church, so he was familiar with the people who made

Faith | 291

**ABOVE:** The original St Columba Church in 1928. It remains on its wedge-shaped site at the northern end of the Grey Lynn shops and has been converted into several retail spaces. AUCKLAND LIBRARIES HERITAGE COLLECTIONS, 4-03772

**RIGHT:** The interior of the original St Columba Church, 1922. AUCKLAND LIBRARIES HERITAGE COLLECTIONS, 4-03783

**ABOVE:** The new St Columba Church, **1932.** AUCKLAND LIBRARIES HERITAGE COLLECTIONS, 4-03780

**RIGHT:** The fine interior of the new St Columba Church, **1931.** AUCKLAND LIBRARIES HERITAGE COLLECTIONS, 4-03774

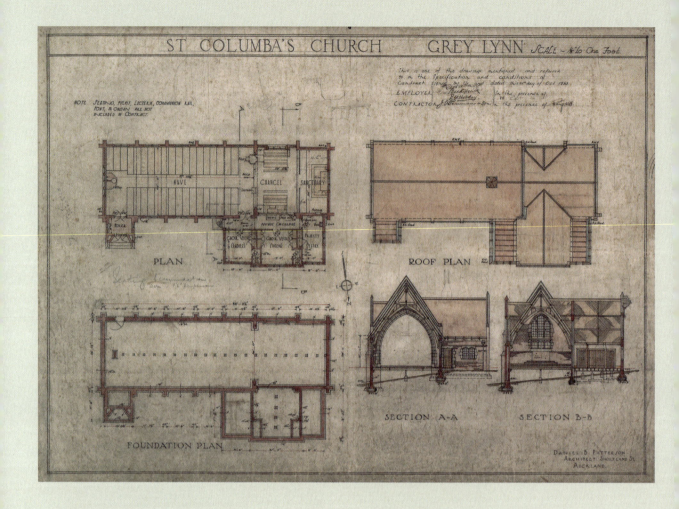

St Columba Church was designed by well-known Auckland architect Daniel B. Patterson, who was responsible for designing a number of Auckland churches including St David's on Khyber Pass Road.
COURTESY JANE MATTHEWS

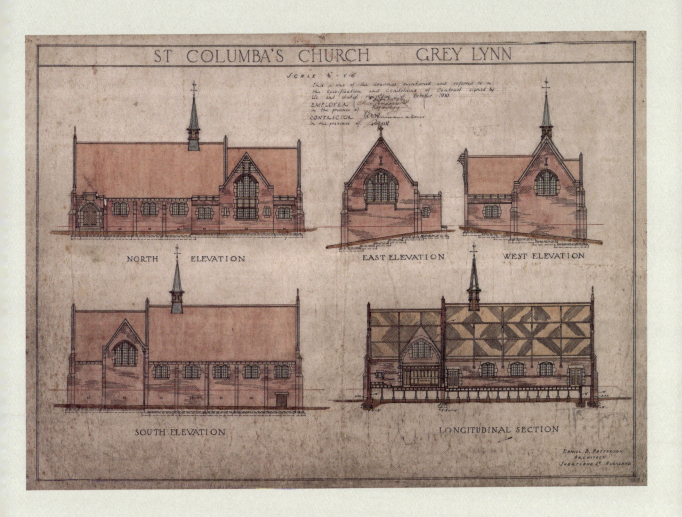

the inner-west suburbs home. He was a keen sportsman: he played rugby and cricket, and was at home in the saddle, owning several horses. He also acted, sang, sailed and boxed. His wide range of interests no doubt helped him to connect with a variety of people, including non-churchgoers.[71]

Known as the 'sporting parson', in 1914 he spoke at the St Columba Hall on novel subjects including 'Church and Racing' and 'Church and Sport', attracting substantial audiences and considerable publicity.[72] He discussed the ethics of betting and proffered the opinion that betting was not necessarily evil, but, individual circumstances determined whether or not betting could be considered morally permissible.[73] His opinions did not meet with the approval of the church authorities, however, and he was censured by the Anglican Social Questions Commission.[74]

Calder was one of a number of radical vicars sent to St Columba, where they were appreciated by a community that was more open-minded and accepting than most. Others included Reverend John Maclean, who served at St Columba in the 1970s and 1980s and who is remembered for his work in fostering connections between the church and Pacific Island communities.[75] During this time St Columba became one of the first Anglican churches in New Zealand to offer services in Tongan after John Tamahori, a Māori missionary who had spent time in Tonga, began preaching to the Tongan congregation in 1974. Tongan services continue today at St Columba.[76] When the St Columba Hall was erected in 1910 it was on an ideal and quiet site, but over the years Great North Road had become noisy with vehicles, including the trams, struggling up the hill and descending with brakes squealing.[77] By late 1927 plans were being made for the purchase of a quieter site further along Surrey Crescent.[78] Dedicated in 1931, St Columba Church was set back from the road and its surrounding gardens provided a peaceful approach to the beautiful brick and stone church.[79]

Three other churches were built in Grey Lynn and Westmere at this time. In 1927 the St Columba parish erected St Cuthbert's Hall at 8 Faulder Avenue to serve the growing Westmere community, and in 1929 a Mission Hall was built at the top of Tuarangi Road and used by the Reading Brethren.[80]

In 1928 the Salvation Army extended its presence in Grey Lynn by erecting a hall on the corner of Richmond Road and Castle Street. Dryden Street was already home to the Salvation Army Bethany Centre, which opened in 1913, and the Newton Corps barracks had opened in Ponsonby Road near the intersection of Crummer Road in 1893.[81]

At the Ponsonby end of the district a group of spiritualists known as the

Spiritual Scientists opened a church in 1929, relocating from Karangahape Road, where they had been holding meetings since 1913, led by Australian psychic orator John McLeod-Craig. The new church, at 43 Mackelvie Street on the corner of Rose Road, was soon renamed the Christian Spiritualist Church.[82] It remained there until 2003, when it was moved to Portage Road in New Lynn and renamed the Mackelvie West Spiritualist Church, in memory of its long history in Mackelvie Street.[83]

When the Mackelvie Street church was first built it was one of a number of spiritualist churches in the city, and it was not the only one with a presence in the street. From the mid-1920s the Church of True Spiritual Light held regular services in the Forresters Hall in Edinburgh Street, Newton, as well as a weeknight public circle in Mackelvie Street at the residence of herbalist and spiritual healer Jessie Clayton, also known as Nurse Clayton.[84] In the early 1930s these weeknight gatherings were relocated to Clayton's home at 5 Dickens Street in Grey Lynn.[85]

Also during the 1930s a Gospel hall was built on Coleridge Street near the junction with Great North Road, where it served as a Brethren Church until 1960. It was then bought by the Auckland Rosicrucian Order, a mystical fraternity that is part of the Ancient Mystical Order Rosae Crucis (AMORC), formed in New York in 1915 and founded on the teachings of an older European Rosicrucian order.[86] The order continues to meet in the hall to this day.

In 1935 the Dunnottar Memorial Hall was built at the corner of Garnet Road and Faulder Avenue in Westmere as an extension of St Stephen's Presbyterian Church in Ponsonby.[87] It was also used for interdenominational services in 1940, and from the 1960s to the 1980s it was rented by a group of Brethren who had split from the Exclusive Brethren.[88]

In 1935 the former Costley Training Institute on Richmond Road, which had served as an Anglican children's home through the 1910s and 1920s, became the New Zealand headquarters of the newest branch of the Church Army, an international organisation of lay evangelists. The Church Army had made a small start in New Zealand in 1926 when a Church Army officer came to serve in the Waiapu diocese, concentrating his work on remote railway and roading workers' camps.[89]

In 1933 a flying column of the Church Army was sent from England to travel the country demonstrating their work and promoting the establishment of a New Zealand division.[90] After two years' missionary work in New Zealand, the group returned home and the New Zealand branch was founded soon afterwards, beginning with a day of continuous prayer in the small chapel that

Faith | 297

The Anglican Children's Home soon after it opened in the former Costley Training Institute building on Richmond Road in 1909.
AUCKLAND LIBRARIES HERITAGE COLLECTIONS, NZG-19091215-0031-03

had been built alongside the children's home in 1913.[91] This chapel would soon be renamed St Michael and All Angels.[92]

The former children's home, which now housed not only the New Zealand Church Army headquarters but also men's and women's residential training schools for Church Army recruits, became known as Carlisle House after the founder of the Church Army, Reverend Wilson Carlisle.[93] Here men and women were prepared for missionary work in diverse settings, from remote workers' camps to prisons and parishes. During the Second World War, 75 Church Army missionaries were sent to tend to the military both here and overseas.[94]

Although the property at 90 Richmond Road has been associated with the religious organisations for much of its history, it was originally built as a home and training institution for boys. It was one of a number of substantial Auckland buildings funded from the bequests of eccentric and wealthy Aucklander Edward Costley, who died in 1883. Costley was born in Ireland and came to New Zealand in the late 1830s, living initially at the Bay of Island. He was one of the earliest settlers in Auckland; he invested in land and buildings, and eventually amassed a considerable fortune. Kind and generous, he lived a very frugal lifestyle.[95]

The institute that bore his name took in the most promising boys from the government-run residential industrial schools for neglected, destitute and criminal children. Opened in 1886, the building initially had accommodation for 25 boys as well as quarters for the manager. A large workshop and gymnasium were added later. Life at the institute was busy. Days were spent either working

**The opening of the Salvation Army Hall at the corner of Richmond Road and Castle Street, 1928.** ALEXANDER TURNBULL LIBRARY, *NEW ZEALAND HERALD*, 6 FEBRUARY 1928

as apprentices or attending Richmond Road School, followed by evening lessons with the manager and carpentry classes four nights a week. There were also long lists of chores to be completed. Sundays were spent at Sunday school and church. Occasional entertainments helped break the monotony.

By the mid-1890s the intake of boys was declining and the Costley Training Institute had a number of vacancies — the government was moving away from institutional care and children were more commonly boarded out with foster families. Rules were bent to allow children to be admitted direct from the community to fill vacancies. By 1906 maintenance costs were rising, and with occupancy declining the institute was running at a loss. The decision was made to close the institution and sell the building. At the end of 1908 the Costley Training Institute closed its doors and the property was sold to the Anglican Church, which reopened it as a children's home.[96]

By this stage most denominations were represented by just one or two churches in the district, but there were three Methodist churches — all built before the Methodist Union of 1913 joined the branches of Methodism together.[97] Two of the three were within a few blocks of each other on Great North Road — one built as a Wesleyan Methodist Church in 1883 and the other by the Primitive Methodists in 1898. Each had its own small, loyal congregation, but it was inefficient to have such duplication and in 1930 the

Faith | 299

The congregation outside the Grey Lynn Presbyterian Church at the corner of Great North Road and Crummer Road, c. 1980.
PRESBYTERIAN ARCHIVES

former Arch Hill Wesleyan Methodist Church, which had started life in Cooper Street before moving to Great North Road, was closed and relocated to sit alongside the Richmond Methodist (formerly Primitive Methodist) Church, where it served as a Sunday school.[98] Two decades later the Great North Road church erected by the Primitive Methodists half a century earlier was closed and sold.[99]

This consolidation of church properties within the Methodist denomination gave the one remaining Methodist church in the area a better chance of survival — something that other denominations also needed to consider. By the 1950s it was no longer necessary to have a church of one's denomination within walking distance — car ownership was increasing and public transport was affordable and fairly frequent. Even if an extensive walk was required on a Sunday morning to get to church, the provision of well-formed roads and footpaths made this easier than it had been in the nineteenth century when the foundations of the first churches in the district were laid.

With dwindling congregations, the Presbyterian Church decided to sell St Peter's on Great North Road and St Mungo's in Francis Street and combine the congregations at a new brick church on the corner of Great North and Crummer roads. The final service at St Peter's was held in June 1950 and the building was bought by the Auckland Watersiders' Silver Band committee for a band room and dance hall.[100] The Presbyterians used the former Primitive Methodist Church in Great North Road for their services until their new church opened in 1956.[101]

In 1954 St Mungo's was offered for sale and in 1957 the Auckland Wrestling Association bought it to use as a gymnasium for wrestling clubs. It later became home to the Auckland Repertory Theatre, and later still to the Westmere Congregational Christian Church of Sāmoa (now the Western Springs Congregational Christian Church of Sāmoa), the second branch of this church in the Grey Lynn area; the other is located in Sussex Street.[102]

Not all congregations were shrinking. The presence of two Catholic schools in the area — St Joseph's on Great North Road and Sacred Heart College for boys (now St Paul's) on Richmond Road — had no doubt attracted families of the faith to Grey Lynn, as was reflected in the strength of the congregation at Grey Lynn's only Catholic church. Work began on the new St Joseph's in 1959 and it opened in 1961.[103] Designed by modernist architect Guy Chambers, the building has a three-finned bell tower topped with a tall cross that can be seen for miles. The building has windows in abstract-patterned stained glass and the Way of the Cross is presented in a mosaic frieze around the walls, both designed by artist Milan Mrkusich.[104]

Through the second half of the twentieth century, many of the struggling churches in Arch Hill, Grey Lynn and Westmere were reinvigorated by the arrival of immigrants from the Pacific Islands, large numbers of whom settled in the area. The Pacific had been a successful missionary field through the nineteenth century, resulting in an extensive conversion to Christianity, and Pasifika migrants were in general more pious than the established New Zealand population.[105]

The churches had an important role in helping Pasifika immigrants adjust to life in New Zealand. James Yandall, who later lived on Dryden Street, was one of the early post-war Pacific Island immigrants; he arrived from Apia in 1946 with his brother. He recalled disembarking in Auckland to a welcome from a representative of the London Missionary Society (LMS), an organisation that had converted many Samoans to Christianity in the nineteenth century. The LMS representative invited Yandall and his fellow passengers to attend Beresford Street Congregational Church (now Hopetoun Alpha). Yandall recalled that English language services were held in the mornings, while the afternoons were given over to services for the various Pacific Island groups.[106]

The following year Newton Pacific Islanders' Congregational Church was established in the Newton Congregational Church building in Edinburgh Street, off Karangahape Road. It was an important touchstone for Pacific Islanders. Ministers arrived from the Pacific to preach to the various congregations that worshipped there. There was an English language service as well as services in the languages of the Samoan, Cook Island, Niuean and Tokelauan congregations.[107] In the late 1960s the Pacific Island Congregational

Faith | 301

Churches joined the Presbyterian Church, and the Edinburgh Street church became known as the Pacific Islanders' Presbyterian Church.[108]

But many Pasifika immigrants were members of other denominations, and at first the local churches tried to cater for them by welcoming them into existing congregations. It was often an uneasy fit as language, culture and worship practices were different. Some of the city churches did, however, make efforts to provide more appropriate services, and as they grew in number and confidence, the congregations were able to create church-based facilities that met their needs and were close to where they lived.

This was the case for the Catholic Samoans, who began meeting in 1957 in a Catholic Social Services building at the corner of Pitt and Wellington streets, where they were ministered to by Father Louis Schwehr, the only Catholic priest in New Zealand at the time who could speak Samoan. Through fundraising efforts, the local Catholic Samoan community bought St Clare, a former maternity home in Williamson Avenue on the southeast corner of Mackelvie Street, and converted it into a Catholic Samoan centre complete with a small chapel and a meeting room.

The centre opened its doors in 1964 and around 200 people attended meetings at the centre each week. It was too small for large gatherings, however, so Mass and large socials were held at nearby St Joseph's Church, which became the first Catholic church in New Zealand to hold Mass in Samoan and in accordance with Samoan customs. The Samoan centre also catered for a Tongan congregation of around 50 who worshipped monthly at the chapel.[109]

The Turou Cook Island Catholic Centre opened on Great North Road, near the corner of Coleridge Street, in 1967, and continues to serve the Cook Island community. From 1985 to 1996, Turou was home to two Cook Island Sisters of St Joseph of Cluny who ministered to the Cook Island population.[110]

Some groups were able to establish themselves in under-utilised churches that had been built in the nineteenth and early twentieth centuries but were now struggling to survive, including the Seventh-day Adventist Church in Mackelvie Street. The first Seventh-day Adventist Pacific Island congregation met initially in a hall in Newton in 1951, but four years later they were in need of larger premises for the nearly 200 people attending. At the same time there were empty pews at the large Seventh-day Adventist Church in Mackelvie Street, so the congregation moved.

This was a godsend for the church, which had been offered for sale two years earlier when its membership had dropped below 40.[111] With the rising numbers of Pasifika migrants, services were now overcrowded, and in 1966 a new building with accommodation for 450 was erected behind the old church.[112]

The Grey Lynn Presbyterian Church, erected in the 1950s at the corner of Great North and Crummer roads to replace St Peter's and St Mungo's, also had

The exterior and interior of the newly completed St Joseph's Church in 1962. The striking design was by architect Guy Chambers and the stained-glass windows are by Milan Mrkusich.
AUCKLAND LIBRARIES HERITAGE COLLECTIONS, 1528-62058, 1528-62059

Faith | 303

Vaine Mo'onia Tongan Methodist Church at the corner of Richmond Road and Sackville Street. PATRICK REYNOLDS

space to spare. In the 1970s the Tokelauan and Tuvaluan communities were welcomed to worship at the church and it became a centre for these Pacific Island communities in Auckland. The decline in Pākehā attendance eventually led the elders to gift the church to the Tokelauan and Tuvaluan church members.[113]

The Baptist Church that started life in Garnet Road before twice moving on Richmond Road was also invigorated by the arrival of Pacific Island immigrants. In 1965 Reverend R. F. Gaskell noted that he and other ministers in this multicultural community needed to do much more than just write sermons and visit the sick in order to meet the needs of the community. Many new immigrants needed not only spiritual help but also activities that fostered community connections, and advice on non-spiritual matters, including tenancy and property purchase agreements.

The church had developed a range of facilities to meet the social and cultural needs of the community. A tennis court had been formed on which basketball was also played and there was an electronic rifle range and facilities for badminton, table tennis, chess and gymnastics. A boys' club operated on Thursday nights, attended by up to 40 boys, many of them recent immigrants from the Pacific Islands who did not otherwise attend the church. Church social workers were always on hand so that the boys had someone to talk to if they had any problems.[114] Now known as the Grey Lynn Community Church, it continues to provide a wide range of activities and groups catering to the needs of the church community, including a Christian preschool.

Celebrating White Sunday at the Congregational Christian Church of Sāmoa on Sussex Street, Grey Lynn, in 2000. GLENN JOWITT COLLECTION, TE PAPA TONGAREWA MUSEUM OF NEW ZEALAND, O.041142

St Jude's Methodist Church (formerly known as the Richmond Primitive Methodist Church) at the corner of Richmond Road and Sackville Street also had a dwindling congregation, as did the Kingsland Trinity Methodist Church. The two churches had been sharing a minister since 1970 and by the mid-1980s the Central Methodist Circuit decided to merge the two congregations, with the faithful of St Jude's attending services at the Kingsland Church from 1987. St Jude's was then handed over to a Tongan Methodist fellowship that had been meeting at the Kingsland Trinity Methodist Church on Sunday afternoons since the 1970s.[115] The new congregation expanded and raised funds for a much larger church complex.

In 1993 the 111-year-old St Jude's Church was demolished and the Sunday school building behind, which had been built in 1883 in Cooper Street as the Arch Hill Wesleyan Methodist Church, was sold and moved to Schofield Street where it was converted into a residence. In their place the Vaine Moʻonia (the True Vine) church arose. It was opened in 1994 by King Tāufaʻāhau Tupou IV and Queen Halaevalu Mataʻaho ʻAhomeʻe of Tonga, who had donated funds to the church, at an elaborate ceremony that featured singing by the 80-member Royal Tongan Choir, who flew in for the event.[116]

Vaine Moʻonia comes under the administration of the New Zealand Methodist Church, but there are also three other Methodist churches in Grey Lynn catering to Tongan communities. Two are branches of different Methodist churches based in Tonga and the other is run by an independent church

Faith | 305

Roasting pigs for the feast that followed the White Sunday service at the Free Church of Tonga, Grey Lynn, in 2000. GLENN JOWITT COLLECTION, TE PAPA TONGAREWA MUSEUM OF NEW ZEALAND, O.041145

organisation based in New Zealand. This multiplicity of churches catering to Tongan Methodists arose from the complicated history of Methodism in Tonga.

The Wesleyan Methodist Missionary Society brought Methodism to Tonga in the 1820s and in 1885 a new Free Church of Tonga was established, independent of the Methodist Church of Australasia, while the Wesleyan Church in Tonga remained linked to the Methodist Church of Australasia. In the 1920s Queen Sālote Tupou III united the two churches under the name Free Wesleyan Church of Tonga, but not all were happy and the resulting schism resulted in three Tongan churches — Free Wesleyan Church of Tonga (Siasi Uēsiliana Tauʻatāina ʻo Tonga), Free Church of Tonga (Siasi ʻo Tonga Tauʻatāina) and Church of Tonga (Siasi ʻo Tonga) — each with their own practices and administration.[117]

The independent United Church of Tonga was established in Grey Lynn in 1977 to provide a place where all Tongan Methodists could worship without having ties to either the New Zealand Methodist administration or the Methodist Churches of Tonga. The church bought the Anglican Church property in Richmond Road where the 90-year-old former Costley Training Institute stood with the small Church of St Michael and All Angels alongside. The church building was altered and extended, before being reopened in late 1979 by King Tāufaʻāhau Tupou IV and dedicated to the memory of his mother, Queen Sālote III.[118] The church property was named Lototonga, and is the centre of the United Church of Tonga, which now has seven Auckland branches, as well as one in Christchurch and five in Australia.[119]

A New Zealand branch of the Free Church of Tonga was established in some houses in Crummer Road at the corner of Turakina Street in 1975.[120] In 1990 a Church of Tonga was built at 84 Sackville Street.[121]

Just as some Tongan church communities preferred to set up New Zealand branches of their home churches, so too did one of the local Samoan church communities. A New Zealand branch of the Congregational Christian Church of Sāmoa (Ekalesia Fa'apotopotoga Kerisiano Sāmoa) was established in Grey Lynn in 1962 by a congregation that met at the Pacific Islanders' Congregational Church (later the Pacific Islanders Presbyterian Church) but wanted to have greater control over their own affairs.

They initially met at a home in Grey Lynn with just 20 people attending their first service. In 1968 they built a church on Sussex Street, the first purpose-built Congregational Christian Church of Sāmoa in New Zealand.[122] This large building, with a capacity of 550, has been considerably extended since.[123] At the time of its fiftieth anniversary in 2012 it was one of 73 New Zealand churches affiliated with the Congregational Christian Church of Sāmoa.[124]

Possibly the most imposing church building in the area is the Sione Uesile (John Wesley) Church at the corner of King and Dean streets in Arch Hill, which was opened in 1975 by the Samoan Methodist Congregation. The completion of the three-storey concrete-block building, with its church on the top floor and community centre below, was an impressive achievement for the 105-strong congregation.[125] Its simple, modernist concrete-block form referenced the government buildings erected in Sāmoa during the 1950s and 1960s.[126]

In the 1970s the Rastafari faith came to New Zealand via reggae, the music genre that emerged in Jamaica in the late 1960s and became associated with the Rastafari faith in the early 1970s, partly through Jamaica's most famous reggae musician and Rastafarian, Bob Marley. Marley's visit to Auckland and huge concert at Western Springs in 1979 piqued local interest in the Rastafari faith, and a Twelve Tribes of Israel house was established on Surrey Crescent soon after. It was formally blessed by Prophet Gad (Vernon Carrington), the founder of the movement in Jamaica, in 1986.[127] There was later a Twelve Tribes of Israel headquarters on Pollen Street.[128]

In the mid-1980s a large Mormon church was also built on Surrey Crescent.

Despite the influx of new worshippers from the Pacific Islands, not every struggling church could be saved from closure. The Church of Christ in Francis Street became home to the Samoan Assembly

Faith | 307

of God, but when the church's plans to expand met local opposition, it moved elsewhere and the building became home to the Wellpark College of Natural Therapies, part of a collection of businesses and organisations promoting spiritual and physical health that found a natural home in Grey Lynn. When the college later moved to Albany the church was demolished.[129]

The Salvation Army Hall on Richmond Road and St Cuthbert's Anglican church in Westmere were too large for their existing congregations and too small to cater to the needs of growing Pacific Island congregations. The hall was sold and converted into an artist's studio and later a residence. St Cuthbert's struggled on for years, but when attendance on Sundays fell to just five or six people the decision was made to close. It was sold in 2007 and converted into a house, and the small congregation was encouraged to attend St Columba, where a new side chapel was formed in memory of St Cuthbert's.[130]

In 1990 the Buddhist Centre on the corner of Warnock Street and Richmond Road at the West Lynn shops was opened in a former art gallery by the Friends of the Western Buddhist Order (now known as Triratna Buddhist Community), an organisation formed in England in 1967. Unlike most other Buddhist organisations, the Friends of the Western Buddhist Order (FWBO) was formed by Westerners who sought to teach the essential ideas and practices

**ABOVE:** The exterior of Sione Uesile (John Wesley) Church, at the corner of King and Dean streets in Arch Hill. JANE USSHER

**OPPOSITE:** The church's interior. JANE USSHER

308 | **The Near West**

of Buddhism in a way suited to modern society. The New Zealand FWBO was started in Mairangi Bay in 1970 at the home of recent British immigrant Akshobhya (Warren Karno-Atkins), who had been ordained into the Order in Britain 1969. It appears to have been the first FWBO group active outside Britain. The Buddhist Centre moved from Grey Lynn to Mount Eden in 2023.[131]

In the past few decades, the Samoan, Tongan, Tuvaluan, Tokelauan and Cook Island communities in the Arch Hill, Grey Lynn and Westmere areas have decreased in number, but the area remains a strong spiritual home for numerous Pacific Island families, many of whom travel from other parts of Auckland to worship in the places where they first put down roots in Aotearoa and formed lively church congregations.

# Mothers and babies

Bethany Hospital on Dryden Street in Grey Lynn in 1976. AUCKLAND LIBRARIES HERITAGE COLLECTIONS, CL-19761027-04-01

The Bethany Centre, which stood for nearly a century on Dryden Street (formerly known as Owen Street), was one of six similar institutions in New Zealand established by the Salvation Army. Opened in 1913, it replaced a much smaller Salvation Army maternity home for unwed mothers on Vermont Street, Ponsonby, which had opened in 1897. The new building accommodated 30 women and provided maternity services to poor and unwed women as well as to private patients, whose fees helped support the institution.[132]

The rhetoric of nineteenth-century homes that took in pregnant unmarried women was often dominated by a 'saving fallen women' trope, but in the early twentieth century the focus changed to saving babies and their mothers. The birth rate was falling, and as historian Margaret Tennant has written, 'even "illegitimates" began to have their value'.[133]

But the Salvation Army had always had a more enlightened attitude to social work and warmly welcomed all women needing their services.[134] With no reliable form of contraception, unplanned pregnancies were not uncommon and to be single and pregnant was considered shameful.

Maternity services went through a major change in New Zealand through the Bethany era. Births at home or in small, unregulated private maternity homes were the norm at the turn of the twentieth century, but high maternal death rates led to government intervention to improve standards and access to modern care. By the 1930s most women were giving birth in maternity hospitals attended by qualified staff and where more effective forms of pain relief were available. In 1937 around 100 women a year were giving birth at Bethany, second only in Auckland to St Helen's Maternity Hospital.[135]

But Bethany's services set it apart from other maternity hospitals. For example, it was one of the first hospitals not only to allow but also to encourage fathers to be present at the birth of their children. They also worked with other community and charitable organisations such as the Auckland Parents Centre, which ran antenatal classes at which fathers were welcome.[136] These services were available to both married and unmarried women giving birth at Bethany.

Unmarried women could stay longer, sometimes for several months before and after the birth of their babies.[137] In October 1970 Bethany opened a school for pregnant school-aged girls — at the time 25 per cent of its residential clients were aged between 12 and 17, so there was a clear need. The school was also open to school-aged expectant mothers who were not Bethany residents.[138]

For single women at Bethany, decisions had to be made about the future for them and their babies. Some married the baby's father, while others found a way to keep their babies, or made other arrangements for their care, including fostering or adoption. Adoption was fairly rare in early twentieth century New Zealand, but it rose markedly after the Second World War, reaching a high point in the late 1960s and early 1970s — in 1969, 6 per cent of babies born in New Zealand were adopted.[139] Closed adoptions had been the norm, but from 1973 Bethany residents were encouraged to opt for an open adoption in which the birth parents were given information about adoptive parents and could select who would adopt their baby. If both parties agreed, a meeting could be arranged and the parties could keep in touch if they wished. This removed some of the uncertainty and worry for both parties.[140]

Bethany was not the only institution caring for single pregnant women in Grey Lynn. Just two blocks away, on the corner of Surrey Crescent and Firth Road (now the site of Cohaus), was the interdenominational Motherhood of Man Movement (MOMM) maternity hospital, Fairleigh, which opened in 1954 in a substantial villa where Mrs Annie Butterworth had formerly run the Fairleigh private maternity home; the building has recently been relocated to the Browning Street frontage of Cohaus.

Like Bethany, the maternity hospital catered for private, fee-paying married women, as well as single pregnant women who came to MOMM for help. MOMM was established in 1942, initially as a war measure to help single pregnant women who left their homes in order to conceal their pregnancies. MOMM arranged for them to stay with families, providing household help in return for board. By the time MOMM had opened Fairleigh, its primary aim of caring for pregnant unmarried women and assisting them to keep their babies had shifted and it was now running a successful adoption agency.

Problems arose in the early 1950s, when it was discovered that Mr and Mrs Bovaird, president and treasurer of MOMM, had been mismanaging the organisation and stealing from it. Worse still, they had been refusing to assist young women who wanted to keep their babies, in clear breach of the organisation's rules. They were swiftly expelled from their positions and MOMM reviewed its practices.[141]

The Bovaird episode damaged MOMM's reputation, but the organisation rallied and continued its work. The numbers of adoptive parents applying to MOMM for babies declined through the 1960s, while the numbers of unmarried pregnant women applying for help increased. Babies waiting for adoption were having to be boarded out. Meanwhile the supply of free maternity services increased when National Women's Hospital opened in 1964. As the demand for private maternity services at Fairleigh fell, so did MOMM's income. Fairleigh had become uneconomic and closed in 1968; it reopened soon afterwards as a hostel for women and babies and continued in this role for a decade.[142]

Bethany closed its hospital in the mid-1970s, but it remained an important support for single mothers, providing education programmes and residential care for those in need until its closure in 2011.[143]

Faith | 311

09

# The visual arts

**PREVIOUS PAGES:** Julian
Dashper, *The Colin
McCahons*, 1992.
CHARTWELL COLLECTION,
AUCKLAND ART GALLERY
TOI O TĀMAKI, 2001
C2001/1/27/3

If the walls of many Grey Lynn, Arch Hill and Westmere houses could speak, they would tell stories of creative endeavour. For a while in the 1980s and 1990s it seemed that if you lived in a flat in Grey Lynn you were either in a band, or one of your flatmates was in a band, or you or someone in your flat was an aspiring artist. Creative types were everywhere. But it didn't all start in the last decades of the twentieth century. The creative spirit that is evident in the people of Grey Lynn, Arch Hill and Westmere today has a long history.

In the nineteenth century there was considerable scope in homes, workplaces and elsewhere for those with a passion for domestic and technical arts. At home, girls were taught to sew and cook and boys learnt woodworking.

Industrial settings also provided an avenue for creative expression. In the 1860s, for example, George Boyd's brick and tile works in Arch Hill was producing not only utilitarian products for the building industry but also ornamental vases and flower pots.[1] Many of these ended up in local homes, and were used for flower arrangements that could then be painted.

Some locals devoted their spare time to artistic pursuits, including Harold Young, a lithographer for the *Auckland Star* who lived in Leighton Street in the late nineteenth and early twentieth centuries, and who benefited from the philanthropic activities of Sir John Logan Campbell, who founded Auckland's first school of art in 1878.[2] It offered free art tuition in the original Auckland Museum building at the northern end of Princes Street in the city.[3]

Young attended the school in the mid-1880s and was taught by artist Kennett Watkins. His work was shown at the New Zealand Art Students Association exhibition, and at the end of the 1890s it appeared in the Auckland Society of Arts annual exhibition.[4] Young designed a series of stamps in the 1890s, and won competitions for the design of the certificate awarded to the best exhibits at the Auckland Industrial and Mining Exhibition 1898–99. Early in the new century his winning design graced a souvenir card to mark the 1901 visit of the Duke and Duchess of Cornwall and York.[5]

**The visual arts** | 315

LEFT: Harold Young, *Ponsonby Road Reservoir Corner*, 1899. AUCKLAND ART GALLERY TOI O TĀMAKI, PURCHASED 1936, 1936/26/11

OPPOSITE ABOVE: Brushmaker Charles Augustus Brown and shipping company proprietor Ernest Charles Binns had busy working lives but they devoted some of their spare time to photography and took many photographs of Grey Lynn during the late nineteenth and early twentieth centuries. They formed a local photography club (probably the Auckland Camera Club). Some members of the club are pictured here. AUCKLAND WAR MEMORIAL MUSEUM TĀMAKI PAENGA HIRA

OPPOSITE BELOW: Edward Friström, *Gum Trees, Great North Road, Grey Lynn*, 1903. This painting is a view of the road now known as Tuarangi Road, the original Great North Road. AUCKLAND ART GALLERY TOI O TĀMAKI, BEQUEST OF MR E. EARLE VAILE, 1956, 1956/6/4

In 1913, then in his mid-fifties, Young left the *Auckland Star* to become a commercial artist. He produced many watercolour landscapes of Auckland and the Waitākere Ranges, and he wrote and illustrated poetry.[6] Several of his artworks are in the Auckland Art Gallery Toi o Tāmaki collection, including views of Grey Lynn, Coxs Creek and Western Springs that date from the late nineteenth century, when he lived in Grey Lynn.[7]

Artists living in other parts of Auckland were inspired by the landscape of the district. Swedish-born Edward Friström (Clas Edvard Friström) came to New Zealand in the early twentieth century from Australia, where he had been a photographer and artist.[8] He lived in St Marys Bay and Mount Eden and initially worked from a studio in Queen Street. From there he ventured west, where he painted landscapes, including views of Tuarangi Road and Western Springs.[9] In 1911 he took up a position teaching drawing and painting at Elam School of Art. A number of his New Zealand paintings are held in public collections throughout the country.[10]

Friström had a big impact on his student Ida Eise, who was raised in Mackelvie Street, one of two children of warehouseman Frederick Gustav (George) Eise and his wife Emma (née Cox).[11] Ida attended Grey Lynn College, where she was dux. A scholarship awarded in 1907 helped her study

Ida Eise (seated at front) with fellow art students, c. 1914–16. AUCKLAND WAR MEMORIAL MUSEUM TĀMAKI PAENGA HIRA, PH-1975-1-13

at Elam School of Art at a time when most female artists came from well-off backgrounds.[12]

By 1915 Eise was teaching art at New Plymouth College, the beginning of a long teaching career. In 1920 she returned to teach at Elam and moved back into the family home on Mackelvie Street, where she would spend the rest of her life. She was at Elam in 1949 when a fire in the Symonds Street building forced its painting and sculpture departments to relocate to the former Newton West School on Great North Road.[13] Eise retired in 1960 and spent the next year on a tour of Europe with her former pupil, acclaimed New Zealand artist Lois White.[14]

In her retirement, Eise taught one day a week at the Auckland Society of Arts.[15] She was a regular exhibitor at the society and won its prestigious Bledisloe Medal for landscape painting in 1936 and 1949. She was made a Member of the Order of the British Empire in 1976 for services to art and her work is represented in major public collections.[16] She left a bequest to the Auckland Society of Arts to support artists of the future, through the Ida Eise Painting Award.[17]

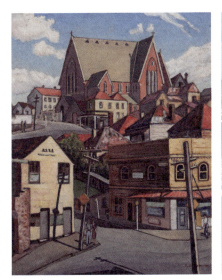 

**LEFT:** *Auckland Cityscape*, painted by Jack Hutchison around 1950, shows St Benedict's Church in Newton viewed from near the intersection of East and South streets, where the motorway runs today. AUCKLAND ART GALLERY TOI O TĀMAKI, PURCHASED 1988, 1988/27/3

**RIGHT:** Peter Siddell, *Homecoming*, 1976. Siddell's paintings are not of actual places but rather are made up of elements adapted from his memory, including the houses he saw on his paper run when he was a child in the 1940s and living on Scanlan Street. *Homecoming* shows what appears to be the house that stands at the corner of Ponsonby and Crummer roads. The view beyond, with its volcanic cone and variety of timber houses, comprises familiar elements of the area. AUCKLAND ART GALLERY TOI O TĀMAKI, PURCHASED 1977, 1977/6

Teaching was a common adjunct to a career in the arts, particularly for those living in working-class areas like Arch Hill, Grey Lynn and Westmere. But there were many other ways to earn a regular income. Artist Jack Hutchison, for example, worked in a factory for many years as well as painting and making pottery. He attended the Canterbury College School of Art in the 1920s and 1930s, in the era when it was the most progressive art school in the country.[18] He exhibited at the Canterbury Society of Arts from 1941, and in 1944 he submitted two works he had painted in the Pacific when on active service.[19]

On his return from the war he moved to Grey Lynn, living on Richmond Road, Scanlan Street and finally Rose Road, where he died in 1987.[20] Several of his paintings from the 1940s and 1950s are held in Auckland Art Gallery collection and feature Auckland's urban landscapes and industrial scenes.

Sir Peter Siddell was also inspired by urban landscapes. Born in Grey Lynn in 1935, he grew up in Scanlan Street. Siddell's English father was a wharfie who was barely literate and the Siddell home had few books and no art, but Siddell's mother made up for this by taking him to the Grey Lynn Library, Auckland City Art Gallery and Auckland War Memorial Museum.[21]

Siddell showed an early talent for drawing, and his skills were further developed during his school years at Newton West School, Richmond Road School, Newton Central School, Pasadena Intermediate and Mount Albert Grammar School.

But being an artist was 'quite foreign' to his family, and he left school at 16 to become an apprentice electrician, a trade he followed for a decade before retraining as a teacher. His love of art was rekindled in his thirties, by which time he was married to artist Sylvia Siddell (née Bartlett). Although he spent

**The visual arts** | 319

his married life initially in Blockhouse Bay and then Mount Eden, the place where he spent his childhood was his greatest source of inspiration.[22] His works are held in major collections.

The potter Len Castle was born in 1924 at Fairleigh, the maternity home on Surrey Crescent run by his maternal grandmother, Annie Butterworth. Castle's father, Frank, was brought up in Ponsonby, Freemans Bay and Grey Lynn, and his mother, Cora, spent much of her childhood in Grey Lynn.[23] Soon after Len's birth the Castle family moved to a new subdivision in Westmere Crescent.[24]

As a child Len explored the natural world, fossicking among the mangrove-edged inlets, clambering over lava flows, investigating caves and bringing home treasures to display in the basement playroom.[25] He made clay marbles, digging the raw material out of a deposit on Westmere beach and firing his creations, which often exploded, in the electric oven at home. These early experiments led to a life working with clay. After completing a Bachelor of Science degree in 1946 and training as a science teacher, he took a night class in pottery at Avondale College with the artist Robert Field, an influential teacher who played a major role in the development of studio pottery in New Zealand.[26]

Castle began making pots in his spare time, utilising a nearby deposit of clay. The room that had housed his nature museum now served as his first studio, where he wedged clay and threw and press-moulded pots which he had fired at the Crum Brick Pipe and Tile Works in New Lynn in return for a few bottles of beer.[27]

He first exhibited in 1949, when eight of his pots featured in the Auckland Society of Arts annual exhibition.[28] In the 1950s he built a new workshop equipped with an oil-fired kiln at the bottom of the garden. Here he developed his skills as a potter, making use of local clay and gathering glaze materials on trips out to Te Henga Bethells Beach.[29]

It was a time of growth for local craft and design. The mass-produced imported homewares fashionable in the 1930s had become scarce in the 1940s with wartime restrictions on imports, and there was new interest in locally produced products, including handmade pottery.[30] There were also changes afoot in the way contemporary art was marketed.

In 1949 New Zealand's first dealer gallery, the Helen Hitchings Gallery, opened in Wellington and soon craft and design shops began to appear in the larger cities, providing an avenue for craftspeople to market their wares and increasing knowledge and appreciation of local artistry. Castle's work was soon represented in these galleries and specialist retailers.[31]

**Len Castle throwing a pot in 1958.** NEW ZEALAND WOMAN'S WEEKLY

320 | The Near West

British potter Bernard Leach's seminal 1940 publication *A Potter's Book* was a major influence on Castle's work and on the generations of potters that followed. In 1956 Castle won a fellowship from the Association of New Zealand Art Societies, and went to St Ives in England to work with Leach. On his return he began lecturing in science at the Auckland Teachers' College and devoted his spare time to potting. By 1963 he had exhibited work at the Auckland Art Gallery and Otago Museum, and his work was available at all the major dealer galleries and specialist craft shops in the country. With a promising future as a potter, he resigned from his teaching position and moved to Titirangi. He went on to become one of New Zealand's most influential potters.[32]

Theo Schoon was one of a number of artists who came to New Zealand ahead of the Second World War. Of Dutch heritage, he was born and raised in Java in what was then the Dutch East Indies — now the Republic of Indonesia. When he was 11, he and his younger brother were sent to live with relatives in Holland to complete their education. Schoon attended art school in Rotterdam and in 1936, aged 20, he returned to the cultured Javanese city Bandung.[33] But war clouds were gathering over Europe, and the Schoon family left Java for New Zealand in February 1939. It was intended to be a temporary stay, but after the Japanese invasion of the Dutch East Indies and the subsequent declaration of independence Java was forever changed, and so they remained in New Zealand.[34]

Schoon attended Canterbury College School of Art and got about with the arty set, to whom he was a flamboyant, exotic and entertaining addition, known for his displays of Javanese dancing.[35] He spent much of the 1940s living in Christchurch and Wellington, and from 1946 to 1948 was employed by the Canterbury Museum to record Māori rock drawings in the South Island, an artform that had fascinated him since he first saw depictions of them in Otago Museum. Schoon considered the rock drawings to be art, an opinion that aligned him with the modernist movement internationally but for which there was not much sympathy in New Zealand's conservative art circles.[36]

In the early 1950s he collaborated with Len Castle and decorated some of Castle's forms.[37] Schoon introduced the potter to the central North Island geothermal field that inspired Castle's later work.[38]

Schoon lived an insecure and itinerant life in New Zealand, but found relative stability from the mid-1950s to the mid-1960s through the kindness of his friend Martin Pharazyn, who bought a house at 12 Home Street and invited him to live there for as long as he wished.[39] At Home Street Schoon began to explore a new obsession with decorated Māori gourds.[40]

322 | The Near West

Theo Schoon in his garden at Home Street, 1961. COURTESY CHRISTINE FERNYHOUGH

Schoon's decade-long residence in Arch Hill was a productive time artistically. As well as carved gourds and pottery decoration, he produced drawings and paintings in which his experiences of the previous nomadic decade coalesced.[41] He also shared his ideas about art. Home Street was just two blocks from the Elam School of Art, which was then housed in the former Newton West School, and this brought Schoon into contact with a new generation of student artists, whom he entertained at his home.[42]

For a time, Schoon was a key influence on one of New Zealand's most celebrated modernist artists, Gordon Walters. Walters had accompanied Schoon on expeditions to record rock drawings in 1946, and the two maintained a correspondence.[43]

While Schoon was living in Home Street another influential artist came to live nearby. In 1960 Colin and Anne McCahon moved with their four children from the Titirangi bush to Partridge Street in Arch Hill.[44]

Colin and Anne (née Hamblett) met at the Otago School of Art in the 1930s. Anne was three years ahead of Colin and graduated top of her class. Her work had been well received at Otago Art Society and Wellington Sketch Club exhibitions in the 1930s.[45] In 1939 she established a shared studio and gallery in Dunedin with Doris Lusk and Mollie Lawn.[46] After her marriage to McCahon

The visual arts | 323

in 1942 and the arrival of the first of their children in 1943, her career as an artist largely gave way to domestic demands. She took on part-time work as an illustrator for the *New Zealand School Journal*, a Department of Education publication that featured the work of many of New Zealand's leading writers and illustrators.[47]

When the McCahons moved to Arch Hill, Colin was the keeper and deputy director of Auckland City Art Gallery.[48] McCahon's artwork changed when he came to live in the city; the trees of the Titirangi years gave way to the rooflines of the city, evident in his new 'Gate' series paintings.[49]

The family enjoyed the buzz of the neighbourhood, with its many students and Māori and Pacific Island residents, and the influence of Māori culture can be seen in McCahon's early Arch Hill work.[50] In 1962 his 'Koru' series included Māori words, and in subsequent work he incorporated not just Māori words but also designs and references to Māori history. McCahon's biographer Peter Simpson notes that this was probably partly the result of connections with Māori who lived in his Partridge Street neighbourhood, as well as the influence of several friends with an interest in Māori culture and history, including Schoon and Buster Black (Pihama), a young Māori artist who became a close friend after McCahon taught him at an art class at Auckland City Art Gallery.[51]

Colin McCahon at home in Partridge Street, Arch Hill, 1968. His wife Anne is partly visible through the window. ARTS HOUSE TRUST, 12.178

Artist Paul Tangata photographed in front of two of his paintings in 2012. NEW ZEALAND HERALD

Increasing numbers of Pacific Islanders were now coming to Auckland, but few of their artists gained a foothold in the local art scene until the 1980s. There were exceptions, of course, and one of these was Grey Lynn resident Paul Tangata (known to his family as Pomani). Tangata was born in Atiu in the Cook Islands in 1941, the son of a Cook Islands Christian Church minister.[52] He spent much of his childhood on the islands of Ma'uke and Rarotonga before moving to New Zealand in the mid-1950s with his family. They settled in Leighton Street in Grey Lynn, and Tangata attended Seddon Memorial Technical College, then located in the city where Auckland University of Technology is today.[53]

He showed great promise in art and was encouraged by his art teacher to continue his studies at Elam. In 1965 he became the first Pacific Island artist to graduate with a degree in fine art.[54] As a student he held a well-received solo exhibition at the Uptown Gallery in the city, and this was followed by an exhibition at the Barry Lett Gallery towards the end of 1965 during his honours year.[55] Given that most artists work for years before gaining a solo exhibition, this was a remarkable achievement.

Part of the appeal of Tangata's work was its Pacific Island feel, with its watery patterns and abstract tropical plants and flowers.[56] He won a scholarship

**The visual arts** | 325

to study at the East–West Center in Honolulu and graduated in 1967 with a master's degree in fine arts, after which he returned to New Zealand to complete a diploma in teaching.[57]

After teaching briefly in Rarotonga and at Auckland Technical Institute, he was encouraged to return to the Cook Islands to stand for election in 1968 as member of Parliament for Atiu, one of the 15 islands in the scattered Cook Islands archipelago. It had been just three years since the Cook Islands had gained independence, becoming self-governing in free association with New Zealand. Painting gave way to politics and Tangata served as an MP from 1972 until 1977 and then took on an administrative role in the Cook Islands government. In the late 1980s he returned to his parents' house in Leighton Street in Grey Lynn, where he resumed painting. In 2012 his work was included in *Home AKL*, an Auckland City Art Gallery exhibition of Auckland artists with Pacific heritage.[58]

In 1995 a group of Tongan women formed a Tongan Women's Crafts Cooperative to keep traditional Tongan arts alive in New Zealand. Working from the former Costley Training Institute in Richmond Road, they gathered to socialise and make tapa cloth, or ngatu as it is known in Tonga. Soon they were running courses and travelling to schools where they demonstrated the craft, passing their skills on to a new generation.[59]

The cultural mix of Grey Lynn provided inspiration for photographer Glenn Jowitt, whose photographs depicted an intimate portrait of Pacific cultures both here and in the islands. Jowitt studied photography at Ilam School of Fine Arts in Christchurch in the late 1970s, and soon afterwards moved to Grey Lynn. He photographed people in the Grey Lynn and Ponsonby communities in their homes, churches and at social events, and many of his photographs have been reproduced in books and magazines. When Jowitt died in 2014 he left behind a collection of striking images, some of which are held in the collection of the Museum of New Zealand Te Papa Tongarewa.[60]

As other parts of the city were reshaped, many artists came to the area from the 1970s on. The designation of gully land for a new motorway affected neighbouring Newton, whose rundown, city-end housing grew more so as landlords saw no point in improving condemned properties. They became home to a number of artists, attracted by cheap rent and proximity to the city, but as the motorway pushed its way through, the displaced residents of Newton looked for elsewhere to live, some finding their way to Arch Hill and Grey Lynn.

Other factors also affected the supply of cheap inner-city housing. The

Glenn Jowitt in the backyard of his home in Sackville Street, Grey Lynn, in 1982.
PHOTO BY PETER ADAMS, WWW.PETERADAMS.COM, COURTESY GLENN JOWITT CHARITABLE TRUST

number of flats in the inner suburbs shrank in the 1980s as run-down flats in Freemans Bay, Parnell and Ponsonby were snapped up by young owner-occupiers keen to renovate. Rental housing in Grafton was depleted by the expanding university and hospital as well as by motorway development. As rents rose, some moved west to Grey Lynn and Arch Hill, where affordable rentals could still be found. Others had reached the point in their lives where they wanted to buy a house and put down roots. In the 1980s a number of people who had spent parts of their youth living in cool flats in Parnell, Grafton, Freemans Bay or Ponsonby found themselves saddled with mortgages and raising children in Grey Lynn.

Tony Fomison, who had been living in Gunson Street in Freemans Bay, was among the artists on the move from the changing inner-west suburbs. Freemans Bay was remembered by another Gunson Street resident, silversmith Wallace Sutherland, as the centre of a thriving creative community who

LEFT: Matt McLean with one of his large, delicately balanced sculptures, c. 2010. COURTESY MATT MCLEAN

RIGHT: Richard McWhannell working in his Grey Lynn studio in 2012. PHOTO BY KALLAN MACLEOD, COURTESY RICHARD MCWHANNELL

socialised and supported one another with ideas and materials.[61] Now there was a partial transplant of this community to Grey Lynn and Arch Hill. Potters Matt and Kate McLean moved from Ryle Street to Cockburn Street in the 1980s, while their near neighbours Richard McWhannell and his actress partner Donogh Rees moved to Baildon Road. McWhannell had attended the Ilam School of Fine Arts in the early 1970s before moving to Auckland later in the decade.[62]

Rees was born in Auckland and spent her childhood in Auckland and Fiji before attending the Theatre Corporate Drama School. Her long career as an actor has spanned live theatre, film and television — for several years she was beamed into New Zealand living rooms as nurse Judy Brownlee on *Shortland Street*.[63]

In 1980 Fomison moved to Chamberlain Street in Grey Lynn where his good friend Allen Maddox was a frequent visitor.[64] Maddox, too, ended up living in Arch Hill and Grey Lynn in the 1980s, first in Monmouth Street, and after some time away, for several months in Dryden Street while he was making prints at Muka Studio.[65]

Both Maddox and Fomison had a reputation for wild living, but they were also committed and prolific artists.[66]

Like Theo Schoon, Fomison was interested in Māori rock art, a passion that grew in 1959 when he was employed to provide a more detailed record of Māori rock art in Canterbury. Fomison was also acutely interested in Pacific art. While living in Freemans Bay and Grey Lynn he came in close contact with Pacific Island cultures and was fascinated by a tatau (Samoan tattoo) that he saw on a man in Ponsonby. This led to a meeting with tatau artist Su'a Sulu'ape

Tony Fomison painting *The Ponsonby Madonna* mural for the chapel at St Paul's College on Richmond Road in 1982–83. The mural is now in the collection of the Auckland Art Gallery Toi o Tāmaki. A print of the work has been installed in the chapel. COURTESY E. H. MCCORMICK RESEARCH LIBRARY, AUCKLAND ART GALLERY TOI O TĀMAKI. PHOTOGRAPHER UNKNOWN. IMAGE COURTESY THE FOMISON FAMILY

Paulo II, a member of one of two 'āiga (extended families) who had practised the art in Sāmoa since the 1700s. Sulu'ape had come to Auckland in 1974, two years after his cousin and fellow tatau artist Su'a Tavui Pasina Iosefo Ah Ken.[67]

Fomison and Sulu'ape got to know each other over several months and Sulu'ape consented to give Fomison a pe'a tatau, the densely patterned tattoo that adorns men from the lower torso to the knees. Fomison was joined in this by his friend Fuimaono Tuiasau, the New Zealand-born son of Samoan parents who had immigrated to New Zealand in the 1950s, and the two men supported each other as they received their markings.[68] The process was documented in a celebrated series of photographs by Mark Adams, later published in the book *Tatau*.

Fomison mentored a new generation of artists. The Samoan artist Fatu Feu'u recalled Fomison's encouragement and the way he instilled in him a responsibility to do as he had done and help the next generation to follow.[69] It was a time of birth and growth for Māori and Pacific artists working in a number of genres, something that Feu'u fostered as one of the founders of the Tautai Contemporary Pacific Arts Trust, which supports Pasifika artists.[70]

**The visual arts** | 329

One of the best-known artists to benefit from Fomison's encouragement was John Pule, who was born in Niue in the early 1960s and immigrated to New Zealand with his family at the age of two.[71] The family initially stayed with an aunt in Kingsland, but soon moved to Arch Hill and then over the Great North Road ridge to Crummer Road. In the late 1960s they moved to South Auckland but retained links with the inner-city suburbs through visits to relatives and family friends.[72]

Pule had enjoyed art at school and continued to draw while working at the Westfield abattoirs and then for the Railways Corporation loading hazardous goods onto wagons. After his boss saw some of his art, he encouraged him to think about his future. Pule left soon after to explore his creativity.[73] He became involved in the 1980s inner-city live poetry scene, which was centred on the Poets' Place just off Karangahape Road, along with regular poetry nights at the Globe Hotel in Wakefield Street and later at the Gluepot in Ponsonby.

It was a lively scene, and he was soon writing poetry and painting with his new friends. Tony Fomison attended one of Pule's poetry readings and invited him to his house on Chamberlain Street, where Pule met other artists. He became a frequent visitor there and also visited other local artists, including Colin McCahon, who was then living on Crummer Road.[74]

Fomison left Grey Lynn in 1985 when he was awarded the Rita Angus Residency in Wellington. He spent part of the following year at Barry Brickell's Driving Creek property in Coromandel before returning to Auckland, staying in a basement flat at Sue Gee and Miles Hargest's house in Lincoln Street, Ponsonby, before buying a house at 90 Williamson Avenue in 1988.[75] After Fomison died in 1990, Pule moved into his house, where he lived for the next two years. During this time he went back to Niue — his first visit since leaving as a small child — a trip that provided inspiration for his art and writing.[76] He spent much of the following decades living in Grey Lynn; his art can be seen in a mural on a building at the northern corner of the intersection of Great North Road and Williamson Avenue.[77] He returned to Niue and in 2015 built a home there, but he makes regular trips back to Grey Lynn.[78]

Early in the new century Pule collaborated with Grey Lynn fashion designer Doris de Pont to create designs for her winter 2004 textile collection *Let's*

Doris De Pont and John Pule at the launch of *Let's Gather Here* at New Zealand Fashion Week in 2004. COURTESY DORIS DE PONT

330 | The Near West

*Gather Here*. De Pont has worked with a number of artists, including Paul Hartigan, who works from a studio in Grey Lynn, and photographer Sally Tagg, who lived on Surrey Crescent during the early 2000s.[79]

De Pont learned to sew as a child and went on to design and make clothes to sell while studying at the University of Auckland. In 1984 she established her own retail store in the city. Her work quickly gained attention and featured in magazines, and was sought after by Auckland trendsetters.[80] By the early 1990s she and her husband Tejo van Schie were parents and had moved to Grey Lynn.[81] In 1994 de Pont set up a new business, DNA, with the fabric designer Adrienne Foote and later she began collaborating with artists to create new textile designs for her independent label. She retired from fashion in 2008 and completed a degree in museums and cultural heritage, after which she founded the New Zealand Fashion Museum.[82]

Māori artists from Grey Lynn were also making their mark. The skills of Inia Taylor (Ngāti Raukawa), who moved to Grey Lynn in the 1990s, were put to use in the film industry, where he designed tattoos, costumes and props for local productions, including *Once Were Warriors* and *Xena: Warrior Princess*. He later established the Grey Lynn tattoo studio Moko Ink. Two of his artworks occupy prominent positions in public spaces in Grey Lynn: *Potatau* (dark door), a carved macrocarpa entrance, has stood at front of the Grey Lynn Community Centre since 2004.[83] A gateway by Taylor was installed at the entrance to the Sculptura collection of works by local artists in Grey Lynn Park's Rose Gully Road in 1996. The Sculptura project kicked off in 1993 with works by Barbara Ward, Fatu Feu'u and Richard McWhannell, later joined by Taylor, Charlotte Fisher, Andrew de Boer and Giuseppe Romeo.[84]

Since the 1970s Grey Lynn has been home to a number of important women artists, including Annette Isbey (née Graham), who painted from a studio at the back of a property in West View Road from the 1970s until a few years before her death in 2022.[85] Isbey studied art part-time at Elam in the late 1940s while working as a dental nurse in Waterview. Her husband Eddie was president of the Watersider Workers' Union in New Zealand and later member of Parliament for Grey Lynn and then Papatoetoe. For many years Annette's life was dominated by bringing up their children and acting as an unpaid secretary to her husband, a role that wives of MPs were expected to perform. This left little time for painting, but after their children grew into adulthood Isbey was able to devote herself to her art.[86]

One of Isbey's contemporaries, Jacqueline Fahey, moved to Grey Lynn soon

**The visual arts** | 331

 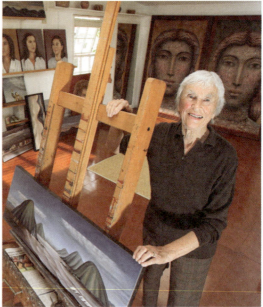

after the death of her husband, the psychiatrist Fraser McDonald, in 1994.[87] The move was a turning point in her career, which had begun when she studied art in the late 1940s and early 1950s at Canterbury University College. While living in Porirua in the 1950s she painted a series entitled 'Suburban Neurosis', which focused on the stifling effects of societal expectations of women, depicting everyday domestic scenes with all their untidiness and chaos.[88] When she moved to Grey Lynn in the mid-1990s, her paintings of domestic interiors largely gave way to other subjects, and her Grey Lynn neighbourhood featured prominently in a number of her paintings. Fahey has written two memoirs, *Something For the Birds* and *Before I Forget*, and a novel, *Cutting Loose*.[89]

Gretchen Albrecht faced similar challenges as a solo mother early in her career. Albrecht attended Elam School of Art, where half the painting teachers were women, including Grey Lynn local Ida Eise. During her time at Elam Albrecht became a mother, but despite her marriage ending not long after, she managed to complete her studies thanks to her determination and her parents' willingness to care for her son.[90] Colin McCahon arranged a solo show of Albrecht's drawings at Ikon Gallery in 1964 and she subsequently trained to be an art teacher and taught at Kelston Girls' High School while continuing to exhibit. In 1970 she married Elam graduate James Ross and the following year won a two-year teaching fellowship at Elam.[91] James Ross held his first solo exhibition in 1974.

In 1982 the couple moved to Grey Lynn from Titirangi, where Gretchen had lived for 15 years, and she has remained in the neighbourhood ever since.

**ABOVE LEFT:** Jacqueline Fahey in her Grey Lynn home in 2013. ARTS HOUSE TRUST

**ABOVE RIGHT:** Annette Isbey in her studio in 2012. STUFF MEDIA LTD

**OPPOSITE ABOVE:** Gretchen Albrecht in her Grey Lynn studio in 1992. PHOTO BY ROBIN MORRISON, COURTESY GRETCHEN ALBRECHT

**OPPOSITE BELOW:** Richard McWhannell, Barbara Ward and Fatu Feu'u, the first three artists to be commissioned for Sculptura, the Grey Lynn Park sculpture project, 1990. SCULPTURA: THE GREY LYNN PARK SCULPTURE PROJECT

**LEFT:** Paul Hartigan in his Grey Lynn Studio in 2005. ARTS HOUSE TRUST, 13.142

**RIGHT:** Mervyn Williams in his Wilton Street studio in 1984. PHOTO BY MICHAEL GILLIES, COURTESY MERVYN WILLIAMS

Mervyn Williams and Paul Hartigan also repurposed former Grey Lynn industrial buildings as studios: Williams, the former Sharpe Brothers soft drink factory in Grey Lynn, and Hartigan, a shop. Williams grew up in Auckland and attended Avondale College, where his art skills were recognised by Robert Field. After he left school at 15 to help support his family, Williams began working in the display department at the Auckland department store Milne & Choyce.[92] When he sold his first artwork at 17 it made him determined to become a full-time artist, and he enrolled at Elam School of Fine Arts in the late 1950s. Williams developed an international expressionist style.[93] In recent years he has created digitally produced paintings as well as free-standing sculptures.[94]

Paul Hartigan was brought up in New Plymouth in a creative family headed by his Egyptian single mother. There wasn't much money in the household but he found opportunities for creativity where he could. Hartigan showed an early entrepreneurial streak, and when he was 16 he and a friend opened an underage venue to provide an alternative to the church groups and occasional dances that were the mainstay of teenage social life. Called the Blue Room, it featured a large, brilliantly coloured mural painted by Hartigan, who also designed a logo for the venue.

Hartigan was encouraged by his art teacher at New Plymouth Boys' High School and found inspiration at the city's Govett-Brewster Art Gallery. His next step was to attend Elam, where he experimented with different media. After art school he worked as a screenprinter in a wallpaper factory in Melbourne and in 1974 he returned to Auckland. He and Philip Peacocke set up Snake

Studios in Darby Street in the city, designing and screenprinting fabrics for fashion boutiques as well as T-shirts and other merchandise. This would be one of several creative commercial enterprises that have provided an income for Hartigan over the years.

By the time he moved to Snake Studios in Great North Road, Grey Lynn, in the mid-1990s Hartigan was a well-established artist working in a number of different mediums, producing drawings, paintings, prints, ceramics and neon art.[95]

✕

Simon Shepheard got a taste for creating art from a mobile studio after throwing in his job as a lecturer at Elam and travelling north with his wife and young son in tow, parking his motorhome at his favourite surfing spots and painting outdoors. At the end of this two-year road trip he settled in Grey Lynn, but he continued to create his art in a variety of locations from his motorhome. His work is inspired by the locations he visits and frequently incorporates discarded objects he finds along the way.[96]

Jeweller Sofia Tekela-Smith has called Grey Lynn home for much of the past three decades. Of Rotuman heritage, she spent much of her childhood on Rotuma and came to Auckland in the early 1980s. Her work, using traditional Pacific materials including bone, stone and shell, explores her multicultural heritage and her place in the world.[97]

Grey Lynn artists and Elam School of Fine Arts lecturers Jim Speers and Lisa Crowley create art around busy teaching schedules. The couple spent a year living in Westmere in 2008 before moving to Grey Lynn.[98] Speers is one of several present or former Grey Lynners to have been awarded the prestigious Frances Hodgkins Fellowship (2000); the others are Gretchen Albrecht (1981) and John Ward Knox (2015).[99]

Many other artists have had a relatively short presence in the area. Kinetic sculpture artist Phil Price lived in Selbourne Street in the mid-1990s before returning home to Christchurch, and the following decade painter Karl Maughan and his wife, author Emily Perkins, lived in the street for seven years before moving to Wellington.[100]

Sofia Tekela-Smith wearing one of her necklaces in 2005. PHOTO BY MARTI FRIEDLANDER, COURTESY GERRARD AND MARTI FRIEDLANDER CHARITABLE TRUST

**The visual arts** | 335

With so many artists living in the area, it was inevitable that Grey Lynn and its people would be referenced in art. The painter Julian Dashper was part of a new generation of artists who employed humour and popular culture in their work. Dashper attended Elam in the late 1970s. By the mid-1980s he was working from a studio in Grey Lynn, where he created the 'Grey' series of paintings, including *The Grey in Grey Lynn*.[101]

✕

Through the 1970s and 1980s, Grey Lynn and Westmere became home to several established potters, who relished the increased opportunities to sell directly to the public that the area gave them. For many, the move to the residential inner suburbs prompted a change in the style of their work — sometimes born of the need to consider the effect on nearby neighbours of firing a kiln — and the cheap-to-rent commercial buildings at the city end of Grey Lynn made great studios.

In around 1980 Warren Tippett moved to Grey Lynn from Albany, where he had lived briefly after moving from Colville on the Coromandel Peninsula. Tippett was known for his wood-fired and salt-glazed stoneware, some of which featured combed surfaces or slip and brush decoration. But in built-up Grey Lynn, the smoke from a wood-fired kiln was a problem. He switched to electric firing and experimented with a lower-temperature glaze colour palette that was bolder and more urban. Tippett had a studio out the back of his Prime Road home and held regular open days selling his latest work to friends and

**ABOVE:** Karl Maughan in his Grey Lynn Studio in 2006. ARTS HOUSE TRUST, 13.155

**OPPOSITE:** *Warren Tippett, 1967,* by Marti Friedlander. AUCKLAND ART GALLERY TOI O TĀMAKI, GIFT OF MARTI FRIEDLANDER, WITH ASSISTANCE FROM THE ELISE MOURANT BEQUEST, 2001, 2000/28/133

A photo by Rika Fukushima of Louise Rive working in her Old Mill Road studio, mid-1990s. COURTESY LOUISE RIVE

visitors.[102] Potters Matt and Kate McLean also moved to Grey Lynn in around 1980, from Freemans Bay. Grey Lynn offered an affordable option, with more space for backyard workshops and kilns. Matt built a kiln and began making the large sculptural works for which he is well known. Both Matt and Kate have worked as tutors at Artstation (now Studio One — Toi Tū) at the top of Ponsonby Road, where they built a huge wood-fired kiln in 1978.[103]

Louise Rive and Chuck Joseph met at the University of Auckland in the 1970s, when Rive was studying printmaking and Joseph was training to be a teacher. After teaching in Tolaga Bay and Northland, where they also took art classes, they bought a property with a shop and adjoining bungalow at the junction of Garnet and Old Mill roads in 1981.

With two small children, life was busy. Joseph began teaching part-time to keep the family afloat and painted local scenes in and around Westmere and Western Springs when time allowed. In 1987 they opened their shop and studio, Edge City, by which time they were both working in clay.[104] The couple still has a presence in Westmere, where they have a studio and small shop fronting Garnet Road.

Potters Andrew and Jeannie Van der Putten were part of a thriving community of Coromandel potters whose dominant style was rustic wood-fired pieces. Their move to Grey Lynn in the 1980s prompted a change to something

338 | The Near West

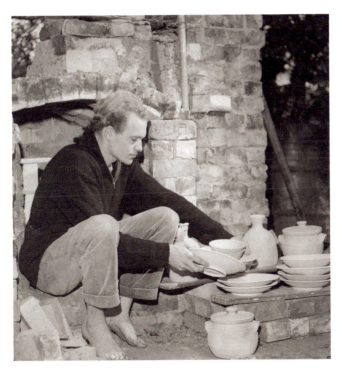

LEFT: Potter Jeff Scholes, 1965. ARCHIVES NEW ZEALAND TE RUA MAHARA O TE KĀWANATANGA, A79033

RIGHT: Andrew and Jeannie van der Putten at their home and studio in Selbourne Street, Grey Lynn, 1988. COURTESY ANDREW AND JEANNIE VAN DER PUTTEN

more refined. Like Rive and Joseph, their Surrey Crescent property included a shop on the street front.[105] After they moved to Huia in 2005 their house was bought by the photographer Sally Tagg. More recently, Kirsten Dryburgh has established a pottery studio at her home on Sherwood Avenue, where she sells direct to the public.

From the 1980s a number of buildings at the commercial- and industrial-dominated city end of Grey Lynn and Arch Hill were converted into studios, some with an adjoining retail space. Jeff Scholes, who had established himself as a potter in the 1970s at Te Henga Bethells Beach, later moved to St Marys Bay, where he set up a pottery at home. But the cramped backyard and close proximity of neighbours was not ideal, so in 1980 he bought a large villa on Mackelvie Street and converted the street-front room into a gallery.

At Bethells he had made stoneware pots in a style that drew on his early training at Barry Brickell's Coromandel pottery. Now, in the city, his works were inspired by earthenware pottery from other parts of the world and fired at a lower temperature that allowed brighter colours to enter his glaze palette. Having his own showroom meant that he no longer had to please the pottery shops and galleries and was now in direct contact with his customers. This gave him freedom to try new techniques and gauge the public response, which in turn encouraged him to develop a new style — from red earthenware he moved to white clay, and he switched from gas to electric firing.[106]

The visual arts | 339

**OPPOSITE:** John Croucher blowing glass in his studio in the late 1970s. COURTESY SANNE HANSEN

**BELOW:** Stephen Bradbourne (left) and Isaac Katzoff at Monmouth Glass Studio, Arch Hill, 2015. COURTESY STEPHEN BRADBOURNE, MONMOUTH GLASS

Scholes was soon joined on Mackelvie Street by jeweller Daniel Clasby, who occupied the upper floor of the building, and New Zealand art glass pioneers John Croucher, Garry Nash and Anne Robinson of the Sunbeam Glass Co-operative, which had been established in Jervois Road by Croucher in the 1970s.[107] They created art glass by melting sand from Mount Somers in the South Island, producing clear glass due to the sand being relatively free of iron.[108] Sunbeam's furnace was kept going day and night, and Nash lived on-site to keep an eye on things.

In 2000 glass artist Peter Viesnik established Viz Glass on Monmouth Street, Arch Hill, in the former Gloria glass studio run by Ruth Allen and Vivienne Bell.[109] Viesnik had immigrated from England in the 1970s and taught himself to work in hot glass, initially from a studio in Devonport. He was later joined at Viz Glass by Isaac Katzoff, who had studied art at Southern Illinois University.[110] In 2012 Katzoff and Stephen Bradbourne formed Monmouth Glass, which operated from the same studio as Viz Glass. Bradbourne had started out in ceramics but soon became interested in glass, and in 1992 he began working at Sunbeam Glass on Mackelvie Street, which by then was run by Garry Nash.

Bradbourne's passion for glass was shared with his ceramic and glass artist partner, Emily Siddell, daughter of the painters Peter and Sylvia Siddell. The pair had both studied at Carrington Polytechnic (now Unitec) in the late 1980s and early 1990s and lived on Prime Road, Grey Lynn, for several years in the 1990s before moving to Sandringham.[111]

The Monmouth Street studio moved to Henderson in 2019 and a retail shop was opened on Great North Road near the corner of Ponsonby Road.[112]

The inexpensive commercial spaces of Grey Lynn and Arch Hill that had provided great artists' studios for many years are now few and far between.

The visual arts | 341

10

# The performing and literary arts

**PREVIOUS PAGES:** Chris Knox performing outside the Grey Lynn post office in the late 1990s.
COURTESY DAVID TIPPETT

In 2015 the music writer Russell Brown observed that census data had shown that Grey Lynn was still the songwriting capital of New Zealand. It's an area that has many associations with music and musicians — some stretching back well beyond living memory.[1]

Music was very much a part of life for many nineteenth- and early twentieth-century households, and children often learned to play the piano or some other instrument. People entertained family and friends with songs and music, and music was a major part of any entertainment, fundraiser or church service held in the district.

Some even made instruments. In 1841 John Cox made his home on the lonely banks of Coxs Creek, where he cleared scrub and planted vegetables. Cox was more than a brickmaker and gardener, however. He also played, built and repaired violins, sometimes using local wood, and a number of his violins were sent to London for sale in 1861.[2]

Local musicians enjoyed many opportunities to perform. Gordon Lanigan, who was born in Francis Street in 1906, came from a musical family. His father Edward played in a string band, mainly in Ponsonby and Herne Bay, and Gordon learned to play the violin and piano as a child, later adding the saxophone. In the late 1920s he and a cousin were providing the accompaniment to silent movies at the Adelphi Theatre on the corner of Richmond Road and Tutanekai Street. Three different films were shown each week, and the pair had to be adaptable, the film synopsis guiding their music choices. Lanigan recalled many visits to Marbeck's music library on Selbourne Street to borrow suitable sheet music.[3]

Alfred Marbeck was a talented pianist who taught music, played in the movie theatres in the city and conducted the Lyric Theatre Orchestra in the 1920s.[4] He loaned his substantial collection of sheet music to other musicians.[5] In the 1930s Marbeck, his wife, Eileen (also a talented musician), and her brother established the city music store that is now run is by their grandson.[6]

But change was afoot for the theatre musicians.[7] In March 1929 the first

**The performing and literary arts** | 345

**ABOVE:** The Adelphi Picture Theatre opened on Richmond Road on the southern corner of Tutanekai Street in 1928.
MUSEUM OF TRANSPORT AND TECHNOLOGY

**LEFT:** In 1914 the Empress Theatre (later known as the Avon and Newton) was the first cinema to open in Grey Lynn, at the city end of Great North Road. This was during the silent film era when live musicians provided the accompaniment.
AUCKLAND WAR MEMORIAL MUSEUM TĀMAKI PAENGA HIRA, PH-NEG-M106(ABCD)

**BELOW:** The splendid interior of the Cameo Cinema. When it opened in 1929 records rather than live music provided the accompaniment, but after just a few months sound equipment was installed and the first talkie, *The Singing Fool*, was screened.
AUCKLAND WAR MEMORIAL MUSEUM TĀMAKI PAENGA HIRA, PH-NEG-RMS-SOP FRONTISPIECE-0 (DUPE)

Gordon Lanigan (front row, second from right) playing in Ted Croad's band at the Orange Ballroom on Newton Road. PHOTO BY JIM WARREN, COURTESY CHRIS BOURKE

'talkie' was screened at the Paramount Theatre in Wellington to great acclaim.[8] A month later the first talkies were shown at the Regent and Strand theatres in Auckland. Sound equipment was expensive and was not immediately installed in the smaller suburban theatres, but by the mid-1930s Grey Lynn's two cinemas — the Adelphi in West Lynn and the Grey Lynn Cinema (later known as the Cameo) at the Surrey Crescent shops — were both showing movies with sound.[9] Accompaniment by musicians was no longer required.

Technology did not replace all live music, of course. Lanigan played frequently at dances such as those held at St Columba and St Joseph's. He also played saxophone with Ted Croad's 12-piece band, which performed at the Orange Coronation Ballroom on Newton Road in the 1940s, and was one of the top jazz musicians of his day.[10] Such was the demand for Lanigan's services that he sometimes played seven nights a week as well as holding down his regular job.[11]

Some people made a living from their music. Music was in the blood of Grey Lynn resident Carl Hellriegel, whose multi-instrumentalist father Julius to came to New Zealand in 1903, via Australia, from the small German town of Einöllen in the West Palatinate (Westpfalz) area that was well known for its many travelling musicians.[12]

**The performing and literary arts** | 347

The Hellriegels settled in Grey Lynn in 1910 — initially in Sussex Street and later in Millais Street and then Dickens Street.[13] Julius worked as a musician and music teacher, and also loaded rail freight in the city. He performed with the Bohemian Orchestra, which played regularly from 1914 to 1937 — one of a number of groups to which he belonged, many of them with his son, Carl, who began playing in Adeane's Orchestra with his father as a teenager. The two also took in students. Julius taught cornet and slide trombone and Carl the violin.[14]

In the early 1920s Carl and his cousin Henry Engel entertained passengers on the Pacific mail route plied by the *Niagara*, the fastest of the New Zealand-owned Union Steam Ship Company vessels.[15] In the 1930s Carl became the conductor of the St John Ambulance Orchestra in which Julius played trombone and clarinet. In 1946 Carl was selected to play in New Zealand's first state-funded orchestra, the Wellington-based National Broadcasting Service Symphony Orchestra (later the New Zealand Symphony Orchestra).[16] The family musical legacy continues today, most notably through Julius's great-granddaughter Jan Hellriegel, an award-winning Auckland singer-songwriter who lived for a while on Richmond Road.[17]

There was also a more local orchestra, the grandly titled Westmere Symphony Orchestra, which was active in the early 1930s, playing concerts in local halls.[18] This amateur group was conducted by Beryl Debenham, who taught piano and violin from a studio in her family's home on Nottingham Street, Westmere.[19]

From the 1940s immigrants from the Pacific Islands settled in Grey Lynn and Arch Hill, bringing new sounds to the district. Music and faith were very much a part of life for many Pasifika people, including the Yandall family. Tanuvasa James Yandall arrived in New Zealand from Sāmoa as a young man in 1946; he married Nova Phineas soon after and started a family. He attended Christian rallies, where he learned the gospel songs he taught to his young family. Sunday school at the Pacific Islanders' Congregational Church (later known as the Pacific Islanders' Presbyterian Church) in Newton provided further opportunities for singing. His four daughters — Caroline, Adele, Mary and Pauline — entered singing competitions held by the Sunday School Union, and sang with the Friendly Road choir on Radio 1ZB. Their parents encouraged them to sing to entertain visitors to their Dryden Street home, and took them to talent quests.[20] Caroline, Adele and Mary performed as the Yandall Sisters and made their first recordings in 1966 — including *Samoa Ea*, their album of Samoan songs, recorded with Bill Sevesi and His Islanders — while they were still attending Auckland Girls' Grammar School.

The Yandall Sisters, Pauline, Adele and Mary, recording an overdub in the 1970s. COURTESY AUDIOCULTURE

The Yandall Sisters had a polished performing style reminiscent of the American group The Supremes, and became regular performers on television. They also worked as backing singers for EMI, and their cover of American song 'Sweet Inspiration' was a local hit in 1975.[21] By this stage the youngest sister, Pauline, had joined the group and they quickly became household names.[22]

With their family backing and strong Christian faith, the Yandall Sisters were professional and well behaved — unlike some musicians who lived briefly in Grey Lynn in the mid-1960s. The PleaZers (not to be confused with local band the Pleasers) was formed in Brisbane from members of the Auckland band The London Brothers (Billy Bacon, aka Billy London, and Bob Cooper) and Brisbane band The G Men. The PleaZers soon moved south to Sydney, where they were spotted by Auckland's Eldred Stebbing, who signed them to his Zodiac label.[23] The band arrived in Auckland in mid-1965 and moved into a Northland Street house that Stebbing had rented for them. They were in the mood for some fun, and the result was visits from the police and fire service and a litany of complaints from neighbours.

One of Stebbing's other signings at this time was the west Auckland band the La De Da's, who played some elaborate tricks on the PleaZers. The La De

**The performing and literary arts | 349**

ABOVE: Toy Love, 1979–80. The band members are, from left, Chris Knox, Mike Dooley, Paul Kean, Jane Walker and Alec Bathgate. MAURICE LYE

OPPOSITE: Toy Love performing, probably at the Gluepot in Ponsonby, in 1979. From left: Paul Kean, Alec Bathgate, Chris Knox. ANTHONY PHELPS

Da's would arrive at Northland Street when they knew the band was out and create mayhem. One day a prank call resulted in an undertaker arriving at the house to pick up a corpse, something the unimpressed undertaker took up with Stebbing. Eventually Stebbing moved the band closer to home in Herne Bay, where he could keep a better eye on them.[24]

Long-term Grey Lynn resident Chris Knox was brought up in Invercargill but moved to Dunedin in early 1970s to study at the University of Otago. He soon dropped out and assembled the punk band The Enemy, which performed with the exuberant and outrageous Knox out front on vocals.[25] The Enemy moved north in the late 1970s but soon fell apart, and band members Knox and Alec Bathgate with Paul Kean, Jane Walker and Mike Dooley formed the punk rock band Toy Love, based in a flat on Grey Lynn's Williamson Avenue.

After being signed to the music label WEA, in 1980 the band had a brief foray to Australia, where they recorded in Sydney's EMI Studios. The tour and recording did not live up to expectations, however, and the experience led Knox to eschew formal recording studios. He adopted a do-it-yourself approach using a second-hand TEAC 4-track recorder that he bought for $400. It was later put to good use recording Knox's subsequent band Tall Dwarfs (Chris Knox and Alec Bathgate), as well as many of Knox's solo compositions and a plethora of early bands recording under the Flying Nun label.[26]

350 | The Near West

The Legion of Frontiersmen Hall on Bond Street was a popular band practice space, used by Split Enz among others. The Chills' *Rolling Moon* and The Clean's *Boodle Boodle Boodle* and *Getting Older* were recorded there in the 1980s. Pictured outside the hall in 1982 are (from left) Chris Knox, Martin Phillips, David Kilgour and Doug Hood. ROBERT SCOTT

Following their stint in Sydney, Knox and his partner, the sculptor Barbara Ward, flatted on Grey Lynn's Jessel Street with Toy Love's manager and soundman Doug Hood, and his partner, photographer Carol Tippet. The quirky video for the Tall Dwarfs song 'Nothing's Going to Happen', using scraps of TVNZ film and experimenting with stop-motion animation and a range of household items, was filmed in the house. They also recorded and released a bizarre single, including a song about Bob the Jessel Street cat ('Bobzilla') and a Christmas song ('Worst Noel') under the name The Jessels.[27]

Knox and Ward bought a house near the top of Hakanoa Street in the mid-1980s, and it became a focus of the creative community that gathered around them.[28] For several years in the 1980s Knox was in charge of distribution for Flying Nun Records in Auckland — he was just the right sort of character for this voluntary job.[29] His contribution and that of many other unpaid helpers allowed the record label to survive its early years. Knox also created art for the label, lent his 4-track recorder to various Flying Nun bands, and put up band members from other parts of the country at his home when they were in Auckland on tour. It was a small world, and there were often just a few degrees of separation between one Flying Nun band and another.[30]

One of the early bands to utilise Knox's 4-track recorder was The Clean, which recorded its EP *Boodle Boodle Boodle* in Arch Hill at the Legion of

352 | The Near West

Frontiersmen Hall at the bottom end of Bond Street, with the assistance of Knox and Hood's technical expertise (Hood had been The Clean's original singer). Knox provided the cover artwork based on a photograph Tippet had taken of the band fully clothed and sopping wet in the bath.[31]

Over the coming years Knox continued his various creative pursuits. His 1989 love song 'Not Given Lightly' became well known and his *Max Media* comic strip was published by the *New Zealand Herald* for 15 years.

Knox suffered a major stroke in 2009, but his house continued to be a gathering place for artists, many of whom rallied around to help. Despite having only fleeting commercial success himself, Knox's influence on other musicians and artists has been significant. Both local and international musicians gave their time to record a tribute album, *Stroke: Songs for Chris Knox*, to raise money to support his recovery.[32]

There were plenty of other bands about. Grey Lynn was a colourful place that attracted colourful people, including singer-songwriter Linn Lorkin. Originally from Tokoroa, she had worked in Europe and New York for many years. She returned to New Zealand in 1985 with her young son, followed by his father, Hershal Herscher, a musician from New York.[33] They subsequently settled in Grey Lynn and Lorkin continued to write and perform, including in local bands the Jews Brothers Band and French Toast, both of which feature Herscher.[34] Lorkin published her memoir, *The Redhead Gets the Gig*, in late 2022.

Some bands that had been intertwined in other parts of the city ended up in Grey Lynn. Brothers Todd and Marc Hunter, who later formed the band Dragon, and Graham Brazier and Dave McArtney, who formed Hello Sailor, lived a drug-fuelled bohemian lifestyle in a notorious St Marys Bay party house known as Mandrax Mansion in the early 1970s.[35] Dragon then moved to Murdoch Road, where their guitarist, Ray Goodwin, recorded a demo tape of songs written by Brazier and McArtney.[36]

Hello Sailor played its first Auckland gig in Grey Lynn at Dunlop's gym in July 1975, and although the band would later break up, core members Brazier (who lived in the terrace houses on Great North Road near the Grey Lynn shops for several years), McArtney and Harry Lyons teamed up again in 2009 to record *Surrey Crescent Moon*, their last album together. As ever, Brazier's lyrics were fed by what was around him. Featuring vocals by New Zealand-born Samoan fashion designer and fa'afāfine Lindah Lepou, 'Friday Night Fa'afāfine' is a song about a man who is fascinated by a fa'afāfine he sees at the Grey Lynn (Surrey Crescent) shops pedestrian crossing.[37]

The performing and literary arts | 353

**OPPOSITE:** Hershal Herscher (left) and Linn Lorkin recording the Jews Brothers album *Live at Gerhard's Café* in 1994. PHOTO BY DAVID LEGGE, COURTESY LINN LORKIN AND CHRIS BOURKE

**BELOW LEFT:** Robert Key and Graeme Jefferies of The Cakekitchen outside Jefferies' flat on Crummer Road in 1988. JONATHAN GANLEY

**BELOW RIGHT:** Able Tasmans, 1996. From left: Craig Mason, Leslie Jonkers, Graeme Humphreys, Jane Dodd and Peter Keen. GRAEME HILL

In the 1980s and 1990s the colourful, creative vibe of Grey Lynn attracted people from elsewhere in Auckland as well as other parts of New Zealand. Many musicians outside Auckland felt the pull towards the city and its potential for larger live audiences.

When brothers Graeme and Peter Jefferies, of the post-punk bands Nocturnal Projections and This Kind of Punishment, moved to Auckland in 1982, they lived first on Paget Street in Freemans Bay and then Fourth Avenue in Kingsland. When that house sold they moved to O'Neill Street in Ponsonby. Their next Auckland flat was on Williamson Avenue in Grey Lynn.[38]

Graeme Jefferies had lived for a short time in 1979 on Wellpark Avenue, on the border of Grey Lynn and Westmere, where he wrote one of his first songs, 'Nothing That's New'. It was recorded several years later and released on his solo album *Messages for the Cakekitchen* in 1988.[39] After a period overseas he returned to Grey Lynn in the late 1980s, when his solo project morphed into a band known as The Cakekitchen. Like many Grey Lynn locals, he was also involved in side projects — he joined his Crummer Road flatmate, drummer Craig Mason, in his band The Sombretones (from which he enlisted his first drummer for The Cakekitchen, Robert Key).[40] Mason later joined Able Tasmans and was one of several members of the band who lived in Grey Lynn from the 1980s.

The performing and literary arts | 355

Able Tasmans formed in the early 1980s after Graeme Humphreys and Craig Baxter, who had been in Whangārei band Sister Ray, moved to Auckland. Baxter and Humphreys initially performed as a duo, but they were soon joined by Sister Ray's former bass player, Dave Beniston. Various friends were brought in to help record their first EP, *The Tired Sun*, including Peter Keen from Auckland band Raucous Laughter. By the time they released their first full album, *A Cuppa Tea and a Lie Down*, in 1987, Keen had become a core member of Able Tasmans along with Leslie Jonkers.[41]

Grey Lynn's Crummer Road became home to many members of the band's evolving line-up: when they released *Hey Spinner!* (featuring the song 'Grey Lynn') in 1990, band members Peter Keen, Graeme Humphreys and Leslie Jonkers were living in houses along the street. Ron Young later lived on Potatau Street in Arch Hill. Bass player Jane Dodd had earlier lived in Grey Lynn for a while, too, after leaving Dunedin, where she had played in bands including The Chills and The Verlaines.[42]

Various guests appeared on their recordings, and the band's full sound set them apart from other Flying Nun bands of the era.[43] They went on to record two further albums before going their separate ways in 1997.[44] Flying Nun founder Roger Shepherd was a great fan of the band — two years after they folded, Flying Nun released an Able Tasmans compilation, *Songs from the Departure Lounge*.[45] In 2006 Humphreys and Keen released *The Overflow*, which featured several of their former bandmates along with Grey Lynn local Victoria Kelly.[46]

×

Both budding and established musicians have spent much time writing in bedrooms, lounges, sleepouts and sheds.[47] The songs on the Strawpeople's album *Vicarious*, for example, emerged from the spare room at Fiona McDonald's Grey Lynn flat in 1997.[48] Local ska band The Managers wrote *The Grove Street Tapes* (2010) in the basement of a punk flat on Grey Lynn's Grosvenor Street.[49]

Sheds could also provide space for recording. Grey Lynn band Goodshirt was formed after Gareth Thomas installed a recording studio in the laundry of the flat rented by his friends Rodney and Murray Fisher. The trio recorded the demos that got them air time on bFM and 96dot1 next to the washing machine. They became a four-piece with the addition of drummer Mike Beehre, and their first album, *Good*, emerged from the shed in 2001, followed soon after by the number-one single 'Sophie'. They were then booked to record at a professional studio, but after five weeks they returned to the shed to complete their second album, *Fiji Baby*.[50] The song 'Slippy' from their first album was

Goodshirt band members Rodney Fisher and Gareth Thomas.
GARETH SHUTE

written about taking the bus from Richmond Road to the city.[51]

Boh Runga has spent many years living in Grey Lynn and Westmere since she and Andrew Maclaren left their home town of Christchurch in 1992 to further their musical ambitions, forming the band Stellar* a couple of years later. Runga was raised in a musical household — her father played piano with a Māori showband and her mother was a nightclub singer.[52] Her younger sister, the musician Bic Runga, also lived in Grey Lynn for a few years.[53]

British producer Tom Bailey, best known as a member of British band Thompson Twins that achieved international fame in the 1980s, was brought in to produce Stellar*'s first album, *Mix*, which was recorded in 1998 at various locations, including a house on Warnock Street, Westmere, where Boh Runga and Maclaren lived. Success followed quickly, with Runga winning the award for Most Promising Female Vocalist at the 1999 New Zealand Music Awards and Stellar* winning Most Promising Group. The band took home an even bigger haul of awards the following year.[54] Stellar* went on to release three further albums, and Runga released a solo album in 2009. She has collaborated with various other musicians, including Anika Moa and Hollie Smith, with whom she released an album in 2013. During this time she also began designing jewellery, launching her first range in 2007.[55]

Alas, some local musicians who found commercial success also met

The performing and literary arts | 357

Street Chant — from left Emily Littler (Edrosa), Billie Rogers and Chris Varnham — outside 41 Sussex Street, three doors along from Littler's grotty flat where she wrote 'Pedestrian Support League' and where they recorded the album *Hauora* on which the song features. PHOTO BY KEVA RANDS, COURTESY STREET CHANT

challenges they were unable to overcome. Daniel Bolton moved from the North Shore to Ponsonby with his Telecaster guitar, an effect pedal and a 4-track recorder and then moved to Grey Lynn. He spent many hours alone in his bedroom, writing and recording songs that would ultimately become his six-song EP *Jesus I Was Evil*, which he released under his stage name Darcy Clay, a persona with a penchant for Formula One-style jumpsuits, large Elvis-style sunglasses and cheap, long wigs. Bolton was something of an outsider, preferring to do things on his own and in his own way.[56]

The title track 'Jesus I Was Evil' was rough and ready, its amusing lyrics detailing past transgressions and redemption. It quickly became a hit after Bolton dropped off a demo tape at the student radio station bFM, which added it to their playlist. The song climbed the national charts to number five, and a backing band was cobbled together to perform live, including as the support act for British band Blur.[57]

The success of the song garnered some international interest, but he never made the leap from suburban bedroom to world stage. Sadly, Bolton took his own life in March 1998 at the age of 25. Later that year he was posthumously named the most promising male vocalist at the New Zealand Music Awards.[58] Fellow Grey Lynn 4-track enthusiast Chris Knox would later write 'I Wanna Look Like Darcy Clay', a song that appears on his 2000 album *Beat*.

Living in a grotty Grey Lynn flat could be grim, particularly in the

**LEFT:** Darcy Clay performing at the bFM Summer Series, c. 1995. EJ MATHERS

**RIGHT:** Diggy Dupé in the laundromat in the Grey Lynn (Surrey Crescent) shops. PHOTO BY TOM GRUT, COURTESY AUDIOCULTURE

winter. Emily Littler of Street Chant recalled writing the band's Silver Scroll-nominated song 'Pedestrian Support League' about feeling depressed and paranoid after coming home to live in a dingy flat after a lengthy tour overseas.[59] They recorded their Taite Prize-winning 2016 album *Hauora* with Bob Frisbee in the Grey Lynn villa that is pictured on its cover.[60]

Hip Hop artist Diggy Dupé, who was born in Auckland to Niuean parents, has written about growing up in a poor household in Arch Hill and Grey Lynn. His song 'CT & T' recalls the many occasions when a cup of tea and toast was all there was to eat after the meagre household income had been depleted by gambling.[61]

By the 1990s well-established musicians who had long since left the cheap flats of their youth behind were also moving into the area. Sir Dave Dobbyn moved to Grey Lynn in the 1990s. Brought up in Glen Innes, he attended Sacred Heart College with Ian Morris and Peter Urlich, with whom he formed Th' Dudes in the 1970s. The band DD Smash followed in the 1980s, and then a solo career. Over the years he has received numerous awards for his music, including more Silver Scroll awards than any other artist.[62]

Of course Grey Lynn, Arch Hill and Westmere were part of a vast swathe of 'dry' suburbs west of Ponsonby at the time, so if you wanted to see a band at a pub you would have to go elsewhere. Grey Lynn was not far from the licensed music venues in Ponsonby, the city and Parnell, but there were also opportunities to perform locally at parties or at the annual Grey Lynn Park

The performing and literary arts | 359

Dave Dobbyn performing at Christmas in the Park in Hastings in 2022.
NEW ZEALAND HERALD

Festival, which has been a springtime staple since 1984. In the 1990s musicians sometimes performed at the short-lived but much-loved Gerhard's Café at the Grey Lynn shops.

Many locals breathed a sigh of relief when Grey Lynn voted to go wet in 1996, but it would be mainly small wine bars and restaurants rather than large pubs that would provide alcoholic beverages to the people of the area. In recent years Freida Margolis, Malt and the Grey Lynn Returned Services Club have hosted small gigs, and buskers entertain shoppers at the weekly Grey Lynn Farmers' Market. Gigs have also been held at other venues, including the Grey Lynn Bowling Club, where Shayne Carter's band Dimmer performed a live version of their 2004 album *You've Got to Hear the Music*.

Carter returned to the Grey Lynn Bowling Club in 2006 to record his album *There My Dear* with a host of other musicians, including Anika Moa and Bic Runga.[63] While Carter is very much a Dunedinite, he also lived in various parts of Auckland for 25 years. Grey Lynn was home for some of that time, including several years in which he lived in a sleepout at a friend's house or worked as one of Chris Knox's caregivers.[64]

But the days of cheap flats in the area were numbered. Grey Lynn ska-punk band The Poisoners wrote about rising house prices and gentrification in their song 'Grey Lynn', from the self-titled 2008 album.[65] Many people who had enjoyed the creative vibe of Grey Lynn and Arch Hill in the 1980s and 1990s feel a sense of sadness at the changes in the community and the exponential

Goodnight Nurse, c. 2006. From left: Paul Taite, Joel Little and Jaden Parkes. COURTESY GARETH SHUTE

rise in property prices. Some had day jobs that enabled them to remain in the area, or had sufficient financial success to be able to afford to stay.

Some earlier creative residents who had been able to put down roots in the area and raise families created a new generation interested in the arts. Joel Little, for example, spent much of his childhood living on Dryden Street, having arrived there as a seven-year-old in 1990 with his sister and parents. His mother, Trish Scott, was the former guitarist for the late-1970s Auckland punk band Suburban Reptiles (she was also known as Sissy Spunk at this time); and his father, Paul Little, was a magazine journalist and editor who went on to write books and establish a small publishing firm in the early 2000s while living on neighbouring Schofield Street.[66]

Joel Little has fond memories of growing up in Grey Lynn and later named his record label Dryden Street. While attending Western Springs College he began writing songs in the sleepout at the back of his house with school friend Jaden Parkes. With Paul Taite, who answered their advertisement for a bass player, they formed post-punk band Goodnight Nurse. The band was part of a sponsored schools tour in 2004 and travelled the country, playing at 120 high schools. After releasing two albums, the band split. Little went on to become well known for his award-winning collaborative work with Lorde, Broods and Ellie Goulding, among others.[67] He and his wife Gemma have recently set up the recording studio and performance space Big Fan, in Kingsland, as a not-for-profit to support emerging artists.

Reggae, the music style that emerged from Jamaica in the late 1960s, arrived in New Zealand in the early 1970s through overseas recordings. The Grey Lynn bands Back Yard and Unity were among the first to play reggae music in New Zealand, in the mid-1970s. Back Yard featured Toni Fonoti, who was born in New Zealand to Samoan parents, while Unity was Tigilau Ness's band.[68] Members of both bands would go on to become major figures in local reggae — Back Yard reformed as Herbs, and Ness formed Unity Pacific.

**The performing and literary arts** | 361

Ness was born in New Zealand in 1955 to Niuean parents. In the mid-1970s he was introduced to the music of Bob Marley when friends bought the album *Natty Dread*. Ness responded to the biblical lyrics as well as to the music, which he felt had a Pacific vibe, and saw parallels in the struggle against prejudice and oppression of Marley's people and his own.[69]

For Ness and other reggae fans, 1979 was an important year. On 16 April Bob Marley and the Wailers played before a crowd of nearly 22,000 at Western Springs, and after the concert Ness and his wife, Miriama, invited the Wailers back to their house in Grey Lynn for a meal — Ness recalled that, after preparing the umu, he discovered with some embarrassment that his guests were vegan.[70]

Reggae, with its messages of resistance, redemption, faith, love and peace, resonated particularly with Māori and Pasifika, and Marley's concert provided a huge boost to the local music scene. Some became interested in the Rastafarian faith with which reggae is associated. A local chapter of the Twelve Tribes of Israel, a conservative Rastafarian organisation founded in Jamaica that counted Bob Marley as a member, was established in Surrey Crescent in 1980 and soon an old villa in Pollen Street was up and running as a headquarters offering consciousness-raising dance parties, craft group meetings, and budgeting and employment training services.

The Twelve Tribes of Israel house band entertained visitors at regular events as well as playing elsewhere in the city. The suburbs of Grey Lynn and Ponsonby were the centre of reggae in Auckland at the time. By the early twenty-first century New Zealanders were reputedly the world's largest consumers of reggae music per capita, and its adoption by Māori and Pasifika and the development of a New Zealand variant infused with Polynesian sounds and lyrics were central to its success here.[71]

Ness's son Che (known as Che Fu) lived for much of his childhood with his grandmother in Ponsonby, while maintaining close contact with his Māori mother and Niuean father in Grey Lynn.[72] Che started his musical journey with friends at Western Springs College (then known as Seddon High School) in The Lowdown Dirty Blues Band, which morphed into Supergroove. He has had a successful solo career and has collected numerous music awards.[73]

Tigilau Ness and his son Che Fu in 2011. Ness, often referred to as the Grandfather of Reggae, kept his creative fire burning while his children grew up. In 2003 he recorded his first album with Unity Pacific. STUFF MEDIA LTD

Feleti Strickson-Pua also came from a creative Grey Lynn family. He is the son of Reverend Mua Strickson-Pua, whose parents had emigrated from Sāmoa, and Linda Strickson-Pua, whose father was part of the wave of British post-war immigration to New Zealand. Mua Strickson-Pua grew up in Grey Lynn but left to study social work at Massey University in

**The performing and literary arts** | 363

Palmerston North. On his return he moved to 12 Home Street, Arch Hill, where artist Theo Schoon had lived in the 1950s and 1960s.

Mua began writing poetry while at university, and it became a life-long passion. The verbal rhythms appealed to young Feleti, who was encouraged to start rapping by his cousin Malo Luafutu (better known as Scribe), who lived with the family for a year.[74] Feleti was soon performing in a band called Fa'atasi. At one of their gigs he met Donald McNulty, a student at Western Springs College, and together they wrote songs that they performed at poetry nights organised by Mua at the Dead Poets Café in Karangahape Road.[75]

Meanwhile McNulty and several other Western Springs College pupils formed the band Nesian Mystik and were joined by Feleti Strickson-Pua. The band met with early success, with their single 'Nesian Style' charting at number 10 in 2001. Four albums and numerous awards followed.[76]

Nesian Mystik's song 'Brothaz' featured on the soundtrack to the film *Sione's Wedding* (2006), a comedy about a group of Samoan friends from Grey Lynn. The script was written by Grey Lynn locals Oscar Kightley (who also plays Albert) and James Griffin, both of whom are prolific screenwriters.

Māori culture and language have had a champion in musician, filmmaker, television presenter and writer Moana Maniapoto (Ngati Tūwharetoa, Te Arawa), who lived in Grey Lynn for a number of years before moving to

**Nesian Mystik performing in Aotea Square in 2010.** GARETH SHUTE

364 | The Near West

Muriwai in 2011. She has carved her own path, recording and performing from the early 1980s. By the late 1980s she was fronting Moana and the Moahunters and incorporating te reo Māori into her songwriting, as she continues to do today with her band Moana and the Tribe.[77]

Others who had flatted in Grey Lynn in their youth, or had other connections with the area, have returned to the area to settle down and raise families. Fiona McDonald lived in various Grey Lynn flats in her younger years and eventually bought a house in Westmere.

Composer, performer and producer Victoria Kelly lent her considerable skills to a variety of musical endeavours, including some connected to Grey Lynn. She moved to Grey Lynn in the early 2000s and then to Westmere with her husband Ashley Brown, founder and cellist of NZTrio, who she married in 2004. Brown and Kelly later moved back to Grey Lynn, where their house has a large music room. Kelly is a well-established composer working in genres from pop to classical and creating film soundtracks, having completed the prestigious composing for film course at the University of Southern California. One of her recent works is a secular requiem, featuring the words of some of her favourite poets and inspired by Anne Noble's photography, performed at the Auckland Arts Festival in 2023.[78]

There is still a lively creative vibe in the area. Musicians still practise and

Moana and the Tribe performing at the Stołeczna Estrada Cross Culture Warsaw Festival in September 2013. From left: Kemara James Kennedy, Moana Maniapoto and Laurence Tanetiu Kershaw.
STOŁECZNA ESTRADA CROSS CULTURE WARSAW FESTIVAL

The performing and literary arts | 365

**OPPOSITE ABOVE:** Victoria Kelly at home in 2023. STUFF MEDIA LTD

**OPPOSITE BELOW:** Benee performing at the Laneway Festival in 2020. STUFF MEDIA LTD

**BELOW LEFT:** A scene from Warwick Broadhead's film *Rubbings from a Live Man*, made with director Florian Habicht and director of photography Christopher Pryor and released in 2008. PHOTO BY FRANK HABICHT, COURTESY FLORIAN HABICHT

**BELOW RIGHT:** Michael Hurst and Jennifer Ward-Lealand in a production of *King Lear* in 2023. NEW ZEALAND HERALD

write in bedrooms, sheds and lounges, and artists create visual feasts, but they are more likely to be either middle-aged homeowners or their offspring, nurtured in households where creativity is valued.

One of the more recent musical success stories to emerge from a Grey Lynn villa is Stella Bennett, better known as Benee. In 2019, while still a teenager, she collected four New Zealand Music Awards, and she gathered a further three in 2020. That year she also won an APRA Silver Scroll for her hit song 'Glitter'.[79] Benee is part of the deep well of talent that has always existed in the neighbourhood.

Theatre has always been a strong part of the Grey Lynn creative ecosystem. One of the most famous practitioners was the flamboyant Warwick Broadhead, who lived his life as a work of art. Born in 1944, Broadhead grew up in Mount Roskill and attended St Paul's College on the edge of Grey Lynn. As a young gay man he moved to Sydney, where he studied dance and embarked on a theatrical life of his own making. Returning to New Zealand in the 1970s he started The Full Moon Follies, a performance group that put on theatrical events every full moon. Broadhead went on to perform in and orchestrate various elaborate amateur theatrical performances and solo shows throughout New Zealand and in many parts of the world, including over 500 performances of Lewis Carroll's *The Hunting of the Snark*.

From the late 1970s until around 2008 he lived at 59 Selbourne Street, in

**The performing and literary arts | 367**

gay-friendly Grey Lynn, and at one stage he decided he loved his house so much that he should marry it — which he did at an extraordinary ceremony, only to divorce it several years later when he moved to Waiheke Island. Broadhead died in 2015 at the age of 70, having just begun a series of shows entitled *Monkey*, through which he intended to tell, in monthly instalments, the ancient Chinese story of the Monkey King.[80]

Theatre power couple Te Atamira Jennifer Ward-Lealand and Michael Hurst have spent many years in Grey Lynn and Westmere. Ward-Lealand appeared in the classic television soap *Close to Home* and was performing at Wellington's Downstage theatre while she was a student at Wellington Girls' High School. She later moved north to study with Auckland's Theatre Corporate.[81] Hurst was born in England and his family moved to Christchurch in the mid-1960s, when he was at primary school. After school he trained at Christchurch's Court Theatre before moving to Auckland to join Theatre Corporate.[82] Ward-Lealand and Hurst have each worked extensively in film television and theatre and have taken on governance roles in theatre organisations, Ward-Lealand most notably as president of the actors' union Equity.[83]

Actor and playwright Oscar Kightley's connection to Grey Lynn goes back to the early 1970s, when he lived there briefly after arriving from Sāmoa at the age of four. Although his family subsequently moved to Te Atatū, Kightley returned to Grey Lynn in the mid-1990s.[84] He was the co-writer (with James Griffin) and actor in the 2006 box office hit *Sione's Wedding* and its sequel, *Sione's 2: Unfinished Business*, which also features many scenes shot in Grey Lynn. In 2022 a 'prequel' television series, *Duckrockers*, was produced.

Kightley has written and appeared in many other film, television and stage productions, including as part of The Naked Samoans, the comedy group behind the award-winning animated series *Bro'Town* and numerous live comedy shows. He has also written and appeared in dramas and documentaries, the most recent of which is his feature-length film *Dawn Raid*, about the South Auckland music label of the same name. Kightley has received numerous awards over the years and his work has ensured that many stories about Pacific immigrants coming to New Zealand and adapting to life here are seen on screen and stage.[85]

The Naked Samoans comedy group in 2006. Oscar Kightley is at bottom right. NEW ZEALAND HERALD

**M**any writers have made the Grey Lynn, Arch Hill and Westmere area their home. Author Vincent O'Sullivan grew up in Westmere and went on to become one of New Zealand's best-known writers. His novel *All This By Chance* is partly set in Westmere. Similarly, in the 1950s Derek Hansen spent part of his childhood living in Grey Lynn, which inspired several of his novels set in Auckland. Food writer Julie Le Clerc grew up at the seaward end of Garnet Road in Westmere and opened the Garnet Road Foodstore in the late 1990s. Former journalist Stacy Gregg, who lived in Westmere for several years in the late 1990s and then again in the 2010s, used a corner table there to write her best-selling books for junior readers.[86] More recently she has penned books a few doors down at the Seabreeze Café in the company of Point Chevalier author Nicky Pellegrino, who wrote at the next table.[87] Other writers find that home provides a quiet sanctuary for crafting books. Among them are award-winning writer Stephanie Johnson, romance novelist Jackie Ashenden and art writer and novelist Andrea Hotere.

Dominic Hoey grew up on Firth Road in the 1980s, an era when many local children of his generation had musician parents, so there were always instruments and equipment that could be picked up.[88] He started rapping as a teenager and adopted the name Tourettes when he was 19.[89] He has released several rap albums, three books of poetry, a play and a novel, *Iceland*, set in Grey Lynn during the early 2000s. It tells the story of a couple of artists trying to survive as the suburb changes around them, imperilling their creativity and future.[90] Hoey mourns the loss of aspects of the Grey Lynn of this childhood and youth. He now lives in Titirangi, where he mentors troubled teens and continues to write. His second novel, *Poor People with Money*, was published in 2022.[91]

The area is also home to people who are working in wider creative fields such as the film and television industry, journalism, advertising and design. Award-winning documentary filmmaker Shirley Horrocks, for example, has lived in Grey Lynn since about 1980 with her husband Roger Horrocks, a writer, university lecturer and filmmaker who played a key role in the development of the study of film and television in New Zealand.[92]

Grey Lynn may no longer have the struggling artist vibe that it had in the 1980s and 1990s but it remains a place where creativity is valued. Today's creative residents are more likely to be established in their fields and many are bringing up a new creative generation.

**The performing and literary arts | 369**

# Afterword

The life of a suburb is like a net anchored to the sea floor — it exists in a particular place but is affected by what's happening around it. Sometimes it remains relatively still, gently registering the rhythmic tidal comings and goings, like the repeating pattern in the weekday departures of workers and their eventual return several hours later, or a gentle push or pull from other parts of the city.

But the net is also affected by other surrounding forces — some as dramatic as storms, rips and swirls. In Grey Lynn, Arch Hill and Westmere, we see this process in the industries that flooded in during the nineteenth century, often 'offensive' trades that were later expelled from the increasingly closely settled city where their soot and smells had become intolerable — the area was both near enough to the city but also far enough away. The abattoirs, boiling-down works and brickmakers were held in the sparsely settled suburban net for a time, until they, too, were washed out to more distant parts as houses sprang up and new residents gushed in.

New technologies and their relative affordability led to a surge of residential development in the early twentieth century. Suburbs on the electric tramlines grew at pace and the net was now well populated with workers and their families. This in turn encouraged light industry to further swell the net as manufacturers looked for places to expand or start from scratch.

Again the proximity to the city was important, but so too was the availability of a local workforce. Clothing, bedding and furniture factories were set up and the place bubbled over with soft-drink manufacturers. Other household needs were met by factories producing yeast and vinegar, processed dairy products and cereals. A large laundry factory drew in dirty linen and clothing from the city and suburbs, washed it clean and dispatched it back to from where it came.

Families grew up in the timber houses that sprang up on the green fields west of the city, and were served by the schools, churches and shops that were built to cater for their needs. The early generations of locals grew older, and some moved on while others remained until the end of their days. The tides brought new residents in, including those from rural Māori communities and the islands of the Pacific. Waves of post-war migrants were drawn to the inner-west suburbs of the city, where cheap housing was available. Swirls and eddies brought in other residents — there was an increase in the number of student flats through the latter decades of the twentieth century, and as more and more gay and lesbian people found the neighbourhood receptive and supportive, the epithet People's Republic of Grey Lynn alternated with Gay Lynn.

More recently rising property prices have drawn in more affluent residents and local schools now abound with the children of professionals. The Pacific flavour of the suburb has been diluted as the families that immigrated here have sold up and left.

The area today is the culmination of everything that has gone before, and though there has been much change there has also been much continuity — evident in the survival of the original housing stock, which is either approaching its first century, or surpassed that milestone decades ago.

So what does the future hold? There will undoubtedly be both continuity and change as the residents of Grey Lynn, Arch Hill and Westmere continue to define the unique place these suburbs hold in the city of Auckland, the Auckland region, New Zealand and the wider world.

# Notes

## Introduction

1 Nicholas Reid, 'Thomas and Mary Poynton — New Zealand's first Catholic Laity', *The Australian Catholic Record*, January 2011, pp.19, 20 and 21.

2 Jack Lee, *Hokianga* (Auckland: Hodder & Stoughton, 1987), 69; Duncan Moore, Barry Rigby and Matthew Russell, *Old Land Claims* (Wellington: Waitangi Tribunal, 1997), 123; Deeds index 1A — Map A [Auckland], BAJZ A1660 23662 Box 788a 1A R22764169, Archives New Zealand, Folio 544.

3 Deeds register book 2D [Eden County] — Folio 1-759, BAJZ A1660 23641 Box 667a 2D Part 1 R22764048, Archives New Zealand, Auckland, Folio 428; Deeds register book 3D [Eden County] — Folio 461-933, BAJZ A1660 23641 Box 670a Part 2 R22764051, Archives New Zealand, Auckland, Folios 479 and 482; Deeds index A3 — Folio 1-308 [copy of A1660/791a] [Eden County, Auckland], BAJZ A1660 23662 Box 824a A3 Part 1 R22764207, Archives New Zealand, Auckland, Folio 156.

4 Although the land transfer from Burn to Gow was not formally completed until 1870 and the subsequent sale from Gow to Baildon was completed in 1887, it is clear that an agreement to transfer ownership of lot 79 to Baildon had been made much earlier. In 1865, William Baildon made a claim to vote based on his ownership of lot 79 in Home Street and in 1867 Nathaniel Gow made a claim to vote based on his ownership of his house in Home Street on lot 78. *New Zealander*, 7 April 1865, p.6; *New Zealand Herald*, 6 April 1867, p.6; Deeds Deeds index 14A — Folio 518-938 [Eden County, Auckland], BAJZ A1660 23662 Box 858a 14A Part 3 R22764241, Archives New Zealand, Auckland, Folio 722; Deeds register book 25D [Eden County], BAJZ A1660 23641 Box 697a 25D R22764078, Archives New Zealand, Auckland, Folio 177; Deeds register book R24 [Auckland] — Folio 480-958 [Deed 103938 split between volume 1 and 2], BAJZ A1660 23641 Box 46a Part 2 R22763427, Archives New Zealand, Auckland, Folio 581; *Auckland Star*, 10 September 1917, p.8; 24 November 1917, p.9; *New Zealand Herald*, 11 April 1933, p.12

5 Newton Electoral Roll, 1884, p.2; *Auckland Star*, 24 November 1917, p.9.

6 *Daily Southern Cross*, 25 July 1876, p.3; *Auckland Star*, 24 November 1917, p.9.

7 *New Zealand Herald*, 17 August 1928, p.14; 11 April 1933, p.12

8 *Auckland Star*, 22 April 1902, p.2; 29 April 1922, p.5.

9 *Auckland Star*, 4 January 1882, p.2.

10 Richard S. Hill, *The Colonial Frontier Tamed: New Zealand Policing in Transition, 1867–1886* (Wellington: Government Printer, 1989), 266–67; *New Zealand Herald*, 25 August 1880, p.6; *Observer*, 25 December 1880, p.132; 11 May 1895, p.2; *Auckland Star*, 17 February 1887, p.4.

11 *New Zealand Police Gazette*, 13 April 1887, p.72; *Wises New Zealand Post Office Directory*, 1890, p.26.

12 *Auckland Star*, 5 March 1886, p.2.

13 *Auckland Star*, 8 June 1888, p.3; Paul Christoffel, 'Prohibition and the Myth of 1919', *New Zealand Journal of History* 42, no. 2 (2008): 156; the Eden electorate was the only New Zealand electorate to match Grey Lynn's 91-year dry stretch. Eden voted dry in 1908 and was one of the three last electorates to vote wet. http://archive.electionresults.govt.nz/electionresults_1996/pdf/6.1%20Return%20of%20Local%20Restoration%20Poll%20Votes.pdf; http://archive.electionresults.govt.nz/electionresults_1999/e9/html/e9_partXII.html.

14 Eden Electoral Roll, 1899, p.4.

15 G. W. A. Bush, *Decently and in Order: The Centennial History of the Auckland City Council* (Auckland: Collins, 1971), 143; *New Zealand Herald*, 26 November 1874, p.1; 13 May 1882, p.4.

16 *Auckland Star*, 23 February 1893, p.8; Eden Electoral Roll, 1893, p.4.

17 *Wises New Zealand Post Office Directory*, 1903, p.62; *New Zealand Herald*, 27 July 1925, p.10; *Gisborne Herald*, 28 September 1946, p.8.

18 Grey Lynn Electoral Roll, 1931, p.139; Certificate of Title NA582/183, Land Information New Zealand; *New Zealand Herald*, 12 May 1903, p.4.

19 *Auckland Star*, 21 February 1918, p.10; 10 September 1918, p.6; 4 August 1943, p.4; William Tidswell Ellis online cenotaph record, https://www.aucklandmuseum.com/war-memorial/online-cenotaph/record/C23452

20 Damian Skinner, *Theo Schoon: A Biography* (Auckland: Massey University Press, 2018), 156, 166.

21 Certificate of Title NA582/181, Land Information New Zealand.

22 Melani Anae (ed.), *Polynesian Panthers: Pacific Protest and Affirmative Action in Aotearoa New Zealand 1971–1981* (Wellington: Huia, 2015), 111.

23 Certificate of Title, NA582/183, Land Information New Zealand.

## Chapter 1: Geological and Māori history

1 Bruce W. Hayward, Graeme Murdoch and Gordon Maitland, *Volcanoes of Auckland: The Essential Guide* (Auckland: Auckland University Press, 2011), 2.

2 David Simmons, *Greater Māori Auckland* (Auckland: Bush Press Communications, 2013), 30–31, 67.

3 Ibid., 69.

4 Hayward, Murdoch and Maitland, *Volcanoes of Auckland*, 134, 135.

5 Kaaren Hiyama, *High Hopes in Hard Times: A History of Grey Lynn and Westmere* (Auckland: Media Studies Trust, 1991), 1.

6 Hayward, Murdoch and Maitland, *Volcanoes of Auckland*, 53; George Graham, 'The Account of Kupe and Tainui', *Journal of the Polynesian Society* 28 (1919): 116.

7 Simmons, *Greater Māori Auckland*, 47.

8 Hayward, Murdoch and Maitland, *Volcanoes of Auckland*, 49, 141–43.

9 Malcolm McKinnon (ed.), *New Zealand Historical Atlas* (Auckland: Bateman, 1997),4a, 8b.

10 Atholl Anderson, *The First Migration: Māori Origins 3000BC–AD1450* (Wellington: Bridget Williams Books, 2016), 15.

11 Ngarimu Blair, *Te Rimu Tahi: Ponsonby Road Masterplan — Māori Heritage Report*, June 2013, p.3.

12 McKinnon, *New Zealand Historical Atlas*, 12a, 13a.

13 *New Zealand Herald*, 12 May 1939, p.10.

14 R. C. J. Stone, *From Tamaki-makau-rau to Auckland* (Auckland: Auckland University Press, 2001), 2.

15 Western Springs Lakeside Te Wai Ōrea Development Plan, pp.30, 40.

16 Margaret Anne Kawharu, Statement of Evidence to High Court, 2 June 2020, p.31, https://ngatiwhatuaŌrākei .com/wp-content/uploads/2021/02/2-BOE-M-A-Kawharu.pdf

17 Blair, *Te Rimu Tahi*, 6, 12.

18 Hiyama, *High Hopes*, 2.

19 Blair, *Te Rimu Tahi*, 6, and Auckland Unitary Plan, Schedule 12, Sites and Places of Significance to Mana Whenua Schedule, item 001.

20 Paul Moon, *The Struggle for Tamaki Makaurau: The Maori Occupation of Auckland to 1820* (Auckland: David Ling, 2007), 104.

21 Auckland Unitary Plan, Schedule 12, Sites and Places of Significance to Mana Whenua Schedule, item 004; Simmons, *Greater Māori Auckland*, 153.

22 Blair, *Te Rimu Tahi*, 6.

23 Personal communication with Taura Eruera, February 2024.

24 Moon, *The Struggle for Tamaki Makaurau*, 83–94.

25 Ibid., 94–95.

26 Ani Pihema, Ruby Kerei and Steven Oliver, 'Te Kawau, Āpihai', *Dictionary of New Zealand Biography*, first published in 1990. Te Ara — the Encyclopedia of New Zealand, https://teara.govt.nz/en/biographies/1t42/te-kawau-apihai

27 Agnes Sullivan, *Maori Gardening in Tamaki Before 1840, Vol. 1*, 104.

28 Ibid., 104–05.

29 Hiyama, *High Hopes*, 3, 4; Sullivan, 105; Margaret Anne Kawharu, Statement of Evidence to High Court, 2 June 2020, p.24, https://ngatiwhatuaŌrākei .com/wp-content/uploads/2021/02/2-BOE-M-A-Kawharu.pdf

30 Sullivan, Appendix 9, lv–lx.

31 Hiyama, *High Hopes*, 4.

32 Stone, *From Tamaki-makau-rau to Auckland*, 100–01.

33 Lucy Mackintosh, *Shifting Grounds: Deep Histories of Tāmaki Makaurau Auckland* (Wellington: Bridget Williams Books, 2021), 40.

34 Ibid., 103, 180–82.

35 Margaret Anne Kawharu, Statement of Evidence to High Court, 2 June 2020, p.38, https://ngatiwhatua Ōrākei .com/wp-content/uploads/2021/02/2-BOE-M-A-Kawharu.pdf

36 Statement of Evidence of Ngarimu Alan Huiroa Blair on behalf of Ngāti Whātua Ōrākei Trust, 2 June 2021, p.6.

37 Stone, *From Tamaki-makau-rau to Auckland*, 216–17.

38 Pihema, Kerei and Oliver, 'Te Kawau, Āpihai'.

39 Stone, *From Tamaki-makau-rau to Auckland*, 216; Judith Binney, Vincent O'Malley and Alan Ward, *Te Ao Hou: The New World 1820–1920* (Wellington: Bridget Williams Books, 2018), 27, 28.

40 Stone, *From Tamaki-makau-rau to Auckland*, 258; Simmons, *Greater Māori Auckland*, 8; Report of the Waitangi Tribunal on the Ōrākei Claim (Wai-9), 1991, p.16.

41 Stone, *From Tamaki-makau-rau to Auckland*, 254, 255, 256, 258, 259.

42 Melissa Matutina Williams, *Panguru and the City: Kāinga Tahi, Kāinga Rua: An Urban Migration History* (Wellington: Bridget Williams Books, 2015), 18.

43 Ibid., 103–05, 124.

44 New Zealand Population Census, 1956, Vol. 1, p.43; New Zealand Population Census, 1971, Supplement 2a, p.59.

45 Ibid.

46 Ben Schrader, *The Big Smoke: New Zealand Cities 1840–1920* (Wellington: Bridget Williams Books, 2016), 191–93.

47  *Wises New Zealand Post Office Directory*, 1955, p.157.

48  Michael King, 'Cooper, Whina', *Dictionary of New Zealand Biography*, first published in 2000. Te Ara — the Encyclopedia of New Zealand, https://teara.govt.nz/en/biographies/5c32/cooper-whina

49  Michael King, *Whina: A Biography of Whina Cooper* (Auckland: Hodder & Stoughton, 1983), 164, 165.

50  Ibid., 170–72.

51  Ibid., 175, 176.

52  King, 'Cooper, Whina'.

53  Athol Anderson, Judith Binney and Aroha Harris, *Tangata Whenua: A History* (Wellington: Bridget Williams Books, 2016), 358, 359.

54  Melani Anae (ed.), *Polynesian Panthers: Pacific Protest and Affirmative Action in Aotearoa New Zealand 1971–1981* (Wellington: Huia, 2015), 111.

55  Melani Anae, Lautofa Iuli and Leilani Tamu eds., *Polynesian Panthers: Pacific Protest and Affirmative Action in Aoetearoa New Zealand 1971–1981* (Wellington: Huia, 2015), 60–61, 63, 73, 77, 83, 84–85.

56  Cybèle Locke, 'Māori Sovereignty, Black Feminism and the New Zealand Trade Union Movement', in *Indigenous Women and Work: From Labour to Activism*, ed. Carol Williams (Champaign: University of Illinois Press, 2012), 255.

57  Anderson, Binney and Harris, *Tangata Whenua*, 359–360, 375.

58  Cybèle Locke, 'Māori Sovereignty, Black Feminism and the New Zealand Trade Union Movement', in *Indigenous Women and Work: From Labour to Activism*, ed. Carol Williams (Champaign: University of Illinois Press, 2012), 255.

59  www.stats.govt.nz

60  Ibid.

## Chapter 2: Farming

1  R. C. J. Stone, *From Tamaki-makau-rau to Auckland* (Auckland: Auckland University Press, 2001), 280.

2  Ibid., 270, 279.

3  From: John Cox, Auckland To: Colonial Secretary Date: 15 December 1841, AGCO 8333 Box 9 1841/1604 R22804084, Archives New Zealand, Wellington.

4  When John and Jane Cox arrived at Coxs Bay they had at least two sons, Edmund James and Alfred John, both born in Sydney. They had a further two sons, George and Frank. *New Zealand Herald*, 12 August 1887, p.3; Births Deaths and Marriages, Birth Record 1849/2045; New South Wales Baptism, No. 502, Vol. 21 and No. 344 Vol. 25a.

5  *Daily Southern Cross*, 2 December 1875, p.1.

6  Crown grants 3G — Folio 901-1594 [Eden County, Auckland], BAJZ A1660 23663 Box 962a 3G Part 3 R22764319, Archives New Zealand, Auckland, Folios 1230 and 1232.

7  *Daily Southern Cross*, 6 July 1844, p.2; 5 October 1844, p.4; 4 January 1845, p.3.

8  Crown grants 3G — Folio 1-426 [Eden County, Auckland, Original], BAJZ A1660 23663 Box 958a 3G Part 1 R22764315, Archives New Zealand, Auckland, Folios 258, 60, 366; Crown grants 3G — Folio 430-900 [Eden County, Auckland], BAJZ A1660 23663 Box 960a 3G Part 2 R22764317, Archives New Zealand, Auckland, Folios 563, 565, 585, 587, 701, 703, 792; Crown grants 3G — Folio 901-1594 [Eden County, Auckland], BAJZ A1660 23663 Box 962a 3G Part 3 R22764319, Archives New Zealand, Auckland, Folios 935, 1318, 1497, 1549, 1230, 1232.

9  Trevor Bentley, *Cannibal Jack: The Life and Times of Jacky Marmon, a Pakeha Maori* (Auckland: Penguin, 2010, 219–10; Roger Wigglesworth, 'Marmon, John', *Dictionary of New Zealand Biography*. Te Ara — the Encyclopedia of New Zealand, www.TeAra.govt.nz/en/biographies/1m14/marmon-john

10  Jack Lee, *The Old Land Claims in New Zealand* (Kerikeri: Northland Historical Publications Society, 1993), 3–4.

11  Jack Lee, *Hokianga* (Auckland: Hodder & Stoughton, 1987), 69.

12  While the Kapowai Peninsula land had been declared Crown land in 1844 when Whytlaw was granted scrip in return for it, the old land claim was not settled for decades. Māori living at Kapowai claimed that it had never been sold and various investigations by old land claims commissioners variously accepted or rejected this. Finally in 1920, some 76 years after Whytlaw's scrip payment, the Kapowai Peninsula was returned to local Māori. Moore, Rigby and Russell, 57; and Lee, *The Old Land Claims*, 4.

13  *New Zealander*, 14 March 1846, p.2.

14  Deeds register book 3D [Eden County] — Folio 461-933, BAJZ A1660 23641 Box 670a Part 2 R22764051, Archives New Zealand, Auckland, Folios 596-597.

15  *Jane Gifford* and *Duchess of Argyle* 150th Anniversary Committee, *Documents Relating to the* Jane Gifford *and* Duchess of Argyle *1842–1992*, Auckland, 1992, pp.11–13, 22–23, 34; Scotland Census 1841, Parish: Paisley Low; ED: 20A; Page: 22; Line: 1310, 1360, 1410, 1460.

16  No primary source recording the death of Margaret McNair has been found, but the Davies family tree (Rosyskye) on Ancestry.com.au records that Margaret died on board the *Duchess of Argyle* on 26 August 1842. *Jane Gifford* and *Duchess of Argyle* 150th Anniversary Committee, p.23.

17    Mary Anne was born in 1843 at Coromandel, as was James in the 1840s. Jessie and Peter were born in 1848 and 1851 respectively. Births Deaths and Marriages, Birth Record 1851/1369; Marriage Record 1869/4515; Death Records 1909/676 and 1915/644.

18    *New Zealand Herald*, 30 May 1921, p.8.

19    Kaaren Hiyama, *High Hopes in Hard Times: A History of Grey Lynn and Westmere* (Auckland: Media Studies Trust, 1991), 8, 10; *New Zealander*, 27 April 1861, p.3.

20    *Daily Southern Cross*, 28 April 1866, p.7.

21    *Daily Southern Cross*, 4 April 1863; *Auckland Star*, 12 February 1887, p.2; 19 March 1890, p.4; 6 February 1891, p.1; 17 January 1901, p.8; *New Zealand Herald*, 30 May 1921, p.8; Deeds register book 7D [Eden County], BAJZ A1660 23641 Box 676a 7D R22764057, Archives New Zealand, Auckland, Folio 811; Deeds register book R2 [Auckland] — Folio 1-483 [Deed 78765 split between two volumes], BAJZ A1660 23641 Box 2a R2 Part 1 R22763383, Archives New Zealand, Auckland, Folio 471; Waitemata Electoral Roll 1880–1, p.22 and 1900, p.40; *Wises New Zealand Post Office Directory*, 1894–1895, p.759; Ian B. Madden, *Riverhead: The Kaipara Gateway* (Auckland: Riverhead Jubilee Association, 1966), 174.

22    *Auckland Star*, 2 April 1894, p.2.

23    Deeds register book R7 [Auckland] — Folio 1-477 [Deed 88409 split between volume 1 and 2], BAJZ A1660 23641 Box 11a R7 Part 1 R22763392, Archives New Zealand, Auckland, Folio 287-288; Deeds register book R8 [Auckland] — Folio 480-957 [Deed 87924 split between volume 1 and 2], BAJZ A1660 23641 Box 14a R8 Part 2 R22763395, Archives New Zealand, Auckland, Folio 862; Deeds register book 27M — Mortgages, BAJZ A1660 23641 Box 747a 27M R22764137, Archives New Zealand, Auckland, Folio 13; *New Zealand Herald*, 16 May 1885, p.6.

24    *New Zealand Herald*, 19 March 1909, p.1; 7 July 1899, supplement, p.4; Deeds register book 22D [Eden County], BAJZ A1660 23641 Box 694a 22D R22764075, Archives New Zealand, Auckland, Folio 81; Births Deaths and Marriages, Death Record 1909/696.

25    Rose Dale interviewed by Kaaren Hiyama, 3 June 1990, Auckland Libraries Heritage Collections, OH-1355-003; Grey Lynn Electoral Roll 1905–1906, p.19; 1911, p.107; 1928, p.142; 1946, p.141 and Ponsonby Electoral Roll 1954, p.169.

26    Deeds register book 2D [Eden County] — Folio 760-1699, BAJZ A1660 23641 Box 688a 2D Part 2 R22764049, Archives New Zealand, Auckland, Folios 1627-1628.

27    1851 Scotland Census, Parish: Ceres; ED: 8; Page: 30; Line: 12; Roll: CSSCT1851_85; Year: 1851.

28    This was the second daughter of George and Euphemia Wilson to have been given the name Euphemia Arnot. It would appear that their first daughter of that name, who was born in Ceres, Scotland, in 1842, died sometime after the Scottish census of 1851, and their baby daughter born in Melbourne in 1855, was given the same name. The New Zealand death record for Euphemia Arnot (also spelled Arnott) Wilson records that she was 28 years old when she died in 1883. This confirms that she was born in 1855 rather than 1842. 1851 Scotland Census, Parish: Ceres; ED: 8; Page: 30; Line: 12; Roll: CSSCT1851_85; Year: 1851 and Births Deaths and Marriages, Death Record 1883/2371.

29    Births Deaths and Marriages, Birth Record 1858/2494.

30    Suburbs of Auckland Electoral Roll, 1857, p.39.

31    Births Deaths and Marriages, Death Record 1883/4855.

32    *New Zealand Herald*, 8 May 1868, p.3; *Auckland Star*, 12 August 1926, p.14.

33    Deeds register book 22D [Eden County], BAJZ A1660 23641 Box 694a 22D R22764075, Archives New Zealand, Auckland, Folio 810.

34    The lease on Archibald Wilson's farm was not relinquished until 1887, by which time the land had been gifted to George and to Archibald Wilson's daughters. Deeds register book R23 [Auckland] — Folio 480-958 [Deed 103463 split between volume 1 and 2], BAJZ A1660 23641 Box 44a R23 Part 2 R22763425, Archives New Zealand, Auckland, Folios 910-911; Deposited Plan 17365, Land Information New Zealand; *Auckland Star* 27 March 1924, p.7; *New Zealand Herald*, 13 October 1932, p.12.

35    Deeds register book 20D [Eden County], BAJZ A1660 23641 Box 691a 20D R22764072, Archives New Zealand, Auckland, 602-603.

36    Births Deaths and Marriages, Death Records 1883/4855 and 1884/3649; *Auckland Star*, 6 August 1884, p.2.

37    By this stage Sarah had married and was known as Sarah Elizabeth Atwood. Deeds register book R29 [Auckland], BAJZ A1660 23641 Box 52a R29 R22763433, Archives New Zealand, Auckland, Folios 916-917; Deeds register book R15 [Auckland] — Folio 480-958 [Deed 98174 split between volume 1 and 2], BAJZ A1660 23641 Box 28a R15 Part 2 R22763409, Archives New Zealand, Auckland, Folios 894-895.

38    Deeds register book R40 [Auckland] — Folio 480-958 [Deed 121612 split between volume 1 and 2], BAJZ A1660 23641 Box 69a R40 Part 2 R22763450, Archives New Zealand, Auckland, Folios 711-713.

39    Ibid.

40    *Auckland Star*, 18 July 1871, p.2; *Richmond Baptist Church Silver Jubilee Souvenir*, p.3.

41  *New Zealander*, 27 April 1861, p.3; *Daily Southern Cross,* 21 February 1963, p.1.

42  One of Joseph Young's sons, William John Young, died in 1873, although his other two children survived him. *New Zealand Herald*, 11 September 1880, p.4; Births Deaths and Marriages, Death record 1880/1691; Lisa Truttman, 'Arch Hill — Why?', https://timespanner. blogspot.co.nz/2012/06/arch-hill-why.html, Mike Taylor comments dated 30 July 2012.

43  Harris, Benjamin of Auckland — part lot 20, section 7, suburbs Auckland, ABWN A1825 26710 Box 369 3888 R25398541, Archives New Zealand, Auckland; Harris, Benjamin of Auckland — part lot 20, section 7, suburbs Auckland, ABWN A1825 26710 Box 369 3889 R25398542, Archives New Zealand, Auckland.

44  Truttman, 'Arch Hill — Why?', Timespanner comments dated 27 June 2012.

45  Ibid., Mike Taylor comments dated 30 July 2012.

46  *New Zealander*, 22 June 1861, p.2; *Daily Southern Cross*, 20 February 1863, p.1.

47  The property was referred to as Meadow Farm in an 1867 land transaction following the death of George McElwain. Deeds register book 23D [Eden County], BAJZ A1660 23641 Box 695a 23D R22764076, Archives New Zealand, Auckland, Folio 11.

48  Heather M. Murdoch-Hall, *Killin Connections: A family history of Richard McElwain and Mary Ann née Hughes of Killin, County Louth, Ireland, and their descendants* (Auckland: self-published, 2013), 28.

49  W. E. C. Fleming, *Armagh Clergy 1800–2000* (Dundalk: self-published, 2001), 195; Murdoch Hall, *Killin Connections*, 28.

50  Murdoch-Hall, *Killin Connections*, 28.

51  Quoted in Una Platts, *The Lively Capital: Auckland 1840–1865* (Christchurch: Avon Fine Prints, 1971), 87.

52  Murdoch-Hall, *Killin Connections*, 28.

53  Mark Derby and Warwick Tie, 'Feculent Hovel: Auckland's First Gaol 1841–1865', *Counterfutures* 3 (2017): 23–24, 26–27, 42, 43, 48.

54  Deeds register book 17D [Eden County], BAJZ A1660 23641 Box 688a 17D R22764069, Archives New Zealand, Auckland, Folios 449-450; Murdoch-Hall, *Killin Connections*, 28.

55  Murdoch-Hall, *Killin Connections*, 38.

56  *Daily Southern Cross*, 28 May 1848, p.2.

57  *New Zealander*, 17 October 1857, p.1.

58  *New Zealander*, 17 October 1857, p.1; 24 July 1858, supplement, p.2; *New Zealand Herald*, 1 October 1866, p.4.

59  *New Zealander*, 25 March 1863, p.2.

60  Deeds register book 16D [Eden County], BAJZ A1660 23641 Box 687a 16D R22764068, Archives New Zealand, Auckland, Folios 563, 564; Deeds register book 19D [Eden County], BAJZ A1660 23641 Box 690a 19D R22764071, Archives New Zealand, Auckland, Folios 883, 884; Deeds register book 21D [Eden County] — Folio 476-938 [Deed 37582 split between volume 1 and 2], BAJZ A1660 23641 Box 693a 21D Part 2 R22764074, Archives New Zealand, Auckland, Folios 726, 727.

61  Deeds register book 23D [Eden County], BAJZ A1660 23641 Box 695a 23D R22764076, Archives New Zealand, Auckland, Folios 10-13; Certificate of Title NA32/8, Land Information New Zealand, Auckland.

62  At the time of his death John and Eliza Billington had one son, three spinster daughters and a married daughter. *Auckland Star*, 27 February 1889, p.5; Deeds register book 25D [Eden County], BAJZ A1660 23641 Box 697a 25D R22764078, Archives New Zealand, Auckland, Folios 583-584; BILLINGTON John — Richmond, Auckland — Gentleman, BBAE A48 1569 Box 17 442 R21442113, Archives New Zealand, Auckland.

63  Deeds register book 21D [Eden County] — Folio 476-938 [Deed 37582 split between volume 1 and 2], BAJZ A1660 23641 Box 693a 21D Part 2 R22764074, Archives New Zealand, Auckland, Folio 907; *Auckland Star*, 6 November 1872, 7 January 1873, p.2; p.3; 27 June 1885, p.7; 21 July 1887, p.5; 15 February 1897, p.2; *Daily Southern Cross*, 26 April 1871, p.1; *New Zealand Herald*, 29 October 1872, p.3.

64  Roger Wigglesworth, 'Montefiore, John Israel', *Dictionary of New Zealand Biography*, first published in 1990. Te Ara — the Encyclopedia of New Zealand, https://teara.govt.nz/en/biographies/1m50/montefiore-john-israel

65  Crown grants 3G — Folio 1-426 [Eden County, Auckland, Original], BAJZ A1660 23663 Box 958a 3G Part 1 R22764315, Archives New Zealand, Auckland, Folios 236, 238, 240.

66  Deeds register book 2D [Eden County] — Folio 1-759, BAJZ A1660 23641 Box 667a 2D Part 1 R22764048, Archives New Zealand, Auckland, Folios 571-577.

67  Crown grants 3G — Folio 1-426 [Eden County, Auckland, Original], BAJZ A1660 23663 Box 958a 3G Part 1 R22764315, Archives New Zealand, Auckland, Folio 244; Deeds register book 2D [Eden County] — Folio 1-759, BAJZ A1660 23641 Box 667a 2D Part 1 R22764048, Archives New Zealand, Auckland, Folios 572-573.

68  Crown grants 3G — Folio 1-426 [Eden County, Auckland, Original], BAJZ A1660 23663 Box 958a 3G Part 1 R22764315, Archives New Zealand, Auckland,

Folios 242, 246, 248; Deeds register book 2D [Eden County] — Folio 1-759, BAJZ A1660 23641 Box 667a 2D Part 1 R22764048, Archives New Zealand, Auckland, Folios 571-574.

69   *Daily Southern Cross*, 5 October 1844, p.1.

70   Deeds register book 2D [Eden County] — Folio 1-759, BAJZ A1660 23641 Box 667a 2D Part 1 R22764048, Archives New Zealand, Auckland, Folios 574-577.

71   *New Zealander*, 6 October 1858, p.3; R. C. J. Stone, 'Williamson, James', *Dictionary of New Zealand Biography*, first published in 1990. Te Ara — the Encyclopedia of New Zealand, https://teara.govt.nz/en/biographies/1w27/williamson-james

72   Deeds register book 2D [Eden County] — Folio 1-759, BAJZ A1660 23641 Box 667a 2D Part 1 R22764048, Archives New Zealand, Auckland, Folios 731-732; Deeds register book 3D [Eden County] — Folio 461-933, BAJZ A1660 23641 Box 670a Part 2 R22764051, Archives New Zealand, Auckland, Folios 523-524.

73   G. W. A. Bush (ed.), *The History of Epsom* (Auckland: Epsom & Eden District Historical Society, 2006), 42; *New Zealander*, 18 September 1850, p.4; 22 September 1852, p.1; *Daily Southern Cross,* 17 March 1857, p.2.

74   *New Zealander*, 11 July 1855, p.2.

75   *New Zealander*, 18 September 1855, p.1.

76   *Auckland Star*, 6 July 1926, p.9.

77   Stone, 'Williamson, James'.

78   *Daily Southern Cross*, 13 December 1865, p.1 and 1 February 1867, p.1.

79   *New Zealand Herald,* 13 April 1868, p.1 and *Auckland Star*, 6 July 1926, p.9.

80   *Cyclopedia of New Zealand*, Vol. 2 (Christchurch, 1902), 98; J. O. Wilson, *The New Zealand Parliamentary Record 1840–1984* (Wellington: Government Printer, 1985), 212.

81   *New Zealand Herald*, 5 May 1971, p.1; *Daily Southern Cross*, 19 March 1872, p.2.

82   *Daily Southern Cross*, 19 March 1872, p.2.

83   *New Zealand Herald*, 20 June 1877, p.3; 25 February 1889, p.10.

84   *Auckland Star*, 30 September 1876, p.4.

85   *New Zealand Herald*, 21 January 1885, p.3.

86   Neville and Rosha Peacocke, *The Peacocke Family in New Zealand and Australia* (Mount Maunganui: N. J. F. and R. A. Peacocke, 1980), 37.

87   *New Zealand Herald*, 21 January 1885, p.3.

88   Dick Scott, *Stock in Trade: Hellaby's First Hundred Years 1873–1973* (Auckland: Southern Cross Books, 1973), 26–27; *New Zealand Herald*, 16 May 1885, p.6; *Daily Southern Cross*, 2 December 1875, supplement p.1.

89   Lily Lee and Ruth Lam, *Sons of the Soil: Chinese Market Gardeners in New Zealand* (Auckland: Dominion Federation for New Zealand Chinese Commercial Growers, 2012), 13.

90   *New Zealand Herald*, 16 February 1878, p.2.

91   Lee and Lam, *Sons of the Soil*, 327; *New Zealand Herald*, 2 September 1881, p.5; 25 November 1881, p.5.

92   *New Zealand Herald*, 16 February 1878, p.2; *Auckland Star*, 8 July 1889, p.2.

93   *Auckland Star*, 25 June 1878, p.3. Other parts of the Young family farm were subsequently leased to other Chinese market gardeners. Deeds register book D12 [Queens, Coromandel Counties] — Folio 1-479 [Deed 73324 split between volume 1 and 2], BAJZ A1660 23641 Box 721a D12 Part 1 R22764102, Archives New Zealand, Auckland, Folios 416-418; Deeds register book R5 [Auckland] — Folio 1-539 [Deed 81892 split between volume 1 and 2], BAJZ A1660 23641 Box 7a R5 Part 1 R22763388, Archives New Zealand, Auckland, Folios 75-76; Deeds register book R22 [Auckland] — Folio 1-479 [Deed 102442 split between volume 1 and 2], BAJZ A1660 23641 Box 41a R22 Part 1 R22763422, Archives New Zealand, Auckland, Folio 306.

94   Lee and Lam, *Sons of the Soil*, 324–25, 327; Certificate of Title NA 22/106, Land Information New Zealand; *Auckland Star*, 26 August 1881, p.3; 13 April 1894, p.1.

95   Lee and Lam, *Sons of the Soil*, 328; *New Zealand Herald*, 16 October 1930, p.14.

96   *Auckland Star*, 25 June 1878, p.3; *New Zealand Herald,* 7 June 1881, p.6; *Thames Advertiser*, 27 July 1893, p.3.

97   *Auckland Star*, 1 September 1881, p.3; 3 March 1883, p.2.

98   *Auckland Star*, 27 March 1889, p.5; 28 February 1889, p.5.

99   *Auckland Star*, 27 March 1889, p.5; 2 May 1889, p.2.

100  *Auckland Star*, 5 May 1888, p.5.

101  Ibid.

102  *Auckland Star*, 18 February 1890, p.8; 8 March 1890, supplement, p.2.

103  *Auckland Star*, 5 May 1892, p.8; 14 November 1893, p.2.

104  James Ng, *Windows on a Chinese Past, Vol*. 3 (Dunedin: Otago Heritage Books, 1999), 123.

105  In 1888 Thomas Quoi was interviewed on the subject of Chinese in New Zealand and stated that Chinese market gardeners in Auckland had earned £2–3 per week in the past but were now earning far less. *Auckland Star*, 5 May 1888, p.5.

106  Ng, *Windows on a Chinese Past*, 123.

107  *New Zealand Herald*, 14 February 1878, p.3.

108  *Auckland Star*, 28 February 1878, p.3.

109 *Auckland Star*, 14 January 1909, p.4.

110 R. C. J. Stone, *Makers of Fortune: A Colonial Business Community and Its Fall* (Auckland: Auckland University Press, 1973), 41, 173, 179–80, 182, 184–85, 186, 187; Stone, 'Williamson, James'.

111 *Auckland Star*, 16 January 1884, p.2.

112 Rose Dale interviewed by Kaaren Hiyama, 3 June 1990, Auckland Libraries Heritage Collections, OH-1355-003.

## Chapter 3: Residential development

1 *New Zealander*, 11 December 1858, p.2.

2 Deed Blue 53, Land Information New Zealand, Auckland.

3 Ibid.; *New Zealander*, 24 August 1859, p.3.

4 Crown grants 3G — Folio 901-1594 [Eden County, Auckland], BAJZ A1660 23663 Box 962a 3G Part 3 R22764319, Archives New Zealand, Auckland, Folios 1230, 1232.

5 William Brown purchased lots 1 and 2 in 1855 for £261 and then sold them in 1858 for £400. But not everyone made money. Samuel Jackson and William Aitken made a loss of £58 when they bought and sold lots 1 and 2 in quick succession in 1858. The subsequent purchasers, Stannus Jones and Thomas Craig, made the substantial sum of £293 after owning the land for just six months. Deeds register book 4D [Eden County] — Folio 431-877 [Deed 5999 split between volume 1 and 2] BAJZ A1660 23641 Box 672a 4D Part 2 R22764053, Archives New Zealand, Auckland, Folios 678, 678; Deeds register book 6D [Eden County] BAJZ A1660 23641 Box 675a 6D R22764056, Archives New Zealand, Auckland, Folio 643.

6 While the *New Zealander* states that all the lots were sold at the auction, the Deeds Indexes reveal that some lots remained unsold and some of Michael Wood's remaining lots were sold to pay his creditors in 1866. *New Zealander*, 18 December 1858, p.3 and 28 March 1866, p.2.

7 *Daily Southern Cross*, 26 November 1858, p.2.

8 Arber purchased the land in April 1859 for £11/15 and sold it in August 1859 for £16/16. Deeds register book 8D [Eden County], BAJZ A1660 23641 677a 8D R22764058, Archives New Zealand, Auckland, Folios 452, 453.

9 Deeds register book 8D [Eden County], BAJZ A1660 23641 677a 8D R22764058, Archives New Zealand, Auckland, Folio 74; Deeds register book 16D [Eden County], BAJZ A1660 23641 Box 687a 16D R22764068, Archives New Zealand, Auckland, Folio 760.

10 Deeds register book 8D [Eden County], BAJZ A1660 23641 677a 8D R22764058, Archives New Zealand, Auckland, Folio 94; Deeds register book 11D [Eden County], BAJZ A1660 23641 Box 680a 11D R22764061, Archives New Zealand, Auckland, Folio 177; Deeds register book 20D [Eden County], BAJZ A1660 23641 Box 691a 20D R22764072, Archives New Zealand, Auckland, Folio 169; *Observer*, 13 December 1902, p.18; *Press*, 3 July 1918, p.9.

11 *New Zealander*, 28 March 1866, p.2.

12 *Daily Southern Cross*, 7 June 1872, p.3.

13 *Daily Southern Cross*, 3 May 1865, p.5; *Auckland Star*, 29 October 1875, p.3; Deeds Blue 26, Land Information New Zealand.

14 *Daily Southern Cross*, 3 May 1865, p.5.

15 Census, 1878, Table XXIII.

16 Census 1891, Population and Houses, p.3.

17 *New Zealand Herald*, 9 December 1882, p.5; *Auckland Star*, 8 December 1882, p.2.

18 *Auckland Star*, 24 September 1883, p.2.

19 *New Zealand Herald*, 14 March 1883, p.4; *Auckland Star*, 24 September 1883, p.2.

20 *New Zealand Herald*, 25 September 1883, p.5; *Auckland Star*, 24 September 1883, p.2.

21 *New Zealand Herald*, 24 September 1883, p.2.

22 *Auckland Star*, 24 September 1883, p.2.

23 Ibid.

24 The board adopted clause 156 of the Road Board Act 1882, which stipulated the 66-foot minimum street width. *New Zealand Herald*, 25 September 1883, p.5.

25 *Auckland Star*, 28 September 1883, p.4.

26 *Auckland Star*, 26 September 1883, p.2; 16 October 1883, p.2.

27 These smaller subdivisions included the Marshfield Estate and the Sackville and Westmoreland Street subdivisions. Kaaren Hiyama, *High Hopes in Hard Times: A History of Grey Lynn and Westmere* (Auckland: Media Studies Trust, 1991), 27.

28 *New Zealand Herald*, 5 October 1883, p.8; 24 November 1884, p.8; DP 322, Land Information New Zealand.

29 *Auckland Star*, 9 October 1883, p.4.

30 R. C. J. Stone, *Makers of Fortune: A Colonial Business Community and Its Fall* (Auckland: Auckland University Press, 1973), 123.

31 *New Zealand Herald*, 11 October 1883, p.4.

32 Stone, *Makers of Fortune*, 125.

33 *Auckland Star*, 24 October 1883, p.3.

34 *Auckland Star*, 1 November 1883, p.2.

35 Stone, *Makers of Fortune*, 107–08, 137 and 227.

36 *New Zealand Herald*, 27 March 1886, p.3.

37 *New Zealand Herald*, 20 June 1887, p.12; 20 June 1887, p.12.

38 Stone, *Makers of Fortune*, 127–28.

39 Ibid., 186.

40 *Auckland Star*, 5 March 1885, p.2.

41 *Auckland Star*, 14 September 1893, p.8.

42 *New Zealand Herald*, 8 May 1901, p.5.

43 *Auckland Star*, 11 August 1903, p.5.

44 *Auckland Star*, 30 January 1902, p.2; 6 May 1902, p.8; 26 April 1905, p.8; *New Zealand Herald*, 27 April 1905, p.8; 1 February 1908, p.8.

45 Certificate of Title 139/4, 220/274, 225/67 and 234/46, Land Information New Zealand; *New Zealand Herald*, 12 October 1912, p.14; 28 January 1913, p.1; 21 January 1914, p.1; *Auckland Star*, 2 August 1911, p.2; 11 October 1912, p.2; 11 October 1913, p.1.

46 Certificate of Title 31/80, 139/4, 387/63, 389/156, Land Information New Zealand; *Auckland Star*, 5 July 1924, p.5.

47 *Auckland Star*, 15 March 1884, p.2.

48 *New Zealand Herald*, 5 April 1884, p.1.

49 *Auckland Star*, 13 January 1903, p.8; 14 January 1924, p.7; *Cyclopaedia of New Zealand*, 326–27.

50 Buildings and Sites — Primary Schools — Auckland — Newton Central, BCDQ A739 1050 Box 252a 7/11 Part 1 R23970054, Archives New Zealand, Auckland, 30 October 1919.

51 Ibid.; Extract from *New Zealand Gazette* No. 46, 13 May 1920.

52 *New Zealand Herald*, 1915, p.4.

53 Jeremy Salmond, *Old New Zealand Houses 1800–1940* (Auckland: Reed, 1986), 112, 202.

54 Ibid., 92.

55 Ibid., 73–77.

56 Ibid., 86.

57 Patrick Reynolds, Jeremy Salmond and Jeremy Hansen, *Villa: From Heritage to Contemporary* (Auckland: Random House, 2012), 20, 23.

58 Ibid., 26, 29–30.

59 Ibid., 39.

60 Salmond, *Old New Zealand Houses*, 168–69.

61 Reynolds, Salmond and Hansen, *Villa*, 34.

62 Nicole Stock, ed., *Bungalow: From Heritage to Contemporary* (Auckland: Godwit, 2014), 19.

63 Jeremy Ashford, The *Bungalow in New Zealand* (Auckland: Viking, 1994), 16; Stock, *Bungalow*, 20.

64 Stock, *Bungalow*, 19, 25; Reynolds, Salmond and Hansen, *Villa*, 26.

65 Certificate of Title, 139/4, Land Information New Zealand.

66 *New Zealand Herald*, 12 May 1904, p.6.

67 *New Zealand Herald*, 5 May 1910, p.6.

68 DP 3147, Land Information New Zealand, Auckland; *Auckland Star*, 3 February 1909, p.5.

69 *Auckland Star*, 15 March 1909, p.5; Deposited Plan 4755, Land Information New Zealand.

70 Deeds register book R5 [Auckland] — Folio 1-539 [Deed 81892 split between volume 1 and 2], BAJZ A1660 23641 Box 7a R5 Part 1 R22763388, Archives New Zealand, Auckland, Folio 436; Deeds register book R83 [Auckland] BAJZ A1660 23641 Box 132a R83 R22763513, Archives New Zealand, Auckland, Folios 259, 308, 346.

71 *New Zealand Herald*, 9 March 1914, p. 12; 16 March 1915, p.3.

72 *New Zealand Herald*, 3 November 1923, p.4.

73 Ibid.

74 *New Zealand Herald*, 21 July 1923, p.16; *Auckland Star*, 17 December 1923, p.10.

75 *New Zealand Herald*, 4 August 1923, p.13.

76 In Warwick Avenue 47 houses were erected in 1924 and 1925. Of these 18 were built by speculative builders. Building Permit index cards, Warwick Avenue 1924 and 1925, ACC 433 Box 3 Item 3 Record 73866, Auckland Council Archives.

77 The Westmere Estate Extension included Westmere Crescent, Oban Road and the northern side of Lemington Road, while the Westmere Park Estate comprised Sunny Brae Crescent, Winsomere Crescent, Westmere Park Avenue, Weona Place and the western part of Lemington Road. *Auckland Star*, 31 October 1925; *New Zealand Herald*, 9 October 1926, p.21.

78 *Auckland Star*, 31 October 1925, p.5; 3 October 1931, p.7; *New Zealand Herald*, 9 October 1926, p.21; map of Westmere Park Estate.

79 Valuation Field Sheets, Lemington Road, Auckland Council Archives, ACC 213 Box 88 Item 88a Record 328451, Allotment 123 of 9/10 Section 9 and Allotment 78 of 9/10 Section 9.

80 *New Zealand Herald*, 22 August 1914, p.12; 30 August 1915, p.4.

81 G. W. A. Bush, *Decently and in Order: The Centennial History of the Auckland City Council* (Auckland: Collins, 1971), 215.

82 Ibid., 287.

83 Ben Schrader, *We Call It Home: A History of State Housing in New Zealand* (Wellington: Bridget Williams Books, 2016), 35, 37, 43.

84 Streets in the Casey Estate include Moira, Tawariki and Mokau Streets, Parawai Crescent and parts of Richmond Road and Hukanui Crescent. *Auckland Star*, 11 December 1937, p.8; 23 May 1938, p.9.

85 *Auckland Star*, 25 July 1936, p.5; *New Zealand Herald*, 18 March 1937, p.10.

86 A few examples of multi-unit houses were built earlier in Grey Lynn, including some recently demolished early twentieth-century semi-detached housing in Hadlow Terrace.

87 New Zealand Population Census 1961, Vol. 9, Dwellings and Households, p.11; New Zealand Census of Population and Dwellings, 1981, Regional Statistics Series Bulletin, Central Auckland, p.160.

## Chapter 4: Infrastructure and local government

1 *New Zealander*, 5 July 1848, p.2.

2 Ibid; G. W. A. Bush, *Decently and in Order: The Centennial History of the Auckland City Council* (Auckland: Collins, 1971), 30, 31.

3 Bush, *Decently and in Order*, 30.

4 Martin McLean, *Auckland 1842–1845: A Demographic and Housing Study of the City's Earliest European Settlement* (Wellington: Regional Archaeology Unit for Science and Research Directorate, Department of Conservation, 1989), 52.

5 Una Platts, *The Lively Capital: Auckland 1840–1865* (Christchurch: Avon Fine Prints, 1971), 40–42.

6 Bush, *Decently and in Order*, 31–32.

7 Ibid., 31–32; G. T. Bloomfield, *The Evolution of Local Government Areas in Metropolitan Auckland 1840–1971* (Auckland: Auckland University Press, 1973), 41.

8 Bush, *Decently and in Order*, 33–37, 40–46.

9 Bloomfield, *Evolution*, 45, 47.

10 *Daily Southern Cross*, 14 February 1860, p.3.

11 *New Zealander*, 23 February 1862, p.3.

12 *New Zealand Herald*, 11 April 1864, p.3, *Daily Southern Cross*, 17 May 1865, p.4; *New Zealander*, 22 October 1863, p.5; 26 December 1863, p.6; 16 July 1864, p.2; 29 September 1864, p.4.

13 Turnpike Act 1866; *New Zealand Herald*, 17 December 1866, p.4.

14 *New Zealand Herald*, 28 June 1866, p.3.

15 *Auckland Star*, 29 August 1923, p.9.

16 *Daily Southern Cross*, 4 August 1868, p.3; *New Zealand Herald*, 4 January 1868, p.3.

17 Bloomfield, *Evolution*, 127.

18 *Daily Southern Cross*, 4 August 1868, p.3; *New Zealand Herald*, 26 July 1871, p.2.

19 Bloomfield, *Evolution*, 124.

20 Ibid., 47–48, 110, 125; Bush, *Decently and in Order*, 189; Deeds index 1A — Map A [Auckland], BAJZ A1660 23662 Box 788a 1A R22764169, Archives New Zealand, Folio 542.

21 Inwards letters. 18 September 1874 — 1 March 1875 — FJ Jones, Auckland — Newton Highway Board. Requests funds to carry out essential repair work on Richmond Road. Mr Albright [Allwright] recommends expenditure of £100. Reports that contractors have completed road works, ACFM 8180 Box 28 623/75 R22426893, Archives New Zealand, Auckland, 18 September 1874.

22 Ibid., 29 October 1874 and 1 March 1875; *New Zealand Herald*, 27 May 1876, p.2.

23 Arch Hill Road Board Minute Book 1890–1903, ARH 001, Item 1, Auckland Council Archives, 6 September 1897, 6 December 1897, 1 May 1898 and 6 November 1899.

24 *Auckland Star*, 5 March 1884, p.2.

25 Arch Hill Road Board Minute Book 1890–1903, ARH 001, Item 1, Auckland Council Archives, 8 January 1900, 5 February 1900, 4 July 1904, 4 August 1904, 3 April 1905, 5 June 1905, 4 September 1905 and 6 November 1905.

26 Bloomfield, *Evolution*, 46–47.

27 *New Zealand Herald*, 28 May 1870, p.1; *Daily Southern Cross*, 26 April 1871, p.1.

28 *New Zealand Herald*, 10 February 1973, p.1; *Auckland Star*, 25 November 1874, p.2.

29 Bush, *Decently and in Order*, 119; *New Zealand Herald*, 13 August 1873, p.4.

30 *Daily Southern Cross*, 10 December 1874, p.3.

31 *Auckland Star*, 5 June 1874, p.2; *Daily Southern Cross*, 10 December 1874, p.10.

32 *Daily Southern Cross*, 10 December 1874, p.3.

33 *Auckland Star*, 27 January 1873, p.2; *New Zealand Herald*, 21 July 1873, p.3; David E. Newton, 'Germ Theory', in *The Gale Encyclopedia of Public Health, Vol. 1*, ed. Laurie J Fundukian (Farmington Hills, MI: Gale, 2013), 390–92. Gale Virtual Reference Library, http://link.galegroup.com/apps/doc/CX@&^)%))!!)/ GVRL?u=learn&sid=GVRL&xid=9dda23ce

34 *Daily Southern Cross*, 4 August 1874, p.3.

35 *Daily Southern Cross*, 10 December 1874, p.3.

36 *Auckland Star*, 25 November 1874, p.2.

37 *Appendices to the Journals of the House of Representatives*, 1875, H-22, p.2.

38 *Daily Southern Cross*, 8 March 1870, p.5.

39 *Auckland Star*, 25 November 1874, p.2.

40 *Auckland Provincial Government Gazette*, Vol. 22, 1873, p.9; *Auckland Star*, 25 November 1874, p.2; *Daily Southern Cross*, 26 November 1874, p.3; *New Zealand Herald*, 3 December 1874, supplement, p.1.

41 *Auckland Star*, 16 November 1874, p.2; *Daily Southern*

*Cross*, 20 July 1876, p.3; *New Zealand Herald*, 30 December 1876, p.3.

42 Bush, *Decently and in Order*, 129–31.

43 *New Zealand Herald*, 13 December 1879, p.6.

44 *Auckland Star*, 26 January 1886, p.4; 11 October 1887, p.5; *New Zealand Herald*, 12 January 1889, p.3.

45 Arch Hill Road Board Minute Book, 1890–1903, ARH 001 Minutes, Item 1, Box 1, Auckland Council Archives, Auckland, New Zealand, 1 February 1897; *New Zealand Herald*, 28 August 1901, p.5.

46 *Daily Southern Cross*, 28 October 1853, p.2; 10 March 1854, p.2; 20 June 1874, p.5.

47 *Auckland Star*, 26 November 1877, p.2.

48 *New Zealand Herald*, 3 May 1877, p.2.

49 *Auckland Star*, 26 November 1877, p.2.

50 Ibid.

51 *New Zealand Herald*, 27 November 1877, p.3.

52 *New Zealand Herald*, 26 November 1877, p.2; Bush, *Decently and in Order*, 143.

53 Arch Hill Road Board Outward Correspondence Book, 1877–1913, ARH 002 Letter Books, Item 1, Box 1, Auckland Council Archives, Auckland, New Zealand, 3 August 1882.

54 *Auckland Star*, 8 August 1882, p.3.

55 Ibid.

56 *Daily Southern Cross*, 21 May 1874, supplement, p.1; *New Zealand Herald*, 5 August 1879, p.5; 9 March 1880, p.6.

57 Arch Hill Road Board Outward Correspondence Book, 1877–1913, ARH 002 Letter Books, Item 1, Box 1, Auckland Council Archives, Auckland, New Zealand, 2 September 1886.

58 *Auckland Star*, 26 June 1889, p.8; 27 June 1889, p.5; 5 September 1889, p.5.

59 Arch Hill Road Board Minute Book, 1890–1903, ARH 001 Minutes, Item 1, Box 1, Auckland Council Archives, Auckland, New Zealand, 20 February 1895; Government Loans to Local Bodies Act 1886.

60 Arch Hill Road Board Outward Correspondence Book, 1877–1913, ARH 002 Letter Books, Item 1, Box 1, Auckland Council Archives, Auckland, New Zealand, 5 July 1886.

61 Ibid., 15 September 1886.

62 For an explanation of the modes of dealing with bodily wastes in the nineteenth century, see Pamela Wood, *Dirt: Filth and Decay in a New World Arcadia* (Auckland: Auckland University Press, 2005), 92–112.

63 Arch Hill Road Board Minute Book, 1903–1913, ARH 001 Minutes, Item 2, Box 1, Auckland Council Archives, Auckland, New Zealand, 4 November 1907.

64 *New Zealand Herald*, 12 January 1886, p.6; *Auckland Star*, 26 January 1886, p.4; Newton Borough Council Minute Book [B], 1891–1897, GLB 001 Minute Books, Item 1, Box 1, Auckland Council Archives, Auckland, New Zealand, 29 October 1894.

65 *Auckland Star*, 27 April 1886, p.2.

66 Newton Borough Council Minute Book [B], 1891–1897, GLB 001 Minute Books, Item 1, Box 1, Auckland Council Archives, Auckland, New Zealand, 7 March 1892.

67 *New Zealand Herald*, 8 April 1886, p.4.

68 Arch Hill Road Board Outward Correspondence Book, 1877–1913, ARH 002 Letter Books, Item 1, Box 1, Auckland Council Archives, Auckland, New Zealand, 24 August 1888.

69 *Auckland Star*, 16 January 1884, p.2.

70 *Auckland Star*, 28 December 1878, p.3; 29 June 1886, p.6.

71 *Auckland Star*, 27 April 1886, p. 2.

72 *Auckland Star*, 21 January 1887, p.2; 13 July 1887, p.1; *New Zealand Gazette*, 1887, p.841.

73 *New Zealand Herald*, 12 January 1886, p.6; Jennifer King, *Sign of Service: A Jubilee History of the Auckland Electric Power Board 1922–1972* (Auckland: Wilson and Horton, 1972), 3.

74 Rollo Arnold, *New Zealand's Burning: The Settlers' World in the Mid-1880s* (Wellington: Victoria University Press, 1994), 115.

75 *New Zealand Herald*, 7 October 1886, p.5.

76 King, *Sign of Service*, 2.

77 *Auckland Star*, 29 June 1886, p.2.

78 *New Zealand Herald*, 12 January 1889, p.3.

79 *Auckland Star*, 13 December 1898, p.8; 6 May 1899, p.6; Arch Hill Road Board Minute Book, 1890–1903, ARH 001 Minutes, Item 1, Box 1, Auckland Council Archives, Auckland, New Zealand, 5 March 1900 and 2 April 1900; Arch Hill Road Board Outward Correspondence Book, 1877–1913, ARH 002 Letter Books, Item 1, Box 1, Auckland Council Archives, Auckland, New Zealand, 30 July 1906; Arch Hill Road Board Minute Book, 1903–1913, ARH 001 Minutes, Item 2, Box 1, Auckland Council Archives, Auckland, New Zealand, 2 September 1912 and 31 March 1913.

80 *Grey River Argus*, 16 July 1878, p.2; *Auckland Star*, 13 July 1878, p.3; 4 January 1882, p.2.

81 *New Zealand Herald*, 15 July 1878, p.2.

82 *Auckland Star*, 24 September 1875, p.2.

83 *New Zealand Police Gazette*, 23 April 1879, p.71; 30 May 1883, p.95.

84 *Auckland Star*, 15 July 1878, p.2

85 *Auckland Star*, 15 July 1878, p.2; 8 October 1878, p.3.

86 *New Zealand Herald*, 9 October 1878, p.3.

87 *Auckland Star*, 4 January 1882, p.2.

88 Owen J. Cherrett, *Without Fear or Favour: 150 Years Policing Auckland 1840–1990* (Auckland: New Zealand Police and L. Patrick Hunter, 1989), 28–29.

89 Ibid., 29, 30; Richard S. Hill, *The Colonial Frontier Tamed: New Zealand Policing in Transition 1867–1886* (Wellington: Government Printer, 1989), 272, 273.

90 Richard S. Hill, *The Iron Hand in the Velvet Glove: The Modernisation of Policing in New Zealand 1886–1917* (Palmerston North: Dunmore Press, 1995), 7; Graeme Dunstall, *A Policeman's Paradise?: Policing a Stable Society 1918–1945* (Palmerston North: Dunmore Press, 1999), 2.

91 *Appendices to the Journals of the House of Representatives*, 1878, H-13, p.11.

92 Hill, *The Colonial Frontier Tamed*, 267; *Auckland Star*, 13 August 1885, p.2; 26 January 1886, p.2; 23 August 1892, p.4.

93 *New Zealand Police Gazette*, 13 April 1887, p.72; *Wises New Zealand Post Office Directory*, 1890, p.26.

94 *Appendices to the Journals of the House of Representatives*, 1887, H-5, p.8; 1887, H-9, p.2.

95 *New Zealand Herald*, 16 February 1889, p.4; 8 January 1891, p.4; 24 February 1904, p.4; *Auckland Star*, 4 July 1900, p.5.

96 See, for example, *New Zealand Herald*, 4 August 1892, p.5; *Auckland Star*, 11 April 1893, p.2.

97 *New Zealand Herald*, 28 July 1902, p.5.

98 *Auckland Star*, 17 January 1898, p.8; *New Zealand Herald*, 18 January 1898, p.4.

99 *New Zealand Herald*, 26 January 1898, p.4.

100 *New Zealand Herald*, 24 February 1904, p.4; 4 August 1905, p.7.

101 *New Zealand Herald*, 13 February 1906, p.5; *New Zealand Police Gazette*, 4 April 1906, p.118.

102 *Appendices to the Journals of the House of Representatives*, 1912, D-1, p.86.

103 *Auckland Star*, 7 August 1911, p.4; *Wises New Zealand Post Office Directory*, 1913, p.129.

104 *Auckland Star*, 5 August 1911, p.9; Cherrett, *Without Fear or Favour*, 43; Dunstall, *A Policeman's Paradise?*, 217; Susan Butterworth, *More Than Law and Order: Policing a Changing Society 1945–92* (Dunedin: Otago University Press, 2005), 136.

105 Dunstall, *A Policeman's Paradise?*, 56, 296; Bill Grieve interviewed by Kaaren Hiyama, 5 and 17 March 1990, Auckland Libraries Heritage Collections OH-1355-002.

106 Cherrett, *Without Fear or Favour*, 39.

107 Police — Grey Lynn Police Station, BBFY A1179 1054 Box 375b 17/49 Part 3 R22702520, Archives New Zealand, Auckland, 11 March 1943, 17 March 1943, 19 September 1946, 6 November 1946.

108 *Appendices to the Journals of the House of Representatives*, 1959, H-16, p.18; 1960, H-16, p.20.

109 Police — Grey Lynn Police Station, BBFY A1179 1054 Box 375b 17/49 Part 3 R22702520, Archives New Zealand, Auckland, 11 August 1980.

110 Butterworth, *More than Law and Order*, 241; Auckland Scrapbook, August 1969, p.31.

111 Melani Anae, 'All Power to the People: Overstayers, Dawn Raids, and the Polynesian Panthers', in *Tangata O Le Moana: New Zealand and the People of the Pacific*, eds Sean Mallon, Kolokesa Māhina-Tuai and Damon Salesa (Wellington: Te Papa Press, 2012), 226, 227–28, 230.

112 Butterworth, *More than Law and Order*, 193–95; www.beehive.govt.nz/release/government-offers-formal-apology-dawn-raids

113 Police — Grey Lynn Police Station, BBFY A1179 1054 Box 375b 17/49 Part 3 R22702520, Archives New Zealand, Auckland, 23 July 1985, 1 November 1983.

114 www.stuff.co.nz/auckland/local-news/8735332/New-policing-team-hitting-the-beat

115 www.nzherald.co.nz/nz/police-on-the-move-auckland-central-relocating-hq-after-51-years-in-cbd/AWCQ353FM7LC2R4RXNNAQARMFE

116 *New Zealand Herald*, 16 April 1900, p.5; 20 April 1900, p.5; 24 April 1900, p.5; 26 April 1900, p.5; Bush, *Decently and in Order*, 123–24; *Appendices to the Journals of the House of Representatives*, 1901, H-31, p.5.

117 Slaughtering and Inspection Act 1900.

118 *New Zealand Herald*, 17 May 1901, p.5.

119 Ibid.

120 *Auckland Star*, 15 November 1901, p.3.

121 *Auckland Star*, 29 November 1901, p.2.

122 Public Health Act 1900, section 82; *Appendices to the Journals of the House of Representatives*, 1902, H-31, p.36.

123 *Auckland Star*, 30 November 1908, p.6.

124 *New Zealand Herald*, 7 October 1903, p.6.

125 Ibid.

126 Ibid.

127 Bush, *Decently and in Order*, 145.

128 *New Zealand Herald*, 24 April 1900, p.5.

129 *New Zealand Herald*, 18 April 1900, p.5.

130 *New Zealand Herald*, 18 April 1900, p.5.

131 *New Zealand Herald*, 21 April 1900, p.5.

132 *New Zealand Herald*, 23 June 1903, p.3.

133 Bush, *Decently and in Order*, 125; *New Zealand Herald*, 19 December 1905, p.6.

134 *New Zealand Herald*, 18 September 1919, p.9.

135 *New Zealand Herald*, 9 November 1921, p.7.

136 *Meola Reef Reserve Te Tokaroa Development Plan* (Auckland, 2018), 16; *New Zealand Herald*, 16 April 1927, p.12; 6 March 1943, p.6; *Auckland Star*, 16 March 1943, p.2.

137 Graham Stewart, *The End of the Penny Section: When Trams Ruled the Streets of New Zealand* (Wellington: Grantham House, 1993), 62.

138 Ibid., 69.

139 *New Zealand Herald*, 18 November 1902, p.6; Stewart, *The End of the Penny Section*, 65, 66, 234.

140 *Auckland Star*, 17 July 1902, p.4; *New Zealand Herald*, 12 May 1903, p.4.

141 *Auckland Star*, 7 July 1903, p.3; 3 November 1903, p.3.

142 *New Zealand Herald*, 17 July 1906, p.6; 5 May 1910, p.6.

143 Auckland City Libraries, *Pt Chevalier Memories 1930s–1950s* (Auckland: Point Chevalier Historical Society, 2010), 60.

144 Stewart, *The End of the Penny Section*, 86–87.

145 Grey Lynn Borough Council Streets and Other Committees Minute Book, 1911–1914, GLB 002 Committee Minutes, Item 2, Box 2, Auckland Council Archives, Auckland, New Zealand, p.117.

146 *New Zealand Herald*, 20 November 1906, p.3.

147 Stewart, *The End of the Penny Section*, 132.

148 Neil Rennie, *Power to the People: 100 Years of Public Electricity Supply in New Zealand* (Wellington: Electricity Supply Association of New Zealand, 1989), 38.

149 King, *Sign of Service*, 4, 5; *New Zealand Herald*, 12 June 1896, supplement, p.4; *Auckland Star*, 11 April 1888, p.8.

150 King, *Sign of Service*, 7.

151 Rennie, *Power to the People*, 39.

152 Bush, *Decently and in Order*, 164; *Auckland Star*, 6 April 1909, p.4; 5 August 1909, p.3.

153 Bush, *Decently and in Order*, 164; *Observer*, 7 October 1911, p.2.

154 John E. Martin, *People, Politics and Power Stations* (Wellington: Electricity Corporation of New Zealand, 1998), 42; Bush, *Decently and in Order*, 164–65; *New Zealand Herald*, 28 October 1913, p.8; 13 January 1914, p.5.

155 *New Zealand Herald*, 28 October 1913, p.8; 22 December 1913, p.5; 13 January 1914, p.5.

156 *Auckland Star*, 24 January 1914, p.9.

157 *Auckland Star*, 1 January 1920, p.5; 17 June 1921, p.7; 17 June 1922, p.11; 7 November 1922, p.4; *New Zealand Herald*, 9 May 1922, p.8.

158 *New Zealand Herald*, 2 June 1903, p.7; 2 August 1904, p.3; *Auckland Star*, 4 August 1903, p.3.

159 *Auckland Star*, 29 August 1905, p.3.

160 *Auckland Star*, 8 May 1906, p.2.

161 *New Zealand Herald*, 8 May 1906, p.7; *Auckland Star*, 15 May 1906, p.2.

162 *New Zealand Herald*, 9 June 1911, p.7; *Auckland Star*, 15 April 1913, p.9.

163 Bloomfield, *Evolution*, 134, 135.

164 *Auckland Star*, 23 February 1911, p.7.

165 Bloomfield, *Evolution*, 134, 135.

166 *New Zealand Herald*, 19 June 1908, p.7.

167 *Auckland Star*, 26 February 1908, p.5; 2 May 1908, p.8.

168 *Auckland Star*, 31 October 1916, p.4.

169 Bush, *Decently and in Order*, 332; Lisa Truttman, 'A Night Cart Timeline', https://timespanner.blogspot.com/2009/09/night-cart-timeline.html

170 Bush, *Decently and in Order*, 189.

171 *New Zealand Herald*, 23 December 1891, p.6.

172 *Auckland Star*, 9 January 1892, p.2.

173 Ibid.

174 Bush, *Decently and in Order*, 190.

175 *Auckland Star*, 6 September 1901, p.6.

176 *Auckland Star*, 22 January 1904, p.5; 7 May 1904, p.6.

177 Bush, *Decently and in Order*, 192.

178 *Auckland Star*, 16 March 1906, p.3.

179 *Auckland Star*, 28 February 1906, p.6.

180 There were 2767 registered voters in Grey Lynn and of the 708 legal votes cast 384 opposed amalgamation and 324 supported it. *Auckland Star*, 11 May 1906, p.2.

181 *New Zealand Herald*, 9 May 1906, p.5.

182 *Auckland Star*, 25 January 1906, p.3.

183 *Auckland Star*, 12 May 1906, p.7.

184 Bush, *Decently and in Order*, 193, 194.

185 Ibid., p.126; *Auckland Star*, 11 October 1912, p.2; 30 October 1912, p.9.

186 Arch Hill Road Board Minute Book, 1903–1913, ARH 001 Minutes, Item 2, Box 1, Auckland Council Archives, Auckland, New Zealand, 31 March 1913; Bush, *Decently and in Order*, 194.

187 Bush, *Decently and in Order*, 194.

188 *New Zealand Herald*, 6 October 1919, p.6.

189 *Auckland Star*, 9 November 1918, p.2; *New Zealand Herald*, 18 November 1918, p.6.

190 Geoffrey W. Rice, *Black Flu 1918: The Story of New Zealand's Worst Public Health Disaster* (Christchurch: Canterbury University Press, 2017), 32.

191 Rose Road had 74 houses at the time and there were six deaths recorded in the street by 25 February 1919 (*Auckland Star*, 25 February 1919, p.5).

192 *Auckland Star*, 15 December 1913, p.12; New Zealand Herald, 30 October 1920, p.1; Thames Star, 15 December 1913, p.4.

193 *New Zealand Herald*, 30 October 1920, p.1.

194 Linda Bryder, '"Lessons" of the 1918 Influenza Epidemic in Auckland', *New Zealand Journal of History* 16, no. 2 (1982): 97.

195 Bush, *Decently and in Order*, 262; Bryder, 'Lessons', 120, 121.

196 Graham Bush, *From Survival to Revival: Auckland's Public Transport since 1860* (Wellington: Grantham House, 2014), 141–45.

197 Ibid., 153.

198 Auckland Scrap Book, Auckland City Libraries, January 1979, p.36.

199 Bush, *Decently and in Order*, 383.

200 West Lynn Character and Heritage Study, Auckland, 2004, p.16.

201 Barry Gustafson, *Labour's Path to Political Independence* (Auckland: Auckland University Press, 1980), 13–14.

202 David Hamer, *The New Zealand Liberals: The Years of Power, 1891–1912* (Auckland: Auckland University Press, 1988), 262; Frank Rogers, 'Fowlds, George', *Dictionary of New Zealand Biography*, first published in 1993. Te Ara — the Encyclopedia of New Zealand, https://teara.govt.nz/en/biographies/2f17/fowlds-george

203 Barry Gustafson, 'Payne, John', *Dictionary of New Zealand Biography*, first published in 1996. Te Ara — the Encyclopedia of New Zealand, https://teara.govt.nz/en/biographies/3p18/payne-john

204 Sandra Coney, 'Melville, Eliza Ellen', *Dictionary of New Zealand Biography*, first published in 1996. Te Ara — the Encyclopedia of New Zealand, https://teara.govt.nz/en/biographies/3m51/melville-eliza-ellen

205 Erik Olssen, 'Lee, John Alfred Alexander', *Dictionary of New Zealand Biography*, first published in 1998. Te Ara — the Encyclopedia of New Zealand, https://teara.govt.nz/en/biographies/4l8/lee-john-alfred-alexander; *New Zealand Herald*, 16 May 1938, p.11; *Auckland Star*, 2 March 1939, p.16.

206 Olssen, 'Lee, John Alfred Alexander'.

207 *New Zealand Herald*, 27 April 1932, p.14; *Auckland Star*, 5 September 1935, p.8; Grey Lynn Electoral Roll, Supplementary No. 1, 1938, p.55.

208 Cybèle Locke, *Comrade: Bill Andersen — A Communist, Working-Class Life* (Wellington: Bridget Williams Books, 2002), 199–200; Melani Anae, ed., *Polynesian Panthers: Pacific Protest and Affirmative Action in Aotearoa New Zealand 1971–1981* (Wellington: Huia, 2015), 111; *Grey Lynn Live Wire*, September 1964–March 1967, Wilfred (Bill) McAra Papers, Special Collections, University of Auckland, A-139.

## Chapter 5: Industry and business

1 *Daily Southern Cross*, 18 November 1843, p.1; 25 November 1843, p.2.

2 *Daily Southern Cross*, 20 January 1844, p.2; 17 August 1844, p.3; *New Zealander*, 25 April 1846, p.3; 19 September 1846, p.1.

3 *New Zealander*, 26 September 1846, p.4; Western Springs — site of waterworks and abattoirs, n.d., ACC 015 City Engineer's Plans 1862–1993, Record No 1131-1, Auckland Council Archives, Auckland, New Zealand.

4 *Auckland Star*, 3 February 1932, p.6; 3 February 1932, p.6.

5 *Auckland Star*, 3 February 1932, p.6.

6 Kaaren Hiyama, *High Hopes in Hard Times: A History of Grey Lynn and Westmere* (Auckland: Media Studies Trust, 1991), 10; *Auckland Star*, 3 February 1932, p.6.

7 *Auckland Star*, 3 February 1932, p.6.

8 Ibid.

9 Ibid.

10 *New Zealander*, 12 June 1852, p.3.

11 *New Zealander*, 4 April 1849, p.1.

12 Hazel Petrie, *Chiefs of Industry: Māori Tribal Enterprise in Early Colonial New Zealand* (Auckland: Auckland University Press, 2006), 168–70, 171.

13 Ibid., p.6.

14 *Auckland Star*, 3 February 1932, p.6.

15 *New Zealand Herald*, 1 June 1876, p.2; *Auckland Star*, 11 August 1887, p.5.

16 *Auckland Star*, 11 August 1887, p.5; 24 October 1887, p.8; 3 February 1932, p.6.

17 *New Zealand Herald*, 1 November 1889, p.5; *Auckland Star*, 27 November 1998, p.5.

18 *Daily Southern Cross*, 24 September 1862, p.3.

19 *Daily Southern Cross*, 28 January 1863, p.3.

20 *New Zealander*, 11 January 1862, p.1; 22 November 1962, p.3; *Daily Southern Cross*, 16 July 1862, p.3.

21 *Daily Southern Cross*, 16 January 1863, p.2; 26 January 1863, p.3.

22 *Daily Southern Cross*, 24 September 1864, p.6; 2 January 1865, p.5.

23 *Daily Southern Cross*, 2 January 1865, p.5; 9 April 1866, p.3; *Auckland Star*, 23 January 1886, p.2.

24 *Daily Southern Cross*, 2 January 1865, p.5.

25 Ibid.; *New* Zealand *Herald*, 10 January 1865, p.4.

26 *Daily Southern Cross*, 2 January 1865, p.5; 31 January 1965, p.7.

27 *Daily Southern Cross*, 2 January 1865, p.5.

28 *New Zealander*, 31 January 1865, p.7.

29 *Daily Southern Cross*, 2 January 1865, p.5.

30 Simon Best, 'Early Brickmaking in New Zealand', http://bickler.co.nz/bricks/history.php

31 *Daily Southern Cross*, 2 January 1865, p.5.

32 *New Zealander*, 31 January 1865, p.7.

33 *New Zealand Herald*, 10 January 1965, p.4.

34 *Daily Southern Cross*, 7 July 1865, p.5; *New Zealand Herald*, 11 July 1865, p.5.

35 *Daily Southern Cross*, 2 October 1866, p.3; 24 October 1866, p.2.

36 *Daily Southern Cross*, 3 June 1868, p.3; *New Zealand Herald*, 17 August 1868, p.3.

37 *New Zealand Herald*, 2 April 1869, p.3.

38 *New Zealand Herald*, 14 June 1869, p.3.

39 *Daily Southern Cross*, 7 June 1872, p.3; *Observer*, 8 March 1890, p.12.

40 *Daily Southern Cross*, 23 March 1865, p.5.

41 *Auckland Star*, 15 June 1872, p.2.

42 *Auckland Star*, 25 January 1889, p.1.

43 *New Zealand Herald*, 10 January 1893, p.4; *Ohinemutu Gazette*, 6 October 1909, p.1.

44 *Daily Southern Cross*, 21 October 1862, p.2; *New Zealander*, 13 December 1862, p.1; *New Zealand Herald*, 7 August 1908, p.7.

45 *Daily Southern Cross*, 16 November 1864, p.4.

46 *New Zealand Herald*, 8 April 1865, p.7; 6 January 1871, p.6; 18 January 1873, p.1; *Daily Southern Cross*, 14 September 1967, p.2.

47 *Auckland Star*, 18 November 1873, p.2.

48 *Auckland Star*, 1 December 1873, p.2.

49 *New Zealand Herald*, 26 November 1874, p.1.

50 *Daily Southern Cross*, 4 November 1876, p.2; *New Zealand Herald*, 15 November 1876, p.2.

51 *New Zealand Herald*, 26 October 1893, p.5.

52 *Auckland Star*, 15 October 1894, p.3.

53 Ibid.

54 Dinah Holman, *Newmarket: Lost and Found*, revised ed (Auckland: Bush Press, 2010), 89, 90, 93.

55 *Daily Southern Cross*, 10 March 1854, p.2.

56 *Daily Southern Cross*, 20 June 1874, p.5.

57 G. W. A. Bush, *Decently and in Order: The Centennial History of the Auckland City Council* (Auckland: Collins, 1971), 143; Auckland Libraries Heritage Collection Map 1343.

58 Dick Scott, *Stock in Trade: Hellaby's First Hundred Years 1873–1973* (Auckland: Southern Cross Books, 1973), 13, 26.

59 *New Zealand Herald*, 13 May 1882.

60 Scott, *Stock in Trade*, 27.

61 *New Zealand Herald*, 26 July 1888, p.5.

62 *Auckland Star*, 24 July 1888, p.5.

63 Scott, *Stock in Trade*, 26.

64 Ibid., 27.

65 *Industries of New Zealand (Illustrated): An Historical and Commercial Review: Descriptive and Biographical Facts, Figures and Illustrations: An Epitome of Progress: Business Men and Commercial Interests* (Auckland: The Arthur Cleave Publishing Company, 1898), 330.

66 *Auckland Star*, 16 October 1884, p.2; Deeds register book R11 [Auckland] — Folio 482-958 [Deed 88786 split between volume 1 and 2], BAJZ A1660 23641 Box 20a R11 Part 2 R22763401, Archives New Zealand, Auckland, Folios 879-890.

67 *New Zealand Herald*, 7 October 1882, p.5; 9 March 1886, p.5; *Auckland Star*, 23 March 1886, p.4.

68 *New Zealand Herald*, 1 September 1882, p.1; 15 September 1882, p.6; 7 October 1882, p.5; 20 November 1882, p.6; 22 December 1882, p.6; *Auckland Star*, 18 November 1882, p.2.

69 Lisa J. Truttman, *Leathermakers: The Gittos Family of Tanners and Leather Merchants, Part 3* (Auckland: Lisa Truttman, 2006), n.p.; *Part 4* (2008), n.p.

70 *New Zealand Herald*, 16 May 1885, p.6.

71 Ibid.

72 Ibid.

73 G. E. Alderton (ed.), *The Resources of New Zealand* (Whangārei: Alderton & Wyatt, 1898), 122.

74 Ibid., 123.

75 *Auckland Star*, 11 July 1922, p.6; *Franklin Times*, 18 July 1922, p.5; *New Zealand Herald*, 5 April 1893, p.6

76 *Auckland Star*, 2 April 1897, p.1; 18 July 1900, p.8.

77 *New Zealand Herald*, 28 April 1891, p.6.

78 *New Zealand Herald*, 18 April 1874, p.3.

79 *New Zealand Herald*, 12 December 1910, p.6.

80 *Auckland Star*, 8 July 1910, p.2.

81 *Auckland Star*, 3 October 1927, p.9.

82 *Auckland Star*, 26 November 1906, p.5.

83 Bush, *Decently and in Order*, p.145.

84 Scott, *Stock in Trade*, 87, 102, 103; *New Zealand Herald*, 10 February 1911, p.7.

85 *New Zealand Herald*, 19 November 1901, p.3.

86 *Auckland Star*, 15 September 1885, p.3; 6 January 1920, p.5; 20 October 1937, p.3; Hiyama, *High Hopes*, 45; Holman, *Newmarket*, 274.

87 *New Zealander*, 21 January 1857, p.2; *Daily Southern Cross*, 9 October 1855, p.2; 28 July 1957, p.1; 10 November 1857, p.2; *Auckland Star*, 11 November 1878, p.3.

88 Deeds index 1A — Map A [Auckland], BAJZ A1660 23662 Box 788a 1A R22764169, Archives New Zealand, Folio 543.

89 *Daily Southern Cross*, 8 July 1862, p.3.

90 *New Zealand Herald*, 11 March 1864, p.3.

91 *Daily Southern Cross*, 12 January 1865, p.5.

92 Ibid.

93 Ibid.

94 *Auckland Star*, 11 November 1878, p.3.

95 *Daily Southern Cross*, 12 January 1865, p.5.

96 Ibid.

97 *Daily Southern Cross*, 12 March 1873, p.1; *Auckland Star*, 26 January 1880. p.3; Auckland Libraries Heritage Collections Map 4497-3.

98 *Auckland Star*, 16 February 1876, p.3; 10 December 1877, p.3; 9 December 1890, p.1.

99 *Auckland Star*, 10 December 1877, p.3; Gail Lambert, *New Zealand Pottery: Commercial and Collectable*, 2nd edition (Auckland: Heinemann, 1999), 143, 145.

100 *Auckland Star*, 13 August 1881, p.3; 9 March 1882, p.1; *New Zealand Herald*, 19 April 1883, p.5.

101 *New Zealand Herald*, 6 May 1884, p.6.

102 R. C. J. Stone, *Makers of Fortune: A Colonial Business Community and Its Fall* (Auckland: Auckland University Press, 1973); *Auckland Star*, 25 October 1889, p.2; *New Zealand Herald*, 20 November 1890, p.8.

103 *Auckland Star*, 11 August 1891, p.5.

104 *Auckland Star*, 31 July 1886, p.5; 4 November 1886, p.2.

105 DP 2711, Land Information New Zealand; *Auckland Star*, 13 July 1901, p.1; 18 January 1902, p.3; 7 May 1910, p.9; *Wises New Zealand Post Office Directory*, 1898–1899, p.62; 1913, p.71.

106 *Industries of New Zealand*, 289, 290; *New Zealand Herald*, 24 November 1967.

107 *New Zealand Herald*, 24 November 1967.

108 *Auckland Star*, 27 October 1888, p.2; 3 February 1893, p.2.

109 *Industries of New Zealand*, 290.

110 Ibid.

111 Cunitia Evelyn Wilkinson, 'The Tattersfield Family of Auckland, New Zealand', https://tattersfield.one-name.net/?page_id=83

112 *Evening Star*, 4 October 1899, p.2; *New Zealand Herald*, 13 June 1904, p.4; *Wises New Zealand Post Office Directory*, 1903, p.62.

113 Wilkinson, 'The Tattersfield Family'.

114 *New Zealand Herald*, 23 December 1919, p.9; 3 June 1930, p.6.

115 *New Zealand Herald*, 30 January 1920, p.2; 31 March 1920, p.2; 26 February 1931, p.5.

116 *Auckland Star*, 25 October 1919, p.22; 4 February 1922, p.12.

117 *New Zealand Herald*, 27 March 1922, p.8; 13 October 1922, p.1; Fred C. Symes (ed.), *Auckland Expanding to Greatness* (Auckland, 1962), 86.

118 Wilkinson, 'The Tattersfield Family'; *Auckland Star*, 8 November 1924, p.24.

119 Certificate of Title NA 265/212, Land Information New Zealand; *Wises New Zealand Post Office Directory*, 1924, p.133.

120 Symes, *Auckland Expanding to Greatness*, 86; E. Waterfield, 'Recollections of Tattersfield Ltd', *Auckland Waikato Historical Society Journal*, no. 61 (September 1992): 25; *Press*, 11 December 1948, p.9; 29 May 1959, p.13.

121 Alderton, *Resources of New Zealand*, 36.

122 *Auckland Star*, 22 October 1900, p.8; 18 October 1910, p.1.

123 *New Zealand Herald*, 10 June 1907, p.6.

124 *Auckland Star*, 11 January 1908, p.1.

125 Ian Cumming, *Glorious Enterprise: The History of the Auckland Education Board 1857–1957* (Christchurch: Whitcombe & Tombs, 1959), 639, 649.

126 *Auckland Star*, 14 August 1906, p.3.

127 *New Zealand Herald*, 2 April 1919, p.6; *Auckland Star*, 17 October 1931, p.11.

128 *Auckland Star*, 21 January 1925, p.1.

129 *Auckland Star*, 23 November 1920, p.4; 15 December 1920, p.9.

130 *Sun*, 17 June 1915, p.5; *Auckland Star*, 17 December 1923, p.3; 25 March 1925, p.11.

131 *Auckland Star*, 11 December 1925, p.11.

132 *Auckland Star*, 7 August 1894, p.5; Grey Lynn Electoral Roll 1905-1906, p.10; Auckland Libraries Heritage Collections 226-7640.

133 *Auckland Star*, 7 August 1894, p.5; Grey Lynn Electoral Roll 1905–1906, p.10; *Wises New Zealand Post Office Directory*, 1912, p.157..

134 *Auckland Star*, 8 January 1909, p.1; 6 April 1914, p.12.

135 *New Zealand Herald*, 10 January 1923, p.14; *Auckland Star*, 13 February 1923, p.7.

136 *Auckland Star*, 27 May 1920, p.1; 31 January 1929, p.22.

137 https://karmadrinks.co/nz/journal/growers/we-started-something-1

138 *Auckland Star*, 5 June 1929, p.4.

139 *New Zealand Herald*, 14 June 1928, p.7; *Auckland Star*, 7 August 1929, p.9.

140 Jean-Marie O'Donnell, '"Electric Servants" and the Science of Housework: Changing Patterns of Domestic Work, 1935–1956', in *Women in History 2: Essays on Women in New Zealand*, eds Barbara Brookes, Charlotte Macdonald and Margaret Tennant (Wellington: Bridget Williams Books, 1992), 169, 170, 171, 178, 180.

141 *Auckland Star*, 18 June 1928, p.10; 7 August 1929, p.9.

142 *Auckland Star*, 18 June 1928, p.10.

143 *Auckland Star*, 29 July 1929, p.1.

144 *New Zealand Herald*, 5 April 1935, p.7.

145 *New Zealand Herald*, 12 February 1938, p.16; *Auckland Star*, 29 March 1939, p.8.

146 Grant Gillanders and Robyn Welsh, *Wired for Sound: The Stebbing History of New Zealand Music* (Auckland: Bateman, 2019), 14, 44.

147 Ibid., 44, 48, 50, 53.

148 Ibid., 53–58.

149 Ibid., 62.

150 Ibid.

151 Bryan Staff and Sheran Ashley, *For the Record: A History of the Recording Industry of New Zealand* (Auckland: Bateman, 2002), 44, 72.

152 Ibid., 80.

153 Peter E. W. Robson, *A History of the Aerated Water Industry in New Zealand 1845–1986* (Auckland: New Zealand Soft Drink Manufacturers Association, 1995), 33, 40; Murray R. Frost, *Cordially Yours: Life Stories from the Soft Drink Industry* (Hamilton: Peter Robson, 2006), 21, 76.

154 Robson, *History of the Aerated Water Industry*, 33.

155 *New Zealand Herald*, 11 December 1920, p.10.

156 David Sharpe, *Remember that Heavenly Ginger Beer? A History of Sharpe Brothers* (Melbourne: David Sharpe, 1992), 1–2, 3–5, 11, 13, 17–18, 29–30, 266–69.

157 Ibid., 32.

158 Ibid., 49, 60, 85.

159 Frost, *Cordially Yours*, 78; O'Donnell, 'Electric Servants', 169.

160 Sharpe, *Remember that Heavenly Ginger Beer?*, 2, 176, 266.

161 Ibid., 266.

162 Ibid., 129; *New Zealand Herald*, 13 November 1923, supplement, p.38.

163 Sharpe, *Remember that Heavenly Ginger Beer?*, 131, 266.

164 Frost, *Cordially Yours*, 55, 74–75.

165 Ibid., 78.

166 Ibid., 77, 79.

167 Robson, *History of the Aerated Water Industry*, 94, 95, 96.

168 *New Zealand Herald*, 8 January 1931, p.12.

169 *Auckland Star*, 6 July 1929, p.11; *New Zealand Herald*, 5 June 1930, p.7; www.nzicecream.org.nz/history-nz-1930.htm

170 *Press*, 27 January 1931, p.12; *Star* (Christchurch), 5 July 1932, p.12.

171 *Waikato Times*, 1 October 1932, p.13 (supplement); *Gisborne Herald*, 31 August 1950, p.4.

172 *New Zealand Herald*, 13 November 1923, supplement, p.28; *Auckland Star*, 15 August 1944, p.6.

173 www.heritage.org.nz/the-list/details/672

174 *Auckland Star*, 24 August 1897, p.3; 23 April 1901, p.2; *New Zealand Herald*, 11 April 1901, p.6.

175 *New Zealand Herald*, 27 December 1911, p.14; 24 May 1940, p.9.

176 *New Zealand Herald*, 29 October 1910, p.3; *Auckland Star*, 4 April 1911, p.7; Grey Lynn Borough Council Streets and Other Committees Minute Book, 1911–1914, GLB 002 Committee Minutes, Item 2, Box 2, Auckland Council Archives, Auckland, New Zealand, 11 November 1912, p.86.

177 *New Zealand Herald*, 5 October 1859, p.5.

178 *Daily Southern Cross*, 31 May 1872, p.3; *Auckland Star*, 3 June 1972, p.3; 6 January 1874, p.3; 25 February 1892, p.8.

179 *Auckland Star*, 13 January 1882, p.3; *New Zealand Herald*, 7 November 1883, p.1.

180 *Auckland Star*, 31 March 1902, p.6; *New Zealand Herald*, 6 June 1902, p.8; 19 January 1903, p.8.

181 *Auckland Star*, 1 June 1916, p.2.

182 *New Zealand Herald*, 19 December 1919, p.4.

183 *Cyclopedia of New Zealand*, Vol. 2, Christchurch, 1902, p.389.

184 *Auckland Star*, 10 August 1886, p.2.

185 *Auckland Star*, 6 September 1906, p.4; 26 June 1907, p.3; *New Zealand Herald*, 26 June 1907, p.4.

186 *New Zealand Herald*, 2 June 1880, p.6; 12 May 1903, p.4; *Auckland Star*, 4 June 1903, p.5; *Auckland Star*, 4 October 1904, p.8; 25 May 1912, p.15.

187 Character/Heritage Study: Grey Lynn, 2004, pp.27–29

188 *New Zealand Herald*, 24 July 1906, p.6; *Auckland Star*, 5 May 1910, p.9; Auckland Libraries Heritage Collections Map 3115.

189 *Cyclopedia of New Zealand*, Vol. 2, Christchurch, 1902, p.389; *New Zealand Herald*, 1 July 1905, p.8; 15 August 1905, p.3; Auckland Libraries Heritage Collections 226-7641.

190 *Wises New Zealand Post Office Directory*, 1907, p.91; *Auckland Star*, 24 October 1905, p.4; 6 February 1906,

191 *New Zealand Herald*, 31 July 1906, p.3; *Auckland Star*, 20 November 1926, p.15.

192 Character/Heritage Study: West Lynn, 2004, p.22.

193 Map G7 — 31st August 1919 and Map G8 — 6 August 1919, ACC 014 City of Auckland Map, Auckland Council Archives, Auckland, New Zealand.

194 *Auckland Star*, 8 October 1930, p.10; *New Zealand Herald*, 17 January 1931, p.13.

195 *Wises New Zealand Post Office Directory*, 1924, p.114; *New Zealand Herald*, 18 December 1922, p.8.

196 *Sun*, 11 July 1927, p.3; *Auckland Star*, 9 May 1931, p.11.

197 Russell Stone, *As It Was: Growing Up in Grey Lynn and Ponsonby Between the Wars* (Auckland: David Ling, 2017), 69–70.

198 *Auckland Star*, 24 October 1907, p.1; *New Zealand Herald*, 11 August 1910, p.1; *Wises New Zealand Post Office Directory*, 1908, p.64; 1912, p.84; 1913, p.71; 1914, p.68.

199 Stone, *As It Was*, 70, 71.

200 Alec Brown, *Town Milk: A History of Auckland's Town Milk Supply* (Auckland: New Zealand Milk Corporation Limited, 1992), 17–18, 19; *New Zealand Herald*, 26 September 1900, supplement, p.3.

201 *New Zealand Herald*, 12 March 1898, p.3.

202 Proposed zoning of western districts — Civic Survey data and map showing existing users in Grey Lynn, Arch Hill and portions of Point Chevalier and Ponsonby, 1930, ACC 005 Town Planning Maps with T.P. Numbers 1908–1984, Item 104, Auckland Council Archives, Auckland, New Zealand.

203 Proposed zoning of western districts — Civic Survey data and map showing existing users in Grey Lynn, Arch Hill and portions of Point Chevalier and Ponsonby, 1930–1930, ACC 005 Item 104 Record TP 77 Record ID 484333, Auckland Council Archives.

204 Bush, *Decently and in Order*, 290–92; Plan showing proposed zoning scheme for Grey Lynn, Arch Hill and part Ponsonby districts, 1934, ACC 005 Town Planning Maps with T.P. Numbers 1908–1984, Item 397, Auckland Council Archives, Auckland, New Zealand.

205 Bush, *Decently and in Order*, 383.

206 Stone, *As It Was*, 83.

207 Ibid., 83.

208 Nancy M. Taylor, *The Home Front*, Vol. 2 (Wellington: Historical Publications Branch, 1986), 784, 813–14, 815, 829, 830.

209 Russell Stone, 'Auckland Business, 1841–2004: Myth and Reality', in *City of Enterprise: Perspectives on Auckland Business History*, eds Ian Hunter and Diana Morrow (Auckland: Auckland University Press, 2006), 241.

210 *Wises New Zealand Post Office Directory*, 1953–54, p.170a; Gael Ferguson, *Building the New Zealand Dream* (Palmerston North: Dunmore Press, 1994), 212–14.

211 NA 185/252, NA 413/176, NA 1089/165, Land Information New Zealand; Auckland Scrap Book, December 1967, p.22.

212 Ibid.

213 Ibid.

214 *Wises New Zealand Post Office Directory*, 1970–71, p.271.

215 *New Zealand Herald*, 6 May 2007; NA588/212 and NA62D/683, Land Information New Zealand.

216 *Auckland Star*, 22 July 1936, p.4; Sheffield Radio Limited, BADZ A35 5586 Box 275b 1936/156 R207746 , Archives New Zealand, Auckland, Annual Return 1940.

217 Sheffield Radio (NZ) Ltd, BBNZ A1762 5181 Box 14403 70607 87154 R3728993, Archives New Zealand, Auckland, Annual Returns 1979, 1980, 1981.

218 Taylor Aumua, 'Tales of Homage: The Pua Brothers of Grey Lynn', 19 November 2019, https://tpplus.co.nz/community/tales-of-homage-the-pua-brothers-grey-lynn; https://collection.waikatomuseum.org.nz/objects/6741/shower-curtain

219 DP 41011 and NA 591/44, Land Information New Zealand.

220 Auckland Scrap Book, July 1957, p.184.

221 *Auckland Star*, 17 December 1945, p.1; *Wanganui Chronicle*, 14 September 1950, supplement, p.18.

222 Sean Millar, *The Bus Builders of Auckland* (Auckland, 2007), 43; Auckland Scrap Book, July 1957, p.184.

223 Auckland Scrap Book, July 1957, p.184

224 Auckland Scrap Book, December 1962, p.225; May 1970, p.231; *Auckland Star*, 14 November 1983, Sec. B, p.6.

225 *Wises New Zealand Post Office Directory*, 1970–71, p.306.

226 *Wises New Zealand Post Office Street Directory*, 1964–1965, p.216.

227 Auckland Council Geomaps, 1959 aerial; Aerial Photograph of City of Auckland, 1975, ACC 022 Aerial Photographs of Auckland City 1974–1975, Item 108, Box 6, Auckland Council Archives, Auckland, New Zealand.

228 *Inner City News*, 13 May 1988.

229 *Sunday Star Times*, 13 April 2003, p.25; *New Zealand Herald*, 22 March 2017, www.nzherald.co.nz/property/art-couples-brush-with-fame/DLNIJARUK2TVK57UJMRB7TOZ44

230 *The Local Rag*, 1 August 1998; https://

christchurchartgallery.org.nz/exhibitions/muka-studio-lithographs

231 *New Zealand Herald*, 22 March 2017, www.nzherald.co.nz/property/art-couples-brush-with-fame/DLNIJARUK2TVK57UJMRB7TOZ44

232 Ibid.

233 Ibid.

234 *Auckland City Harbour News*, 27 November 1996, p.4.

235 *The Local Rag*, 1 August 1998.

236 *New Zealand Herald*, 13 August 1987, p.5.

237 *Sunday Star Times*, 12 August 2012, p.32; *Auckland City Harbour News*, 5 April 1990, p.5.

238 Murray Cammick, 'Rip it Up', *Audioculture*, 21 May 2014, www.audioculture.co.nz/scenes/rip-it-up

239 Helen Wilson, 'Te Wa Whakapaoho i te Reo Irirangi: Some Directions in Māori Radio', in *Sound Alliances: Indigenous Peoples, Cultural Politics and Popular Music in the Pacific*, ed. Philip Hayward (London: Bloomsbury Academic, 1998), 129; *Te Maori News* 4, no. 17 (1995): 4; *North & South* (August 1999): 28.

240 www.scoop.co.nz/stories/BU0807/S00365/george-fm-future-proofed.htm

241 *Rip It Up*, 1 August 1983, p.34.

242 Ben Howe, 'A Short History of Arch Hill Recordings and So On', 17 May 2010, www.stuff.co.nz/entertainment/3703527/Guest-Blog-Ben-Howe-of-Arch-Hill

243 Personal communication with Bob Mahoney and Anna Wallis, February 2024.

244 www.liquidstudios.co.nz; https://stoppress.co.nz/news/peter-van-der-fluit-we-put-liquidstudios-creative-director-hot-seat

245 www.recordedmusic.co.nz/portfolio/about-recorded-music

246 John Singleton, 'Auckland Business: The National and International Context', in *City of Enterprise: Perspectives on Auckland Business History*, eds Ian Hunter and Diana Morrow (Auckland: Auckland University Press, 2006), 20; Peter Brosnan and Moira Wilson, 'How Does New Zealand Compare Now? International Comparisons of Disaggregated Unemployment Data', *New Zealand Journal of Industrial Relations* 14 (1989): 241, 244, 245.

247 *Broadsheet*, April 1988, p.6.

248 *New Zealand Woman's Weekly*, 19 November 1984, pp.4–5; Michael Bassett, *The Mother of All Departments: The History of the Department of Internal Affairs* (Auckland: Auckland University Press, 1997), 226.

249 *Auckland Star*, 2 April 1907, p.1.

250 Auckland Scrap Book, January 1984, pp.151–52, *Inner City News*, 9 October 1984, p.5; *Bay News*, June 2005, p.12; *New Zealand Listener*, 12 June 1982, p.63.

251 Cushla Dodson, 'Moa Unlimited', *Broadsheet*, January–February 1988, pp.30–31.

252 Michael Davis and Kathy Waghorn, *Making Ways: Alternative Architectural Practice in Aotearoa* (Auckland: Objectspace, 2010), 139–41; email communication with Chris Fox, 28 July 2023.

253 http://garnetstation.com/events/dinner-with-the-singing-chef

254 *Wises New Zealand Post Office Directory*, 1964–65, p.82 and 1970–01, p.90.

255 Stevan Eldred-Grigg, *Pleasures of the Flesh: Sex and Drugs in Colonial New Zealand 1840–1915* (Wellington: Reed, 1984), 210; Greg Ryan, 'Drink and the Historians', *New Zealand Journal of History* 44, no. 1 (2010): 40.

256 *New Zealand Herald*, 2 June 1880, p.6.

257 Licensing Act 1873, Section 17; *New Zealand Herald*, 5 June 1878, p.3; *Auckland Star*, 5 June 1877, p.2.

258 *New Zealand Herald*, 20 March 1877, p.2; *Auckland Star*, 8 February 1879, p.1.

259 *New Zealand Herald*, 20 March 1877, p.2.

260 *Auckland Star*, 4 February 1881, p.3; 7 June 1881, p.3; 6 September 1881, p.3.

261 Ministry for Culture and Heritage, 'Beginnings', https://nzhistory.govt.nz/politics/temperance-movement/beginnings

262 *Auckland Star*, 23 December 1885, p.3; *New Zealand Herald*, 19 March 1927, p.12; 13 May 1933, p.14; J. Malton Murray and J. Cocker, *Temperance and Prohibition in New Zealand* (London: The Epworth Press, 1930), 241–42.

263 *New Zealand Herald*, 3 October 1878, p.2.

264 *New Zealand Herald*, 22 June 1885, p.4.

265 *New Zealand Herald*, 18 November 1880, p.4.

266 *Auckland Star*, 18 January 1993, p.2; *New Zealand Herald*, 25 January 1883, p.4.

267 Licensing Act 1881, section 13.

268 *Auckland Star*, 5 March 1886, p.2.

269 *Auckland Star*, 9 March 1886, p.2.

270 *Auckland Star*, 3 December 1883, p.2; 3 June 1886, p.2; 4 June 1887, p.5; 6 June 1892, p.2; 8 May 1895, p.8.

271 *Auckland Star*, 5 September 1901, p.6; 6 September 1901, p.3.

272 *Auckland Star*, 4 September 1901, p.4; 5 September 1901, p.5.

273 *New Zealand Herald*, 3 September 1901, p.3; 5 September 1901, p.5.

274 *New Zealand Herald*, 4 September 1901, p.1.

275 *Auckland Star*, 9 December 1901, p.5 ;6 July 1903, p.4.

276 *Auckland Star*, 13 March 1903, p.2; 4 June 1903, p.5.

277 *New Zealand Herald*, 2 December 1905, p.6; *Auckland Star*, 12 March 1906, p.5.

278 Ministry for Culture and Heritage, 'Beginnings'.

279 Paul Christoffel, 'Prohibition and the Myth of 1919', *New Zealand Journal of History* 42, no. 2 (2008): 156.

280 Ibid., 157.

281 *New Zealand Herald*, 11 April 1919, p.5; 8 December 1922, p.8; 5 November 1925, p.10; 15 November 1928, p.12.

282 Richard Newman, 'New Zealand's Vote for Prohibition in 1911', *New Zealand Journal of History* 9, no. 1 (1975): 62–63, 69–70.

283 Ibid.

284 Licensing Act 1908, sections 28 and 146; Sale of Liquor Act 1962, Part X, sections 232; Sale of Liquor Act 1989, Section 251.

285 6714 voters supported restoration while 6404 voted for no licence. *Appendices to the Journals of the House of Representatives*, 1935, H-33b, p.23.

286 *Appendices to the Journals of the House of Representatives*, 1946, H-38, p.33; Local Restoration Polls Act 1990, section 19 (1).

287 The Eden electorate was the only New Zealand electorate to match Grey Lynn's 91-year stretch as a dry area. Eden voted dry in 1908 and was one of the three last electorates to vote wet. http://archive.electionresults.govt.nz/electionresults_1996/pdf/6.1%20Return%20of%20Local%20Restoration%20Poll%20Votes.pdf; http://archive.electionresults.govt.nz/electionresults_1999/e9/html/e9_partXII.html

288 Graeme Hutchins, *Your Shout: A Toast to Drink and Drinking in New Zealand* (Auckland: Hodder Moa, 2009), 63–65, 70, 108.

## Chapter 6: Education

1 Russell Stone, *As It Was: Growing Up in Grey Lynn and Ponsonby Between the Wars* (Mangawhai: David Ling Publishing Ltd, 2017), 95.

2 Helen May, *School Beginnings: A Nineteenth Century Colonial Story* (Wellington: NZCER Press, 2005), 22–24, 26, 40, 42.

3 Statistics of New Zealand, 1861, Table 16.

4 May, *School Beginnings*, 85–88.

5 Ibid., 88–89, 91–92, 97–98, 105–106.

6 Ibid., 80.

7 Ian Cumming, *Glorious Enterprise: The History of the Auckland Education Board 1857–1957* (Christchurch: Whitcombe & Tombs, 1959), 21, 29.

8 Ibid., 30–31.

9 Ibid., 36–8.

10 Ibid., 36.

11 *New Zealand Herald*, 13 April 1937, p.12.

12 Cumming, *Glorious Enterprise*, 84–85.

13 Ibid., p.87.

14 Ibid., 84–92.

15 Ian and Alan Cumming, *History of State Education in New Zealand 1840–1975* (Wellington: Pitman, 1978), 49.

16 May, *School Beginnings*, 168.

17 Roger Openshaw, Greg Lee and Howard Lee, *Challenging the Myths: Rethinking New Zealand's Educational History* (Palmerston North: Dunmore Press, 1993), 86.

18 May, *School Beginnings*, 215.

19 Ibid., 149–150, 152.

20 *New Zealand Herald*, 23 January 1877, p.3; Cumming, *Glorious Enterprise*, 100.

21 Cumming, *Glorious Enterprise*, 68; *Auckland Star*, 29 March 1873, p.3; 18 October 1877, p.3.

22 *New Zealand Herald*, 1 February 1876, p.3.

23 *New Zealand Herald*, 23 August 1877, p.2.

24 Ibid.; School History — Newton West, YCBD A688 5023 Box 1760c 449/37 R7204520, Archives New Zealand, Auckland, 13 May 1937.

25 *New Zealand Herald*, 27 January 1880, p.5; Original School Plans — Newton West, YCBD A688 19843 Box 1657d R7207599, Archives New Zealand, Auckland.

26 *Appendices to the Journals of the House of Representatives*, 1884, E-1, p.12, 46.

27 *Auckland Star*, 23 January 1883, p.2.

28 *Appendices to the Journals of the House of Representatives*, 1884, E-1, p.46 and Auckland Star, 23 November 1883, p.3.

29 *Auckland Star*, 10 July 1883, p.2.

30 *Wise's New Zealand Post Office Directory*, 1892–93, p.421; *New Zealand Herald*, 25 January 1884, p.8; Auckland Education Board — Minutes of Proceedings — 25 May 1883–19 December 1884, YCAF A433 5491 Box 4a R1512139, Archives New Zealand, Auckland, 28 September 1883; Deeds register book R5 [Auckland] — Folio 1-539 [Deed 81892 split between volume 1 and 2], BAJZ A1660 23641 Box 7a R5 Part 1 R22763388, Archives New Zealand, Auckland, Folios 105-106.

31 *New Zealand Herald*, 29 January 1884, p.5; 27 January 1885, p.6; 24 April 1888, p.4.

32 *New Zealand Herald*, 14 July 1888, supplement, p.1; *Auckland Star*, 8 August 1935, p.8, *Auckland Star*, 5 November 1888, p.4.

33 Stone, *As It Was*, 85; Original School Plans — Richmond Road, YCBD A688 19843 Box 1666l R7207690, Archives New Zealand, Auckland; May, *School Beginnings*, 42–43.

34 Auckland Education Board School History (indexed), YCBD A688 20033 Box 2475a 1 R7208429, Archives New Zealand, Auckland, pp.234, 237, 239, 240.

35 Rory Sweetman, *A Fair and Just Solution? A History of the Integration of Private Schools in New Zealand* (Palmerston North: Dunmore Press, 2002), 24

36 *New Zealand Tablet*, 13 June 1884, p.17.

37 Diane Strevens, *MacKillop Women: The Sisters of St Joseph of the Sacred Heart, Aotearoa New Zealand, 1883–2006* (Auckland: David Ling Publishing Ltd, 2008), 33, 49.

38 Ibid., 51, 52; *St. Joseph's Convent School, Grey Lynn, Centennial of the Auckland Foundation of the Sisters of St. Joseph of the Sacred Heart, 1984* (Auckland: D. Rogers, 1984), 23.

39 *New Zealand Herald*, 2 November 1885, p.3; *New Zealand Tablet*, 13 November 1885, p.13.

40 *New Zealand Herald*, 2 November 1885, p.3; 4 March 1886, p.5; *St. Joseph's Convent School*, p.13.

41 Tony Waters, *Confortare: A History of Sacred Heart College, Auckland 1903–2003* (Auckland: Sacred Heart College, 2003), 17.

42 Ibid., 13–14.

43 Ibid., 20.

44 Ibid., 21–22.

45 Ibid., 22, 24.

46 Ibid., 25, 26, 28, 38, 39.

47 *Auckland Star*, 30 April 1902, p.5.

48 Inspection of Schools — Inspection and Registration of Private Primary Schools — Seventh Day Adventist School Grey Lynn, BCDQ A739 1050 Box 1307a 22/2 R23977454, Archives New Zealand, Auckland, 15 May 1918.

49 Ibid., 17 November 1927, 6 December 1927, 19 December 1928, 4 February 1931.

50 *Auckland Star*, 18 January 1886, p.3.

51 *Auckland Star*, 20 February 1897, p.1; 20 February 1897, p.5; 18 December 1899, p.8; *New Zealand Herald*, 5 March 1898, p.3.

52 *Auckland Star*, 30 April 1902, p.5; *New Zealand Herald*, 4 August 1903, p.8; 8 August 1903, p.3; 6 February 1904, p.7.

53 Edith Mary Paul Taylor was born in 1871 and Inez Laura Taylor was born in 1876. Births, Deaths and Marriages register, 1871/14265 and 1876/15345.

54 J. M. R. Owens, 'Taylor, Richard', in *Dictionary of New Zealand Biography*, first published in 1990. Te Ara — the Encyclopedia of New Zealand, https://teara.govt.nz/en/biographies/1t22/taylor-richard

55 Postcard to Miss Ida Eise [Grey Lynn College], QAAI A1036 4554 Box 1a R928996, Archives New Zealand, Auckland.

56 *New Zealand Herald*, 24 December 1907, p.5.

57 Elizabeth S. Wilson, 'Eise, Ida Gertrude', *Dictionary of New Zealand Biography*, first published in 1998. Te Ara — the Encyclopedia of New Zealand, https://teara.govt.nz/en/biographies/4e6/eise-ida-gertrude

58 *Auckland Star*, 19 December 1910, p.6.

59 *Auckland Star*, 17 September 1902, p.4.

60 *Auckland Star*, 12 September 1902, p.4.

61 *New Zealand Herald*, 15 November 1906, p.7; *Auckland Star*, 22 February 1907, p.4.

62 Cumming, *Glorious Enterprise*, 220

63 May, *School Beginnings*, 194; Cumming, *Glorious Enterprise*, 220–221.

64 John F. Roberts (ed.), *Newton West School Diamond Jubilee: Sixty Years 1877–1937* (Auckland, 1937), 5.

65 *New Zealand Herald*, 20 September 1906, p.4.

66 *New Zealand Herald*, 30 November 1906, p.6.

67 *Auckland Star*, 19 April 1907, p.3.

68 *Auckland Star*, 17 January 1908, p.4; *New Zealand Herald*, 23 January 1908, p.8.

69 *Auckland Star*, 6 March 1908, p.2.

70 *New Zealand Herald*, 23 July 1908, p.7; 10 June 1909, p.6; *Auckland Star*, 14 October 1909, p.6.

71 *New Zealand Herald*, 10 June 1909, p.6.

72 Ibid.; *Auckland Star*, 17 June 1909, p.3; 23 July 1909, p.2.

73 *Auckland Star*, 11 May 1910, p.4; 9 June 1910, p.7.

74 *Auckland Star*, 9 February 1911, p.5; *New Zealand Herald*, 21 April 1911, p.8.

75 Original School Plans — Grey Lynn Primary, YCBD A688 19843 Box 1643b R7207489, Archives New Zealand, Auckland.

76 Dorothy Dowgray and John Dowgray, *100 Years of Learning: Grey Lynn School Centenary 1910–2010* (Auckland, 2010), 4.

77 *Auckland Star*, 28 February 1913, p.7.

78 *Appendices to the Journals of the House of Representatives*, 1913, E-2, pp.xiv, xviii.

79 *New Zealand Herald*, 19 May 1898, p.3; 23 February 1907, p.3; 11 July 1912, p.8.

80 *New Zealand Herald*, 22 April 1899, p.3.

81 Auckland Education Board School History (indexed), YCBD A688 20033 Box 2475a 1 R7208429, Archives New Zealand, Auckland, p.238.

82 *Westmere School (Richmond West) Golden Jubilee 1914–1964* (Auckland: Reliance Printery, 1964), 10.

83 *New Zealand Herald*, 23 July 1914, p.10.

84 *Auckland Star*, 5 August 1914, p.4.

85 *St. Joseph's Convent School Centennial*, pp.13, 15.

86 *Auckland Star*, 26 November 1918, p.6.

87 Sister Anne Marie Power, *Sisters of St. Joseph of the Sacred Heart: New Zealand Story 1883–1983* (Auckland: The Sisters, 1983), 143.

88 Ibid., 147, 149.

89 Tania Mace, *A History of St James Kindergarten 1913–2013* (Auckland: St James Kindergarten, 2013), 2, 3, 4, 14, 16, 17, 18, 20.

90 *New Zealand Herald*, 14 March 1918, p.7.

91 *Northern Advocate*, 1 July 1918, p.2.

92 Stella Younie, *Golden Jubilee Newton Central School 1924–1974* (Auckland, 1974), 1.

93 Roberts, *Newton West School Diamond Jubilee*, 7.

94 Charles S. Morris, *Newton Central School: Commemorating 25 Years of Service* (Auckland, 1947), 3.

95 Younie, *Golden Jubilee Newton Central School*, 2; Early School History 1817–, YCBD A688 20033 Box 2469c R7208436, Archives New Zealand, Auckland, Newton Central School.

96 Younie, *Golden Jubilee Newton Central School*, 2.

97 *New Zealand Herald*, 11 February 1919, p.4.

98 *New Zealand Herald*, 8 March 1919, p.10.

99 *New Zealand Herald*, 21 March 1919, p.5.

100 *New Zealand Herald*, 18 April 1922, p.6; 30 August 1922, p.8.

101 *New Zealand Herald*, 26 April 1922, p.6.

102 *New Zealand Herald*, 19 March 1928, p.10.

103 Auckland Education Board School History (indexed), YCBD A688 20033 Box 2475a 1 R7208429, Archives New Zealand, Auckland, pp.237, 238, 239.

104 Ibid., p.239.

105 *New Zealand Herald*, 20 October 1926, p.12; 12 February 1929, p.12.

106 *New Zealand Herald*, 1 August 1929, p.8

107 *Auckland Star*, 7 March 1928, p.8.

108 *New Zealand Herald*, 15 July 1935, p.11; 13 March 1937, p.19.

109 *Auckland Star*, 8 August 1935.

110 *Auckland Star*, 7 March 1931, p.11.

111 *Poverty Bay Herald*, 14 January 1932, p.4; *Manawatu Standard*, 14 March 1932, p.6.

112 Helen May, *I Am Five and I Go to School: Early Years Schooling in New Zealand 1900–2010* (Dunedin: Otago University Press, 2011), 102–03; *New Zealand Herald*, 2 June 1932, p.10; Coral Ridling interviewed by Kaaren Hiyama, 24 February 1990, Auckland Libraries Heritage Collections, OH-1355-001.

113 *Auckland Star*, 11 July 1945, p.4.

114 Tania Mace, *For the Children: A History of the Auckland Kindergarten Association 1908–2016* (Auckland: Auckland Kindergarten Association, 2016), 115–16.

115 Helen May, *The Discovery of Early Childhood* (Wellington: NZCER Press, 2013), 392.

116 Younie, *Golden Jubilee Newton Central School*, 17.

117 Cumming, *Glorious Enterprise*, 456, 458.

118 Ibid., 459, 460.

119 Younie, *Golden Jubilee Newton Central School*, 17; *Kowhai School 75th Jubilee*, p.25; *Auckland Star*, 6 September 1944, p.6.

120 *New Zealand Herald*, 24 March 1942, p.6.

121 *Appendices to the Journals of the House of Representatives*, 1943, E-2, p.7.

122 *New Zealand Herald*, 3 March 1942, p.6.

123 Frank Churchward, Mary Fitzgerald, Joy Glasson, Tunny McFadyen and Helen Villers, *Richmond Road School 1884–1984* (Auckland: Richmond Road School Publications, 1994), 11.

124 Cumming, *Glorious Enterprise*, 639, 649.

125 R. C. J. Stone and N. A. C. MacMillan, *Tradition and Change: Mt Albert Grammar School: The First Seventy-five Years* (Auckland: Mount Albert Grammar School, 1997), 14, 15.

126 Waters, *Confortare*, 50.

127 Ibid., 122–24.

128 Matt McEvoy, *The Grey Lynn Book: The Life and Times of New Zealand's Most Amazing Suburb* (Auckland: Paul Little Books, 2015), 153.

129 Ibid.

130 Pat Gallagher, *The Marist Brothers in New Zealand, Fiji and Samoa 1876–1976* (Auckland: New Zealand Marist Brothers Trust Board, 1976), 129–30.

131 *Ashburton Guardian*, 17 January 1949, p.6; www.auckland.ac.nz/en/creative/about-the-faculty/elam/about-elam/history.html

132 Cumming, *Glorious Enterprise*, 629.

133 Mace, *A History of St James Kindergarten*, 24.

134 Inspection of Schools — General — Annual Reports — Senior Inspector of Schools, Auckland, BCDQ A739 1050 Box 1300a 22/1/22 Part 1 R23977426, Archives New Zealand, Auckland, Auckland District Annual Report 1964.

135 Mace, *A History of St James Kindergarten*, 30.

136 Churchward et al., *Richmond Road School*, 4.

137 Ibid., 32.

138 Courtney B. Cazden, *The Whole Language Plus: Essays on Literacy in the United States and New Zealand* (New York: Teachers College Press, 1992), 226, 227.

139 Younie, *Golden Jubilee Newton Central School*, 1; School History — Newton Central, YCBD A688 5023 Box 2100g 1/261/24 R7204519, Archives New Zealand, Auckland, newspaper clipping, 7 December 1972.

140 School History — Newton Central, YCBD A688 5023 Box 2100g 1/261/24 R7204519, Archives New Zealand, Auckland, 7 December 1972.

141 Karen Vaughan, 'Daring to be Different: The Rise and Fall of Auckland Metropolitan College', *New Zealand Annual Review of Education* 11 (2001): 87–88.

142 Karen Vaughan, *Beyond the Age of Aquarius: Reframing Alternative Education* (Wellington: NZCER Press, 2004), 32.

143 Ibid., 37.

144 Inspection of Schools — Inspection and Registration of Private Secondary Schools — Auckland Alternative Secondary School, BCDQ A739 1050 Box 1342d 22/11 R23977642, Archives New Zealand, Auckland, newspaper clippings, 7 February 1973 and 10 March 1973.

145 Ibid., 10 March 1973; 31 July 1973.

146 Ibid., 17 February 1976; 5 May 1977; 10 February 1978; 27 February 1978.

147 Karen Vaughan, 'Daring to be Different', 88–99.

148 Inspection of Schools, 27 February 1978; 22 February 1978.

149 Inspectors Reports — Westmere, YCBD A688 5023 Box 2051b 1/566/34 R7205326, Archives New Zealand, Auckland, School Inspection Report, 15, 16, 17 October 1979; Dowgray, *100 Years of Learning*, 54.

150 Morris, *Newton Central School*, 17, 18; School History — Newton Central, 7 December 1972.

151 Sweetman, *A Fair and Just Solution?*, 42.

152 Ibid., 40, 41–42.

153 Ibid., 42.

154 Bee Dawson, *Sir Brother Patrick Lynch: A Life in Education and New Zealand's Integrated Schools 1976–2016* (Auckland: Wairau Press, 2018), 41.

155 Sweetman, *A Fair and Just Solution?*, 164–65.

156 St Paul's Integration Agreement, www.education.govt. nz/our-work/information-releases/issue-specific-releases/integration-agreements-for-state-integrated-schools

157 Education Review Office Report, Grey Lynn School, 1997.

158 Ibid.

159 Dowgray, *100 Years of Learning*, 74.

160 Education Review Office Report, Grey Lynn School, 1998 and 2001.

161 Education Review Office Report, Grey Lynn School, 2001 and 2005.

162 Education Review Office Reports, St Paul's College, 1993, 1997, 2002, 2003.

163 www.stuff.co.nz/national/education/69864348/how-aucklands-st-pauls-college-is-fighting-back

164 www.stuff.co.nz/auckland/70818832/aucklands-st-pauls-college-sells-land-for-4m

165 *Auckland City Harbour News*, 4 April 2014.

166 *Te Kura o Newton Newton Central School 1923–2023* (Newton Central School, 2013), 64.

167 Te Kura o Newton Newton Central School 1923–2023, 64; Inspectors Reports — Newton Central YCBD A668 5023 Box 2027b 1/261/34 R7205053, Archives New Zealand, Auckland, 1985, p.1; Education Review Office Report, Newton Central School, 2014, https://ero.govt. nz/institution/1392/newton-central-school

168 'Taingakawa: Opening of the New Learning Environment Newton Central School', www.newton. school.nz/wp-content/uploads/2018/10/The-History-of-TE-AKA-PU%CC%84KA%CC%84EA-2018.pdf

169 Dowgray, *100 Years of Learning*, 91; ET80829_03 12 1997 — Grey Lynn School AAHY 27073 R25649649, Archives New Zealand, Wellington.

170 https://hail.to/westmere-schoolte-rhu/article/DbUltgq

171 www.aogafaasamoa.school.nz/about_us.html

172 www.mataagaogaamata.com/about1-c1×1t

173 Education Review Office Report, Grey Lynn School, 2000; *East and Bays Courier*, 22 August 2008, p.5.

174 Helen May, *Politics in the Playground: The World of Early Childhood in Aotearoa New Zealand* (Dunedin: Otago University Press, 2019), 215, 226.

175 *Evening Post*, 8 September 1897, p.1.

176 *Auckland Star*, 25 November 1879, p.2 and 2 December 1915, p.4.

177 *Appendices to the Journals of the House of Representatives*, 1881, E-1, p.14.

178 Ibid., 1882, E-1, p.12; 1883, E-1, p.13; *New Zealand Herald*, 7 January 1884, p.11.

179 *New Zealand Herald*, 7 January 1884, supplement, p.3; Appendices to the Journals of the House of Representatives, 1885, E-1, p.16.

180 *Auckland Star*, 20 June 1884, p.2.

181 Births Deaths and Marriages, Death Record 1903/2295.

182 *New Zealand Herald*, 27 April 1889, p.5.

183 *New Zealand Herald*, 22 July 1895, p.4.

184 *Auckland Star*, 4 December 1894, p.5

185 Ibid.

186 *Auckland Star*, 10 September 1895, p.5.

187 *Auckland Star*, 9 September 1895, p.2.

188 *New Zealand Herald*, 22 July 1895, p.4.

189 *New Zealand Herald*, 10 April 1896, p.6.

190 *New Zealand Times*, 3 May 1900, p.5.

191 *Observer*, 18 April 1903, p.4; *Auckland Star*, 8 April 1903, p.8.

192 In 1895 there were 11 female heads of schools and 116 male heads of schools and in 1905 there were 6 female heads of schools and 133 male heads of schools in the Auckland Education Board area. *Appendices to the Journals of the House of Representatives*, 1896, E-1, 1906, E-1, xi.

193 Rollo Arnold, 'Women in the New Zealand Teaching Profession, 1877–1920', in *Reinterpreting the Educational Past*, eds Roger Openshaw, Gary Hermansson and David McKenzie (Wellington: New Zealand Council for Educational Research, 1987), 46.

194 Esther Irving, 'Haselden, Frances Isabella', *Dictionary of New Zealand Biography*, first published in 1993. Te Ara — the Encyclopedia of New Zealand, https://teara. govt.nz/en/biographies/2h17/haselden-frances-isabella; *New Zealand Herald*, 5 May 1888, p.3; *Auckland Star*, 4 October 1889, p.4.

195 *New Zealand Herald*, 28 April 1896, p.3; 21 March 1939, p.11.

196 Cumming, *Glorious Enterprise*, 542–43; Jo Aitken, 'Wives and Mothers First: The New Zealand Teachers' Marriage Bar and the Ideology of Domesticity, 1920–1940', *Women's Studies Journal* (January 1996): 86, 87.

197 *Auckland Star*, 18 February 1931, p.9; Aitken, 'Wives and Mothers First', 83.

198 Aitken, 'Wives and Mothers First', 89.

199 *New Zealand Herald*, 7 May 1931, p.10.

200 *Appendices to the Journals of the House of Representatives*, 1933, E-2, p.23.

201 Grey Lynn Schools Committee Minute Book [Grey Lynn School and Richmond West School (Westmere)], AFOU A1709 23417 Box 7a R22856895, Archives New Zealand, Auckland, 13 July 1931, 14 December 1931, 13 March 1932.

## Chapter 7: Sport and recreation

1 *Auckland Star*, 1 January 1873, p.2.

2 *Auckland Star*, 1 January 1873, p.2; 1 January 1874, p.2.

3 *Auckland Star*, 19 April 1879, p.2; 5 January 1884, p.5; *New Zealand Herald*, 30 January 1884, p.5.

4 *Auckland Star*, 29 December 1885, p.4.

5 See, for example, *New Zealand Herald*, 18 March 1879, p.3; 7 February 1881, p.6; *Auckland Star*, 10 December 1880, p.2.

6 *New Zealand Herald*, 18 November 1878, p.2; Auckland Star, 9 December 1878, p.2.

7 *Auckland Star*, 2 October 1883, p.2; 25 October 1883, p.2; *New Zealand Herald*, 16 November 1885, p.4.

8 *New Zealand Herald*, 29 July 1881, p.6.

9 *New Zealand Herald*, 12 August 1881, p.3; Certificate of Title NA25/65, Land Information New Zealand; R. C. J. Stone, *Makers of Fortune: A Colonial Business Community and Its Fall* (Auckland: Auckland University Press, 1973), 179, 180, 182; *New Zealand Herald*, 9 December 1882, p.1.

10 G. W. A. Bush, *Decently and in Order: The Centennial History of the Auckland City Council* (Auckland, 1971), 189.

11 *Bay of Plenty Times*, 10 March 1883, p.2; *New Zealand Herald*, 22 October 1883, p.5.

12 *New Zealand Herald*, 22 October 1883, p.5.

13 *New Zealand Herald*, 15 January 1879, p.3; 11 September 1882, p.3; 27 August 1887, p.6; *Auckland Star*, 24 July 1880, p.3.

14 *New Zealand Herald*, 1 May 1886, p.6.

15 Jim Allnatt, *Auckland Cricket 1841–1901: The Victorian Era* (Auckland: self-published, 2008), 50, 61.

16 Ibid., 129.

17 Greg Ryan and Geoff Watson, *Sport and the New Zealanders: A History* (Auckland: Auckland University Press, 2018), 57; *New Zealand Herald*, 1 June 1874, p.2.

18 Ryan and Watson, *Sport and the New Zealanders*, 56–59.

19 *Auckland Star*, 14 September 1883, p.2.

20 *Auckland Star*, 13 May 1881, p.3; 25 July 1881, p.2; 6 April 1883, p.2; 7 September 1883, p.2.

21 *Auckland Star*, 4 July 1884, p.2; 4 August 1885, p.2; 2 August 1886, p.4.28 May 1891, p.4.

22 Paul Neazor, *Ponsonby Rugby Club: Passion and Pride* (Auckland: Celebrity Books, 1999), 25, 26, 27.

23 *Auckland Star*, 6 April 1903, p.5; *New Zealand Herald*, 25 March 1909, p.8.

24 Neazor, *Ponsonby Rugby Club*, 29.

25 *100 Years Auckland Rugby: Official History of the Auckland Rugby Football Union* (Auckland: The Union, 1983), 285–86.

26 *New Zealand Herald*, 5 June 1897, p.6; Terry Maddaford, *The First 100 Years: The Official Centenary History of the Auckland Football Association 1887–1987* (Auckland: The Association, 1987), 10.

27 *Auckland Star*, 19 April 1907, p.3.

28 *NZ Truth*, 20 July 1912, p.3.

29 *Auckland Star*, 21 April 1900, p.6.

30 *Auckland Star*, 30 May 1885, p.2; *New Zealand Herald*,

17 May 1899, p.7; 20 May 1899, p.7; 11 April 1900, p.3; 21 June 1900, p.3.

31  *Auckland Star*, 23 May 1901, p.3; 16 August 1901, p.2.

32  *New Zealand Herald*, 2 September 1901, p.3; *Auckland Star*, 29 August 1902, p.2.

33  www.nzlacrosse.com/nz-history

34  *Auckland Star*, 9 April 1904, p.4; *New Zealand Herald*, 23 September 1907, p.6; DP 831, Certificate of Title NA49/295, Land Information New Zealand.

35  Ryan and Watson, *Sport and the New Zealanders*, 103; Sandra Coney, *Standing in the Sunshine: A History of New Zealand Women Since they Won the Vote* (Auckland: Viking, 1993), 244.

36  *New Zealand Herald*, 28 March 1904, p.3.

37  John Carter, *Bowls Through the Decades: The Proud History of Over 100 Years of Bowls in New Zealand* (Auckland: Bowls New Zealand Incorporated, 2013), 13.

38  Ibid., p.223.

39  *Observer*, 26 November 1904, p.18.

40  *New Zealand Herald*, 23 July 1906, p.7.

41  *Auckland Star*, 6 November 1906, p.12.

42  *Auckland Star*, 6 September 1907, p.2; 11 November 1907, p.3.

43  *New Zealand Herald*, 23 September 1907, p.1; 4 October 1910, p.8.

44  Sally Blundell, 'Hunting the Jack', *New Zealand Geographic*, November–December 2008; *New Zealand Herald*, 17 June 1905, p.7; 18 November 1909, p.8; *Auckland Star*, 17 December 1904, p.7; 11 November 1909, p.2; 18 November 1909, p.6.

45  *New Zealand Herald*, 5 November 1906, p.3.

46  *Auckland Star*, 28 October 1910, p.7.

47  *Auckland Star*, 28 October 1910, p.7; *New Zealand Herald*, 21 November 1910, p.7.

48  *Auckland Star*, 20 March 1926, p.10.

49  *New Zealand Herald*, 27 November 1941, p.11.

50  Michael R. Watts, *The Dissenters: The Crisis and Conscience of Nonconformity* (Oxford: Claredon Press, 2015), 187; Margaret West and Ruth Fawell, *The Story of New Zealand Quakerism 1842–1972* (Auckland: Yearly Meeting of the Religious Society of Friends, 1973), 95.

51  *Auckland Star*, 12 August 1913, p.8; *New Zealand Herald* 17 April 1915, p.4.

52  *Auckland Star*, 22 May 1912, p.7, 4 April 1913, p.8.

53  *Auckland Star*, 27 March 1914, p.2.

54  *Auckland Star*, 12 August 1913, p.8.

55  *New Zealand Herald*, 10 May 1913, p.10; 24 April 1914, p.4; 31 March 1915, p.4; *Auckland Star*, 12 August 1913, p.8.

56  *New Zealand Herald*, 5 August 1915, p.5.

57  *Auckland Star*, 17 May 1941, p.4; Grey Lynn Schools Committee Minute Book [Grey Lynn School and Richmond West School (Westmere)], AFOU A1709 23417 Box 7a R22856895, Archives New Zealand, Auckland, 13 July 1931, 14 December 1931, 13 March 1932.

58  *Auckland Star*, 7 September 1907, p.10.

59  *New Zealand Herald*, 24 April 1915, p.5; 13 May 1915, p.3.

60  *New Zealand Herald*, 24 April 1915, p.5; 13 May 1915, p.3.

61  *Auckland Star*, 10 April 1916, p.7.

62  *Observer*, 29 June 1918, p.10.

63  *Auckland Star*, 24 April 1920, p.20.

64  *Auckland Star*, 16 May 1923, p.9; 17 September 1924, p.9.

65  *Auckland Star*, 17 March 1926, p.9; *Wises New Zealand Post Office Directory*, 1926, p.84.

66  Maddaford, *The First 100 Years*, 15, 16; *Auckland Star*, 28 March 1923, p.9.

67  *Auckland Star*, 14 May 1915, p.7.

68  John Coffey and Bernie Wood, *Auckland: 100 Years of Rugby League 1909–2009* (Wellington: Huia, 2009), 3.

69  Ibid., 2.

70  John Haynes, *From All Blacks to All Golds: Rugby Leagues Pioneers* (Christchurch: John Haynes, 1996), 51; John Coffey and Bernie Wood, *The Kiwis: 100 Years of International Rugby League* (Auckland: Hachette, 2007), 408; Coffey and Wood, *Auckland*, 3, 4.

71  Coffey and Wood, *Auckland*, 4; Grey Lynn Electoral Roll, 1908, p.98; Grey Lynn Supplementary Electoral Roll, 1908, p.73.

72  Bruce Montgomerie, *Those Who Played Rugby League for New Zealand 1907–2004* (Sydney: Bruce Montgomerie, 2004), 204, 242; Coffey and Wood, *The Kiwis*, 37.

73  Coffey and Wood, *Auckland*, 19.

74  Ibid., 18–19.

75  www.richmondroversrugbyleague.com/history.html

76  *New Zealand Herald*, 17 April 1914, p.10; 16 April 1915, p.8.

77  *Auckland Star*, 6 April 1914, p.12; 24 April 1916, p.12.

78  *New Zealand Herald*, 13 May 1915, p.3.

79  *Auckland Star*, 14 May 1915, p.7; 5 May 1916, p.3; 4 May 1917, p.7.

80  *Auckland Star*, 5 May 1922, p.6; Coffey and Wood, *Auckland*, 137–39.

81  *New Zealand Herald*, 24 June 1903, p.3.

82  *New Zealand Herald*, 8 March 1904, p.3; *Auckland*

*Star*, 12 February 1904, p.4; *Appendices to the Journals of the House of Representatives*, 1906, C-10, p.5; 1907, C-10, p.4; 1908, C-10, p.3.

83 *Auckland Star*, 27 February 1906, p.6; *Appendices to the Journals of the House of Representatives*, 1908, C-10, p.3.

84 *Auckland Star*, 16 November 1901, p.4.

85 *Auckland Star*, 4 June 1907, p.7.

86 *New Zealand Herald*, 12 November 1906, p.8; 20 September 1907, p.6; 28 March 1908, p.4; 5 May 1908, p.6.

87 *Auckland Star*, 5 February 1909, p.3; *New Zealand Herald*, 26 June 1909, p.8.

88 Grey Lynn Domain Vesting Act 1909.

89 *New Zealand Herald*, 8 November 1909, p.4.

90 *Auckland Star*, 7 March 1911, p.7.

91 Bush, *Decently and in Order*, 171; *New Zealand Herald*, 9 April 1915, p.7.

92 *Auckland Star*, 20 January 1926, p.10; *Appendices to the Journals of the House of Representatives*, 1916, E-2, pp.xxi, xxii and xx.

93 *New Zealand Herald*, 13 October 1913, p.5.

94 *New Zealand Herald*, 10 May 1921.

95 *New Zealand Herald*, 10 May 1921, p.9.

96 *New Zealand Herald*, 20 April 1923, p.5; 19 April 1924, p.17; *Auckland Star*, 3 May 1926, p.5.

97 *New Zealand Herald*, 1 April 1927, p.12; 9 May 1927, p.10.

98 Lisa J. Truttman, *The Zoo War: J.J. Boyd's Aramoho and Royal Oak Zoos 1908–1922* (Auckland: Lisa Truttman, 2008), 20, 21.

99 Derek Wood, *A Tiger by the Tail: A History of Auckland Zoo 1922–1992* (Auckland: Auckland City Council, 1992), 4–5, 7, 8, 9; *New Zealand Herald*, 26 September 1911, p.7.

100 Truttman, *The Zoo War*, 48–50.

101 Wood, *A Tiger by the Tail*, 9, 11; *Auckland Star*, 16 June 1922, p.6.

102 *Auckland Star*, 16 June 1922, p.6; 27 June 1922, p.4.

103 See for example *Auckland Star*, 25 July 1922, p.6; *New Zealand Herald*, 25 July 1922, p.3; *Auckland Star*, 29 May 1922, p.4; *Auckland Star*, 25 July 1922, p.4.

104 *Auckland Star*, 20 August 1935, p.9.

105 *New Zealand Herald*, 28 June 1922, p.9.

106 Ibid.

107 Ibid.; *Otago Daily Times*, 11 August 1950, p.8.

108 2454 ratepayers voted in favour and 1013 against. *Auckland Star*, 27 July 1922, p.8.

109 *New Zealand Herald*, 18 December 1922, p.8.

110 Wood, *A Tiger by the Tail*, 167; Bush, *Decently and in Order*, 279.

111 Wood, *A Tiger by the Tail*, 23–25.

112 Ibid., 25, 31, 34.

113 *New Zealand Herald*, 29 August 1924, p.8.

114 *New Zealand Herald*, 18 September 1925, p.10.

115 Ibid.

116 Bill Grieve interviewed by Kaaren Hiyama, 5 and 17 March 1990, Auckland Libraries Heritage Collections, OH-1355-002.

117 Wood, *A Tiger by the Tail*, 38.

118 *Auckland Star*, 10 July 1926, p.11; *New Zealand Herald*, 1 October 1926, p.16.

119 *Auckland Star*, 24 September 1927, p.12.

120 *New Zealand Truth*, 14 January 1926, p.4; *Auckland Star*, 24 September 1927, p.12.

121 *Auckland Star*, 29 September 1927, p.11.

122 *Auckland Star*, 3 February 1928, p.7; *New Zealand Herald*, 4 February 1928, p.12.

123 Maureen A. Bull, *Vintage Motor Cycling: A Record of Motor Cycling in New Zealand from 1899 to 1931* (Masterton: Hedley's Bookshop, 1970), 14–16, 71, 72, 73.

124 A. R. E. Messenger and Douglas E. Wood, *Flat to the Boards: A History of Motor Car Sport in New Zealand from 1901–1940* (Christchurch: Vintage Car Club of New Zealand, 1985), 23–24.

125 Bull, *Vintage Motor Cycling*, 73, 74.

126 Messenger and Wood, *Flat to the Boards*, 7–24; Bull, *Vintage Motor Cycling*, 65–70, 81–85.

127 Messenger and Wood, *Flat to the Boards*, 99; *New Zealand Herald*, 16 March 1929, supplement, p.10; *Auckland Star*, 26 March 1929, p.18.

128 *Evening Star*, 3 December 1929, p.15; *New Zealand Herald*, 20 April 1929, supplement, p.12.

129 *Auckland Star*, 15 March 1929, p.4 and *New Zealand Herald*, 13 September 1929, p.12.

130 *New Zealand Herald*, 2 December 1929, p.13.

131 *Auckland Star*, 19 March 1934, p.14.

132 Reserves and Other Lands Disposal and Public Bodies Empowering Act 1913; *Auckland Star*, 16 December 1913, p.4.

133 Caroline Daley, *Leisure and Pleasure: Reshaping and Revealing the New Zealand Body 1900–1960* (Auckland: Auckland University Press, 2003), 119.

134 Kevin Moran, *The Shape of Swimming and Water Safety Education in New Zealand* (Saarbrucken, 2009), 21.

135 *75th Jubilee of the Ponsonby Amateur Swimming and Lifesaving Club 1908–1983* (Auckland, 1984), 5, 7; *New Zealand Herald*, 15 November 1923, p.11.

136 *New Zealand Herald*, 15 November 1923, p.11; 24 February 1928, p.14.

137 *Auckland Star*, 12 January 1928, p.11.

138 *Auckland Star*, 12 February 1924, p.9, 22 February 1924, p.7; 28 February 1924, p.9; *New Zealand Herald*, 3 March 1924, p.10.

139 *New Zealand Herald*, 10 April 1924, p.6; 29 January 1925, p.6.

140 *New Zealand Herald*, 8 September 1927, p.8; *Auckland Star*, 18 May 1928, p.13.

141 Auckland Scrap Book, Auckland City Libraries, 1952–1954, p.105.

142 *New Zealand Herald*, 18 February 1926, p.11.

143 *Auckland Star*, 21 November 1930, p.5; *New Zealand Herald*, 21 November 1930, p.13; Grey Lynn Electoral Roll, 1928, p.215.

144 *New Zealand Herald*, 8 November 1930, p.8; 21 November 1930, p.13; Grey Lynn Electoral Roll, 1928, p.191.

145 Plan of Cox's Creek reserves showing proposed reclamation and development, 1931, ACC 005 Town Planning Maps with T.P. Numbers 1908–1984, Item 125, Auckland Council Archives, Auckland, New Zealand.

146 *New Zealand Herald*, 20 March 1931, p.14; 5 October 1932, p.15; *Auckland Star*, 19 January 1932, p.9; 6 February 1932, supplement, p.2.

147 *Auckland Star*, 5 February 1934, p.10.

148 Bush, *Decently and in Order*, 281; Mark Derby, 'Camping — The golden age of camping', Te Ara — the Encyclopedia of New Zealand, www.TeAra.govt.nz/en/camping/page-2

149 *New Zealand Herald*, 10 June 1944, p.4.

150 *Auckland Star*, 4 October 1927, p.10; *New Zealand Herald*, 25 July 1927, p.8; 22 April 1929, p.8; 12 May 1933, p.13.

151 *Auckland Star*, 29 October 1934, p.13.

152 *Auckland Star*, 12 September 1928, p.17

153 *New Zealand Herald*, 7 July 1939, p.10.

154 *New Zealand Herald*, 5 June 1897, p.6; Maddaford, *The First 100 Years*, 10.

155 Sandra Coney, *Every Girl: A Social History of the YWCA in Auckland 1885–1985* (Auckland: YWCA, 1986), 160.

156 Ibid., 161; Helen Smyth, *Rocking the Cradle: Contraception, Sex and Politics in New Zealand* (Wellington: Steele Roberts, 2000), 11.

157 Coney, *Standing in the Sunshine*, 242.

158 Coney, *Everygirl*, 163.

159 Coney, *Standing in the Sunshine*, 242–43; Ian Cumming and Alan Cumming, *History of State Education in New Zealand 1840–1975* (Wellington: Pitman, 1978), 249.

160 Louise Shaw, *Making a Difference: A History of the Auckland College of Education 1881–2004* (Auckland: Auckland Universtiy Press, 2006), 44.

161 *Auckland Star*, 17 August 1926, p.19; Coney, *Everygirl*, 176.

162 Coney, *Standing in the Sunshine*, p. 242.

163 Peter Hawes and Lizzie Barker, *Court in the Spotlight: History of New Zealand Netball* (Christchurch: Netball New Zealand, 1999), 13; *New Zealand Herald*, 11 June 1906, p.7; 25 May 1908, p.8.

164 *New Zealand Herald*, 19 June 1912, p.9; 11 September 1912, p.7.

165 *Auckland Star*, 24 June 1927, p.12; 21 October 1930, p.12; 1 August 1940, p.3; *New Zealand Herald*, 7 June 1937, p.17.

166 *New Zealand Herald*, 17 October 1932, p.12; 7 June 1937, p.17; *Franklin Times*, 8 October 1945, p.3.

167 Ryan and Watson, *Sport and the New Zealanders*, 104; Christchurch *Star*, 11 July 1896, p.6; *Press*, 30 September 1897, p.4; *Auckland Star*, 17 September 1898, supplement, p.10; *New Zealand Herald*, 11 August 1899, p.5.

168 *New Zealand Herald*, 29 July 1907, p.8.

169 *New Zealand Herald*, 10 April 1933, p.14.

170 *Auckland Star*, 24 March 1924, p.16.

171 *Auckland Star*, 13 February 1930, p.18.

172 *Auckland Star*, 20 February 1930, p.18.

173 *Auckland Star*, 24 February 1930, p.17.

174 https://thevintagent.com/2017/10/03/from-glorious-to-notorious-the-fay-taylour-story

175 Cleve Dheensaw, *The Commonwealth Games: The First 60 Years 1930–1990* (Auckland: Queen Anne Press, 1994), 35; Joseph Romanos, 'Olympic and Commonwealth games — New Zealand as the Commonwealth Games host', Te Ara — the Encyclopedia of New Zealand, www.TeAra.govt.nz/en/olympic-and-commonwealth-games/page-9

176 *Otago Daily Times*, 18 January 1950, p.2.

177 *Otago Daily Times*, 6 January 1950, p.6.

178 *Otago Daily Times*, 8 February 1950, p.8; 10 February 1950, p.8; *Gisborne Herald*, 13 February 1950, p.4.

179 *Otago Daily Times*, 13 February 1950, p.4.

180 *Otago Daily Times*, 13 February 1950, p.4.

181 Ryan and Watson, *Sport and the New Zealanders*, 204–06, 226.

182 *New Streets — Auckland Fa'a-Samoa*, documentary film, 1982.

183 Neazor, *Ponsonby Rugby Club*, 161–63.

184 Ryan and Watson, *Sport and the New Zealanders*, 229, 244, 245.

185 N. A. C. McMillan, 'Lumley, Bernice and Lumley,

Doreen', *Dictionary of New Zealand Biography*, first published in 1998, updated March, 2006. Te Ara — the Encyclopedia of New Zealand, https://teara.govt.nz/en/biographies/4l18/lumley-bernice

186 Ibid.

187 Ibid.

188 Ibid.

189 Ibid.

190 *Auckland Star*, 25 March 1939, p.23.

191 *New Zealand Herald*, 14 September 1939, p.3 and *Auckland Star*, 7 October 1939, supplement, p.5.

192 McMillan, 'Lumley, Bernice and Lumley, Doreen'.

193 Ibid.

194 Ibid.

195 Paul Tritenbach, *Botanic Gardens and Parks in New Zealand: An Illustrated Record* (Auckland: Excellence Press, 1987), 38.

196 Bush, *Decenctly and in Order*, 185–86.

197 Ibid., 172.

198 *Auckland Star*, 11 March 1938, p.13; *Ponsonby News*.

199 Grey Lynn Electoral Roll, 1946, p.54; www.angelfire.com/super2/westsubs/westsub1.html

200 Montgomerie, 16; Ryan Bodman, *Rugby League in New Zealand: A People's History* (Wellington: Bridget Williams Books, 2023), 137.

201 Steve Landells, 'Les Mills', https://athletics.org.nz/legends/les-mills; www.olympic.org.nz/athletes/phillip-mills

202 Bob Howitt, *Beegee: The Bryan Williams Story* (Auckland: Rugby Press, 1981), 9–11, 13.

203 Dale Husband, 'Bryan Williams: Sidesteps, Tries, and Pioneering', *E-Tangata*, 14 November 2021, https://e-tangata.co.nz/korero/bryan-williams-sidesteps-tries-and-pioneering

204 Howitt, *Beegee*, 21, 22, 27, 28.

205 Ibid., 28, 34.

206 Ibid., 42; Husband, 'Bryan Williams'.

207 Husband, 'Bryan Williams'.

208 Howitt, *Beegee*, 152–53, 154, 155,

209 Ibid., 125, 265.

210 www.allblacks.com/news/sir-bryan-williams-made-life-member-of-new-zealand-rugby

211 Paul Neazor, *Ponsonby Rugby Club: Passion and Pride* (Auckland: Celebrity Books, 1999), 177.

## Chapter 8: Faith

1 *New Zealand Herald*, 24 January 1874, p.3; 10 May 1901, p.10.

2 *Daily Southern Cross*, 21 January 1874, p.3; *New Zealand Herald*, 24 January 1874, p.3; 14 August 1874, p.2; 21 October 1874, p.3; *Auckland Star*, 8 November 1880, p.2.

3 *Daily Southern Cross*, 21 January 1874, p.3; Peter Lineham, *Sunday Best: How the Church Shaped New Zealand and New Zealand Shaped the Church* (Auckland: Massey University Press, 2017), 228.

4 *New Zealand Herald*, 5 August 1874, p.2; 22 January 1876, p.2; *Auckland Star*, 5 July 1886, p.2.

5 *New Zealand Herald*, 5 February 1883, p.5.

6 Lineham, *Sunday Best*, 230, 370–71.

7 Ibid., 230, 370–71.

8 *Auckland Star*, 5 July 1886, p.2.

9 Lineham, *Sunday Best*, 171, 192.

10 *Church Gazette*, January 1877, supplement, p.iv; March 1884, p.24; *Auckland Star*, 25 January 1884, p.4; 8 July 1919, p.8.

11 *Auckland Star*, 12 April 1882, p.2.

12 Census, 1874, Chapter 23, Table II; *Auckland Star*, 12 April 1882, p.2.

13 *Auckland Star*, 25 April 1882, p.2.

14 Of the 72,134 children (exclusive of Chinese) aged between 5 and 15, 7497 attended only Sunday school while 30,584 attended both Sunday School and weekday school. Lineham, *Sunday Best*, 130; Census, 1874, Chapter 79, Table XIII; *Auckland Star*, 5 July 1886, p.2.

15 *New Zealand Herald*, 19 January 1882, p.6; *Auckland Star*, 5 July 1886, p.2.

16 *New Zealand Herald*, 19 January 1882, p.6; 1 July 1882, p.5; 17 July 1882, p.2; 22 November 1882, p.6; 5 February 1883, p.5; *Auckland Star*, 20 December 1886, p.4.

17 *Auckland Star*, 20 December 1886, p.4.

18 *Auckland Star*, 24 January 1894, p.2; 6 April 1894, p.2; 10 April 1894, p.5.

19 *Auckland Star*, 14 November 1882, p.2; 16 December 1882, p.3; Deeds register book R5 [Auckland] — Folio 1-539 [Deed 81892 split between volume 1 and 2], BAJZ A1660 23641 Box 7a R5 Part 1 R22763388, Archives New Zealand, Auckland, Folios 105-107.

20 *Auckland Star*, 10 November 1882 p.3; 14 November 1882, p.2.

21 *Fifty Years of Primitive Methodism* (Thames: Primitive Methodist Book Depot, 1893), 132; *Auckland Star*, 16 December 1882, p.3.

22 W. Greenwood, *For All the Saints: An Account of the Primitive Methodists of Waimate* (Waimate: Wesley Historical Society, 1980), 4; Donald Phillips, 'From Mow Cop to Airedale Street: An Account of the History of Primitive Methodism in Auckland 1849–1913', *Wesley Historical Society Journal* (1996): 2–5, 20.

23 Peter Lineham, *Agency of Hope: The Story of the City*

*Mission 1920–2020* (Auckland: Massey University Press, 2020), 18.

24 *Auckland Star*, 22 May 1883, p.3; 23 January 1884, p.3; 16 November 1893, p.8; 8 August 1935, p.8; *New Zealand Herald*, 17 November 1893, p.6.

25 *Auckland Star*, 16 November 1893, p.8.

26 *Daily Southern Cross*, 8 August 1872, p.3; 7 November 1872, p.2; *New Zealand Herald*, 27 November 1872, p.2; 29 December 1873, p.2; 23 August 1877, p.2; *Auckland Star*, 21 September 1878, p.3; 7 June 1879, p.3.

27 Census figures from 1878 reveal that public worship was held in 831 churches and chapels, 136 schools and 68 dwellings or public buildings. *Census*, 1878, Chapter 152, Table IX.

28 *New Zealand Herald*, 13 December 1882, p.5.

29 *New Zealand Herald*, 1 July 1882, p.4; 4 July 1882, p.4; 26 April 1883, p.5; 13 December 1882, p.5; *Auckland Star*, 22 November 1919, p.5.

30 *New Zealand Herald*, 26 April 1883, p.5.

31 *New Zealand Herald*, 19 November 1883, p.5.

32 *Auckland Star*, 2 April 1884, p.2; 2 July 1884, p.2; 25 July 1910, p.2.

33 *Auckland Star*, 13 September 1884, p.4.

34 *Auckland Star*, 16 August 1884, p.6; 26 September 1884, p.3.

35 *New Zealand Herald*, 22 December 1884, p.5.

36 Helen May, *School Beginnings: A Nineteenth Century Colonial Story* (Wellington: NZCER, 2005), 168, 215.

37 *New Zealand Herald*, 2 November 1885, p.3; *New Zealand Tablet*, 13 November 1885, p.13.

38 Mark Willis, *From Cottages to Congregations: A History of Churches of Christ in New Zealand from 1844–2004* (Tauranga: self-published, 2009), 43.

39 Ibid.; *New Zealand Herald*, 19 January 1887, p.4; *Auckland Star*, 23 August 1890, p.5.

40 *New Zealand Herald*, 28 April 1897, p.4; 10 August 1897, p.3; *Auckland Star*, 23 August 1897, p.2.

41 Noel Clapham (ed.), *Seventh Day Adventists in the South Pacific, 1885–1985* (Warburton, VIC: Signs Publishing, 1985), 19–21; Milton Hook, *Land of the Long White Cloud: Beginnings of Adventism in New Zealand* (Wahroonga: Adventist Education, 2014), 4–5; *New Zealand Herald*, 8 January 1887, p.4.

42 *Auckland Star*, 7 January 1887, p.2; 4 February 1887, p.2; 16 February 1887, p.6.

43 *New Zealand Herald*, 9 February 1887, p.4; 11 April 1887, p.4; *Auckland Star*, 16 February 1887, p.6.

44 Clapham, *Seventh Day Adventists*, 20; Hook, *Land of the Long White Cloud*, 5.

45 David E. Hay, *Samoa 100+ Years: The South Pacific and Beyond: Seventh-day Adventist Churches in the Samoan Islands, NZ, USA and Australia* (Newcastle: David Hay, 2005), 369; *New Zealand Herald*, 11 January 1887, p.2; 16 April 1887, p.4; 25 April 1887, p.6.

46 *New Zealand Herald*, 20 July 1887, p.4.

47 *Auckland Star*, 26 November 1885, p.2; 29 June 1886, pp.2, 3; *New Zealand Herald*, 11 December 1885, p.5; 28 August 1886, p.4; Peter Lincham, *There We Found Brethren: A History of Assemblies of Brethren in New Zealand* (Palmerston North: G.P.H. Society, 1977), 116.

48 *Auckland Star*, 2 August 1898, p.5; *New Zealand Herald*, 19 September 1898, p.5; John Olphert, *Primitive Methodism in Auckland 1849–1913* (Auckland: Wesley Historical Society, 1949), 15; NA62/278, Land Information New Zealand.

49 *Auckland Star*, 21 September 1898, p.4.

50 *New Zealand Herald*, 29 August 1894, p.6; *Richmond Baptist Church Silver Jubilee Souvenir*, p.3.

51 *New Zealand Herald*, 19 April 1898, p.5; *Richmond Baptist Church Silver Jubilee Souvenir*, p.3.

52 *Auckland Star*, 7 February 1888, p.5.

53 *Auckland Star*, 15 October 1898, p.5; 28 January 1899, p.2.

54 *Diamond Jubilee Souvenir: St Peter's Presbyterian Church 1884–1944* (Auckland: St Peter's Presbyterian Church, 1944), 6, 8; *New Zealand Herald*, 4 February 1899, p.5.

55 *New Zealand Herald*, 26 April 1906, p.3.

56 *Auckland Star*, 15 December 1906, p.3.

57 *New Zealand Tablet*, 14 May 1914, p.25; 12 July 1917, p.27; 15 November 1917, p.22; 26 February 1920, p.21.

58 *Press*, 19 April 1952, p.2; *St Joseph's Parish Centennial 1914–2014* (Auckland: St Joseph's, 2014), 8.

59 *Auckland Star*, 18 February 1921, p.6; *New Zealand Herald*, 8 April 1922, p.10; *Richmond Baptist Church Silver Jubilee*, 7–8.

60 *Richmond Baptist Church Silver Jubilee*, 3, 4; *Wises New Zealand Post Office Directory*, 1908, p.96.

61 *Auckland Star*, 12 June 1909, p.12; 8 January 1910, p.6; 12 March 1910, p.6.

62 *New Zealand Herald*, 13 April 1907, p.2.

63 *Auckland Star*, 5 June 1909, p.12.

64 *Auckland Star*, 10 October 1910, p.7.

65 *New Zealand Herald*, 14 November 1910, p.9.

66 *Church Gazette*, August 1908, pp.146–47; *Auckland Star*, 22 June 1910, p.4.

67 *Auckland Star*, 22 June 1910, p.4; *New Zealand Herald*, 10 February 1911, p.6.

68 *New Zealand Herald*, 6 August 1908, p.8; *Auckland Star*, 1 May 1909, p.9.

69  *New Zealand Herald*, 23 April 1910, p.5.

70  Alison Clarke, 'Churchgoing in New Zealand, 1874–1926: How "Mediocre" Was It?', *New Zealand Journal of History* 47, no. 2 (2013): 117; Peter Lineham, *New Zealanders and the Methodist Evangel* (Auckland: Wesley Historical Society, 1983), 23.

71  Lineham, *Agency of Hope*, 29, 30, 31.

72  *Auckland Star*, 3 October 1913, p.2; 31 March 1914, p.4; *New Zealand Herald*, 5 January 1914, p.8; 3 March 1914, p.6.

73  *New Zealand Herald*, 5 January 1914, p.8.

74  *Auckland Star*, 31 March 1914, p.4.

75  Susan Boyd-Bell, *Saint Columba Grey Lynn, Golden Jubilee* (Auckland: Saint Columba, 1981), 13.

76  Ibid; www.stuff.co.nz/auckland/local-news/10276812/Milestone-at-Anglican-church

77  *New Zealand Herald*, 22 October 1927, p.11; 22 February 1930, p.14; 29 March 1981, p.1.

78  *New Zealand Herald*, 22 October 1927, p.11; 15 May 1928, p.13; 14 March 1931, p.12.

79  *New Zealand Herald*, 31 March 1931, p.12.

80  *Church Gazette*, January 1927, p.5; *Grey Lynn Character and Heritage Study*, 29.

81  *Auckland Star*, 31 July 1893, p.2; *New Zealand Herald*, 3 June 1913, p.5; https://archives.salvationarmy.org.nz/article/bethany-centre-girls

82  *New Zealand Herald*, 19 July 1913, p.4; 23 August 1913, p.4; 11 July 1914, p.4; *Auckland Star*, 27 April 1929, p.26; 31 May 1930, p.20.

83  www.mackelviechurch.org.nz/our-history

84  *New Zealand Herald*, 8 March 1924, p.5; 1 October 1925, p.8; *Wises New Zealand Post Office Directory*, 1926, p.96.

85  *Auckland Star*, 4 February 1933, p.6; 9 February 1933, p.1; *Wises New Zealand Post Office Directory*, 1934, p.55.

86  *Auckland Star*, 18 October 1933, p.16; Certificate of Title NA1631/77, Land Information New Zealand; https://amorc.org.au/history

87  *St Stephen's Presbyterian Church, Ponsonby, Auckland: Centennial History 1876–1976* (1976), 3.

88  See, for example, *New Zealand Herald*, 6 July 1940, p.21; 9 November 1940, p.6; Peter Lineham, 'The 1956 Auckland Crisis in the Exclusive Brethren and the Shaping of Taylorism', *Brethren Historical Review* 11 (2015): 72, 73.

89  *Waiapu Church Gazette*, 1 July 1929, p.10; *New Zealand Herald*, 6 September 1935, p.12.

90  *Auckland Star*, 16 May 1933, p.9.

91  *New Zealand Herald*, 30 October 1935, p.16; 5 November 1935, p.12.

92  *New Zealand Herald*, 5 April 1937, p.12.

93  *New Zealand Herald*, 6 September 1935, p.12; 10 November 1937, p.22.

94  *New Zealand Herald*, 24 February 1971, p.8.

95  Matthews and Matthews Architects, *Carlisle House: Draft Conservation Plan* (August 2003), 22.

96  Matthews and Matthews Architects, *Carlisle House*, 4–12.

97  *New Zealand Methodist Times*, 23 August 1913, p.17.

98  *Richmond Avenue Methodist Church: Jubilee Souvenir 1882–1932*; E. W. Hames, *100 Years in Pitt Street: Centenary History of the Pitt Street Methodist Church* (Auckland: Wesley Historical Society, 1966), 48.

99  Hames, *100 Years in Pitt Street*, 67; NA62/278, Land Information New Zealand.

100  Auckland Scrap Book, 1949, p.43.

101  Auckland Scrap Book, 1952, p.194; 1955, p.202.

102  Auckland Scrap Book, 1952, p.194; July 1955, p.183; 1960, p.64. *New Zealand Herald*, 18 July 2011, p.A4.

103  *St Joseph's Parish Centennial 1914–2014*, 15.

104  Bill McKay, *Worship: A History of New Zealand Church Design* (Auckland: Godwit, 2015), 85.

105  Lineham, *Sunday Best*, 21.

106  James Yandall interviewed by Kaaren Hiyama, 12 and 22 June 1990, Auckland Libraries Heritage Collections, OH-1355-010.

107  Cluny Macpherson, 'Pacific churches in New Zealand', Te Ara — the Encyclopedia of New Zealand, www.TeAra.govt.nz/en/pacific-churches-in-new-zealand/print

108  Feiloaiga Taule'ale'ausumai, 'New Religions, New Identities: The Changing Contours of Religious Commitment', in *Tangata o te Moana Nui: The Evolving Identities of Pacific Peoples in Aotearoa/New Zealand*, eds Cluny Macpherson, Paul Spoonley and Melani Anae (Palmerston North: Dunmore Press, 2000), 183, 184.

109  Auckland Scrap Book, 1964, p.219; *St Joseph's Parish Centennial 1914–2014*, 62, 63.

110  www.clunysisters.org.nz/2-uncategorised/31-history-sisters-of-st-joseph-of-cluny-new-zealand

111  Hay, *Samoa 100+ Years*, 368–70.

112  Ibid., 371.

113  www.glpc.org.nz/about-us

114  *Auckland Star*, 8 July 1965, p.19; Auckland Scrap Book, October 1964, p.289.

115  Audrey Wood, *Trinity Methodist Church Kingsland: 150 Years 1853–2003: Celebrating Past Memories and Hope for the Future* (Auckland: Audrey Wood, 2003), 123, 150, 161.

116 Glenn Jowitt, 'Planting the True Vine', *New Zealand Geographic* (July–September 1995).

117 Jane Samson, 'Fijian and Tongan Methodism', in *The Oxford History of Protestant Dissenting Traditions, Volume IV: The Twentieth Century: Traditions in a Global Context*, ed. Jehu J. Hanciles (Oxford: Oxford University Press, 2019).

118 Antoinette Gardiner, 'Carlile House', unpublished manuscript, Social Services file, Children's Home, Richmond Road, Anglican Diocese of Auckland Archives, p.1.

119 http://uctnz.com/about

120 Certificate of Title NA 93/162 and NA 617/281.

121 Samson, 'Fijian and Tongan Methodism'.

122 Taule'ale'ausumai, 'New Religions', 183.

123 Ibid. 192; *Auckland City Harbour News*, 12 December 2012, p.3; Auckland Scrap Book, October 1968, p.187.

124 *Auckland City Harbour News*, 12 December 2012, p.3.

125 Auckland Scrap Book, September 1975, pp.30, 38.

126 McKay, *Worship*, 35.

127 Tony Fala, '"A riddim resisting against the system": Bob Marley in Aotearoa' (unpublished thesis, University of Auckland, 2008), 109, https://researchspace. auckland.ac.nz/bitstream/handle/2292/47268/whole. pdf?sequence=5

128 Jennifer Cattermole, '"Oh reggae but different!": The localisation of roots reggae in Aotearoa', *Home Land and Sea: Situating Music in Aotearoa New Zealand*, eds Glenda Keam and Tony Mitchell (Auckland: Pearson, 2007), 47, 57.

129 *New Zealand Herald*, 1 May 1993, p.1

130 *Auckland City Harbour News*, 22 August 2007, p.5.

131 Sally McAra, *Land of Beautiful Vision: Making a Buddhist Sacred Space in New Zealand* (Honolulu: University of Hawai'i Press, 2007), 15, 18, 36, 46, 177; FWBO Newsletter, July 1972, pp.17, 18, https:// adhisthana.org/wp-content/uploads/2022/03/ FWBO-NEWSLETTER-ISSUE-16-JULY-1972.pdf; We're on the Move in 2023, https://www.youtube.com/ watch?v=gGfGmzLz29M

132 *Auckland Star*, 5 August 1897, p.9; 11 December 1912, p.5; *New Zealand Herald*, 3 July 1913, p.5; 11 July 1938, p.12; Cyril R. Bradwell, *Fight the Good Fight: The Story of the Salvation Army in New Zealand 1883–1983* (Wellington: Reed, 1982), 135.

133 Margaret Tennant, '"Magdalenes and Moral Imbeciles": Women's Homes in Nineteenth Century New Zealand', in *Women in History 2*, eds Barbara Brookes, Charlotte Macdonald and Margaret Tennant (Wellington: Bridget Williams Books, 1992), 68.

134 Ibid., 61, 68.

135 Linda Bryder, *The Rise and Fall of National Women's Hospital: A History* (Auckland: Auckland University Press, 2014), 15, 17, 22.

136 *Auckland Parents Centre Jubilee 1960–1990* (1990), n.p.

137 Margaret Tennant, 'Maternity and Morality: Homes for Single Mothers 1890–1930', *Women's Studies Journal* (August 1985): 35.

138 *Press*, 3 September 1970, p.5.

139 Anne Else, '"The Need is Ever Present": The Motherhood of Man Movement and Stranger Adoption in New Zealand', *New Zealand Journal of History* 23 (2006): 47, 48, 49.

140 Ione Cussen, 'Help Where Help Was Needed — Single Mothers and the Salvation Army Bethany Home in 1960s–1970s Auckland', https://ahi.auckland. ac.nz/2021/08/05/help-where-help-was-needed-single-mothers-and-the-salvation-army-bethany-home-in-1960s-70s-auckland

141 Ione Cussen, '"Children First" — The Motherhood of Man Movement and Single Motherhood in 1940s and 50s New Zealand', *Records of the Auckland Museum* 52 (2017): 2–6.

142 Else, 'The Need is Ever Present', 245, 248, 249.

143 Cussen, 'Help Where Help Was Needed'.

## Chapter 9: The visual arts

1 *Daily Southern Cross*, 12 January 1865, p.5.

2 City of Auckland Electoral Roll, 1896, p.292; 1900, p.210; *Auckland Star*, 3 April 1944, p.2; R. C. J. Stone, 'A Victorian Friendship and Auckland's First School of Art', *Art New Zealand* 30 (Autumn 1984), www.art-newzealand.com/30-1soa

3 http://heritageetal.blogspot.com/2013/04/recording-history-of-fine-arts-library.html

4 *New Zealand Herald*, 27 October 1885, p.4; 7 May 1898, p.5; 23 November 1899, p.6.

5 *New Zealand Herald*, 5 September 1895, p.5; *Auckland Star*, 6 April 1898, p.2; 11 May 1899, p.5; 10 May 1901, p.3.

6 *Auckland Star*, 3 April 1944, p.2.

7 *Auckland Star*, 21 February 1936, p.6.

8 Elizabeth S. Wilson, 'Friström, Clas Edvard', *Dictionary of New Zealand Biography*, first published in 1996. Te Ara — the Encyclopedia of New Zealand, https://teara. govt.nz/en/biographies/3f13/fristrom-clas-edvard

9 The Dunedin Public Art Gallery holds two of Friström's Western Springs landscapes and the Auckland Art Gallery holds a painting of gum trees on Great North Road (this part of Great North Road is now known as Tuarangi Road), Grey Lynn. *New Zealand Herald*, 17 July 1903, p.6; *Wises New Zealand Post Office Directory*, 1904, p.89A; 1913, p.143.

10   Wilson, 'Friström, Clas Edvard'.

11   *Auckland Star*, 26 January 1889, p.7; Births Deaths and Marriages, Births 1889/11691 and 1891/16869; Elizabeth S. Wilson, 'Eise, Ida Gertrude', *Dictionary of New Zealand Biography*, first published in 1998. Te Ara — the Encyclopedia of New Zealand, https://teara.govt.nz/en/biographies/4e6/eise-ida-gertrude

12   *New Zealand Herald*, 15 December 1905, p.7; 20 December 1906, p.7; *Auckland Star*, 21 December 1907, p.8; Anne Kirker, *New Zealand Woman Artists: A Survey of 150 Years* (Tortola: Craftsman House, 1993), 100; Wilson, 'Eise, Ida Gertrude'.

13   *Ashburton Guardian*, 17 January 1949, p.6; www.auckland.ac.nz/en/creative/about-the-faculty/elam/about-elam/history.html

14   Wilson, 'Eise, Ida Gertrude'.

15   Ibid.

16   Ibid.

17   Ibid.

18   *Press*, 8 December 1926, p.6; 13 December 1927, p.16; 14 December 1936, p.13; 17 December 1938, p.8; http://christchurchartgallery.org.nz/artschool125/SelectiveChronology/1920_1930/index.html; http://christchurchartgallery.org.nz/artschool125/SelectiveChronology/1930_1940/index.html

19   *Press*, 15 March 1941, p.9; 10 March 1942, p.8; 16 March 1944, p.2.

20   New Zealand Society of Genealogists Incorporated; Auckland, New Zealand; New Zealand Cemetery Records, Richard Jack Hutchison, 19519.

21   Peter Siddell, *The Art of Peter Siddell* (Auckland: Random House, 2011), 7.

22   Ibid., 13, 15.

23   Len Castle, *Len Castle: Potter* (Auckland: Sang Architects, 2002), 225–29; *New Zealand Herald*, 13 August 1936, p.8.

24   Grey Lynn Supplementary Electoral Roll, 1919, p.10; Grey Lynn Electoral Roll, 1928, p.36.

25   Castle, *Len Castle*, 29.

26   Ibid., 11; Anna K. C. Petersen, 'Field, Robert Nettleton', *Dictionary of New Zealand Biography*, first published in 1998. Te Ara — the Encyclopedia of New Zealand, https://teara.govt.nz/en/biographies/4f10/field-robert-nettleton

27   Castle, *Len Castle*, 11, 237, 241; Douglas Lloyd Jenkins, *At Home: A Century of New Zealand Design* (Auckland: Godwit, 2004), 106.

28   Castle, *Len Castle*, 235.

29   Ibid., 19.

30   Jenkins, *At Home*, 106.

31   Ibid., 138, 139; Castle, *Len Castle*, 31.

32   Castle, *Len Castle*, 31, 241.

33   Damian Skinner, *Theo Schoon: A Biography* (Auckland: Massey University Press, 2018), 11, 23, 28, 37–38, 51.

34   Ibid., 12.

35   Ibid., 62–64, 67–68.

36   Ibid., 98.

37   Castle, *Len Castle*, 31; Skinner, *Theo Schoon*, 146.

38   Len Castle, *Len Castle: Mountain to the Sea* (Napier: Hawke's Bay Museum and Art Gallery, 2008), 7–8.

39   Skinner, *Theo Schoon*, 156.

40   Ibid., 151, 156, 158.

41   Ibid., 9, 145.

42   Ibid., 166–67.

43   Ibid., 78, 81; Lucy Hammonds, 'Gordon Walters: An Expanding Horizon', in *Gordon Walters: New Vision*, ed. Zara Stanhope (Auckland: Auckland Art Gallery Toi o Tāmaki, 2017), 23, 25; Laurence Simmonds, '"The Last Koru": Gordon Walters: A Painting Life', in *Gordon Walters: New Vision*, 56–57; Deidre Brown, 'Pitau, Primitivism and Provocation: Gordon Walters' Appropriation of Māori Iconography', in *Gordon Walters: New Vision*, 104.

44   Skinner, *Theo Schoon*, 167.

45   *Evening Post*, 19 September 1938, p.18; *Otago Daily Times*, 22 November 1940, p.9; 22 June 1942, p.7.

46   https://michaellett.com/exhibition/anne-hamblett

47   Frances Morton, 'The Power of Two: The Woman Behind Colin McCahon', *Metro*, 25 December 2016, www.metromag.co.nz/arts/arts-art-city/the-power-of-two-the-woman-behind-colin-mccahon; 'First School Journal published', https://nzhistory.govt.nz/first-school-journal-published

48   Peter Simpson, *Is This the Promised Land? Vol. 2 1960–1987* (Auckland: Auckland University Press, 2020), 22.

49   Ibid., 22; Lois R. McIvor, *Memoir of the Sixties* (Auckland: Remuera Gallery, 2008), 39; Morton, 'The Power of Two'.

50   Simpson, *Is This the Promised Land?*, 22.

51   Ibid., 33.

52   Mahikiki Tangaroa, 'Paul Pomani Tangata: Pacific Artist Ahead of His Time', in *Cook Islands Art and Architecture*, eds Rod Dixon, Linda Crowl and Marjorie Tuainekore Crocombe (Rarotonga: USP Cook Islands, 2015), 268.

53   Ron Brownson, *Home AKL: Artists of Pacific Heritage in Auckland* (Auckland: Auckland Art Gallery Toi o Tāmaki, 2012), 104, 133; *New Zealand Herald*, 20 June 2016, www.nzherald.co.nz/business/former-grey-lynn-hovel-sells-for-28m-after-makeover/VM55PRMIGM6Z6ZLH7GZZW7XRIE

54  Brownson, *Home AKL*, 104, 133; *New Zealand Herald*, 14 July 2012, www.nzherald.co.nz/entertainment/home-akl-celebrating-pacific-art/I4SDNQQSXJIXR6P7WFK3ALFOBY

55  *Te Ao Hou* (March 1965): 58; Tangaroa, 'Paul Pomani Tangata', 269.

56  Brownson, *Home AKL*, 114.

57  Tangaroa, 'Paul Pomani Tangata', 269.

58  *New Zealand Herald*, 14 July 2012, www.nzherald.co.nz/entertainment/home-akl-celebrating-pacific-art/I4SDNQQSXJIXR6P7WFK3ALFOBY; Taule'ale'ausumai, 'New Religions', 312; Brownson, *Home AKL*, 99.

59  *Central Leader*, 9 February 2005.

60  Athol McCredie, *New Zealand Photography Collected* (Wellington: Te Papa Press, 2015), 290; Athol McCredie, 'Photographer Glenn Jowitt Passes Away', https://blog.tepapa.govt.nz/2014/07/26/photographer-glenn-jowitt-passes-away

61  Jenny Carlyon and Diana Morrow, *Urban Village: The Story of Ponsonby, Freemans Bay and St Marys Bay* (Auckland: Random House, 2008), 384–87.

62  Elizabeth Caughey and John Gow, *Contemporary New Zealand Art, Vol. 1* (Auckland: David Bateman, 1997), 14; www.pggallery192.co.nz/profile/richard-mcwhannell

63  *New Zealand Herald*, 1 February 2005, www.nzherald.co.nz/lifestyle/sisters-staging-it-for-themselves/MHZJTXM3WNI7DCDOBNTB3HXWKQ

64  Ian Wedde (ed.), *Fomison: What Shall We Tell Them* (Wellington: City Gallery Wellington, 2008), 186; email from Richard McWhannell, 13 February 2023.

65  Email from Richard McWhannell, 13 February 2023.

66  Martin Edmond, 'The Militant Artists ReUnion', in *Militant Artists ReUnion*, by Tony Fomison, Philip Clairmont and Allen Maddox (Napier: Hawke's Bay Cultural Trust, 2004), 6; Michael Dunn, 'Fomison Clairmont Maddox', in *Militant Artists ReUnion*, 11, 12; Richard McWhannell, 'Allen Maddox Painter', *Allen Maddox 1948–2000, eds Ian Wedde and* Richard McWhannell (Auckland: Gow Langsford Gallery, 2006), 29, 33.

67  Sean Mallon, 'Samoan Tattooing, Cosmopolitans, Global Culture', in *Tatau*, eds Sean Mallon, Peter Brunt and Nicholas Thomas (Wellington: Te Papa Press, 2010), 16.

68  Ibid., 16,

69  Fatu Feu'u, Shona Jennings, *Fatu Feu'u on Life and Art* (Auckland: Little Island Press, 2012), 51.

70  Elizabeth Caughey and John Gow, *Contemporary New Zealand Art, Vol. 3* (Auckland: David Bateman, 2002), 28.

71  Brownson, *Home AKL*, 132; www.nzherald.co.nz/entertainment/artists-in-residence-where-artists-find-their-happy-place/MRQYPL2O6YHFJ3LKG4I7A2ZXDQ

72  Nicholas Thomas, *Hauaga: The Art of John Pule* (Dunedin: Otago University Press, 2010), 44, 45; Carlyon and Morrow, *Urban Village*, 409.

73  Thomas, *Hauaga*, 46–47.

74  Ibid., 16, 17; Sean Mallon and Pandora Fulimalo Pereira, *Speaking in Colour: Conversations with Artists of Pacific Island Heritage* (Wellington: Te Papa Press, 1997), 89–90.

75  Wedde, *Fomison*, 186; email from Richard McWhannell, 13 February 2023; Certificate of Title NA50C/25, Land Information New Zealand.

76  Thomas, *Hauaga*, 17.

77  Ibid., 15.

78  Dionne Christian, 'Artists in Residence: Where Artists Find their Happy Place', *New Zealand Herald*, 19 May 2018, www.nzherald.co.nz/entertainment/artists-in-residence-where-artists-find-their-happy-place/MRQYPL2O6YHFJ3LKG4I7A2ZXDQ

79  Thomas, *Hauaga*, 15; Angela Lassig, *New Zealand Fashion Design*, (Auckland: Random House, 2010), 92, 94; 'Doris De Pont', www.nzfashionmuseum.org.nz/doris-de-pont

80  Lassig, *New Zealand Fashion Design*, 86–87.

81  Sarah Beresford, 'How Doris De Pont's Bright Pink House Embarrassed Her Kids', *Stuff*, 19 August 2015, www.stuff.co.nz/life-style/home-property/nz-house-garden/70988489/how-doris-de-ponts-bright-pink-house-embarrassed-her-kids

82  'Doris De Pont', www.nzfashionmuseum.org.nz/doris-de-pont

83  *Island Crossings: Contemporary Māori and Pacific Art from Aotearoa New Zealand* (Ipswich, QLD: Global Arts Link, 2000), unpaged; *Central Leader*, 6 August 2004, p.4.

84  *New Zealand Herald*, 9 December 1993, sec.3, p.1; *Auckland City Harbour News*, 21 June 1996, pp.1–2; 17 January 1997.

85  *East and Bays Courier*, 6 April 2012, p.8.

86  *Auckland City Harbour News*, 4 April 2012, www.stuff.co.nz/auckland/local-news/auckland-city-harbour-news/6664784/Art-a-testament-to-a-full-life

87  Jacqueline Fahey, *Before I Forget* (Auckland: Auckland University Press, 2017), 166.

88  Felicity Milburn et al., *Say Something! Jacqueline Fahey* (Christchurch: Christchurch Art Gallery Te Puna o Waiwhetū, 2017), 5, 7, 8, 13; Fahey, *Before I Forget*.

89  Fahey, *Before I Forget*, 166–69; and Gareth Shute,

Insights: New Zealand Artists Talk About Creativity (Auckland: Random House, 2006), 25.

90 Smythe, Insights, 14, 16.

91 Ibid., 21, 26, 285.

92 'A Free Radical', Content: A Magazine by Art + Object 2 (2014): 43.

93 Ibid., 44, 45; 'Mervyn Williams Artist Biography', https://artisgallery.co.nz/artists/williams

94 Edward Hanfling, Michael Dunn and Leonard Bell, Mervyn Williams: From Modernism to the Digital Age (Auckland: Ron Sang Publications, 2014), 291–93; https://artisgallery.co.nz/mervyn-williams; 'A Free Radical', 44, 45; 'Mervyn Williams Artist Biography'.

95 Don Abbott, Vivid: The Paul Hartigan Story (Auckland: RF Books, 2015).

96 Mary-Jane Duffy, 'The Island Over the Sink', Eye Contact, 13 March 2013, https://eyecontactmagazine.com/2013/03/the-island-over-the-sink

97 Pandora Fulimalo Pereira, 'Identities Adorned: Jewellery and Adornments', in Pacific Art Niu Sila: The Pacific Dimension of Contemporary New Zealand Arts, eds Sean Mallon and Pandora Fulimalo Pereira (Wellington: Te Papa Press, 2002), 43–44; Peter Simpson, 'Adornment at Re-Appropriation: The Art of Sofia Tekela-Smith', Art New Zealand (Autumn 2005), www.art-newzealand.com/Issue114/sofia.htm

98 Personal communication with Lisa Crowley, February 2024.

99 Priscilla Pitts and Andrea Hotere, Undreamed of . . . 50 Years of the Frances Hodgkins Fellowship (Dunedin: Otago University Press, 2017), 94, 165, 225.

100 Wolfe and Robinson, Artists @ Work, 212; New Zealand Herald, 1 December 2012, www.nzherald.co.nz/property/grey-lynns-blend-of-character-and-colour/4V CL5L2UWA3AKXYDYGJ4S23W2U

101 www.nzherald.co.nz/nz/curriculum-will-continue-as-death-ends-vitae/ZQO4E3MGIF7N6DBDRZHNU3V ZCM/; http://over-the-net.weebly.com/the-grey-in-grey-lynn.html

102 New Zealand Potter 36, no. 3 (December 1994): 10.

103 Carlyon and Morrow, Urban Village, 399.

104 New Zealand Herald, 23 January 1987; Nadine Rubin, 'My Space: Louise Rive', 11 February 2015, www.nowtolove.co.nz/news/real-life/my-space-louise-rive-6823

105 New Zealand Potter 33, no. 3 (1991): 19, 22.

106 New Zealand Potter 33, no. 2 (1991): 10–11.

107 Carlyon and Morrow, Urban Village, 381; Horizon (July 1987): 15.

108 Hawera Star, 19 August 1986.

109 Email from Peter Viesnik, 17 February 2023.

110 Auckland City Harbour News, 4 December 2012, www.stuff.co.nz/auckland/local-news/auckland-city-harbour-news/8033642/Peter-Viesnik-is-still-blowing-glass-32-years-on; 'About Isaac', https://monmouthglassstudio.com/isaac-katzoff; 'Everyone who loves glassware needs to visit Monmouth's new store', Home New Zealand, 22 August 2019, https://homemagazine.nz/monmouth-new-store-glass-pendants-auckland

111 'About Stephen', https://monmouthglassstudio.com/stephen-bradbourne

112 'Everyone who loves glassware needs to visit Monmouth's new store'.

## Chapter 10: The performing and literary arts

1 www.aucklandmuseum.com/visit/whats-on/lates/late-songs-of-the-city

2 Daily Southern Cross, 10 December 1861, p.3; 19 January 1866, p.5.

3 Gordon Lanigan interviewed by Kaaren Hiyama, 23 March 1990, Auckland Libraries Heritage Collections, OH-1355-005.

4 Auckland Star, 17 February 1922.

5 Gordon Lanigan interviewed by Kaaren Hiyama; Grey Lynn Electoral Roll, 1928, p.131.

6 Nicky Harrop, 'Marbecks', https://www.audioculture.co.nz/articles/marbecks

7 Gordon Lanigan interviewed by Kaaren Hiyama.

8 Evening Post, 1 March 1929, p.5; 15 March 1929, p.5.

9 Auckland Star, 30 May 1930, p.6.

10 Chris Bourke, Blue Smoke: The Lost Dawn of New Zealand Popular Music 1918–1964 (Auckland: Auckland University Press, 2020), 121.

11 Gordon Lanigan interviewed by Kaaren Hiyama.

12 Hellriegel Family History, 6, 10, 11, 13, 16.

13 Auckland West Electoral Roll, 1911, p.49 and Hellriegel Family History, 19.

14 Hellriegel Family History, 22, 23, 26; Auckland Star, 18 May 1910, p.1; New Zealand Herald, 17 February 1921, p.12.

15 Bourke, Blue Smoke, 24.

16 Hellriegel Family History, 26–30; Owen Jensen, The NZBC Symphony Orchestra (Wellington: A.H. & A.W. Reed, 1966), 27, 44; Joy Tonks, The New Zealand Symphony Orchestra: The First 40 Years (Auckland: Reed Methuen, 1986), 44; Joy Tonks, Bravo! The NZSO at 50 (Auckland: Exisle Publishing, 1996), 219; Grey Lynn Electoral Roll, 1949, p.109.

17 Hellriegel Family History, 40–42; Bevan Rapson, 'The Song Lines', Metro, November 2002.

18 Auckland Star, 14 April 1932, p.1; 7 October 1932, p.3.

19 *Auckland Star*, 9 January 1932, p.15.

20 Ian Chapman, *Kiwi Rock Chicks, Pop Stars and Trailblazers* (Auckland: HarperCollins, 2010), 240.

21 John Dix, *Stranded in Paradise: New Zealand Rock and Roll, 1955 to the Modern Era* (Auckland: Penguin, 2005), 134.

22 Ibid., 134.

23 Ibid., 61–62; Grant Gillanders and Robyn Welsh, *Wired for Sound* (Auckland: David Bateman, 2019), 152–53, 154.

24 Gillanders and Welsh, *Wired for Sound*, 154, 156, 159, 160.

25 Roger Shepherd, *In Love with These Times: My Life with Flying Nun Records* (Auckland: HarperCollins, 2016), 47, 48.

26 Ibid., 50–51, 66, 67, 71, 260, 261; 'Toy Love', https:// nzmusic.org.nz/artists/punk-hardcore/toy-love; Andrew Schmidt, 'Doug Hood Profile', *Audioculture*, www.audioculture.co.nz/people/doug-hood

27 Auckland Central Electoral Roll, 1981, p.100; Schmidt, 'Doug Hood Profile'; Lee Borrie, 'Radio With Pictures: History 5', *Audioculture*, www.audioculture.co.nz/scenes/radio-with-pictures-history-5; Shepherd, *In Love with These Times*, 65–66; www.flyingnun.co.nz/blogs/man-on-the-verge-of-a-nervous-breakdown/the-jessels-bobzilla-the-worst-noel-1982-man-on-the-verge-of-a-nervous-breakdown

28 Certificate of Title NA122/92, Land Information New Zealand.

29 Shepherd, *In Love with These Times*, 73, 76–77, 169.

30 Ibid., 70, 73, 74, 75, 77, 91, 95, 109, 180, 259.

31 Ibid., 67–69, 70, 75; Matthew Goody, *Needles and Plastic: Flying Nun Records, 1981–1988* (Auckland: Auckland University Press, 2022), 21, 22.

32 Simon Sweetman, *On Song: Stories Behind New Zealand's Pop Classics* (Auckland: Penguin, 2012), 68–69.

33 Arthur Baysting, 'Linn Lorkin Songwriter', *Music in New Zealand* (Winter 1992): 42, 43–47; Linn Lorkin, *The Redhead Gets the Gig: A Musical Memoir* (Auckland: Steele Roberts, 2022), 276, 278.

34 www.rouge.co.nz/artists/linn-lorkin

35 Dix, *Stranded in Paradise*, 147, 149; Dave McArtney, *Gutter Black* (Auckland: HarperCollins, 2014).

36 The recording was rediscovered decades later and sent to Brazier, who was then living on Great North Road. McArtney, *Gutter Black*, 43, 48–9, 50, 289.

37 McArtney, *Gutter Black*, 282, 286, 288; *Rip It Up*, 1 August 1977, p.8; 1 February 1978, p.17.

38 Graeme Jefferies, *Time Flowing Backwards: A Memoir* (Oakville: Mosaic Press, 2018), 241, 248, 249, 261.

39 Ibid., 286.

40 Ibid., 288.

41 Goody, *Needles and Plastic*, 258, 344.

42 Ibid., 258; Shepherd, *In Love with These Times*, 201.

43 Gareth Shute, *New Zealand Rock 1987–2007* (Auckland: Random House, 2008), 70–71; Shepherd, *In Love with These Times*, 201; www.flyingnun.co.nz/collections/able-tasmans

44 Shute, *New Zealand Rock*, 71.

45 Ibid., 71; Shepherd, *In Love with These Times*, 201.

46 https://humphreysandkeen.bandcamp.com/album/the-overflow

47 Auckland Museum Late 2015, 'Songs of the City', www.aucklandmuseum.com/visit/whats-on/lates/late-songs-of-the-city/the-panel

48 Greg Fleming, 'Strawpeople Part II', *Audioculture*, 1 February 2019, www.audioculture.co.nz/people/strawpeople/stories/strawpeople-part-two

49 'The Managers', https://nzmusic.org.nz/artists/reggae/the-managers

50 Shute, *New Zealand Rock*, 217, 220, 221; Rebecca Barry, 'Goodshirt: Pop of the Tops', *New Zealand Herald*, 6 February 2004, www.nzherald.co.nz/lifestyle/goodshirt-pop-of-the-tops/3BGUDLQGZ3SVLY4A2ITELGT7C4

51 www.nzonscreen.com/title/making-music-goodshirt-2005

52 Shute, *New Zealand Rock*, 185; Peter McLennan, *I Believe You Are A Star: Interviews with New Zealand Musicians, DJs and Artists* (Auckland: Dunbar Noon Publishing, 2013), 64.

53 Michael Larsen, *See Me Go* (Auckland: Penguin, 2003), 209.

54 Mark Roach, 'Stellar* Profile', *Audioculture*, www.audioculture.co.nz/people/stellar

55 https://bohrunga.com/pages/about

56 Matt Martell, 'Ode to Headonism a Surprise Hit', *Sunday Star-Times*, 31 August 1997, sec.F, p.3; Tim Hume, 'Most Promising', *Sunday Star-Times*, 20 April 2008, https://timhume.files.wordpress.com/2011/06/most-promising.pdf; Paul Shannon, 'Darcy Clay: What About It??', https://www.angelfire.com/hi/discordia5/darcyclay.html; 'Feat of Clay', *Sunday Star-Times*, 15 November 2015, sec.E, p.39.

57 Matt Martell, 'Ode to Headonism a Surprise Hit', *Sunday Star-Times*, 31 August 1997, sec.F, p.3; Sweetman, *On Song*, 191, 193, 195; Shannon, 'Darcy Clay: What About It??'.

58 Sweetman, *On Song*, 195; 'Darcy Clay: Ten Years On', *Sunday Star-Times*, 31 January 2009, www.stuff.co.nz/sunday-star-times/entertainment/sunday/382359/Darcy-Clay-ten-years-on

59 Emily Littler, 'Between the Lines: Pedestrian Support League', *The Pantograph Punch*, 11 September 2015, https://pantograph-punch.com/posts/between-the-lines-pedestrian-support-league-street-chant

60 Duncan Grieve, *The Spinoff*, 27 April 2016, https://thespinoff.co.nz/featured/27-04-2016/its-a-mans-world-the-music-industry-an-interview-with-street-chants-emily-edrosa

61 Silke Hartung, 'Diggy Dupé: High Energy Transfer', https://nzmusician.co.nz/features/diggy-dupe-high-energy-transfer; 'Diggy Dupé Highlights Impacts of Gambling in New Track CT&T', https://nzmusic.org.nz/news/artist/diggy-dupe-highlights-impacts-of-gambling-in-new-t

62 'Dave Dobbyn Biography', www.davedobbyn.co.nz/bio

63 Shute, *New Zealand Rock*, 260, 261.

64 Shayne Carter, *Dead People I Have Known* (Wellington: Te Herenga Waka University Press, 2019), 221, 222, 303, 358, 372.

65 www.countingthebeat.gen.nz/2008/11/auckland.html

66 Joel Little, 'Grey Lynn Park', in *Love Letters to the Landscape: 54 Notable New Zealanders Write About the Places in Their Hearts* (Auckland: Paul Little Books, 2016), 57, 59; www.simongrigg.info/the_suburban_reptiles.htm

67 Shute, *New Zealand Rock*, 291; *New Zealand Herald*, 19 September 2013, www.nzherald.co.nz/entertainment/joel-little-doing-the-lordes-work/NV6YRKLHCWBKFQJOEEDYUUP5JQ

68 Brent Clough, 'Oceanic Reggae', in Global Reggae, ed. Carolyn Cooper (Kingston: University of the West Indies, 2012), 267–68; www.audioculture.co.nz/scenes/aotearoa-reggae-timeline

69 Clough, 'Oceanic Reggae', 267–68.

70 Jennifer Dann, 'Twelve Questions with Tigilau Ness', *New Zealand Herald*, 22 November 2016, www.nzherald.co.nz/entertainment/twelve-questions-with-tigilau-ness/4GNKEFJVEB32NWUNRP6JM74YRQ

71 Jennifer Cattermole, '"Oh reggae but different!": The localisation of roots reggae in Aotearoa', in *Home, Land and Sea: Situating Music in Aotearoa New Zealand*, eds Glenda Keam and Tony Mitchell (Auckland: Pearson, 2007), 47, 57; Robbie Shilliam, *The Black Pacific: Anti-Colonial Struggles and Oceanic Connections* (London: Bloomsbury, 2015), 123, 124.

72 Russell Baillie, 'Che Fu', *New Zealand Herald*, 30 June 2000, www.nzherald.co.nz/lifestyle/che-fu/GGRZP3GYI7LGJZNN3YJWBMA5FY

73 Shute, *New Zealand Rock*, 102, 105, 106; Eloise Gibson, 'Music and Business go together for Mr Fu', *New Zealand Herald*, 1 June 2009, www.nzherald.

co.nz/nz/music-and-business-go-together-for-mr-fu/B7VPMOSV4YMGVSBK4REZPMNT64

74 Gareth Shute, 'Scribe Profile', *Audioculture*, www.audioculture.co.nz/people/scribe

75 Gareth Shute, 'Nesian Mystik, Profile', *Audioculture*, www.audioculture.co.nz/people/nesian-mystik

76 Ibid.

77 Wendyl Nissen, *Filling the Frame: Profiles of 18 New Zealand Women* (Auckland: Reed, 1992), 20, 22, 25, 26.

78 *New Zealand Herald*, 13 September 2006, www.nzherald.co.nz/lifestyle/composer-open-to-interpretation/K3KNSX6SQXVWWFKTY66×43UF3U; *Sunday Star-Times*, 29 November 2020, www.stuff.co.nz/life-style/homed/houses/300154071/at-home-with-a-cellist-and-his-centuriesold-colleague

79 Karl Puschmann, 'Benee the big winner at the Aotearoa Music Awards. Again', *New Zealand Herald*, 15 November 2020, www.nzherald.co.nz/entertainment/benee-the-big-winner-at-the-aotearoa-music-awards-again/OMVL3C5NUEODRAYNONBXJCQMRY

80 Peter Calder, 'Stage Veteran's Monkey Business', *New Zealand Herald*, 3 December 2014, www.nzherald.co.nz/nz/peter-calder-stage-veterans-monkey-business/3SRTEFMXAUSNYQYMFEMF7IY72I; 'Thespian Extraordinaire and Creator of Theatrical Extravaganzas', *New Zealand Herald*, 13 January 2015, www.nzherald.co.nz/nz/thespian-extraordinaire-and-creator-of-theatrical-extravaganzas/DRD46DTRSU3IHODZUOES6HKCMU

81 Sam Brooks, 'A Life Shaped by Theatre: Jennifer Ward-Lealand on the Roles that Shaped Her', *The Spinoff*, 11 June 2019, https://thespinoff.co.nz/society/11-06-2019/a-life-shaped-by-theatre-jennifer-ward-lealand-on-the-roles-that-made-her

82 'Michael Hurst Biography', www.michaelhurst.co.nz/bio.html

83 'Jennifer Ward-Lealand Biography', www.nzonscreen.com/profile/jennifer-ward-lealand/biography

84 'Sione's Wedding Press Kit', www.nzfilm.co.nz/sites/default/files/2017-11/Press_Kit_3.pdf; Matt McEvoy, *The Grey Lynn Book: The Life and Times of New Zealand's Most Amazing Suburb* (Auckland: Paul Little Books, 2015), 201.

85 'Oscar Kightley Biography', www.thearts.co.nz/artists/oscar-kightley; 'Oscar Kightley', www.nzonscreen.com/profile/oscar-kightley/biography

86 'Mission Home was Obsession', *New Zealand Herald*, 30 July 2016; 'An Interview with Stacy Gregg', 2010, https://my.christchurchcitylibraries.com/new-zealand-childrens-authors/stacy-gregg

87 'A story that borders on the mythic: Stacy Gregg's new

**406** | **The Near West**

novel', *Read NZ*, 25 September 2018, www.read-nz.org/new-zealand-book-scene/nzbc-stories-details/a-story-that-borders-on-the-mythic-stacy-greggs-new-novel?pageNum=6

88  McEvoy, *Grey Lynn Book*, 95.

89  Jennifer Dann, 'Twelve Questions: Dominic Hoey', *New Zealand Herald*, 16 April 2015, www.nzherald.co.nz/entertainment/twelve-questions-dominic-hoey/PRMHESULPQL73GJR7AXYQA26OI

90  Ethan Sills, 'Stranger than Fiction: Rapper Tourettes' debut novel is not your conventional breakout story', *New Zealand Herald*, 10 June 2017, www.nzherald.co.nz/entertainment/stranger-than-fiction-rapper-tourettes-debut-novel-is-not-your-conventional-breakout-story/XQGVWT57RZFLZYQXZXT5S5SXHM

91  Ibid.

92  Auckland Central Electoral Roll, 1981, p.41; www.nzonscreen.com/profile/shirley-horrocks/biography

# Acknowledgements

A book like this one does not get written and produced without the help of many people. Some have helped in small ways, others have played very significant roles — all are greatly appreciated by me.

I am grateful to Agnes Sullivan for kindly allowing me to use her unpublished work 'Māori Gardening in Tamaki Before 1840'.

Many grateful thanks go to the following people for reading and offering helpful comments on drafts of the following chapters: Taura Eruera, 'Geological and Māori History'; Graeme Burgess, 'Residential Development'; Peter Lineham, 'Faith'; Bob Mahoney/Frisbee, 'The Performing and Literary Arts.

I'm immensely thankful to the many people who answered my questions, hunted out old photos, or assisted in other ways: Jane Matthews, Richard McWhannell, David Tippett, Chris Fox, Emily Littler/Edrosa, Billie Rogers, Lucy Mackintosh, Graham Humphreys, Leslie Jonkers, Lisa Crowley, Sofia Tekela-Smith, Victoria Kelly, Chris Bourke, Simon Grigg, Tom Grut, Anthony Phelps, Denis Radermacher, Louise Rive, EJ Mathers, Kallan MacLeod, Frans Baetens and Magda Van Gils, Gareth Shute, Jane Ussher, Andrew and Jeannie Van Der Putten, Jonathan Ganley, Florian and Frank Habicht, Sanne Hansen, Maurice Lye, Matt McLean, Mervyn Williams, Murray Cammick, Patrick Reynolds, Sol de Sully, Robert Scott, Stephen Bradbourne and Len Bell.

Researching a book like this, and gathering images to illustrate it, requires the assistance of archivists, librarians and museum curators who are always willing to find what's needed and offer advice. My grateful thanks go to the staff of the following organisations: Auckland Libraries, including Sir George Grey Special Collections, particularly Keith Giles; Auckland University Library Special Collections, especially Sarah Cox of the University of Auckland Architecture Archive; Auckland War Memorial Museum Tāmaki Paenga Hira; Auckland Council Archives; Archives New Zealand in Auckland and Wellington; Fletcher Trust Archives; Presbyterian Research Centre; Auckland Catholic Diocese Archive; Carey Baptist College; Katherine Mansfield House and Garden; Land Information New Zealand; Te Toi Uku Clay Works; Auckland Art Gallery Toi o Tāmaki; Museum of New Zealand Te Papa Tongarewa; Glenn Jowitt Charitable Trust; The Arts House Trust; MOTAT; Alexander Turnbull Library; *New Zealand Herald*; Stuff Media Ltd; and Photosport.

Thanks also to my friends Rachel Cooper and Tiki Johnston for their encouragement.

I'm incredibly grateful to the talented team at Massey University Press who have offered a wealth of skills and experience to the development of this book. It is all the better for the many hours the team have devoted to editing, proofreading and designing — and many other things too numerous to mention.

However, the person to whom I owe the greatest debt of gratitude is fellow Grey Lynner and publisher at Massey University Press Nicola Legat, who has been with me every step of the way on this long journey. Thank you for having faith in me, for your unwavering support, and many insightful comments and suggestions — I can't thank you enough.

# About the author

Tania Mace is a freelance historian with a Master of Arts with honours in history. For more than two decades she has worked in the heritage field, researching and writing histories of buildings and places. Her first book was a history of St James Kindergarten (now known as Grey Lynn Kindergarten), written for the centenary in 2013. She has lived in Grey Lynn for more than 30 years.

# Index

Bold page numbers indicate illustrations.

65th Regiment of Foot 61

## A

A. B. Wright and Sons (cnr Great North Rd & Nixon St) **165**, **166–7**

A. Donald and Sons 143, 239: works (Coxs Creek) **182**

abattoirs 16, 55, 98, 100–1, 110–12, 140–2: Auckland municipal (Old Mill Rd) 74, 98–101, **100–1**, 110–11; Newmarket 98, 111, 140

Abbott, Howard 152

Able Tasmans, The 355, **355**, 356

Abrams, Jonas 106

Adams, Mark 329

Adeane's Orchestra 348

Adelphi Theatre (cnr Richmond Rd & Tutanekai St) 345, **346**, 347

Agriculture, Department of 110–11, 144

Ah Chee 52

Ah Cheok 52

Ah Chew 52

Ah Choy 52

Ah Goon 52

Ah Guit 50

Ah Ken, Su'a Tavui Pasina Iosefo 329

Ah Kew 50–51

Ah Kuoi, Fred 272, **272**

Ah Sing 52

Ah Soy 52

Ah Yum 52

Airest Industries 180

Albrecht, Gretchen 332, **333**, 335

alcohol: 'dry' and 'wet' Grey Lynn 16, 162, 193, 359–60; licensing 16, 192–5; prohibition 194–95; temperance movement 16, 192–93, **193**, 285

Alcoholic Liquors Sale Control Act 1893 194

All Golds 241

Allen, Mrs 107

Allen, Ruth 341

Alpha Dye Works 137

amalgamations, local body 8–9, 119–21, 124–25

Amber and Co. (cnr Great North Rd & King St) 180: crèche 180

Ambury, Stephen 173

Ambury's Ltd 173: dairy (cnr Richmond Rd & Surrey Cres) **177**

Anderson, Duncan 254

Anglican Children's Home (90 Richmond Rd) 218, 297, **298**

Anglican Church 291, 299: Anglican Social Questions Commission 296

apartment buildings 191

Arber, George 61

Arch Hill 8, **11**, 13–19, **51**, 62–64, **149**; and amalgamation 120–21; fire brigade 105; night soil 103; water supply 98

Arch Hill Brick and Pottery Works/Brick and Tile Company 148–49, 150, **150**

Arch Hill Farm 43–44, 95; map **45**: subdivision 44

Arch Hill Highway Board 8, 14, 95, 104

Arch Hill Hotel (cnr Great North Rd & Tuarangi Rd) 169, **170**, 192, 193, 194, **194**

Arch Hill Licensing District elections 16

Arch Hill Post Office and Telephone Bureau 171

Arch Hill Recordings 186

Arch Hill Road Board 16, 95–96, 101, 102, 116: and amalgamation 119–21

Arch Hill Studios 186

Arch Hill Wesleyan Methodist Church (Cooper St/Great North Rd) 282, **282**, 283, 289, 305: moved 289, 299–300, 305

Arch Hill Wesleyan Sunday School 233: festival 233

Arch Hill Workingmen's Club 192

Archangels Architects Collective (138 Richmond Rd) **188**, 189

Archibald Clark and Sons 117: factory (Grey Lynn) 154, **155**

Ardern, Jacinda 109

Argyle St 104

Ariki St 16, 107, 156

art school 315

artists, arts and galleries 183–84, 312–41

Arts and Crafts Movement 71

Artstation 338

Ashenden, Jackie 369

Atmore, Harry 217

Auckland Adult School Association Football Club 240

Auckland Agricultural Association 62, 68

Auckland Agricultural Company 54, 233–34

Auckland Alternative Secondary School (Richmond Rd) 221–22

Auckland Amateur Athletic and Cycle Club 253, 269

Auckland Armed Constabulary 106

Auckland Art Gallery Toi o Tāmaki 316, 319, 322, 324, 326: *Home AKL* 326

Auckland Artists Action 127: artworks 128, **128**

Auckland Basketball Association 261

Auckland Charitable Aid Board 192

Auckland City Council 8–9, 16, 53, 64, 95, 96, 97, 98, 138, 233, 255: abattoirs 111, 140, 144; amalgamation with 118–21; district plan 124; district scheme 183; electricity supply 116–17; and influenza epidemic 123; land-use maps 173; local body amalgamations 119, 124–25; pensioner

flats Surrey Cres **86–87**; pensioner villages (Great North Rd; Surrey Cres) 82, 87; sewerage 117–18; slum clearance 30; Super City 124; Unitary Plan 124–25; Western Springs waterworks **99**, 134; workers' homes Old Mill Rd; West View Rd 80–81, **86–87**; zoo 247, 249

Auckland District Hospital Board 102

Auckland District Plan 176

Auckland Domain 234, 235, **237**, 262, **264–65**

Auckland Education Board 200, 207, 208, 212, 214, 217, 221, 228, 229

Auckland Football Association 240

Auckland Girls' Grammar School 257, 261, 269: hockey team 262, **265**; netball **264**

Auckland Kindergarten Association 212, 218, 221

Auckland Laundry Company/New Auckland Laundry Co. (Surrey Cres) 160, **161**, 190

Auckland Metropolitan College 222

Auckland Metropolitan Relief Committee 289

Auckland Metropolitan Spring Show **153**

Auckland Parents Centre 310

Auckland Primary Schools Athletic Association 262

Auckland Province 94: Provincial Council 94, 95, 98, 200

Auckland Repertory Theatre 301

Auckland Rugby League 243

Auckland Rugby Union 235, 246

Auckland Savings Bank 46: ASB Bank 170, (Surrey Cres) 172

Auckland Society of Arts 318, 320

Auckland Speedways Ltd 251

Auckland Studio Potters 339

Auckland Suburban Drainage Board 118

Auckland Super City 124

Auckland Tallow and Blood Manure Company 141–42, 143

Auckland Teachers' Training College 261, 322

Auckland Trade Union Centre 33, 129

Auckland Transport Board 123

Auckland United Friendly Society Cricket Association 256–57

Auckland Watersiders' Silver Band 300

Auckland Wrestling Association 300

Auckland Zoo 172, 246, **246–47**, 248, **248**, 249–50, 270: Elephant House **247**; elephant Jamuna 249, **250**; trams to 114

Auckland: capital 13, 29, 59

automobiles 112, 123–24: motorways 123–24

Averill, Archbishop 218

# B

Back Yard 361
Bacon, Billy (aka Billy London) 349
Baetens, Frans 183, **184**
Baetens, Saskia and Dominiek 183–84
Baildon Rd 172, 290, 328: shops 172
Baildon, George 16, 17, 251
Baildon, Isabella (née Gow) 14, 16
Baildon, Maggie (née Kerr) 16
Baildon, William 14, 16
Ballantine, James 169
Band of Hope 193
Bank of New Zealand 74, 244
Baptist Church (Garnet Rd/Richmond Rd)
   287: Pasifika congregation 304
Barker, Bill 224
Bartram, Fred 127
Basil, Brother 205
Baskerville, Albert 241, 242
Bastion Point occupation (1977–78) 33, 109
Bates, H. W. L. 73
Bathgate, Alec 350, **350**, **351**
Baxter, Craig 356
Bayfield School 217, 229
Beaney and Sons 149–50, 152: exhibit **153**
Beaney family: house **73**
Beaney, Adam 150
Bedingfield, George 143
Beehre, Mike 356
Bell, Vivienne 341
Benee **366**, 367
Beniston, Dave 356
Bennett, Stella *see* Benee
Beresford St Congregational Church 301
Bethany Centre/Maternity Hospital (Dryden
   St) 310, **310**, 311
BFm Summer Series 359
Bill Sevesi and His Islanders 348
Billington, John 46, 52
Binns family: house (13 Francis St) **56–57**, **72**
Binns, Ernest Charles 316, **317**
Binns, Lucy Doris **56**
Black (Pihama), Buster 324
Black, Henry 106, 107
Blockley & Co. (Mackelvie St) 162
Bloomfield Farm 40–41
Blue Room 324
boating 254–55
Bohemian Orchestra 348
Bolton, Daniel 358
Bond St 8, 62, 96, 164, 186, **353**, 353
Borough of Auckland 93–94
Bouchier, Eileen 273
Bovaird, Mr & Mrs 311
Boyd, George 144–45, 148, 150, 315
Boyd, James 55
Boyd, John 246–48
Bradbourne, Stephen 341, **341**
Brazier, Graham 353
brickworks 135, 136, 144, 145, 148–50, 315:
   bricks **150**, **151**
Bridgenorth Tannery (Old Mill Rd) 41,
   142, **143**
Brinsmead, Frank 172

Brisbane St 8, **11**, 13–14, 283, 288
British Empire Games: Auckland Games:
   (1939) 268–69; (1950) 266, **267**
Broadhead, Warwick 367–68
brothels 14, 106
Brotherhood Club 240–41: football team
   **236**
Brown, Ashley 365
Brown, Charles Augustus 154, 156, 316, **317**:
   brush factory (Surrey Cres/Wilton St) 154,
   156, **159**
Brown, Charles Augustus Jr 156
Brown, Eion 185
Brown, Elizabeth **99**, **159**
Browne, Katharine 229
Bryan, Alfred 172
Buckland, William Thorne 13
Buddhist Centre (cnr Richmond Rd &
   Warnock St) 185, 308
Bullock Track 50, 111
bungalows 71, 80: Californian 71
Burgess, Frederick 143
Burgoyne St 95, 183
Burn, David 13–14
Burns St 8, 145
Burrell Demolition (Westmoreland St) 189
buses 123
Butterworth, Annie 311, 320

# C

C. L. Innes & Co. (Great North Rd) 164
café culture 189
Cakekitchen, The 355, **355**
Calder, Rev Jasper 247, 291, 296
Caledonian Brickworks (Coxs Bay) 135, 136,
   150, **151**
Cameo Cinema/Grey Lynn Cinema (Surrey
   Cres) **346**, 347
Cammell, George 169
Cammell, William 169
Cammick, Murray 185, **186**
Campbell, John 208
Campbell, John Logan 315
Canterbury College School of Art 319, 322
Carder, Joshua: shoe factory (cnr Mackelvie
   St & Williamson Ave) 176
Carlisle House 298
Carlisle, Wilson 298
Carr and Haslam (Dickens St) **166–67**, 169,
   183
Carr, Edwin 169
Carter, Shayne 360
carters 165–67, 169
Case, Ed 186
Casey Estate 81, 129
Cashmore Brothers 243
Cashmore's Mill 144, **146**, **147**, 243, 254
Castle St 64, 108–09, 296, **299**: police
   station 108–09: police residences (at nos.
   10, 16) 109
Castle, Cora 320
Castle, Frank 320
Castle, Len 320, **321**, 322
Catholic Basketball Association 262

Catholic Church 285, 288, 289–90, 303:
   Catholic Samoan centre (Mackelvie St)
   303
Cereal Foods factory (Surrey Cres) **161**, 164
Chamberlain Park golf course 257
Chamberlain St 172, 183, 189, 328, 330: no.
   17 184
Chambers, Guy 301, 303
Chan Unui 52
Chapel St: soap and candle factory 138
Chapman St 95, 278, 279
Charitable Aid Board 107
Che Fu **362**, 363
Chelsea Sugar Refinery 115
Chills, The 352
Chinese Immigrants Act 1881 53
Chinese market gardeners 50, **51**, 52–53
Ching Fou 52
Christians Meeting House (Williamson
   Ave) 285
Church Army 297–98
Church of Christ 285: hall and St Mungo's
   Church (Francis St) 291, 307–08
Church of England Temperance Society 192
Church of Jesus Christ of Latter-day Saints
   (178 Surrey Cres) 307
Church of St Michael and All Angels 306–07
Church of Tonga (Siasi 'o Tonga) 306, 307:
   church 84 Sackville St 307
Church of True Spiritual Light 297
churches: 17, 19, 277–309
Citizens' Unemployment Committee
   250–01
Clark, James McCosh 118–19
Clasby, Daniel 341
Clay, Darcy **359**
Clayton, Jessie 297
Clean, The 352–53
Cochrane, Archibald 141
Cockburn St 31, 328: no. 1 32
Cohaus 311
Coleridge St 297, 303
Collins, George 61
Colonial Land and Emigration Commission
   40
Commercial Rd 8, 62, 96, 108, 148, 283
Communist Party 129
Comrades Club 270
Congregational Christian Church of Sāmoa
   (Ekalesia Fa'apotopotoga Kerisiano Sāmoa)
   307: church Sussex St 226, 307; White
   Sunday **305**
Connell and Ridings' auction mart 59
Constable, Marmaduke 136
Conway, Louisa (née Tucker) 45, 46
Coolahan, Hugh 206
Cooper St 8, 62, 107, **282**, 283, 289, 299, 305
Cooper, Bob 349
Cooper, Whina 31, **31**, 32, 33: Māori land
   March 33
Costley Training Institute 297, 298–99,
   306, 326
Costley, Edward 298
cottages, workers' 70
Court, John 249, 256, 260

**Index** | **411**

Court, John Sr 261

Covid-19 227

Cox, John 37–38, 345: squatter's licence 37, **38**; violins 345

Coxs Bay 74, 253–54, **258**: subdivision 59–61; water sports 239, **258**

Coxs Bay Reserve 26, 243, 244, **245**, 255–56, 270

Coxs Creek 16, **38**, 59, 74, 134–35, **147**, 173, **245**, 345: bridge **147**, 243, **245**, 254, 255, **258**, **259**; industries 134–38, 144, **146**, **147**, **182**; mill 144, **146**, **147**; sewerage 118; swimming **258**; typhoid 118

Cracroft St *see* Kirk St

Croad, Ted 347: band **347**

Crosby, Charles 172: grocery (cnr Garnet Rd & Old Mill Rd) 172

Croucher, John 340, **340**

Crowe, William 14, 106, 107

Crowley, Lisa 335

Crummer Road 31, 69, 109, 154, 162, 176, 185, 186, 190, 296, 300, 303, 307, 319, 330, 355, 356

Crummer Road School 207

Crummer, Thomas 47–48

cultural diversity 6–7, 17, 220–21, 266–67: languages 224–26

Curran Street School 217

# D

Dance, Francis 240

Daniells, Arthur 285–86

Daniells, Mary 286

Darbyshire, Sam 270

Darroch, Gavin 283, 285

Dashper, Julian 336

Davis family: house Richmond Rd **73**

Davis, Benjamin: boot factory (Wilton St) 156, 242, 243

*Dawn Raid* (2020) 368

DD Smash 359

de Boer, Andrew 331

De Pont, Doris 330, **330**, 331: DNA company 331

Dead Poets Café (Karangahape Rd) 364

Dean St 14, 180, 242, 307, **308**

Debenham, Beryl 348

Dedwood Highway District 94

Democratic Labour Party 129

Demonstration Flats (Great North Rd) **81**

Dempsey, Arthur 193–94

Depression, Great (1930s) 176, 218, 289: relief schemes 218

depression, 1890s 55

Deviation Rd 8

Dickens St 162, 163, 164, **166**, 169, 183, 348: no. 5 297; no. 43 272

Dilworth, James 48

Dimery, William 165

Dimmer 360

Disraeli St *see* Dickens St

Dobbyn, Dave 359, **360**

Dodd, Jane **355**, 356

Dolphin, Alfred 149

Dominion Compressed Yeast Company 154

Donald, Alexander 143, 238

Donald, James 239

Donnelly, Michael 185

Dooley, Mike 350, **350**

Dorset St 41, 42: no. 28 42

Dougal, Alastair 185

Dragon 353

Dryburgh, Kirsten 339

Dryden St 129, 172, 296, 301, 310, 328, 348, 361: shops 172

Dryden Street record label 361

*Duchess of Argyle* (ship) 40

Dudley, Rev Benjamin 279

Dunne, Constable Patrick 108

Dunnottar Memorial Hall (cnr Garnet Rd & Faulder Ave) 297

Dupé, Diggy 359, **359**

DYC factory (Grey Lynn) **158**, 190

dye works 61

dyeing 137

# E

Eden Cres 162

Eden Terrace 52, 96, 119, **119**, 120, **149**, 194, 235

Eden Vine Hotel 194

Edgar, John 137

Edgar, William 61, 137

Edgar's Creek 61

Edge City 338

Edinburgh St 297, 301, 303

education 196–229: literacy 199, 200–01, 221; Tomorrow's Schools 224

Education Acts (1857) 200; (1877) 201, 285

Edward Mahoney and Sons 69

Eise, Emma (née Cox) 316

Eise, Frederick Gustav (George) 316

Eise, Ida 207, 316, 318, **318**, 332

Elam School of Art 17, 220, 316, 318, 323, 325, 332, 334, 335, 336

Electric Tramways Company 112, 114

electricity supply 115–17: 'products' **139**

Element, George 136

Elgin St 69, 175, 186: Historic Heritage area 175

Elliot, Allan 269

Elliot's Four Square (cnr Old Mill Rd & Garnet Rd) **174**

Elliotts boot factory 242

Ellis, Daisy and William 17

Empress Theatre (aka Avon, Newton; Great North Rd) **346**

Enemy, The 350

Engel, Henry 348

Ensor, Lesley 273

Epiphany Chapel (cnr Chapman St & Nixon St) **276–77**, 278–80, 291: Sunday School 280

Epiphany Church (Karangahape Rd) 278, 280

Eruera, Taura 185

Exclusive Brethren 297

Exler, Moses 148

# F

Fa'atasi 364

Fahey, Jacqueline 331–32, **332**

Fairleigh maternity hospital (cnr Surrey Cres & Firth Rd) 311, 320

farming 34–55: Chinese market gardeners 50, **51**, 52–53; demise 53–55; early farms 41–46; land purchases 37–40; Surrey Hill Estate 46–50

Farrar St 47

Farrell, John 117, 208, 210, 214

fashion design 330–31, 335: New Zealand Fashion Museum 331

Faulder Ave 55, 296, 297: no. 8 296

Faulder, Dinah 111

Faulder, Thomas 46, 50, 117: night-soil collection 96–97

fellmongeries 140, 141, 143

Feu'u, Fatu 329, 331, **333**

Field, Robert 320, 334

Fife St 147, 256

Finance Act 1931 229

fire brigades 105, 120: Grey Lynn **105**, station **116**

First World War 240–41, 291

Firth Rd 69, 311, 369

Firth, Josiah 115: flour mill 115

Fisher, Charlotte 331

Fisher, Rodney 356, **357**

Fisher, Murray 356

Fisherton St 238

flour mills 40, 98, 115, 133–34: Eden Flour Mill 133; Mechanics Bay 133; New Mills 133

Flying Nun label 350, 352, 356

Foley, Francis P. 162: factory (Surrey Cres) 162: Foley's lemonade **162**

Fomison, Tony 183, 327–28, 329, **329**, 330: *The Ponsonby Madonna* 329

Fong Brothers 52

Fonoti, Toni 361

Foote, Adrienne 331

Forresters Hall (Edinburgh St) 297

Fowlds, George 126, 208, 247

Fox, Chris **188**, 189

Francis St 64, 114, 129, 152, 156, 172, 189, 195, 208, 210, 291, 300, 307, 345: nos. 11 & 13 **56–57, 72**

Free Church of Tonga (Siasi 'o Tonga Tau'atāina) 306, 307: church Crummer Rd 307; White Sunday feast **306**

Free Wesleyan Church of Tonga (Siasi Uēsiliana Tau'atāina 'o Tonga) 306, 307

Freida Margolis (Richmond Rd) 360

French Toast 353

French, Neil 19

Friendly Road choir 348

Friendly Societies 256–57

Friends of the Western Buddhist Order 185, 308–09

Frisbee (Mahoney), Bob 186, 359

Frisbee Studio 186

Friström, Edward (Clas Edvard Friström) 316, 317: *Gum Trees, Great North Road,*

*Grey Lynn* 316, **317**
Froebel, Friedrich 214
Full Moon Follies, The 367

# G

G Men, The 349
*Ganges* (ship) 13
gaol: Auckland 44; Mt Eden 45, 127
Garnet Rd 9, 40, 41, 42, 74, **80**, 81, 82, **84–85**, **90–91**, 112, 114, **158**, 172, 176, 189, 208, 212, 218, 240, 241, 249, 287, 290, 297, 304, **338**: night soil 117; rubbish tip 112; shops 172, **174**; trams 90–91, 114, 123
Garnet Road Foodstore 369
gas reticulation 104–05
Gaskell, Rev R. F. 304
Gee, Sue 330
gentrification 7, 33
geology 21–25: Auckland volcanic field 23, **24**; lava flows 23, **24**, 25; Māori origin stories 23; Te Tokaroa Meola Reef **20–21**, 25
George Blockley and Son 164: factory (Mackelvie St) 162
George FM 185
Gerhard's Café (Great North Rd) 189, 360
Gilbert Ave 82
Gittos and Sons 41
Gittos Brothers 142, 143
Gittos, Benjamin 142
glass-making 340–41
Glenmore house 45
Gloria glass studio 341
Gluepot (Ponsonby, 1979) **351**
gold industry 136–37
Goldsbro', George Selwyn 71
Goodfellow, John 137
Goodnight Nurse 361, **361**
Goodshirt 356–57, **357**
Goodwin, Ray 353
Gospel hall (Coleridge St) 297
Government Loans to Local Bodies Act 1886 102
government, local 93, 105, 110–25: amalgamation 118–21
Gow Langsford Gallery (cnr Richmond Rd & Warnock St) 184–5, **185**
Gow, Isabella *see* Isabella Baildon
Gow, Margaret 14
Gow, Nathaniel 14
Graham, John 192
Great North Rd 8, 14, 16, 33, 43, 62, 66, 80, 82, 105, 107, 121, 148, 151, 162, 164, 165, 168, **168**, **170–71**, 172, 175, 176, 180, 186, 189, 192, **194**, 202, 206, 212, 270, 282, 283, 285, 287–88, 288–89, **288–89**, 291, 296, 299–300, **300**, 301, 303, 316, **317**, 318, 330, 335, 341, 346, 353: no. 571 291; apartment buildings 191; Beaney family house **73**; brickworks 144–45; car yards 191; dairy **18**; Demonstration Flats **81**; electricity 116; gas lamps 104; housing **82**, 125; iron foundry 149–50; maintenance **94**, 95–96, 101–02, 119; market gardens 51; shop plans **67**; street lamps 104; toll booth 94,

101–02; trams 17, 114
Great Northern Hotel 192
Greater Auckland Scheme 120: map **119**
Green and Hall record plant 162
Green, Fred 162
Greenwood Ave *see* Larchwood Ave
Greenwood, Robert 68
Gregg, Stacy 369
Grey Lynn School Te Rae o Kawharu (Surrey Cres) 28, **161**, 207–08, **209**, 210–11, **210–11**, 218, 221, 222, 224, 244, 291: bilingual/immersion classes 225; Education Review Office reports 224
Grey Lynn Borough 68–69
Grey Lynn Borough Council 16, 68, 74, 207, 244, 253: and amalgamation 120–21; electricity 116–17; offices **116**; sewerage 117–18; trams 114; war on rats **110**
Grey Lynn Bowling Club (Richmond Rd/Surrey Cres) **161**, **230–31**, **237**, 238–39, 256, 257, 266, 360; croquet lawn 239
Grey Lynn Cinema/Cameo Cinema (Surrey Cres) **346**, 347
Grey Lynn College (Western Park School) 207: postcard **206**
Grey Lynn Community Centre (Richmond Rd) 124, 331
Grey Lynn Community Church (Richmond Rd) 304
Grey Lynn Croquet Club 257
Grey Lynn district plans **178–79**
Grey Lynn Domain Vesting Act 1909 244
Grey Lynn Druids 257
Grey Lynn Farmers' Market 360
Grey Lynn Fire Brigade **105**
Grey Lynn Kindergarten 212, **213**
Grey Lynn Lacrosse Club 235, 237, 238
Grey Lynn Library **289**
*Grey Lynn Live Wire* (newsletter) 129
Grey Lynn Park **6**, 7, 75, **166–67**, 243–44, 246, 256, 270, 272: activities 6; Festival 6, 274, **274**, 360; formation 74; playground 7, 256, **260**; Samoan sports festival 266–67; Sculptura project 331, **333**
Grey Lynn Park Estate 74
Grey Lynn Post Office (Williamson Ave) 172
Grey Lynn Presbyterian Church (cnr Great North Rd & Crummer Rd) **300**, 303–04: Tokelauan and Tuvaluan congregations 304
Grey Lynn Returned Services Club (Francis St) 195, 208, 360
Grey Lynn Unemployed Workers Association 129
Grey Lynn United/Grey Lynn Celtic football club 270
Grey Lynn Wanderers Football Club 241
Grey Lynn Women's Political Organisation 255
Grieve, Bill 249
Griffin, James 364
Griffin, Louis 248, 249
Grosvenor St 356
*Gum Trees, Great North Road, Grey Lynn* 317
Gunson, James 121, 247, 249

# H

Habicht, Florian 367
Hackett, Fred 129
Haden, Andy and Trecha 273
Hakanoa St 48, 74, 186, 187, 352: London plane trees **125**
Halaevalu Mata'aho 'Ahome'e, Queen 305
Halford, George 69
Hall, Tony 162
Halt All Racist Tours (HART) 129
Hamilton Girls' High School 264
Hammond, Reginald 73
Hansen, Derek 369
Harden, Mary (née Haselden) 229
Hargest, Miles 330
Harrison, William 240
Harry Burrage grocery store (Great North Rd) **170–71**
Hartigan, Paul 331, 334, **334**, 335
Haselden, Frances 228, 229
Haslam, William 169
Hauraki Kayak Club 255, 270
Hawke Sea Scouts 255, 270: The Ship clubhouse 255, **259**
He Taonga Films (cnr Williamson Ave & Ariki St) 156
Health Department 111
health/hygiene: bubonic plague 110, 112; influenza 121, 123; rats 110, **110**; *see also* abattoirs; night soil; sewage; typhoid; waterworks
Heap, Sally 257, 261
Helen Hitchings Gallery 320
Hellaby Brothers 74, 140
Hellaby, Richard 141, **141**
Hellaby, William 141
Hellaby's abattoir/meatworks 16, 55, 74, 144, 243, 254: Coxs Creek paddocks **145**; Richmond works **140**; staff **141**
Hello Sailor 353
Hellriegel, Carl 347–48
Hellriegel, Jan 348
Hellriegel, Julius 347–48
Henderson family 121: Elizabeth 121, 123; Wallace 123
Henning, George 251: Henning's Speedway 251
Herbert, Bill 262
Herbs 361
heritage districts/protection 124–25
Hero Parade (later Pride Parade) 6
Herscher, Hershal 353, **354**
Heseltine, Bill 26
Hewitt, Claude 77, 80
Hickson, Theodore W. 62, 234
Higgins, John 138
Hinemoa Rd *see* Hakanoa St
Hobson, Eliza 44
Hobson, Rev Henry Theophilus 44
Hobson, William 29, 44
Hodgkinson, Thomas 77, 80
Hoey, Dominic (Tourettes) 369
Holbrook, Father Henry 289
Holden and Moon 149

**Index** | 413

Holland Cricket Club 234
Holland, James 234
Holland, Sidney 266
Hollis, John 164
Hollis, Walls & Co. (Great North Rd) 162, 164
Holman, W. A. 66, 156, 169
home deliveries 172–3
Home St **10–11**, 13–14, 15, 17, 177: nos. 10 & 12 **10**, 13, **15**, 17, **17**, 19, 322, 323, 364
Hood, Doug 352, **352**, 353
Horrocks, Roger 369
Horrocks, Shirley 369
Hosken Bros 156: ceiling/wallboard factory (Wilton St) 156
Hosken, Joseph 156
Hosken, William 156
Hoskins, Miss F. 207
Hotere, Andrea 369
housing *see* residential development
Howe, Ben 186
Hukarere School 218
Humphreys, Graeme **355**, 356
Hundred of Auckland 93
Hunter, Marc and Todd 353
Hurst, Michael **367**, 368
Hutchison, Jack 319: *Auckland Cityscape* **319**
Hutson, Edwin 241

# I

ice cream 164
Ilam School of Fine Arts 326, 328
immigration, post-war 180, 220–21, 225, 266–67, 301
*Indian Empire* (ship) 137
industry and business 16, 130–95
influenza pandemic 121, 123, 212
infrastructure 93–105, 110–25
iron foundry 149–50
Isbey, Annette (née Graham) 331, **332**
Isbey, Eddie 331
Ivanhoe Rd 82, 274

# J

J. Flower Ltd furniture frame makers 180
J. Gardner Motors 182
J. M. Mennie biscuit makers 214
Jacob, Arthur 251
Jagger and Parker's tannery (Old Mill Rd) **143**, **248**, 250
Jagger, Frank 142, 143
Jagger, Samuel 192
James St *see* Putiki St
*Jane Gifford* (ship) 40
Jasmax architects 226
Jefferies, Graeme 355, **355**
Jefferies, Peter 355
Jensen, Andrew and Christina **72**
Jessel St 352
Jessels, The 352
Jews Brothers Band 353, **354**
Johnson, Joseph 148

Johnson, Stephanie 369
Jones, Francis 97
Jonkers, Leslie **355**, 356
Joseph, Chuck 338
Jowitt, Glenn 326, **327**
*JustArt* exhibition 127

# K

Karangahape Highway District 95
Kark Katte furniture (Garnet Rd) 189
Karma drinks (cnr Williamson Ave & Ariki St) 156
Karno-Atkins, Warren (Akshobhya) 309
Katzoff, Isaac 341, **341**
Kāwharu 26, 28
Kay, John 251
Keals, Richard 69
Kean, Paul 350, **350**, **351**
Keen, Peter **355**, 356
Kelly, Hugh 110
Kelly, John 47
Kelly, Victoria 356, 365, **366**
Kennedy, Kemara James **365**
Keppell St 19, 32
Kershaw, Laurence Tanetiu **365**
Kew Hing 52
Key, Robert 355, **355**
Kightley, Oscar 364, 368, **368**: *Sione's Wedding* series 368
Kilgour, David **352**
Kimber, Henry: butchery (cnr Richmond Rd & Norfolk St) 172
King St 9, 19, 103, 180
Kingsland Trinity Methodist Church 305: Tongan congregation 305
Kingsley St 9, 69, 135: state houses 80; workers' houses 69
Kirk St 8, 183, 192
Knox, Chris **342–43**, 350, **350**, **351**, 352, **352**, 353, 358
Korma Mills hosiery factory (Surrey Cres) **161**
Kowhai Intermediate School 219: bilingual/immersion classes 225; Gāfoa le Ata 225

# L

La De Da's 349–50
Labour Government, First: housing programme 81–82
Labour Party, New Zealand 126, 127, 269
Lanigan, Edward 345
Lanigan, Gordon 345, 347, **347**
Larchwood Ave **60**, 61, 64
Laughton, Jim 221
law enforcement 106–09
Lawn, Mollie 323
Lawry, Frank 48–49
Le Clerc, Julie 369
Leach, Bernard: *A Potter's Book* 322
Leckie, John 61, 135, 136
Leckie's Creek 135, 137; *see also* Edgar's Creek
Lee, Alexander 286

Lee, John A. 127, **127**, 129
Legion of Frontiersmen Hall (Bond St) 352, **352**, 353
Leighton St 315, 325, 326
Leighton's Packaging (300 Richmond Rd) 183, 190
Lemington Rd 172
Lenihan, Bishop 205, 206
Leon, Henry 192
Lepou, Lindah 353
*Let's Gather Here* collection **330**
Leys, William 228
Licensing Acts: (1873) 192; (1881) 193
Lincoln St **122**, 172, 189, 330
Liquid Studios (Richmond Rd) 186
Liston, James 31
literary arts 369
Little, Joel 361, **361**
Little, Paul 361
Littler, Emily **358**, 359
Livingstone St: no. 43 269; tannery and fellmongery 143; Tattersfield plant 152
Local Restoration Polls Act 1990 195
Lock, Les 266
London Brothers, The 349
London Missionary Society 301
Long, Thomas 193
Lorkin, Linn 353, **354**
Lototonga (Richmond Rd) 306
Low and Motion flour mill 40, 98, 133–34: cutters 134; sheep near **54–55**; Western Springs 98
Low, Joseph 133
Lowdown Dirty Blues Band 363
Luafutu, Malo 364
Luck, Bishop 205
Lumley, Annie and William 269
Lumley, Bernice **268**, 268–69
Lumley, Doreen 262, 268, **268**, 269
Lusk, Doris 331
Luv Ya Mowar (cnr Richmond Rd & Hakanoa St) **186**, 187
Lynnhirst Estate 74, 85
Lynton Lodge (45 William Denny Ave) 42, 43
Lyons, Harry 353

# M

MacDermott, Hanna 193
MacDermott, William J. 119, 193
Mackelvie St 129, 154, 156, 162, 164, 176, 206, 286, 299, 303, 316, 318, 339, 341: no. 48 180
Macky, Logan and Caldwell factory (Mackelvie St) 154: plans **156–57**
Macky, Thomas 48
Maclaren, Andrew 357
Maclean, Rev John 296
Maddox, Allen 184, 328
Mahoney, Bob *see* Frisbee, Bob
Mahoney, Constable Thomas 108
Mahoney, Edward 101
Mai FM (Crummer Rd) 185
Maidstone St 180

**414** | **The Near West**

Makgill, Dr Robert 117
Malt (Richmond Rd) 360
Mamata Bakehouse (Richmond Rd) 187
Managers, The 356
Maniapoto, Moana 364–65, **365**
Manual Training School (cnr Richmond Rd
    & Douglas St) 215, **216**
manufacturing 176–77, 180–83
Manukau Cycling Club 262
Maori Women's Welfare League 32
Māori: 1920s–30s 28–30; 1930s on
    30–33; activism 33; arrival and settlement
    25–29; artists 331–33; education 199,
    201, 221, 285; food sources 26, 28–29;
    hostels 30–31, 32; housing needs 31–32;
    intertribal conflict 26, 29; land rights 33;
    music 363, 364–65; place names Auckland
    **27**; populations 30, 33; residents 17, 30;
    rock art 322, 328; te reo Māori 32, 33, 185,
    225; wheat growing/milling 134
Marbeck, Alfred 345
Marbeck, Eileen 345
Marbeck's (Selbourne St) 345
Marist Brothers 205–06, 220
Marist Old Boys rugby team 235
market gardens, Chinese (Great North Rd)
    **51**: deliveries 172
Marley, Bob 307, 363: Bob Marley and the
    Wailers 363
Marmon, Jacky (John) 39, 40
Marsden & Co bedding/mattress/furniture
    makers (Garnet Rd) 156, **158–59**, 189
Marsden, Israel (Jack) and Lily 156
Marshall, John Williams 61
Mason, Craig 355, **355**
Mason, Herbert 202
Mason, William 133
Massey, Horace 73
Master Butchers' Association 111
maternity services 310–11
Mathew, Felton 37
Mattson, Alf 262
Maughan, Karl 335, **336**
Maxwell Ave 64
Mayne, Edward 48
McArtney, Dave 353
McCahon, Anne (née Hamblett) 323, 324,
    **324**
McCahon, Colin 323, 324, **324**, 330, 332
McCauley, John 69
McCoskrie, Miss 218
McDonald, Fiona 356, 365
McDonald, Fraser 332
McElwain, George 44–46; 169: butchery
    (cnr Great North Rd & Nixon St) 169
McElwain, John 445, 6
McElwain, Walter 45
McGilp, Constable 108
McKinstry, William 68, 204
McLean, Kate 328, 336, 338
McLean, Matt 328, **328**, 336, 338
McLellan, Constable 107
McLeod-Craig, John 297
McManus, Kate 106
McMaster, Charles I. 238

McMaster, Charles Jr 238
McNair and Stephens 77
McNair family 40, 287
McNair, Archibald 40, 41
McNair, Eliza (née Crouch) 41
McNair, Elizabeth (née Weadson) 40
McNair, Isaac 54–55
McNair, James 40–41
McNair, Jane (née Russell) 40
McNair, John 41
McNair, Margaret 40
McNair, Martha 41
McNair, Peter 40–41, 54
McNulty, Donald 364
McWhannell, Richard 328, **328**, 331, 332, **333**
Meadow Farm 44, 45, 46: map **45**
Mell, John 234
Melville, Ellen 126–27
Mennie and Dey 69, 214
Mennie, James 69
Mennie, John 214
Mennie's Reserve/Mennie St (later
    Monmouth St) 69
Meola Rd 40: state housing **84–85**
Meola Reef see Te Tokaroa
Meola Reef Reserve 112
military training 203
Mill Creek see Motions Creek
Millais St 66, 69, 73, 162, 163, 165, 348:
    house plan **66**; houses: **72–73**
Mills, Colleen 272
Mills, Donna 272
Mills, Frederick 136
Mills, Les 272, **272**
Mills, Phillip 272
Milne, Herbert 261
Ming Quong 52
Mission Hall (Tuarangi Rd) 296
Mitchell, John 116
Moa Unlimited (Richmond Rd) 187, **187**,
    189
Moa, Anika 360
Moana and the Moahunters 365
Moana and the Tribe 365, **365**
Modelux Factory (Maidstone St) 180
Moko Ink 331
Monmouth Glass Studio (Arch Hill) 341, **341**
Monmouth St 69, 183, 328, 341
Montage Studios (49 Murdoch Rd) 185–6
Monte Christo Smelting Company 136
Montefiore, John 46–48
Mormon Church 307
Morris, Francis 134
Morris, Ian 359
Morrison, Howard 162
Morrow, Thomas 102
Moses, Lance and Esther 164
Moses, Ron 164
Motherhood of Man Movement (MOMM)
    311
Motion, Jane 200
Motion, William 40, 132: house **130**
Motion's mill (Western Springs) **130–31**
Motions Creek 133, 134, 246: saw pit 40;
    tannery 142

Motions Rd 118, 220, 270
Mountain View Rd underpass 124
Mrkusich, Milan 301, 303
Muka studio and gallery (17 Chamberlain
    St) 183, **184**, 328: Muka Youth Prints
    exhibition 184
Mullins, Frank 249
Murdoch Rd 283, 285, 353: no. 49 185
Murray, Alfred 172: grocery shop (cnr
    Richmond Rd & Lincoln St) 172
Murray, Thomas 148
Museum of Transport and Technology
    (MOTAT) 270
music 185–86, 345–67
Myers, Arthur 119, 120

# N

Naked Samoans 368, **368**
Nash, Garry 341
Nash, Mrs 218
Nash, Walter 129
National Broadcasting Service Symphony
    Orchestra 348
National Women's Hospital 311
Nearing, John 169
Nesian Mystik 364, **364**
Ness, Che see Che Fu
Ness, Miriama 363
Ness, Tigilau 361, **362**, 363
New Zealand Constabulary Force 107
New Zealand Educational Institute 228
New Zealand Institute of Architects 81, 86
New Zealand Lacrosse Association 235
New Zealand Symphony Orchestra 348
Newdick Brothers (Great North Rd) 172
Newdick, Herbert 172
Newmarket Borough Council 120
Newton 8
Newton Borough Council 52, 53, 96, 119,
    286: fire brigades 105; night soil 103;
    offices **116**; roading 103; wards 104
Newton Brick and Tile Works (later Newton
    Potteries) 145, 148, **148**, 149, 150, **150**, **151**
Newton Central School Te Kura a Rito o
    Newton (Monmouth St) 19, 69, **214**, 218,
    219, 221, 222, 235: bilingual/immersion
    classes 225
Newton Cricket Club 233, 234
Newton East School 214, 215: recreation 233
Newton Football Club/Newton District
    Football Club 235, **236**
Newton Highway Board 43, 95
Newton Highway District 8, 62, 64, 94–95,
    98
Newton No. 1 and No. 2 schools 202
Newton Pacific Islanders' Congregational
    Church (Edinburgh St) 301
Newton Police Station and Barracks
    (Ponsonby Rd) **108**, 109
Newton Rangers rugby league club 242
Newton School District 201–02: Committee
    202
Newton Schools Committee 214
Newton West School (Great North Rd) 14,

Index | 415

17, **196–97**, 202, 207–08, 214, 215, 219, 244, 283, 285: cadets 203; netball 261; plans **201**; recreation 233; religious services 283, 285; soccer 235
Newton West subdivision 62: plan **63**
Ngā Tamatoa 32, 33
Ngāti Whātua and Ngāti Whātua Ōrākei 26, 28, 29, 33: land gift 13; Ngāti Whātua Rūnanga 185
*Niagara* (ship) 348
Nicholls, Cyprian 164
Nicholson, Freda 164
Nicols, Myra **186**, 187
night soil collection 96–98, 103, 117–18
Nissan Motor Distributors 182–83
Nixon St 95, 165, 169, 183, 278, 279, 280
Nocturnal Projections 355
Norbert, Sister Teresa 212
Norfolk St 172
Norgrove, Charles 172: butchery (Richmond Rd) **171**
Norman, Decima 268, 269
Northcote St *see* Northland St
Northland St 16, 176, 189, 206, 289, 349, 350
Northwestern Motorway 124
Notley St: state housing **84–85**
Nottingham St 348

# O

O'Callaghan, Maurice 121
O'Neil, Michael 186
O'Sullivan, Vincent 369
Ōkahu Bay 118
Old Mill Rd 40, 41, 74, 80, 85, **86**, 98, 100, 110, **130–31**, 133, 142, **143**, 172, 173, **174**, 200, 246, 249, 270, 338: flour mill 133; trams 114
Onehunga Borough Council 246, 247
Open Brethren 286
Opoutukeha (Opou) Coxs Creek 26, 37; *see* Coxs Creek
Orange Ballroom **347**
Orange Coronation Ballroom (Newton Rd) 347
Otago School of Art 323
Oxford St *see* Waima St

# P

Pacific Island Presbyterian Church (Newton) 19
Pacific Islanders' Congregational Church 307, 348
Pacific Islanders' Presbyterian Church 303, 307, 348
Pagan Prints 187
Paisley New Zealand Emigration Society 40
Parker, William 142, 143
Parkes, Jaden 361, **361**
parks/sports grounds 243–46, 274: *see also* Coxs Bay Reserve, Grey Lynn Park, Western Park, Western Springs
Parr, James 120
Partington, Charles and Edward 134:

Western Springs mill 134
Pasadena Intermediate School 219: bilingual/immersion classes 225
Pasifika Festival **271**, 274
Pasifika: 7, 17, **18**, 19, 223: artists 325–26, 329, 330, 335; churches 17, 19, 301, 303–07, 309; education 221; exodus 7; film-making 368; foods **18**, 19; music 348–49, 361–64; overstayer crackdown 33; sports 266–67, 274
Patterson, Daniel B. 294
Paulo II, Su'a Sulu'ape 328–29
Pawson's Four Square (64 Warnock St) **174**, 175, **175**
Payne, John 126
Peacocke, Philip 334
Peacocke, Ponsonby 49–50
Peel St 243
Pellegrino, Nicky 369
Perkins, Emily 335
Pharazyn, Martin 322
Phelan St *see* Meola Rd
Phillips, Martin **352**
Phineas, Nova 348
Phipps, Mr: horse bus service 96, 101, 192
photography club **317**
Pike, James 'Ikity' **141**
place names (road and suburbs) 8–9
PleaZers, The 349
Point Chevalier Association Football Club 270
Poisoners, The 360
police stations: 14, 16, 107–9: Grey Lynn 108–09; Newton 106, 108, **108**; Surrey Hills 107–08
police–community relations 109
polio 227, 254
politics 127–29: electorates 126, 129; voting 126
Pollen St 26, 66, 116, 154, 169, 191
Pollock, Robert 169
Polynesian Panthers 19, 32, 33, 129
Polynesian Resource Centre (Great North Rd) 33, 129: poster **31**
Ponsonby District School Committee 202, 204, 228
*Ponsonby Road Reservoir Corner* (Harold Young) **316**
Ponsonby Rugby Club 267, 273
Ponsonby rugby league club 242
Ponsonby School 202, 217
Ponsonby Swimming Club 254
population growth (Auckland) 62, 64, 68, 107, 126, 202, 218
Porritt, Arthur 266
post office 170
Potatau St 202, 356
Potters Paddock (Alexandra Park) 235
pottery 315, 320–22, 336–39
pound, animal 104
Poynton, Mary 13
Poynton, Thomas 13
Presbyterian Church 19, 283, 285, 300–01
Price, Phil 335
Prime Rd 47, **286–87**, 336, 341

Primitive Methodist Chapel 202, 290–91: moved 290–91
Primitive Methodist Church, Franklin Road 233
Primitive Methodists 202, 233, 281–82, 287: church Richmond Rd 281, **281**, 287; hall 287
Princep St *see* Ariki St
Probert, John 95
Probert's Buildings (Great North Rd) **168**, 169
Produce Markets Ltd 52
Prophet Gad (Vernon Carrington) 307
prostitution 14, 106–07
Pryor, Christopher 367
Pua, Iosefa Sofi 181
Public Health Act 1900 111
Puddle, George 162
Puddle, John 163–64
Pule, John 330, **330**
Purcell, Vaitulutulusinaolemoana 180–81
Purity Products (Mackelvie St) 164: beverages **162**
Putiki St 164, 183

# Q

Quakers 240

# R

R. G. Norris Ltd cabinetmakers 180
racial issues 109: police dawn raids 109: poster *Take a hand against racism* **128**
Rastafarianism 307, 363: Twelve Tribes of Israel house (Surrey Cres) 307, 363
rates 102, 119–20, 121
rats 110, 111, 112: cartoon **110**
Rawene Ave 255
Reading Brethren 296
Real Pictures Gallery (300 Richmond Rd) 183
Recorded Music New Zealand (Richmond Rd) 186
Redshaw, John 1 43
Redshaw, Joseph 143
Redshaw, Robert 143
Redwood, Jack 243
Rees, Donogh 328
Reform Party 126
reggae 307, 361, 363
Regina St: bridge 243, 244, **245**
religion 276–311: church attendance 280, 291, 296
rental housing 86, 327
Renwick, Ces 177, 180
Renwicks upholstery (Richmond Rd/Surrey Cres) 177, 180
Reserves and Other Lands Disposal ...Act 1913 253
residential development 56–89, 129: Arch Hill 62, **63**, 64, 68; heritage 124, house types 70–71, **72–73**, **88–9**; housing shortage 177; modernisation 84, 86; Newton West 62; plans **66**; Surrey Hills

**416** | **The Near West**

Estate 62, 64–68, **68**, 69, 74; Village of Richmond 59, **60**, 61, 68; Well Park Estate 64, **65**, 68
Rich and Dimery (Millais St) 165
Rich, John 165
Richmond Association Football Club 241
Richmond Ave *see* Richmond Rd
Richmond Baptist Church (cnr Baildon Rd & Richmond Rd) 43, **290**
Richmond Bowling Club 238
Richmond Buildings 129, 152, **170**
Richmond Cricket Club 233
Richmond Cruising Club (Richmond Yacht Club) 239, 254–55: clubhouse (Herne Bay) **236–37**
Richmond Hall (Francis St) 208: school 208, 209
Richmond Hill 134–5: subdivision **60**, 61
Richmond Methodist Church 300
Richmond Rd 8, 16, 26, 46, 47, 59, **60**, 61, 64, **99**, 108, 129, 151–52, 154, 156, 165, 172–73, 176–77, 181, **181**, **182**, 183, 184, 186, 187, 189, 191, **204**, 205–08, 211, 215–21, 226, 228, 232, 235, 238, 240, 269, 270, 281, 283, 290–91, 296, 297, **299**, **304**, 305, 306, 308, 319, 326, 345, **346**, 348, 357: no. 90 298; no. 138 **188**; no. 300 190; community centre 124; dairy **177**; Davis family house **73**; early names 8; electricity 116; maintenance 94, 95–96, **102**; market garden 50, shops 172; trams 74, **113**, 114, **122**; Warnock family house **83**
Richmond Road School Te Kura o Ritimana (Richmond Rd/Brown St) 199, 202, **203**, 204, 207–08, 211, 215, **215**, 217–18, 219, 221, 222, 228–29, 244, 281, 282, 299: bilingual classes 33, 225–26; netball 261; Ritimana Te Kōhanga 225–26; rugby 235; swimming 254
Richmond Rovers Rugby League Club 242, **242**, 243, 266, 267, 272
Richmond School (Francis St/Surrey Cres) 208–09, *see* Grey Lynn School
Richmond Swimming Club 257
Richmond Tennis Club 238
Richmond Village subdivision 9, 39, 61, 62
Richmond Ward 104: water supply 98
Ring, Dr William 248
*Rip It Up* magazine (Crummer Rd) 185, **186**
Rive, Louise 338, **338**
roading 94, 95–96, 101–02, **102**, 119
Robert Rew grocery shop **168**
Robert T. Woods clothing factory 154
Robertson, Andrew 175
Robinson, Anne 341
Robinson, Edwin 164
Robinson, Gemma 361
Robinson's ice-cream (Putiki St) 163, 164: truck **163**
Rodwell, William: joinery/furniture factory (cnr Crummer Rd & Mackelvie St) 176
Rogers, Billie **358**
Romeo, Giuseppe 331
Rooney, Andrew 228
Rooney, Emma (née Fletcher) 228–29

Rose Rd 116, 283, 297, 319: influenza 121; no. 26 plan **66**; no. 55 plan **67**
Rosedale School 222
Rosicrucian Order, Auckland 297
Ross, James 332
Rowe, Harold 242
Royal Tongan Choir 305
Roycroft, Albert (AJ) 251
*Rubbings from a Live Man* (Warwick Broadhead) **367**
rubbish disposal/removal 55, 96, 120, 123, 255: destructor 112
Runciman, Rev R. W. 283
Runga, Bic 357, 360
Runga, Boh 357
Russell St *see* Cooper St
Russell, George 47
Russell, Thomas 68
Ryan, Mary 74

# S

Sackville St 48, 74, **89**, 151, 152, **153**, **181**, 190, 281, 282, 291, **304**, 305, 327: no. 84 307
Sacred Heart Boys' School 205
Sacred Heart College (Sussex/Turakina St/ Richmond Rd) 204–05, **204–05**, 219, 220, 235, 285, 301
Salisbury St *see* Castle St
Sālote Tupou III, Queen 306
Salvation Army 296: band 6; Bethany Centre (Dryden St) 296, 310, **310**, 311; hall (cnr Castle St & Richmond Rd) 296, **299**, 308; Newton Corps barracks (Ponsonby Rd) 296
Samoan Assembly of God 307–08
Samoan language classes/preschools 225–6: A'oga Fa'a Sāmoa 226; Mata'aga A'oga Amata 226
Samoan tatau 328–29
Savage St 85, 142, 142
Savage, Michael Joseph 85, 129, 217, 269
Scanlan St 121, 183, 283, 285, 287, 319: roading 104; tannery 142
Schmidt family 32
Scholes, Jeff 339, **339**
schools 199–229: bilingual/immersion units 224–26; Catholic schools 204–06, 223–24; church/missionary 199–200; female teachers 228–29; kindergartens 212, 214, 218; kōhanga reo/bilingual preschools 225–26; Māori names 226; primary 214–15; private 207; sports 235
Schoon, Theo 17, 322, 323, **323**, 324, 328
Schwehr, Father Louis 303
Scott, Stuart **188**, 189
Scott, Trish 361
Scribe 364
Sculptura **333**
Seabreeze Café (Garnet Rd) 369
Seager, Samuel Hurst 71
Second World War 176, 256, 266, 298, 311
Seddon Fields 270
Seddon High School 220

Seddon Technical College (Motions Rd) 219, 220
Sefton Ave 96
Selbourne St 69, **83**, 211, 291, 335, 345: no. 59 367
Selwyn, Don 156
settlers, European 29–30
Seventh-day Adventists 285–86: church (Mackelvie St) 286, 303: camp (Prime Rd) 286, **286–87**; school (Mackelvie St/Great North Rd) 206; Pasifika 303
sewage collection 96–98, 103, 117–18: sewerage systems 117–18, 120
Sexton, Alice 255
Sharpe Brothers (Millais St/Dickens St) 162–63, 334: stoneware jars **163**
Sheffield Radio Company (48 Mackelvie St) 180
Shenkin's cabinet factory (cnr Williamson Ave & Ariki St) 156
Shepheard, Simon 335
Shepherd, Roger 356
Sherwood Ave 46, 74, 240, 339: no. 1 156
Sherwood Estate 74
shops 169–73: (cnr Great North Rd & Pollen St): plan **67**; (cnr Great North Rd & Williamson Ave) **170**
Short, Thomas 172
Siddell, Emily 341
Siddell, Peter 319–20, 341: *Homecoming* **319**
Siddell, Sylvia (née Bartlett) 319, 341
Simmonds and Osborne (Crummer Rd) 162
Simpson, Jane 229
Sione Uesile (John Wesley) Methodist Church (cnr King St & Dean St) 19, 307, **308, 309**
*Sione's Wedding* film series 368
Sipley (Sipeli), Langi 17
Sisters of St Joseph of Cluny 303
Sisters of St Joseph of the Sacred Heart 204–05, 285
Slater, William 136
Slaughtering and Inspection Act 1900 111
Sloane, William 148
smelting, gold 136–37
Smith, Henry Mornington 129
Snake Studios 334–35
soap: Dingman's electric soap 138; Electric 138, **139**
Social Security Act 1938 257
soft-drink manufacturing 162–64
Soho Square 190
Sombretones, The 355
South African War 203
Spayne, Fanny 106
speedway 6, 251, 262, 274
Speers, Jim 335
Spiritual Scientists 297: Christian Spiritualist Church (43 Mackelvie St) 297
Split Enz 352
sports 230–75: athletics 262, 268–69, 272; competitions **264–65**; cricket 233, 234, 256–57, 267; croquet 257; female participants 257, 261–65; golf 257; hockey 262, **265**; kilikiti 267; lacrosse 235, **237**,

**Index** | **417**

238; lawn bowls 238–39; netball 2616–2, **264**, 267; parks/sports grounds 243–46, 256, 270; rugby league 241–43, 246, 272; rugby union 234–35, 238, 246, 273; soccer 235, 240–41; swimming 253–54, 256, 257; tennis 238, 256, 257, 261; water sports 239, **258**

Springbok tour 1981 109

St Benedict's Church (Newton) **319**

St Clare (Mackelvie St) 303

St Columba Church (Surrey Cres/Great North Rd) **161**, 247, **292–95**, 296, 308: Tongan services 296

St Columba Hall (Selbourne St) 211, 291, 296: dances 347; Sunday school 291

St Cuthbert's Hall (8 Faulder Ave) 296, 308

St George's Hall 105, 286

St Helen's Maternity Hospital 310

St Hill, Windle Hill 61

St James (now Grey Lynn) Kindergarten 212, **213**, 214, 218, 221

St James Presbyterian Church (Freemans Bay) 14

St John Ambulance Orchestra 348

St John's College Trust Board 208

St Joseph's Church (Great North Rd) 289, **289**, 301, 302, **302**, 303: Samoan and Tongan congregations 303

St Joseph's Convent (Great North Rd) **284**, 285, **288–89**

St Joseph's Convent School (Great North Rd) 121, 212, **213**, 219, **288–89**, 289, 301; influenza hospital 121

St Jude's Methodist Church (cnr Richmond Rd & Sackville St) 305: Tongan fellowship 305

St Michael's and All Angels 298

St Mungo's Church (Francis St) 300–01

St Paul's College 220, **223**, 223–24, 329; *see also* Sacred Heart College

St Peter's Presbyterian Church (Great North Rd) **284**, 285, 288: moved 288; sold 300

St Stephen's Presbyterian Church (Ponsonby) 297

St Thomas's Church (Union St) 233

Stanish, Nick **188**, 189

Stanley St *see* Dean St

Stanmore Rd 46, 291

state housing: 80–82, **83**, **84–85**, 129: flats (cnr Larchwood Ave & Garnet Rd) **80**; Demonstration Flats (Great North Rd) **81**; houses 80, **84–85**; pensioner units 82

Stebbing, Eldred 60, 349, 350

Stebbing, Margaret 60

Stebbings record plant (Surrey Cres) 160, 162: labels 162, 349

Stellar* 357

Stiles, Simon **190**

stone works 135

Stone, Russell 199

Strawpeople 356

Street Chant **358**, 359

Strickson-Pua, Feleti 363–64

Strickson-Pua, Linda 363

Strickson-Pua, Rev Mua 19, 363–64

Studio One — Toi Tu 338

Studio Two (Great North Rd) 186

Sullivan, Agnes 28

Summit House 180

Sunbeam Glass Co-operative 341

Sunny Brae Cres 141

Supergroove 363

Surrey Bakery (cnr Great North Rd & Elgin St) plans **175**

Surrey Cres 8, 26, 46, 50, 52–53, 82, 96, 109, 111, 117, 154, 160, 162, 164, 173, 176, 177, 186, 207, 208, 211, 238, 249, 256, 296, 307, 311, 320, 331, 338, 347, 353, 359, 360, 363: Auckland Laundry Co. 160; brush/broom factory 154, **156**; cows **34–35**; dairy **177**; flats **86–87**; shops **170**; trams **113**, 114, **170**

Surrey Hills Basketball Club 261

Surrey Hills Cricket Club 233

Surrey Hills Dairy 49

Surrey Hills Estate 46–49, 53–54, 104, 202, 233: games/picnics 233; map unsold lots **75**; recreation facilities 234; subdivision plans **2**, **15**, **68**, 234; sale 233

Surrey Hills farm 8

Surrey Hotel (cnr Great North Rd & Kirk St) 192

Surrey St *see* Scanlan St

Surrey Tennis Club **161**, 256, 257

Surrey Ward 104

Sussex St 47, 69, 242, **284**, 285, 287, 301, 305, 307, 348, **358**

Sussex Ward 104

Sutherland Bridgwater, Vivien 185

Sutherland, Wallace 327

## T

Tagg, Sally 331, 339

Taite, Paul 361, **361**

Tall Dwarfs 350, 352

Tamahori, John 296

Tāmaki Herenga Waka 25–26

Tāmaki-makau-rau 29: Māori place names 27

Tangata, Paul (Pomani) 325, **325**, 326

tanneries 140, 142–43

Tattersfield bedding factory (cnr Sackville St & Richmond Rd) 151–52, **153**, 165, 177, **181**, **182**: chimney 191; staff hostel 177

Tattersfield Brinton Carpets Ltd 152, 154

Tattersfield James 151–52

Tattersfield Textiles 152

Tattersfield, Evelyn 151–52

Tāufaʻāhau Tupou IV, King 305, 306

Tautai Contemporary Pacific Arts Trust 329

Taylor, Alf 270

Taylor, Edith and Inez 207

Taylor, Inia 331

Taylor, Rev Richard 207

Taylour, Fay 262, **263**

Te Kawau 28, 29

Te Rae o Kāwharu 28

Te Rehu 28–29

Te Reweti 29

Te Tokaroa Meola Reef **20–21**: origin 25

Te Wai Ōrea (Western Springs lake) 25, 26, 29: eels 26, 29; *see also* Western Springs

Technical Old Boys Athletic Club 262

Tekela-Smith, Sofia 335, **335**

Tennyson St *see* Turakina St

Th' Dudes 359

Thames Gold Smelting Company Ltd 136–37

*The Colin McCahons* (Julian Dashper) **312–13**

The Pines farm 64, 73

theatre 367–68

This Kind of Punishment 355

Thomas Wong Doo 52

Thomas, Gareth 356, **357**

Thompson, John 106

Tietjens, John 163

tile-making 135–36

timber industry 70: Cashmore's Mill **146**, **147**

Tippet, Carol 352

Tippett Nurseries (cnr Williamson Ave & Northland St) 189

Tippett, David **190**

Tippett, Warren 336, **337**

Tongan Methodists 305–07: churches 306

Tongan Women's Crafts Cooperative 326: ngatu (tapa) 326

Torrens and Sons Cabinetmakers (cnr Williamson Ave & Ariki St) 156

Town and Country Planning Act 176

Town Planning Act 1926 173

Toy Love 350, **350**, **351**

trams 17, 55, 74, 108, 112, **113**, 114–15, **115**, **122**, 123, **170**, 172, **174**, 249, 296: demise 123; at MOTAT 270

trees 125, **125**

Trevarthen, William 242

Triratna Buddhist Community 308

trolley bus **91**

Tuarangi Rd 43, 45, 50, 52, 94–95, 96, 101, 111, 169, 192, **194**, 296, 316, **317**: naming 8; roading 104; trams 114

Tuiasau, Fuimaono 329

Tukituki Muka 26

Turkington, Emma Buckley 255

Turner, Rev George Henry 282

Turnpike Act 1866 94

Turou Cook Island Catholic Centre (Great North Rd) 303

Tutanekai St 48, 74, 172, 182, 255, 345, **346**

Twelve Tribes of Israel: headquarters (Pollen St) 307; house (Surrey Cres) 307

Tyndall, Arthur 129

typhoid 118

## U

unemployment 187, 218, 229, 250–51

United Church of Tonga (Grey Lynn) 306

United Empire Box Company 183

United Methodist Free Church 282–83

Unity 361

Unity Pacific 362, 363

Urlich, Peter 359

# V

Vaine Moʻonia Tongan Methodist Church (cnr Richmond Rd & Sackville St) **304**, 305
van der Fluit, Peter 186
van der Putten, Andrew and Jeannie 338–39, **339**
Van Gils, Magda 183, **184**
van Schie, Tejo 331
Varnham, Chris **358**
Vickery, William 285
Viesnik, Peter 341
Village of Richmond: map **60**; subdivision 59, **60**, 61, 74
villas 70–71
Vinegar Lane 190–91
Viz Glass (Monmouth St) 341

# W

Waiateao 28, 133 *see* Motions Creek
Waima St 8, 14, 106, 287
Waitītiko Meola Creek 26
Waiwai Ltd (Great North Rd) 162, 164
Wakerley, John and Isabella 283
Walker, Henry 101
Walker, Jane 350, **350**
Walmsley, Major James 49
Walters, Gordon 323
Wanganui Girls' College 261
Ward Knox, John 335
Ward, Barbara 331, **333**, 352
Ward, Miss 206
Ward-Leeland, Jennifer **367**, 368
Warnock Brothers' soap & candle works 16, 55, 95, 137, **137**, 138, 143, 181, **181**, **182**, 183: soaps **139**
Warnock St 184, 241, 308, 357: no. 64 174, **174–75**, 175
Warnock, William 137
Warnock, James 137
Warnock, James Sr 137, 247
Warnock, Mary 137, **83**
Warnock, Richard 137, **83**
Warnock, Robert 137
Warwick Ave 42, 218: house building 77
water supply 98, 117, 120, 121: Domain Springs 98; Western Springs 98
Watkins, Kenneth 315
Webber St 26
Webber, A. S. 208
Well Park Estate 64: plan **65**
Wellpark Ave 41, **60**, 61, 64, 355
Wellpark College of Natural Therapies 308
Wells, T. U. 217
Wesleyan Methodist Missionary Society 306
West End Lawn Tennis Club 244, **245**, 256, 257, 266
West End Rd 253–54, 255: bridge 146, **147**, 243, **245**, 254, 255, **258**, **259**; shops 172
West End Seaside Estate 74, **76**, 77, **79**, 144: advert **78**; subdivision plan **76**
West House Farm 46, 111
West Lynn 172, 186–87, 290–91, 308, 347
West Lynn Bakery (Richmond Rd) 187
West St (West Terrace) 14
West View Rd 16, 74, 80, 86, 98, 140, 331
Western Park 233
Western Springs Association Football Club 270
Western Springs College 112, 220, 225, **226**, 227, 361, 363, 364: Ngā Puna o Waiōrea (Māori school) 225; rebuild 227
Western Springs Flax Company 134
Western Springs: campground/swimming pool 256, **258–59**; Empire Games (1950) **267**; flour mill 133–34; greyhound racing 253; improvements plan **252–53**; lake **99**; midget cars **255**; moa bones 26; MOTAT 270; motor racing 251, 262; Pasifika Festival 270, **271**, 274; Reserve 246, 251; sheep near **54–55**; speedway 6, 251, 262, 274; springs 133; sports fields 250–51; stadium 6, **252–53**, 253, **255**, 266–67, **267**, 274, 363; US forces camp 256; waterworks 97, 98, **99**, 100
Western Suburbs Amateur Athletics Club 262, 266, 270, 272, 274
Westmere 8, 9, **20–21**, 55, 74, 77, **84–85**: bungalows 80
Westmere Bakery (cnr Garnet Rd & Lemington Rd) 172
Westmere Congregational Church of Sāmoa 301
Westmere Estate Extension 77: plan **79**
Westmere Independent Order of Oddfellows 257
Westmere Kindergarten 218
Westmere Park Estate 77
Westmere School Te Rehu (Richmond School/Richmond West; Garnet Rd) 208, **209**, 212, 221, 222, 229, 269: bilingual/immersion classes 225; Ngā Uri o Ngā Iwi 225
Westmere Symphony Orchestra 348
Westmoreland St 180, 181, **181**, 182, 189
White, Arthur 69
White, Helen 129
White, Lois 318
Whytlaw, Matthew 39, 40, **59**
Willesden Works 134–35
William Denny Ave 41, 42, 43
Williams, Arthur 273
Williams, Bryan 273, **273**
Williams, Mervyn 127, 184, 334, **334**: poster *Take a hand against racism* **128**
Williamson Ave 69, 74, **116**, 117, 154, 156, 169, **170**, 172, 176, 180–81, 189, 190, 199, 207, 256, 270, 285, 303, 350, 355: no. 90 330; gas reticulation 104
Williamson, James 47–48, 53, 68, 233, 291
Williamson, John 97
Willis, Frederick 134
Willis, Rev. 192
Wilson Bay Farm 41, 42, **42**, **43**
Wilson family 287
Wilson, Archibald 41, 42
Wilson, Christiana (née Porter) 41
Wilson, David **43**
Wilson, Euphemia 41, 43
Wilson, George 41, 42, 43, 55
Wilson, Mary Jane **42**
Wilson, Sarah 41, 42
Wilson, Thomas 42–43
Wilson's paddock 241, 243
Wilton Motor Body Company (18 Westmoreland St) 181–83
Wilton St 64, 156, 159, 182, 243, 332, 334
Winsomere Cres 141
Winstone's 73
Withers, Russell **188**, 189
Wolseley Rd *see* Garnet Rd
Women's Co-operative Bakery 187
Women's Liberal League 228
Women's Parliamentary Act 1919 126
Wood, Cecil 71
Wood, Michael 59, 61
Workers Dwelling Act 1905 69
Wright, Robert 217
writers 369

# Y

Yandall Sisters (Adele, Caroline, Mary, Pauline) 348–49, **349**
Yandall, Tanuvasa James 301, 348
yeast factory 154
Young, Harold 315–16: *Ponsonby Road Reservoir Corner* **316**
Young, Jane 43
Young, Joseph 8, 43–44, 52
Young, Ron 356
Young, William 47

# Z

zoning 86, 173, 176, 183

First published in 2024 by Massey University Press
Private Bag 102904, North Shore Mail Centre
Auckland 0745, New Zealand
www.masseypress.ac.nz

Text copyright © Tania Mace, 2024
Images copyright © as credited, 2024

Design by Kate Barraclough
Cover photograph by Patrick Reynolds

The moral right of the author has been asserted

All rights reserved. Except as provided by the Copyright Act 1994, no part of this book may be reproduced, stored in or introduced into a retrieval system or transmitted in any form or by any means (electronic, mechanical, photocopying, recording or otherwise) without the prior written permission of both the copyright owner(s) and the publisher.

A catalogue record for this book is available from
the National Library of New Zealand

Printed and bound in China by 1010 Printing International Ltd

ISBN: 978-0-9951465-0-1